"A thoughtful, innovative, and ambitious volume with a unique perspective, surprising insights, and inclusive approach to the complexities of global-wide insecurity. In assembling scholars and policymakers at the forefront of non-traditional international security concerns—climate, energy, food, water health, gender, etc.—Gueldry, Gokcek, and Hebron have produced a collection of readings that is simultaneously sophisticated and accessible. It is refreshing to find a textbook that challenges long-held assumptions in this way and complements the more state-centered perspectives on international security. Geared to inform students and engage scholars alike, it is a must-read for anyone interested in gaining a more comprehensive and nuanced understanding of international security."

—Patrick James, Dornsife Dean's Professor of International Relations, University of Southern California, ISA President (2018–2019)

"*Understanding New Security Threats* is a timely, engaging and accessible volume on the complexity of security in the 21st century. Security is not a simple term and this textbook provides students with an understanding of this issue's breadth and its relevance to their world. Gueldry, Gokcek and Hebron assemble an A list line-up of scholars to examine the non-traditional security threats that many students fail to consider when thinking about global security. These authors provide a wonderfully accessible narrative that engages students in the study of these non-traditional threats, while reminding them of the continued relevance of traditional nation-state threats and the interplay between these traditional and non-traditional security concerns. In short, this is the textbook that finally places the notion of security in the complex narrative that is needed for our students."

—Eric K. Leonard, Henkel Family Chair in International Affairs, Shenandoah University, VA

"A comprehensive look into a multitude of 'new' security threats confronting state and non-state actors today. Each chapter clearly illustrates the connectedness of these non-traditional threats, drawing on an impressive number of the most recent reports and scholarly works. The inclusion of discussion questions makes it especially useful for classes, but the quality of the analyses readily contribute to the growing scholarly dialogue around issues of human security as well. This outstanding volume is engaging, insightful, and accessible to a wide audience."

—Carolyn M. Shaw, Wichita State University, KS

"Gueldry, Gokcek, and Hebron have assembled a fascinating set of readings elevating the discussion of "non-traditional" areas of security. In fact, they successfully make the case that these topics are the new normal for those interested in exploring the present and not-too-distant future of security. While climate change, food security, water security and energy security are currently occupying the minds of scholars and policymakers, the authors in this volume push us one step further to think about geoengineering, STEM transformations, and populism and security. This volume is a much-needed and timely addition to our thinking about security in an increasingly fragmented world."

—Cameron G. Thies, Arizona State University, ISA President (2019–2020)

Understanding New Security Threats

This textbook examines non-traditional forms of security and expands the notion of security to include non-state actors and non-human actors.

Proposing an expansive view of non-traditional forms of security that go beyond traditionally recognized issues of threats to state and national territory, this new textbook rests on the following premises:

- traditional state-centered threats, such as nuclear proliferation and espionage, remain a concern;
- old and new threats combine and create interlocking puzzles—a feature of wicked problems and wicked messes;
- because of the global erosion of borders, new developments of unconventional insecurity interact in ways that frustrate traditional conceptual definitions, conceptual maps, and national policies;
- unconventional security challenges which have traditionally been seen as "low politics" or "soft" issues are now being recognized as "hard security" challenges in the twenty-first century;
- many of the so-called "new" threats detailed here are in fact very old: diseases, gender violence, food insecurity, under-development, and crime are all traditional security threats, but deeply modified today by globalization.

The chapters offer local and global examples and engage with various theoretical approaches to help readers see the bigger picture. Solutions are also suggested to these problems. Each chapter contains discussion questions to help readers understand the key points and facilitate class discussion.

This book will be of great interest to students of international security studies, human security, global politics, and international relations.

Michel Gueldry is Professor of International Relations and Sustainability Studies at Middlebury Institute of International Studies, USA.

Gigi Gokcek is Associate Professor of Political Science at Dominican University, USA.

Lui Hebron is an Academic Coach at Instructional Connections, USA.

Understanding New Security Threats

Edited by
Michel Gueldry, Gigi Gokcek and
Lui Hebron

Routledge
Taylor & Francis Group

LONDON AND NEW YORK

First published 2019
by Routledge
2 Park Square, Milton Park, Abingdon, Oxon OX14 4RN

and by Routledge
52 Vanderbilt Avenue, New York, NY 10017

Routledge is an imprint of the Taylor & Francis Group, an informa business

British Library Cataloguing in Publication Data
A catalogue record for this book is available from the British Library

Library of Congress Cataloging-in-Publication Data
Names: Gueldry, Michel R., editor. | Gokcek, Gigi, editor. | Hebron, Lui, editor.
Title: Understanding new security threats / edited by Michel Gueldry,
Gigi Gokcek and Lui Hebron.
Description: Abingdon, Oxon ; New York, NY : Routledge, 2019. |
Includes bibliographical references and index.
Identifiers: LCCN 2018050833 (print) | LCCN 2019000100 (ebook) |
ISBN 9781351590945 (Web PDF) | ISBN 9781351590938 (ePub) |
ISBN 9781351590921 (Mobi) |
ISBN 9781138104723 (hb) | ISBN 9781138104747 (pbk) | ISBN 9781315102061 (ebk)
Subjects: LCSH: Security, International. | National security. | Human security. |
Energy security. | Biosecurity. | Computer security. |
Non-state actors (International relations) | Terrorism--Prevention.
Classification: LCC JZ5588 (ebook) | LCC JZ5588 .U53 2019 (print) |
DDC 355/.033--dc23
LC record available at https://lccn.loc.gov/2018050833

ISBN: 978-1-138-10472-3 (hbk)
ISBN: 978-1-138-10474-7 (pbk)
ISBN: 978-1-315-10206-1 (ebk)

Typeset in Bembo
by Taylor & Francis Books

Contents

Figures

Table

Boxes

Acknowledgments

Many individuals and organizations contributed to advancing this project from our initial conversations to the final product.

First we must thank our energetic contributors for their commitment to the book's vision, their cooperation and patience in tweaking their chapters so that they are consistent with the book's goals, and their prompt responses to our deadlines.

We are grateful to Andrew Humphrys, our excellent editor at Routledge for his stewardship of the book from beginning to end. His extensive professional experience gave us solid guidance, and his wise counsel was invaluable in the process of editing this book.

We extend our warm thanks to the production team at Routledge. Thank you all for your fine work in finalizing the manuscript and seeing it through to publication.

We want to gratefully acknowledge and thank the anonymous reviewers who took the time to read all or parts of the manuscript and provided well-informed comments and suggestions that helped the book greatly.

While we take full responsibility for any errors of facts or any shortcomings, the credit should go to our contributors for any merit that the present volume may have.

Dr. Michel Gueldry would like to thank the Middlebury Institute of International Studies for their generous and consistent support, which has enabled him to complete this project. He thanks his co-editors for being such a solid and fun team.

Dr. Gigi Gokcek would like to thank Dominican University for their generous and consistent support, which has enabled her to complete this project. She also thanks Dr. Gueldry and Dr. Hebron for embarking on this journey and making the experience intellectually stimulating. Finally, she would also like to acknowledge her husband Todd, for his support and encouragement, and for consistently demonstrating patience and grace despite the pressures this project entailed.

Dr. Lui Hebron would like to thank DeVry University and Hult International School of Business for their support, which has enabled him to complete this project. He would also like to extend his appreciation to Michel and Gigi for their generosity of time, energy, and wisdom to this effort. Working with you both has been both professionally satisfying and personally rewarding. Finally, he would like to acknowledge his children, Christian, Dani, and Skyler, for their patience and understanding of his academic pursuits, which frequently infringed on family time.

List of key acronyms

AEO	Authorized Economic Operator
AfD	Alternative für Deutschland
AIDS	Acquired Immune Deficiency Syndrome
API	Application Program Interface
APT	Advanced Persistent Threat
AR	Assessment Report
BPSN	Biopolitical Security Nexus
CC	Climate Change
CCP	Chinese Communist Party
CCPCJC	Commission on Crime Prevention and Criminal Justice
CDR	Carbon Dioxide Removal
CISO	Chief Information Security Officer
COP	Conference of the Parties
C-TPAT	Customs-Trade Partnership against Terrorism
DLP	Data Loss Prevention
DNC	Democratic National Committee
ECOSOC	UN Economic and Social Council
EMEA	Europe, the Middle East and Africa
ETA	Euskadi ta Askatasuna (Basque separatist organization)
EU	European Union
FAO	Food and Agriculture Organization
FGC	Female Genital Cutting
GAO	General Accounting Office
GBV	Gender-Based Violence
GHG	Green House Gas
GRC	Governance, Risk, and Compliance
GCSC	Global Container Supply Chain
GCSS	Global Container Supply Chain Security
HIV	Human Immunodeficiency Virus
ICADIS	Identify, Correct, Analyze, Design, Implement and Sustain
ICT	Information Communication Technology
IGO	Inter-governmental Organization
IMF	International Monetary Fund
IOT	Internet of Things
IPCC	Intergovernmental Panel on Climate Change

IPS	Intrusion Prevention Systems
IR	International Relations (as a discipline)
ISIL	Islamic State of Iraq and the Levant (synonyms: ISIS, Islamic State)
ISIS	Islamic State of Iraq and Syria (synonyms: ISIL, Islamic State)
ISS	International Security Studies
LCL	Less than Container Load
MENA	Middle East and North Africa
NATO	North Atlantic Treaty Organization (aka the Atlantic Alliance)
NCO	Nuova Camorra Organizzata (Newly Organized Camorra)
NF	Nuova Famiglia (New Family)
NGO	Non-governmental Organization
NOCs	National Oil Companies
OECD	Organization for Economic Cooperation and Development
OPM	Office of Personal Management
PII	Personally Identifiable Information
RH	Reproductive Health
RJ	Reproductive Justice
SDGs	Sustainable Development Goals
SMB	Server Message Block
SRHR	Sexual and Reproductive Health Rights
SRM	Solar Radiation Management
TNC	Transnational Crime Organization
UN	United Nations
UNCTAD	United Nations Conference on Trade and Development
UNDP	United Nations Development Programme
UNFCCC	United National Framework Convention on Climate Change
UNICEF	United National International Children's Emergency Fund
UNODC	UN Office on Drugs and Crime
UNSC	United Nations Security Council
USSR	Union of Soviet Socialist Republics
VAW	Violence Against Women
WAF	Web Application Firewalls
WHO	World Health Organization

Contributors

Daniel Addington is Senior Security Analyst and Adjunct Faculty, Grand Canyon University (USA). Daniel is a cybersecurity professional who focuses on the design and security of critical information systems and data. His technical leadership for complex classified systems supporting the national defense has been recognized by the Department of Defense.

Khalid Bachkar is Associate Professor of International Business and Logistics, California State University, Maritime Academy (USA). Khalid's research focuses on transportation logistics and supply chain management, container supply chain logistics and security, ethanol supply chain, and supply chain risk management.

Michael D. Beevers is Assistant Professor of Environmental Studies, Dickinson College (USA). Michael's research specializes in global environmental politics with an emphasis on the linkages between natural resources, security, conflict and peace. He has worked as a consultant for the United Nations Environment Program and the World Resources Institute.

Amy Below is Assistant Professor of Political Science, California State University, East Bay (USA). Amy publishes in the area of foreign policy analysis with an emphasis in the environment/climate change and a regional specialty in the Americas.

Joel R. Campbell is Associate Professor of International Relations, Troy University, Okinawa (Japan). Joel has written numerous articles for academic journals on topics ranging from combating terrorism and money laundering to European Union economic integration and technology policy.

Colin P. Clarke is Affiliate Faculty at Pardee RAND Graduate School (USA). He is also an associate fellow at the International Centre for Counter-Terrorism (ICCT), a non-resident Senior Fellow at the Foreign Policy Research Institute (FPRI), and a lecturer at Carnegie Mellon University. Colin's research focuses on terrorism, insurgency and criminal networks.

Michael A. Davis is Military Attaché, U.S. Embassy, Rome (Italy). A Colonel in the U.S. Army, Michael has served as both a Special Forces officer and Foreign Area Officer. His political-military expertise is drawn from a vast array of international affairs service in combat, operational, and embassy assignments throughout the Middle East, Africa, and Europe.

Jonathan Drake is Director of the Eurasian Security Studies Program, George C. Marshall European Center for Security Studies (Germany). Jonathan is a former artilleryman in the U.S. Army. Lt Colonel Drake has served in various operational and strategic assignments across Europe, the Middle East, Central Asia, and Eurasia.

Adriana Erthal Abdenur is Coordinator of the International Peace and Security Division, Igarapé Institute (Brazil). Adriana has published widely on development and South–South cooperation, the BRICS, and UN affairs. She is also a collaborating researcher at the Brazilian Naval War College in Rio de Janeiro.

Adrienne Formentos is a graduate of Georgetown University. Her research interests include global public health, mental health, global health security, and the overlap of displacement and population health.

Crister S. Garrett is Professor for American Culture and History, University of Leipzig (Germany). Crister's research includes contemporary trends in political, economic, and social reform in a transatlantic context, involving mostly the United States, Germany, France, and Sweden.

Nicole E. Gerring is Faculty member, Wayne State University (USA). Nicole's research expertise includes feminist international relations, women's political empowerment, and sexual and gender-based violence.

Gigi Gokcek is Associate Professor of Political Science and Director of the Honors Program, Dominican University (USA). Gigi researches, teaches, and publishes in the areas of international relations and comparative politics.

Michel Gueldry is Professor of International Relations and Sustainability Studies and Head of Language Studies Program, Middlebury Institute of International Studies (USA). Michel has authored or edited five books.

Lui Hebron is an Academic Coach at Instructional Connections (USA). Lui's research focuses on the areas of political economy (globalization), international relations (ethnicity, conflict and war), and Asian studies (Pacific Rim and China).

Sharad Joshi is Assistant Professor in the Nonproliferation and Terrorism Studies Program (NPTS) at the Graduate School of International Policy and Management (GSIPM), Middlebury Institute of International Studies at Monterey (USA). Sharad's research and teaching focuses on various facets of conflict, terrorism, and non-proliferation matters in South Asia, such as CBRN terrorism; nuclear strategy; and terrorist financing networks.

Christian-Marc Liflände is Head of Cyber Defence Section, Emerging Security Challenges Division at NATO Headquarters, Brussels (Belgium). Before joining NATO International Staff Christian-Marc served in the Estonian Ministry of Defense, including serving as a Director of Policy Planning, and an Adviser to the Minister of Defense.

Mike Manrod is Director of Security, Grand Canyon University (USA). Mike is responsible for leading the security team and formulating the vision and strategy for protecting students, staff and information assets across the enterprise.

Marissa Quie is Lecturer in Politics and Director of Studies at Magdalene College, and Fellow and Director of Studies in Human Social and Political Science at Lucy Cavendish College, Research Associate, Department of Sociology at Cambridge University (United Kingdom). Marissa's current research is on the European politics of aid and migration. Her research engages with the motifs of participation and protection that characterize debates about women and marginalized groups.

Erica Resende is Assistant Professor, Brazilian War College (Brazil), and Affiliate Lecturer, University of Oklahoma (USA). Her research interests are U.S. foreign policy, Critical Security Studies, identity politics, memory and trauma studies, and discourse analysis.

Joe Sanchez is Director of IT Infrastructure Operations, Grand Canyon University (USA). Joe focuses on strategic plan development, implementation, and performance improvements to continuously deliver higher availability of all GCU's IT services.

Jason Sebastiani is Director of IT Networking, Grand Canyon University (USA). Jason is responsible for leading the networking team and directing an architectural strategy that allows for flexibility and maximum network uptime. He oversees all network infrastructure including switches, routers load balancers and firewalls along with the engineers and administrators that configure them.

Serena Simoni is Associate Professor and Director of International Relations Program, Samford University (USA). A native of Italy, Serena's teaching and research interests include International Relations, International Security, Transatlantic Relations, International Organization, and Foreign Policy.

Erika Weinthal is Lee Hill Snowdon Professor of Environmental Policy at the Nicholas School of the Environment, Duke University (USA). Erika specializes in global environmental politics with an emphasis on water and energy.

Neda A. Zawahri is Associate Professor of Political Science at Cleveland State University (USA). Specializing in Middle East and South Asian politics, Neda's research interests include an examination of the management of international river disputes, the role of international institutions in facilitating cooperation, environmental security, and the potential for conflict and cooperation between adversaries.

Prologue

The international relations discipline currently finds itself in a time of great uncertainty, if not under siege. Academics, policymakers, corporate leaders, and the general public alike have increasingly become more vocal in questioning the intellectual contribution and policy value of a branch of knowledge that largely failed to anticipate the collapse of the bipolar world order, the dramatic rise of the People's Republic of China, the ascent of globalism, the emergence of the war on terrorism, and the expanding global refugee crisis.

In like manner, the border-defying dynamic and transnational nature of globalization have profoundly altered how international relations is researched and taught. The deepening interdependence of an ever-changing array of security risks makes it abundantly clear that nation–centric approaches to problem-solving is inadequate to address the myriad of threats to security.

This crisis of faith in the discipline provides an opportune moment to explore new ways of conceptualizing and analyzing our most pressing global problems. Answers to these evolving dynamics are important to academic scholars, policymakers, and non–state actors. In order to better respond to the challenges of operating in a profoundly politicized, complex, and contentious milieu, its actors (states, corporations, IGOs, NGOs, citizens, and epistemic communities) need a richer and more nuanced perspective of global affairs.

By encouraging the intellectual cross-fertilization of diverse fields and divergent perspectives, this innovative approach to learning and research will be better able to address today's pressing international issues. This meeting of the mind among an eclectic group of well-informed professionals with specialized training and practice in military affairs, business, environmental issues, diplomacy, health, history, culture, and cyber-security could potentially facilitate a comprehensive and inclusive understanding of a rapidly changing world and help produce better policy decisions and outcomes.

Part I

Ecosystems and natural resources

Introduction

Yesterday's security debates, today's realities

Michel Gueldry, Gigi Gokcek and Lui Hebron

Security: A central paradigm

The centrality of security for any society explains its stakes and its sheer complexity, and why it lies at the conceptual core of the discipline of international relations, alongside other key concepts such as power, peace, conflict, cooperation, and capability. In his classic *People, States, and Fear*, Barry Buzan explains: "(T)he concept of security is, in itself, a more versatile, penetrating and useful way to approach the study of international relations than either power or peace. It points to a prime motive for behaviour which is different from, but no less significant than, that provided by power. It also leads to a comprehensive perspective which is likewise different from, but no less useful than, that provided by peace" (Buzan 1991, 3; Buzan in Hughes and Meng 2011, 19).

That security also constitutes the foundation of any stable, prosperous society is recognized in countless founding compacts. In *The Federalist* Paper 23, Alexander Hamilton explained: "The principal purposes to be answered by union are these: the common defense of the members; the preservation of the public peace as well against internal convulsions as external attacks; the regulation of commerce with other nations and between the States; the superintendence of our intercourse, political and commercial, with foreign countries" (*Federalist*, December 18, 1787). In a similar vein, Europeans also squarely placed continental peace at the heart of their project of pan-continental integration. On May 9, 1950, five years and one symbolic day after the official surrender of Nazi Germany (May 8, 1945), French foreign minister Robert Schuman articulated in the Schuman Declaration the rationale for Franco-German cooperation and a European coal and steel community as preludes for continental reconciliation and unification. His plea for new efforts toward continental security resonated deeply with war-weary Europeans: "World peace cannot be safeguarded without the making of creative efforts proportionate to the dangers which threaten it. (…) By pooling basic production and by instituting a new High Authority, whose decisions will bind France, Germany and other member countries, this proposal will lead to the realization of the first concrete foundation of a European federation indispensable to the preservation of peace" (Schuman Declaration 1950). The April 18, 1951 Paris Treaty establishing the European Coal and Steel Community (ECSC), the founding document of what over time became the European Union, re-affirms this intimate connection between economic cooperation and the quest for peace among nations. Its preamble states that "world peace may be safeguarded only by creative efforts equal to the dangers which menace it" (ECSC 1951).

A half-century later, after the fall of the USSR (officially on December 26, 1991), the 1992 Maastricht Treaty on the European Union established "a common foreign and security policy" to further its key objective "to promote peace, security and progress in Europe and in the world" (Paragraph 3).

Today, the governing body of the United Nations (UN) is the *Security* Council (aka "Permanent Five," "Big Five," or "P5"), and under the UN Charter (June 25, 1945), "the Security Council has primary responsibility for the maintenance of international peace and security" and "takes the lead in determining the existence of a threat to the peace or act of aggression." The Preamble to this Charter explicitly rejects "the scourge of war" and calls for a very wide mandate to secure "social progress and better standards of life in larger freedom" to further general peace and security. The Charter gives the UN mandates over numerous security issues—climate change, international development, peace operations, human rights, humanitarian assistance, food security, women's and children's rights, global health, governance, international law, nonproliferation and disarmament, drug control, crime prevention and counter-terrorism, sustainability, refugees, etc.—which together constitute today's expansive security kaleidoscope.

Expanded views of security

This complex security agenda points to the trans-national nature of many security threats. Political borders and countries seem like the natural order of things, the evolutionary apex of human societies and territorial social systems, and the best way to organize security. This **Westphalian** view of states still structures our perception, yet nation-states are neither natural, self-evident, nor immutable. In fact, they are born of accidents, chance, and organized violence; they are also problematic, dysfunctional, and challenged in many parts of the world. They are also recent, porous, and blurred by all sorts of flows and forces, from environmental dynamics to technological development, from human and animal migrations to microorganisms contagion (e.g., AIDS, influenza), from terrorist groups to financial flows, and from climate change to the global mass culture. Globalization is therefore both an integrative and fragmenting process. On the one hand, it creates interdependence or, to be more precise, complex and asymmetrical interdependence: some key actors (China, the US, large countries), regions (the West, maritime straits), issues (religion), and resources (oil) affect the global system disproportionately, while others (the silent majority in the Global South, gender issues, etc.) are underplayed by state and other actors who control the hegemonic discourse of security for their own ends. On the other hand, globalization increases the borderlessness of international relations, thereby shaping and transforming security issues in new and unexpected ways.

Therefore, this book proposes an expansive and inclusive view of nontraditional forms of security that goes beyond traditional realist definitions—that is to say, beyond traditionally recognized issues of threats to state and national territory, beyond sovereignty, territorial disputes, geopolitics, and military-diplomatic affairs. According to Korab-Karpowicz,

> Realism, also known as political realism, is a view of international politics that stresses its competitive and conflictual side. It is usually contrasted with idealism or liberalism, which tends to emphasize cooperation. Realists consider the principal

actors in the international arena to be states, which are concerned with their own security, act in pursuit of their own national interests, and struggle for power.

(Korab-Karpowicz 2017)

For millennia, the official actors of politics were city-states, empires, nation-states, rulers, kings, ministers, generals, warriors, strategists, and other "great" men whose enduring enmity and strategies—political, military, economic, technological, and religious-cultural—fully vindicate one of realism's main contentions that while national politics "is the realm of authority and law," international politics, in contrast, is anarchical, "a sphere without justice, characterized by active or potential conflict among states" (Korab-Karpowicz 2017). The traditional realist vernacular also deems functioning states as sovereign, rational, unitary actors. Traditional conflict among nations—the stuff of realist theory—may be termed traditional military war, with its accepted forms (diplomacy, negotiations, treaties and alliances, formal declarations of war and peace, clear time markers), means (uniformed armed forces), and discourse. Today these age-old traditions, war and peace among nations have drastically evolved; dangers and security have morphed, and even change has changed: it is faster, more encompassing, more complex, and more unpredictable than before.

Therefore, our book addresses forms of threats and insecurity that do not have the state as their sole or central referent object, where state actors are but one player among many and must contend with powerful challenges, both trans-state (migrations, technological challenges, global crime and terrorism), sub-state (gender issues, urban misgovernance), and nonhuman (ecosystems dynamics, micro-pathogens). The following typology helps clarify the five broad types of situations that, put together, constitute security *writ large*. Needless to say, these threats overlap and interact.

In order to avoid the hubris of **anthropocentrism**, we acknowledge that human life and international relations are embedded in, and shaped by, planet Earth and ecosystems. Therefore, a first type of security, *environmental security*, describes threats coming from the living planet, such as climate change, environmental issues, and resource attrition (chapters 1–4 herein), and from other forms of life such as microorganisms and diseases (chapter 8).

Second, state-centered *national defense* still matters very much, which focuses on traditional state rivalry, military war, the geostrategic **Great Game** and new areas such as natural resources (water and oil, respectively chapters 3 and 4) and dark operations in cyberspace (chapter 13).

Third, *human, community, and societal security* focuses on widespread issues such as structural and cultural violence, notably gender violence, sexual and public health botheration, forced migrations, and economic and resource injustice (chapters 5–9).

Fourth, *hybrid, mixed forms of insecurity* combine state military dimensions with forms of dislocation (food and water crises, trafficking, radical ideologies), disruptive groups (organized crime, gangs, terrorists, drug cartels, pirates, anti-democratic forces) and technologies affecting civil societies (chapters 7, 10–17).

One last form of security, *ecological security,* deals with the threats, disruptions, and degradations that social systems impose on ecosystems and other forms of life (chapters 1, 2, 8).

Insecurity, risks, and uncertainty

Insecurity is characterized by both risks and uncertainty. In his classic *Risk, Uncertainty and Profit* (1921), Frank H. Knight, one of the founders of the Chicago School of

Economics, drew a distinction between these two concepts that still inspires today's risk analysis literature. Situations marked by *risks* have unknown outcomes, but the probability distribution (the probability of occurrence) of various outcomes is known and quantifiable. A situation is *uncertain* when not only its outcomes but the probability models that govern these outcomes are unknown (Knight 2006, 19–20). For instance, food insecurity will stifle personal and collective development (a recognized, quantifiable risk), but its impact on migrations and, in turn, the impact of migrations on departing and target countries are hard to estimate over time (fluid uncertainty). Movements of people across borders are immediately observable, but their impact is cascading, complex, and may compound other issues.

An inclusive definition of such **multi-scalar** security would also consider the difference between *objective* security (being protected from a dazzling array of dangers, close and far) and *subjective* security (feeling safe according to one's norms and worldview). This raises the important question of the malleability, the mental and social construction (which the theory of constructivism studies) of the referent threats. For instance, the US Center for Disease Control and Prevention (CDC) has identified heart disease as the leading cause of death in the United States, but pro-life advocates insist that abortions are the primary cause of death among Americans, essentially amounting to a legal Holocaust. To provide another example, the US considers itself as a benign hegemon, the indispensable nation for global peace and stability—at least until President Donald Trump redefined America's position in the world. But many in the world see the US either as a malicious menace or a well-meaning but incompetent giant—a bull in a china shop—because its throws its weight around irresponsibly and never faces the consequences of its foreign adventurism, e.g., the Vietnam way, its disastrous 2003 war in Iraq, and its overreaching global war on terror.

Planners and policymakers also draw a distinction between "tame" or "benign" problems and wicked problems. Benign problems can be, and routinely are, extremely complex—for instance, building a new generation of bridges or airplanes—but their commanding rules (the physical property of materials, the laws of physics and flight, the physical parameters surrounding these human artifacts, the laws of nature) are stable, and their behavior is largely predictable. The objectives (weight bearing over a gap), the physical rules (properties of constituent parts), and the environment (water and wind, terrain and geology) for building bridges have not changed since the first day the first bridge was built. Therefore, linear and cumulative progress is possible and easily observable. In contrast, social problems such as violence, poverty, gender discrimination, and racism are murky, their final resolution is elusive, and they can only be "resolved—over and over again" (Rittel and Webber 1973, 160). They are wicked problems because there is no agreement regarding their very existence, their causes, or their solutions. They can even devolve further into wicked messes and became compounded, chronic, and intractable—for example, failed states (such as the Democratic Republic of Congo, Somalia, or Yemen), drug addictions and epidemics (in the US, for instance), or climate change.

Among the ten defining properties of wicked problems (Rittel and Webber 1973, 160–165), several apply to the nontraditional security problems studied in this book. One: There is no definitive formulation of a wicked problem or even its existence. For instance, climate change deniers do not recognize the dominant science or the existence of an **anthropogenic** problem. Other social actors deny women's rights without seeing this as a problem at all, but as the natural, best, or divinely ordered society. Two: Wicked problems have no stopping rule, no clear or final solution, and approaches toward tackling these issues are in degrees of good or bad, or even contradictory. For instance, what should be done to fight violent crime? Disarm the population, as in Australia and Europe, or arm everyone everywhere all the time, as the National Rifle Association recommends in the US? Three: There are no classes of wicked problems (every wicked problem is unique), and every wicked problem can be considered to be a symptom of another problem—for instance, economic hardship and crime, cultural alienation and terrorism, misgovernance and trafficking. In other words, the scope and variables of security have widened considerably, and interrelating forces, factors, and actors make it a fluid and difficult achievement—the ever-receding horizon of public policies.

Risks, uncertainty, and wickedness are all features of the dangers studied in this book. Theodore Parker (1810–1860) was an American transcendentalist, abolitionist, and reformist minister of the Unitarian church who coined the famous expression "The arc of history is long but it bends toward justice," which Dr. Martin Luther King Jr. popularized in his August 1967 speech to the Southern Christian Leadership Conference. Similarly, as wicked problems and wicked messes force actors to constantly revisit the fundamentals of these situations and their own past responses, the metaphor of a "long arc" or ever-widening spirals of action moving toward some form of progress, while constantly revisiting previously covered ground, is a more apt approach for such issues. Finality—resolving some problems once and for all—probably will remain a utopia for many of the issues this book covers. Therefore, security itself has become a more muddled concept.

Security: From realism to complex construct

That security is a central concept does not entail general agreement on what it means, especially as the world and the field of security studies saw a noted evolution from a realist paradigm to mounting challenges to this state-centered view.

The decades stretching from the end of World War II (May 8, 1945: Victory Europe, August 14–15, 1945: Victory Japan) to the collapse of the USSR (December 1991) were marked by the Cold War between the superpowers, their allies, and client states. The distinctive features of these tense decades provided an excellent template for realism. First, the prevalence of conflict, high politics, and fierce ideo-logical rivalry between two super-powers. Second, clearly structured and antagonistic systems of political and military alliances (NATO vs. Warsaw Pact and Communist China). Third, a run-away and economically ruinous arms race and nuclear build-up for mutually assured destruction (MAD) in case of nuclear confrontation. Fourth, occasional brinkmanship between the two super-powers (e.g., the Cuban missile crisis in October 1962). Fifth, a proliferation of proxy wars and regional conflicts—notably Korea, Vietnam, Latin America, the Middle East, Africa in the late 1970s and 1980s, Afghanistan—with direct or indirect involvement of the superpowers through local alliances, client-states, allies, etc. As a result, "During that period most of the literature on security referred to national or state security because of the military (nuclear) balance between the two blocks. But when that period ended, the concept of security has been enlarged to encompass individual, societal, global and human security…" (Díez-Nicolás 2015, 2). Alternative and critical views of security struggled to make themselves heard during the Cold War.

The end of the USSR opened a vast practical and theoretical space for security. In practical terms, peoples then hoped to enjoy the dividends of peace: The end of the arms race allowed for smaller military budgets and stronger social and economic agendas. The 1994 *UN Development Report* opened up the theoretical debate as it stated:

> Behind the blaring headlines of the world's many conflicts and emergencies, there lies a silent crisis—a crisis of underdevelopment, of global poverty, of ever-mounting population pressures, of thoughtless degradation of environment. This is not a crisis that will respond to emergency relief. Or to fitful policy interventions. It requires a long, quiet process of sustainable human development.
>
> (UN Development Programme 1994, iii)

Today many security theorists are uncomfortable with the notion of extending the concept of security to include the many topics that this book covers. *Traditionalists* purport to limit this concept to inter-state military-political perils for the sake of intellectual and pragmatic clarity; *wideners* extend it to inter-state threats from social, economic, and environmental issues; and *deepeners* integrate all sources since insecurity comes from and affects all: states, individuals, private entities, communities and the environment (Martinovsky 2011, 1–2). This book leans toward *widening* and *deepening* definitions of security, and shows the connections between challenges to state and to society. Under pressure from new realities and evolving perceptions, the field of international security studies has significantly diversified since realism and liberalism emerged in their modern form in the wake of the two world wars and the nuclear age. Kaldor explains:

> As Buzan and Hansen point out in their history of international security studies, it was only after 1945 that the term 'security' came to supplant terms like 'war', 'defence' or 'strategy' among both policy-makers and academic circles. This a conceptual shift, they argue, has 'opened up the study of a broader set of political issues, including the importance of societal cohesion and the relationship between the military and on-military threats and vulnerabilities.
>
> (Kaldor 2018, 13; Buzan and Hansen, 2009)

Indeed, even "geopolitics" and "military war," with their apparently clear-cut apparatus of state actors, standing armies, territorial control, formalized diplomacy, etc., are replete with ambiguity. For one thing, the military outcome (who wins, who loses the military conflict?) can be confused and contested, as in the case of November 1918 in Europe, where Germany officially lost the war but waged every single day of war on enemy territory, east and west, seized immense swaths of land in western Russia, Belgium, and France, avoided military operations on its own soil, and kept its military intact and functional until the very end. Another example is the 1980–1988 war between Saddam Hussein's Iraq and the Ayatollah's Iran, which concluded with a political and military draw. For another, a country may win all or most battles and still lose the war, as in the case of the United States in Vietnam from 1959 to 1975, in Iraq since 1990, and in Afghanistan since 2001. For another, military victory (winning the war) does not necessarily lead to political victory (winning the peace), and in yet another twist of fate, a country may win the war and fail to secure peace, and at best reach a stalemate and new issues, for instance France and Britain in 1918, the United States against North Korea in 1953, Israel against many of its Middle East neighbors since 1967, etc.

Some defenders of traditional, realist views seem more state- and military-centered than military strategists and security agencies themselves. In fact, to take only the US, both the Pentagon and intelligence agencies defend *widened* and *deepened* views of threats and security. For instance, in July 2015, the US Department of Defense released the *National Security Implications of Climate Change*, whose findings are unambiguous:

> DoD recognizes the reality of climate change and the significant risk it poses to U.S. interests globally. The National Security Strategy, issued in February 2015, is clear that climate change is an urgent and growing threat to our national security, contributing to increased natural disasters, refugee flows, and conflicts over basic resources such as food and water (…) Global climate change will have wide-ranging implications for U.S. national security interests over the foreseeable future because it will aggravate existing problems—such as poverty, social tensions, environmental degradation, ineffectual leadership, and weak political institutions—that threaten domestic stability in a number of countries.
>
> (Department of Defense 2015, 3)

The DoD sees troubled times ahead, as affected countries will be

> vulnerable to disruption and far less likely to respond effectively and be resilient to new challenges. Case studies indicate that in addition to exacerbating existing risks from other factors (e.g., social, economic, and political fault lines), climate-induced stress can generate new vulnerabilities (e.g., water scarcity) and thus contribute to instability and conflict even in situations not previously considered at risk.
>
> (Department of Defense 2015, 3–4)

The US intelligence community also recognizes these new challenges to statecraft and society. The Office of the Director of National Intelligence (ODNI) is in charge of intelligence integration across the 17 agencies and organizations (e.g., CIA, intelligence services of all branches of the military, etc.) that constitute the US national intelligence community. The National Intelligence Council (NIC) is the ODNI's center for long-term global analysis, and it articulates the intelligence community's best strategic thinking. In 2012, the NIC released its key report *Global Trends 2030*, which sums up the finding of the entire US intelligence community, and identifies key variables, structural trends, and global trajectories. Four megatrends bear direct and substantial implications for security (National Intelligence Council 2012, i–xi). The first megatrend, growing individual empowerment, will bring much good but also causes worry as "all individuals and small groups will have greater access to lethal and disruptive technologies (particularly precision-strike capabilities, cyber instruments, and bioterror weaponry), enabling them to perpetrate large-scale violence—a capability formerly the monopoly of states."

The second megatrend, the diffusion of power, will see the relative decline of the West—especially Europe—and the increased rise of BRIC and other economies, with dire security implications: "Enabled by communications technologies, power will shift toward multifaceted and amorphous networks that will form to influence state and global actions."

Demographic patterns, the third megatrend, will include a drastic swelling of the human population, aging, increased international migrations, and growing urbanization. All will challenge ecosystems, natural resources, economic growth, public policies, institutional capacity and human agency in multiple ways.

The fourth megatrend, the "growing food, water, and energy nexus" raises considerable concerns:

> Demand for food, water, and energy will grow by approximately 35, 40, and 50 percent respectively owing to an increase in the global population and the consumption patterns of an expanding middle class. Climate change will worsen the outlook for the availability of these critical resources. Climate change analysis suggests that the severity of existing weather patterns will intensify, with wet areas getting wetter and dry and arid areas becoming more so. Much of the decline in precipitation will occur in the Middle East and northern Africa as well as western Central Asia, southern Europe, southern Africa, and the US Southwest (...) Many countries probably won't have the wherewithal to avoid food and water shortages without massive help from outside. Tackling problems pertaining to one commodity won't be possible without affecting supply and demand for the others.
>
> (National Intelligence Council 2012, i–xi)

Against this backdrop of system changes, this report identifies six game-changers—five of them *not* related to traditional military threats—with implications for stability and security (National Intelligence Council 2012, i–xi). They are: 1) A crisis-prone and unbalanced global economy, 2) The governance gap for nations and institutions faced with accelerating disruptive changes and an increasing number of subnational and transnational actors with access to technology, financing, and global networks, 3) A wider scope of regional instability because of changing calculations of key players—particularly China, India, and Russia; increasing contention over resource issues; and a wider spectrum of more accessible instruments of war, 4) Regional instability, especially in the Greater Middle East and South-East Asia connected with nontraditional threats such as sluggish economic growth, rising food prices, energy shortages, youth bulges, inequality, lack of infrastructure, education and employment in the absence of a regional hegemon and multilateral security regimes, 5) New technologies (information and social communication, production, automation, health), and 6) the positive global role of the US may be challenged by emerging rivals. We would add that global stability and the US standing are also challenged by mounting domestic issues within the US, notably economic and political polarization, the legalized corruption of institutions (e.g., Congress) by moneyed interests, and the erosion of its democratic character, values, and morals.

Business organizations opine regarding the salience of climate and resource issues and are increasingly active security actors. For instance, the World Business Council for Sustainable Development (WBCSD) is a trend setter for global governance and security. With a membership of about 200 major international corporations, it is a, if not the, leading institutional advocate for Corporate Social Responsibility (CSR). While it is criticized by advocates of "authentic" CSR and alter globalization advocates, and while the behavior or the mission of some of its members falls vastly short of its proclaimed goals of sustainable development, it represents a critical mass of capability, knowledge, and resources. The WBCSD makes a business case for non-traditional risks for private companies, prosperity, and good societies, and proposes market-based solutions: "Access to fresh water is a basic human right and a critical sustainable development challenge. As competing demands for water continue to rise (across agriculture, households, energy, industrial use, ecosystems, etc.), the effects of climate change are exacerbating the challenges associated with water quality and availability" (WBCSD n.d.).

To take another example, in January 2017, the World Economic Forum (WEF, a Swiss non-profit organization dedicated to improving the state of the global economy, and known for its yearly meetings at Davos) released its *Global Risks Report 2017*. Its top five concerns are rising income and wealth disparity, "increasing polarization and intensifying national sentiment," "cultural schisms" that involve "rapid changes of attitudes in areas such as gender, sexual orientation, race, multiculturalism, environmental protection and international cooperation" and that test "social and political cohesion and may amplify many other risks if not resolved." In addition, "disruptive (…) technological change," global governance, and "a cluster of environment-related risks" interact with "conflict and migration" (World Economic Forum 2017, 6–7).

Therefore, the widened and deepened approach that this book embraces has a strong basis in the nature of the world today. It also receives theoretical backing in **critical security theories** such as feminism and critiques of neoliberalism (see chapter 1, 2, 5–6 and 11 for their application to specific issues), the notion of structural violence, and the three generations of human rights.

Theoretical basis: Structural violence and theories of rights

A key aspect of human, community, and societal security is violence understood *largo sensu*. The concept of "structural violence" was popularized by Norwegian scholar-activist Johan Galtung, a founder of the field of peace studies. In his canonic *Violence Peace and Peace Research* (1969), he rejects a narrow definition of violence (defined as intentional and produced by identifiable human agents) because an "unacceptable social order" is incompatible with real peace ("no justice, no peace"). Instead he proposes the concept of structural violence: "Violence is present when human beings are being influenced so that their actual somatic and mental realizations are below their potential realizations (1969, 168). "Somatic" here means "physical" and ranges from various means of bodily restrictions and threats all the way to the direct, active killings of human beings by others. For instance, dying of tuberculosis before the era of modern medicine was not a form of social violence because TB was neither preventable nor curable and was an equal threat to the general population then. Today it is an avoidable or treatable disease, but factors such as underdevelopment, deficient health infrastructure, lack of access and capacity, all aggravated by failed governance, condemn some—and not others—to die from this disease.

When actual threats and dangers are avoidable but keep affecting specific groups, these communities are victim of some form of structural violence, which can be organized by hegemonic groups and countries, or result from complex conditions partially escaping human agency. Its most common forms include sexism, racism, discrimination against minorities and communities, lack of economic opportunity, lack of access to social goods and services (e.g., maternal health care, education, information), etc. Social injustice expresses this organization of structural violence: "There may not be any person who directly harms another person in the structure. The violence is built into the structure and shows up as unequal power and consequently as unequal life chances" (Galtung 1969, 171).

Structural violence is often depersonalized, anonymous, and the results of complex conditions, rather than of direct intention, although such violence does result from structural hegemonic relations that are deliberately cultivated and imposed, hidden and negated. The causal relation may be diluted and indirect, but direct intentionality or malice is not needed for some policies to be recognized as violent. For instance, the following—and much more—constitutes structural violence: pricing out access to drinkable water and food for impoverished communities in the name of private property, capitalistic profit, and free trade; denying medical information and services to a population in the name of religion or traditions; denying equal opportunities to women and girls; evicting farm laborers from the land; slanting the police and justice system against some categories, etc. Peace is more than the absence of overt war or hostility or military triumph against an armed enemy ("negative peace"): it entails the promotion of the structural conditions—institutional-legal, economic, cultural, etc.—for a generally safe, productive, and positive existence ("positive peace") (Webel and Galtung, 2007).

Another way of framing the debate between national security and other forms of security is to consider the relative probability (low, medium, high) and impact (low, medium high) of threat scenarios. Today inter-state war and nuclear war are low probability and high impact in most regions of the world. However, global hunger, lack of access to drinking water, lack or denial of medical services or health insurance, etc. are high probability and high impact, and their current toll is real. One can compare the driving causes of mortality between developed and under-developed countries. According to the National Center for Health Statistics of the CDC, the three leading causes of death in the United States in 2016 were heart disease, cancer, and respiratory diseases (Center for Disease Control 2016). But World Health Organization (WHO) statistics reveal striking differences in the morbidity and mortality patterns between low-income economies, intermediate, and developed countries:

> In high-income countries, 7 in every 10 deaths are among people aged 70 years and older. People predominantly die of chronic diseases: cardiovascular diseases, cancers, dementia, chronic obstructive lung disease or diabetes. Lower respiratory infections remain the only leading infectious cause of death. Only 1 in every 100 deaths is among children under 15 years (…) In low-income countries, nearly 4 in every 10 deaths are among children under 15 years, and only 2 in every 10 deaths are among people aged 70 years and older. People predominantly die of infectious diseases: lower respiratory infections, HIV/AIDS, diarrhoeal diseases, malaria and tuberculosis collectively account for almost one third of all deaths in these countries. Complications of childbirth due to prematurity, and birth asphyxia and birth trauma are among the leading causes of death, claiming the lives of many newborns and infants.
> (World Health Organization 2016)

In response to such dire trends, in 2015 the United Nations promoted the seventeen **Sustainable Development Goals** (SDGs). **Intersectional** linkages among these objectives are especially revelatory of the forces structuring non-military security. A first "WASH" nexus focuses on the interconnection between water, sanitation, and hygiene. A second security nexus focuses on climate change as a general disrupter. Gender inequality also reverberates through the social structure and dynamics, and undermines a prosperous and humane society.

Another fruitful way of considering security is in terms of the types of rights—against what kinds of dangers—a good society should organize to protect its citizens. The international human right lawyer Karel Vašák (1982) articulated the framework of the three generations of rights, inspired by the three main themes of the French revolution: *liberté, égalité, fraternité.*

First-generation rights are based on personal *liberty*; they deal mostly with political rights and participation in political and electoral life, and define classical Liberalism. These "blue rights" restrict public authority and power in their claims against individual citizens: Right to life, equality before the law, freedom of speech, religion, right to a speedy and fair trial, etc. Such rights as to be safe and secure *against* public encroachments, the protection *against* being harassed, imprisoned, executed, silenced, discriminated against, etc. by the government, the police and the courts are thus deemed "negative rights." They are enshrined in key foundational documents as the Magna Carta (1215), the English Bill of Rights (1689), the 1787–91 US Bill of Rights, and the 1789 French Declaration on the Rights of Man and of the Citizen. In terms of security, these rights point to a traditional liberal-pluralist democratic society, protecting individuals against social and state control, minorities against the dictatorship of the majority, and civil society against encroachments from political, police, judicial and bureaucratic power.

Second-generation rights developed with social reformist movements, with the industrial revolution, the Progressive movement, labor rights' movements, democratic socialism (as opposed to authoritarian forms of socialism), the New Deal, Franklin D. Roosevelt's January 11, 1944 State of the Union address to advance his "Second Bill of Rights," and the economic and social rights recognized after World War II. They include the right to work, to associate to defend labor rights, social entitlements, etc. They form the basis of social-democracy. In terms of security, they grant social legislation, socialized medicine, and public education legislation to workers and citizens, against the selfishness of dominant classes and the class war waged by the haves against the have-nots. Economic security constitutes its core.

Third-generation rights go beyond political and economic rights: they include access to a healthy environment and natural resources ("green" rights), cultural rights, intergenerational rights (such as sustainability), and sexual rights. These progressive rights, affirmed by many UN documents such as the 1992 Rio Declaration, invoke a sense of community to advance social solidarity and justice (*fraternity*). The emphasis is on holistic, integrative views of security in ever-widening circles: identity, inter-generational, inter-cultural, and planetary.

The relationship among these three trends is complex as some rights put limits on others and possible conflicts abound. For instance, the right to private property for the haves puts limits on the rights of redistributive tax policies for the have-nots. Conservatives challenge second- and third-generation rights as disguised socialism and state overreach against individual freedom, while Progressives see first-generation rights as a necessary but by no means sufficient foundation for a moderate government, which should not abandon society and nature to the Darwinian forces of the free market, and to the whims of the rich and powerful. Progressives argue that first-generation rights in isolation facilitate social Darwinism, the domination of the few over the many, and are therefore formal, theoretical rights that concrete rights (economic, social, and community justice) should buttress. Therefore, one's theory of right (strictly individual, or collective, or global) informs one's theory of security: narrowly political, widened to economic justice, or more encompassing.

Premises and organization of this book

This book rests on five premises. First, traditional state-centered threats remain very much a concern: examples include nuclear proliferation in India, Iran, Israel, North Korea, and Pakistan; espionage among leading nations; territorial challenges in Crimea, the Middle East, the East China Sea, and the South China Sea; and regional tensions (Koreas, India–Pakistan, and Iran–Saudi Arabia).

Second, old and new threats combine, interact, and create interlocking puzzles—another feature of wicked problems and wicked messes. For instance, climate change (desertification of large swaths of the Syrian territory), misgovernance, economic hardship, overpopulation, factionalism, and the terrorist contagion from neighboring Iraq (all "unconventional" threats) contributed to the Syrian civil war and foreign military intervention, which in turn heightened the (traditional) tension between Russia and the United States, between Iran and Saudi Arabia, and between Iran and Israel.

Third, because of the global erosion of borders among countries and continents, the traditional distinction between external and internal security has become blurred. New developments of unconventional insecurity, such as climate change and gender discrimination, interact in ways that frustrate traditional conceptual definitions, conceptual maps, and national policies. States and other security actors have to innovate and combine forces in often unexpected ways. As "non-physical security, diversification of threats, and the salience of identity are key effects of globalization in the security realm" (Cha 2000, 391–392), the new security environment in the twenty-first century is essentially **intermestic** (international and domestic) and combines more variables, dimensions, and instruments, including military or military-grade resources mobilized by non-state actors such as criminal gangs, irredentist movements, and terrorists. State capacities and behavior, while remaining central, are no longer the sole source of dangers (e.g., nuclear proliferation) and remedies (e.g., public health policies).

Fourth, unconventional security challenges will likely shape our future. Indeed, while the dominant discourse long considered such concerns as "low politics" or "soft" issues, failed to register them as "systemic threats," and often deprioritized them in comparison to traditional, state-centered threats, they are now morphing into—and increasingly recognized as—"hard security" and "high politics" challenges in the twenty-first century. For instance, the massive migrations affecting Europe over the past few decades feed nationalistic, anti-Islamic forces; the rise of the authoritarian, anti-democratic right; electoral volatility; Brexit; and the possible unraveling of the European Union and the Western alliance. To take another example, the AIDS epidemic is seriously straining the family structure, social fabric, and economic development of many sub-Saharan countries. The rate of infection in the population and its structural impact worsens the further south one travels: Botswana, Lesotho, Malawi, Mozambique, Namibia, South Africa, Swaziland, Zambia, and Zimbabwe suffer from a rate of infection affecting 10–15 percent of the general population. In these countries, the virus incapacitates and kills millions of workers, parents, and citizens; it creates generations of orphans, undermines community life, jeopardizes agriculture production and governance structures, causes immense suffering and is a national, regional, and global security risk.

Our last premise is that the future already happened, in several ways. For one, many of the so-called "unconventional" or "new" threats detailed in this book are in fact very old: diseases, gender violence, food insecurity, under-development and crime are traditional threats—but deeply modified today by globalization, which warrants fresh examination. Two, recent trends give clues as to what tomorrow holds: for instance, climate change is not some future threat, it has been affecting many regions for some time, and will only worsen. Three, as sci-fi writer William Gibson stated, "The future has arrived—it's just not evenly distributed yet" (Gibson 1999). Dominant countries, regions, social groups, gender and race live in different geographical and social places and different time frames from the dominated. In particular, the powerful can externalize their nega-tivities—pollution, etc.— and insulate themselves from the worst forms of contemporary problems, which hit other actors and locales with full force. The problems addressed in this book are only too real and agonizing for too many places and groups, but still a threat scenario for others.

The 17 following chapters are organized into three Parts.

Part I recognizes that all human affairs are first and foremost embedded on this Earth and in natural ecosystems, and deals with climate change and natural resources. Chapters 1 and 2 deal with climate change as a major "threat multiplier" and ways to address it; chapters 3 and 4 delve into the interlocking issues surrounding water security and energy.

Part II continues with human and community security issues. Chapter 5 focuses on the biological and sexual politics imposed on females by societies, and the resistance that women oppose. Chapter 6 argues that there really is no "safe zone" for women, even among the so-called "first world" or "world of peace" that realists deem safe because they see no threat of inter-state war there. Chapter 7 examines food as another key natural resource, as a core condition of human security, and compares the food safety policy of three economic and demographic giants: China, India, and Brazil. Chapter 8 puts invisible foes and micro-enemies under the microscope, exposes their old impact on communities and politics, and explores their security implications today and the role of international organizations in global health. Chapter 9 tackles the heart-wrenching drama of massive global migrations and their cascading consequences.

Part III shows the salience of sub-state and trans-state actors for territorial and community security. Chapters 10–12 detail the threats posed by religious extremists and terrorists, organized crime and trafficking, the feminization of mafias in Italy, and their deleterious impact on Italy's government, society, and international action. Chapters 13–16 examine interrelated aspects of our technological world: cyberspace threats, artificial intelligence, scientific and technological development, and the vul-nerabilities of global logistical networks made possible by trade globalization and information technology. Chapter 17 plumbs the depth of today's democratic crisis, and contrasts "liberal-democratic security" organized around human rights, the rule of law, and open borders, with "populist security" organized around tribal, nation-alist, identity and economic anxieties.

All chapters offer local, regional, and global examples and engage with various theoretical approaches to help readers draw the big picture. Remedies and solutions are suggested. Key specialized concepts are highlighted in **bold** in each chapter and compiled in the final glossary. After each chapter, questions help readers understand key points and connect with threats presented in other chapters. They also invite more theoretical discussions (beyond the empirics of each "silo" issue), and hopefully facilitate class discussion. The final glossary and list of key acronyms should help with the proliferation of concepts.

We hope that this book helps readers grow intellectually, and also as complex, sensitive, and moral human beings seeking to lessen the pain and strengthen the good around them.

Questions for discussion

1   Why is security a key concept of international relations? And why is there no agreement on a common definition or contents? With what practical consequences?
2   What are "wicked problems" and "wicked messes," and how do these concepts apply to security issues?
3   What are key security mega trends identified by leading global actors?
4   How do you personally assess the various types and forms of global insecurity in terms of probability, likely impact, and urgency? Justify your assessment and policy recommendations.
5   Apply the concept of structural violence to your own country or situation, and discuss your findings.

References

Buzan, Barry. 1991. *People, States and Fear: An Agenda for International Security Studies in the Post-Cold War Era.* London: Harvester Wheatsheaf.

Buzan, Barry. 2011. "The National Security Problem in International Relations." 18–23 in Christopher W. Hughes and Lai Yew Meng, eds. *Security Studies: A Reader.* London: Routledge.

Buzan, Barry and Lene Hansen. 2009. *The Evolution of International Security Studies.* Cambridge University Press.

Center for Disease Control (CDC). 2016. "The Three Leading Causes of Death in the United States in 2016." National Center for Health Statistics. https://www.cdc.gov/nchs/fastats/lea ding-causes-of-death.htm

Cha, Victor D.May 2000. "Globalization and the Study of International Security." *Journal of Peace Research* 37(3): 391–403.

Department of Defense. July 23, 2015. "National Security Implications of Climate-Related Risks and a Changing Climate." RefID: 8–6475571. http://archive.defense.gov/pubs/150724-con gressional-report-on-national-implications-of-climate-change.pdf?source=govdelivery

Díez-Nicolás, Juan. November 3, 2015. "The Perception of Security in an International Comparative Perspective." Real Instituto Elcano *Working Paper 16/2015.*

ECSC. April 18, 1951. Preamble of the 1951 ECSC/Paris Treaty. Council of the European Union https://www.consilium.europa.eu/uedocs/cmsUpload/Treaty%20constituting%20the%20Europ ean%20Coal%20and%20Steel%20Community.pdf

Federalist Papers. Yale Law School Library. The Avalon Project. http://avalon.law.yale.edu/18th_ century/fed23.asp

Galtung, Johan. 1969. "Violence, Peace, and Peace Research." *Journal of Peace Studies* 6(3): 167–191.

Gibson, William. 1999. *Quote Investigator.* https://quoteinvestigator.com/2012/01/24/future-has-a rrived/

Kaldor, Mary. 2018. *Global Security Cultures.* Cambridge, UK: Polity.

Knight, Frank H. 2006 (1921). *Risk, Uncertainty and Profit.* Mineola, NY: Dover Publications.

Korab-Karpowicz, W. Julian. May 24, 2017 (2010). "Political Realism in International Relations." in Edward N. Zalta, ed., *The Stanford Encyclopedia of Philosophy*https://plato.stanford.edu/a rchives/sum2017/entries/realism-intl-relations

Martinovsky, Petr. 2011. "Environmental Security and Classical Typology of Security Studies." *The Science for Population Protection*, 3(2): 1–16. http://www.population-protection.eu/prilohy/ca sopis/11/81.pdf

National Intelligence Council (NIC). December 2012. *Global Trends 2030: Alternative Worlds*, Washington, DC: The Office of the Director of National Intelligence, NIC 2012–00. https:// www.dni.gov/files/documents/GlobalTrends_2030.pdf

Rittel, Horst W. J., and Melvin M. Webber. June 1973. "Dilemmas in a General Theory of Planning." *Policy Sciences* 4(2): 155–169.

Schuman Declaration. May 1950. The Communications Department of the European Commission on Behalf of the EU Institutions: https://europa.eu/european-union/about-eu/symbols/europe-day/schuman-declaration_en

United Nations Development Program (UNDP). *United Nations Development Report.* 1994. http://hdr.undp.org/sites/default/files/reports/255/hdr_1994_en_complete_nostats.pdf

Vašák, Karel. 1982. *The International Dimensions of Human Rights.* New York, NY: Praeger.

Webel, Charles, and Johan Galtung, eds. 2007. *Handbook of Peace and Conflict Studies.* New York, NY: Routledge.

World Business Council for Sustainable Development (WBCSD). n.d. https://www.wbcsd.org/Programs/Food-Land-Water

World Economic Forum (WEF). January 17, 2017. *The Global Risks Report 2017.* Geneva: WEF, https://www.weforum.org/reports/the-global-risks-report-2017

World Health Organization. 2016. "Statistics on Morbidity and Mortality Patterns among Poor, Intermediate and Rich Countries." http://www.who.int/mediacentre/factsheets/fs310/en/index2.html

Chapter 1

Climate change
The existential threat multiplier

Amy Below

Introduction

Though the subject of just one of the many important chapters in this book, climate change (CC) is connected to them all. The security implications of past, present, and future climate-related changes affect health/disease, migration, food availability, political in/stability, and terrorism to name just a few. In fact, CC overlaps with almost every policy area considered in this volume. On the one hand, this heightens the importance of CC as a phenomenon and subject of public policy. This is exemplified by the milieu of actors, from the international to sub-local, that are devoting resources to addressing its causes and impacts. On the other hand, it corroborates the designation of CC as the ultimate "wicked problem" (Head 2008; Termeer, Dewulf, and Breeman 2013), a "wicked social problem" (Grundmann 2016) or even a "super wicked problem" (Lazarus 2009; Levin et al. 2012).

While this dubious designation suggests that there is no consensus as to the specific causes of insecurity or to any particular solutions (in line with the argument presented in the Introduction), this chapter considers what is known about the relationships between CC and the range of security considerations it provokes, in terms of CC as a "threat multiplier." While impacts from CC are not believed to lead to insecurity, particularly violent conflict, on their own, they exacerbate existing vulnerabilities and intensify existing insecurities. This chapter then adopts a discourse and, thus, constructivist framework and the lenses of different international relations theories in an effort to better understand the relationship between CC and security threats. Doing so illustrates the importance of language and perception when conceptualizing what the risk is, who is at risk, who is responsible for mediating that risk and in what way. It, thereby, further complicates our understanding of cause, effect, and the ultimate security risks posed by climate change.

Climate change fundamentals: Science and policy

When humans burn fossil fuels such as coal, oil, and natural gas, carbon dioxide (CO_2) and other gases are released into the atmosphere. Together they behave like a blanket trapping heat that normally would escape into the upper layers of the atmosphere. The result is an increase in the planet's overall global temperature and associated disruptions. The sectors contributing the most **greenhouse gas (GHG)** emissions are transportation (primarily oil for cars, trucks, and airplanes), heating and electricity generation (commonly coal), industrial processing (e.g., cement, steel, and paper factories), and agricultural practices.

Greenhouse gases, specifically CO_2, can also be added to the atmosphere by the elimination of **carbon sinks** (deforestation), their saturation (oceans), and melting (permafrost). Sinks naturally absorb carbon and help regulate the global carbon cycle. Land use change, for example replacing natural areas with buildings, roads and parking lots, causes further loss of sinks. Oceans, the largest sinks on the planet, naturally absorb and store the most carbon. When warmed, however, absorption capabilities are reduced, upsetting natural cycles and absorbing less new **anthropogenic** emissions. This phenomenon is called a **positive feedback loop** (amplification of the cycle) in that warming oceans loose significant capacity to absorb carbon, which means more carbon in the atmosphere. This means an enhanced greenhouse effect, more warming and, in turn, even less absorption. There are also **negative feedback loops** (diminution of the cycle) that naturally regulate and slow the greenhouse effect. For example, cloud cover naturally reflects sunlight and radiates it back into space. Warmer temperatures result in more water in the atmosphere in the form of clouds that increase reflection and cool temperature back down.

While the overall impact of an increase in greenhouse gases is an increase in global temperature, or "global warming," and associated trends (notably more severe and frequent weather phenomena, disruption of carbon and water cycles), this syndrome is not evenly distributed. Some areas may become warmer and others cooler. Thus, the broader term "climate change" gained popularity. However, some argue that "global climate disruption" is the most accurate description of the phenomenon (Holdren 2007) as temperatures and weather patterns have become less predictable and deviate from long-standing expectations. The impacts of a warming planet from extreme heat, droughts, melting polar icecaps, rising sea levels and oceanic thermal expansion (warming oceans that destabilize marine life) to extreme weather events (more severe hurricanes/typhoons and winter storms) will be dispersed around the globe, affecting some areas more than others. The result is that some countries have already felt the impacts of CC and/or fear impending impacts while others continue to see the phenomenon as distant, both physically and conceptually.

What further complicates the matters is the transboundary nature of GHGs. Industrialized nations were, and are, the largest contributors to GHG emissions and developing nations the largest contributors to the reduction of carbon sinks and yet the impacts are being felt around the world. Climate change is, thus, a **multi-scalar** problem. In other words, low-contributor countries are some of those experiencing the most deleterious effects. The United States is one of the world's top three CO_2 emitters—China and India are numbers one and three, respectively. Not only do its emissions travel to other countries (a concern for air and other forms of pollution), but they contribute to overall warming and impacts in countries far from US national borders for instance rising sea levels around small island nations in the South Pacific and droughts in sub-Saharan African nations. The obvious result is grave concern for fairness, equity, and climate justice.

Text box 1.1: Climate justice

Environmental justice is achieved when all people, regardless of identity (race, ethnicity, gender, socio-economic status, age, ability, etc.) can live, work, and play in communities that are safe and free from pollution and life-threatening conditions. Climate justice builds off this ideal argument that all people have the right to live, work, and play in communities not adversely affected by CC. The term also applies to justice for countries. Climate justice would be attained if all countries, regardless of developmental or economic status, were protected from the impacts of CC. Issues of equity and fairness are inextricably linked to climate justice. The search for climate justice has manifested in many forms in climate negotiations including:

- Debates about "differentiation" or the division of the world into two categories: developed or Annex I and developing or non-Annex I
- Common But Differentiated Responsibilities (CBDR): The argument that all countries have a common responsibility to address climate change, but industrialized countries have the greater capability and responsibility to do so
- Funding mechanisms: Requiring developed countries to provide funds for mitigation, adaptation, or capacity building in developing countries
- Inequities in representation in climate negotiations.

The transboundary nature of GHGs and resultant equity concerns meant that some of the first efforts to address CC were international approaches. Beginning in the meteorological community and eventually attracting the attention of politicians (Paterson 1996), the first international agreement, the United Nations Framework Convention on Climate Change (UNFCCC), emerged in 1992 out of the **Earth Summit** in Rio de Janeiro, Brazil. The treaty was relatively weak, requiring no specific or strict behavioral changes, but laying the foundation for the future of the climate regime. The 1997 Kyoto Protocol was the first major step forward requiring concrete actions and GHG emission reductions from industrialized nations. This legally binding treaty called for an average reduction of five percent of 1990 level emissions for the commitment period 2008 to 2012. Developing countries were not required to make similar commitments. In contrast, the 2015 Paris Agreement, the next major treaty, called for commitments (though not legally binding) from all countries, not just industrialized ones. It was hailed as an "historic moment" and "major leap for mankind" (Vidal et al. 2015) for its ability to get almost all countries to sign on. Though President Obama signed on the behalf of the United States, soon after taking office Donald Trump announced his intent to leave the agreement. However, due to stipulations in the agreement, the United States could not officially leave until 2020.

Linking climate change and security

Conceptualizing environmental decline as a security threat is not a recent endeavor. Early connections and uses of the term "environmental security" date back to 1977 with Lester Brown's *Redefining National Security* and the 1987 **Brundtland Report** on *Our Common Future*, respectively. In addition, US government intelligence services were considering the potential outbreak of wars over water scarcity in the Middle East as early as the mid-1980s (Starr 1991). This was part of a growing body of academic scholarship on the links between the environment and security concerns in the 1980s (Galtung 1982; Ullman 1983) that grew and thrived in the 1990s (Dabelko and Dabelko 1995; Gleditsch 1997; Homer-Dixon 1994). It included healthy debate over the merits and implications of linking the two (Deudney 1990; Goldstone 1996; Homer-Dixon and Levy 1995). Ronnfeldt (1997) provides a clear overview of these first three generations of environmental security literature. A unifying thread, however, was the understanding that the relationship was complex, multidimensional, and not deterministic.

Debates over the connections between climate change and security concerns are no different. Disagreement over the merits of making the connections and what those connections look like is arguably even more pronounced given the complexity and scope of CC. There is no consensus as to any universal causal linkages, instead agreement that there is no direct causality between variables. Several intervening variables (i.e., government attention and institutions, public response, environmental feedback loops, etc.) as well as interactions between variables pervade the landscape. As a result, conditions under which CC leads to security concerns are varied, dependent, and context-specific. This conclusion has led to a proliferation of attention to and research on the securitization of CC in order to better understand these complex relationships, especially since the 2007 Intergovernmental Panel on Climate Change (IPCC) Fourth Assessment Report that was the organization's first real focus on the topic (Scheffran and Battaglini 2011).

Text box 1.2: The IPCC

Created in 1988 by the World Meteorological Organization and the UN Environment Program, the IPCC does not conduct its own research, but collects and assesses science related to climate change from around the world and writes reports for policymakers. The IPCC also does not make specific policy recommendations but proposes potential scenarios and implications of action or inaction that policymakers can use to make their own decisions. Almost 200 countries are members of the IPCC and hundreds of scientists and experts compile and write the reports at regular intervals. Each contains four Working Groups on the science of climate change; impacts, adaptation and vulnerability; mitigation and a synthesis report. Though the subject of some controversy over the years, the Assessment Reports remain the quintessential assessment of knowledge on the status of climate change and its impacts. Two recent statements that have received mass media attention were its assertions that 1) warming of the climate is "unequivocal" and it is "extremely likely" (with at least 95% certainty) that human activities are largely responsible and 2) it is "extremely unlikely" that rising temperatures will remain below the 1.5 degrees Celsius increase agreed to in the Paris Agreement. Al Gore, former Vice President of the United States, and the IPCC were co-awarded the Nobel Peace Prize for their work in 2007.

In terms of connections to violent conflict, there is little scholarly evidence to support popularized portrayals of calamitous impacts of climate change. Films like *The Day After Tomorrow* (2004) and *Waterworld* (1995) and even documentaries with titles like *Blue Gold: World Water Wars* (2008) or *Climate for Conflict* (2017) depict violent futures (and present realities) resulting from resource scarcity, primarily water scarcity, or abundance. However, while some studies see linkages with climate change, others (Bernauer and Siegfried 2012; Salehyan 2008; Scheffran et al. 2012) yield little to no support for such direct casual claims suggesting that simple or imminent threats of violence are likely, at least in the short term. It is also important to acknowledge distinctions about the type of conflict that is predicted. For example, most observed conflict has been internal to states or at the sub-state level and not necessarily international in nature (Gleditsch 2012). In addition, some conclude that resource scarcity, particularly of shared waterways, has rarely escalated to violent conflict between nations and can actually facilitate international cooperation (Wolf 1999; Dinar et al. 2012) (see Zawahri's and Weinthal's chapter herein). Thus, it may be more accurate to say that "environmental change *may* increase the risk of violent conflict, though the existing evidence indicates that this is not generally the case" (Gleditsch 2012, 7).

But there is greater consensus on the conceptualization of CC as a "threat multiplier" and the understanding that its impacts will affect different types of in/security. First, instead of being the root or sole instigator of conflict, CC impacts exacerbate existing tensions and scarcities and interact with other variables that culminate in insecurity. It is but one of many stressors. Such was the IPCC's Fourth Assessment Report determination that "Climate change impacts spread from directly impacted areas and sectors to other areas and sectors through extensive and complex linkages" (IPCC 2007, AR 4, Executive Summary WG II, 7.ES). Patricia Espinosa, Executive Secretary of the UNFCCC, echoes these points: "Climate change is the threat multiplier that worsens social, economic, and environmental pressures, leading to social upheaval and possibly even violent conflict" (UNFCCC 2017).

Second, the threats that CC can multiply are recognized as increasingly diverse. In other words, violent conflict between or within nation states is not the only type of security at stake. The most prevalent expansion is the consideration of human security and, thus, the focus on threats to individuals and communities, be it to their physical, socio-cultural, and/or economic wellbeing. Though the concept gained popularity with the 1994 *Human Development Report* (UNDP), it was not explicitly considered by the IPCC until its Fifth Assessment Report (2014) that devoted an entire chapter to climate's impact on human security. A growing literature (academic, governmental, and public) similarly considers how CC affects food security (Hanjra 2010; Lobell et al. 2008; Wheeler and von Braun 2013), human health (Lafferty 2009; McMichael et al. 2006; Patz et al. 2005), and migrations (Frolich 2016; Goodell 2018; Institute for the Study of Diplomacy 2017), for example. (Further discussion of these security threats can be found in chapters by Abnedur and Resende, Gokcek and Formentos, and Campbell in this volume, respectively.)

Given the fact that CC as threat multiplier interacts with multiple other variables, tracing the multitude of ways it can reduce security can be an interminable task. Nonetheless, tracing possible trajectories can be illustrative, both of specific cause–effect relationships and of the second and third-order (cascading) tiers of consequences that can result. One possible thread starts with an area that may already be vulnerable due to weak government institutions, resource scarcity, or demographic stress. Extreme heat or drought, flooding or extreme weather events would, then, exacerbate these conditions by (further) reducing agricultural productivity, for example. If existing institutions are not able to mediate the impacts, the result could be reduced food availability and declining health that could lead to increasing health care costs and/or lost wages (due to the inability to work). The result is a decline in human health and individual/family economic security. Another scenario could lead to a loss of income due to crop failure and eventual migration to neighboring areas in hopes of greater prosperity. If the receiving country or area is also suffering from vulnerabilities and/or if tensions already exist between populations, the result could be perceived or actual inequalities (in treatment or the distribution of resources or services, for example) that could increase physical insecurity or stoke physical violence. Yet another potentiality could be a reduction in a state's agricultural exports and, thus, a decline in national income. Resulting declines in government expenditures could negatively impact a variety of social and subsidized services such as health care, infrastructure, or domestic security. The same fiscal stress could affect a government's ability to reduce underlying climate vulnerabilities and related adaptive capacities, thus further perpetuating the cascade. Similar cascading tiers are possible because of other slow-onset events such as rising sea levels, warming oceans, a decline in fresh water availability, or extreme weather events.

At each stage or "node" of the cascade, however, there is a possibility of interrupting the stream by either stopping it outright or reducing the severity of impacts. Conversely, each "node" contains the potential for aggravating or expediting impacts or creating new or unintended consequences, thereby expanding and intensifying the cascading consequences. Thus, these decision or action nodes become crucial for mediating or adapting to climate change-related insecurity. On the one hand, this suggests many opportunities to stave off deleterious impacts. Government attention, from community to international levels, or the actions of other social forces have great potential to protect individuals and nations from pending insecurity. The other hand suggests a darker reality wherein the cascade turns into a spiral and insecurities multiply, perhaps exponentially.

Two other realities are important to consider when assessing how climate change can reduce security. The first deals with time. With some exceptions, such as extreme weather events, most impacts will not be immediate. They will be delayed, potentially even compounding over time especially if left unattended. This is why it is so difficult to attribute specific outcomes to CC; there are many degrees of temporal separation and opportunities for interactions. The second deals with space. The metaphor of a cascade can operate horizontally as well as vertically. Impacts and insecurities in one area (and attention or inattention to them) can impact other areas. In this way, externalities, or impacts external to a particular community, should be acknowledged. Additionally, insecurities are not and will not be evenly distributed across the globe. Some regions will see warming, others cooling, and others an increase in both extremes. Moreover, areas already vulnerable will likely be hit the hardest. Those most vulnerable are developing countries in the Global South, especially small island nations and countries in Africa and South Asia. Low-income and marginalized communities in these areas as well as those in industrialized countries will be affected more when compared to high-income and socially and politically dominant populations (see Gerring's chapter herein).

Discourse, theory, and climate insecurities

The complexity and variety of potentialities inherent in climate change-related insecurity have a direct impact on discourse and, thus, on how the international community addresses the issue and the policy options members pursue. In this way, *how* climate security is discussed matters. Discourses, or "specific ensembles of ideas, concepts and categorization that are produced, reproduced and transformed in a particular set of practices and through which meaning is given to physical and social realities" (Kamanzi 2014, 14) compete against one another, often with one or a limited set of discourses ultimately dominating policy-making circles. This section builds upon a growing literature on discourse and climate security (Barnett 2001; Detraz and Betsill 2009; Trombetta 2009), compares different discourses and conceptualizations to prominent IR theory, and considers implications for policymaking. In doing so, it considers four criteria posed by McDonald (2013, 43):

1   How the referent object of security is conceptualized
2   Who are conceived as key agents of security
3   How the nature of the threat is defined
4   What responses are suggested for dealing with that threat

In other words, how climate security is discussed determines who is at risk, who is responsible, what the threat is and what should be done to mediate it. To date, prevailing discourses, and thus constructions, have aligned with realist and liberal interpretations of international relations most prominently. This section subsequently adopts a constructivist lens and an emphasis on the social construction of meaning.

Realism

Commensurate with increasing concerns about climate change's threat to national security a tendency has emerged to view impending impacts through a realist lens. Doing so implies a state-centric framework with limited and specific conceptualizations of threats, the threatened, and approaches to reduce/eliminate these threats. The fact that the United Nations Security Council (UNSC); the US State Department, military leaders, CIA officials; the North Atlantic Treaty Organization and even the Nobel Peace Prize Committee have taken up discussion of climate change's threats suggests the adoption of such a conceptualization. Herein, states are the primary concern and unit of analysis. They are at risk of violent conflict either from other states or sub-state actors. States are also the actor best able to protect themselves from said threats. The state apparatus, primarily the military, is best able to provide that protection. In this way, climate change is transformed to a threat on par with terrorism, for example, as military solutions are the most obvious way to protect the state from violent attack.

A similar conceptualization has been adopted by some developing nations who emphasize that the threat is posed by *some particular states*. For example, at the 2007 UNSC debate, countries like Namibia, Papua New Guinea (on the behalf of the Pacific Islands Forum), and Tuvalu argued that the threat from CC is akin to warfare and "just as dangerous as the threat posed to developing countries by guns and bombs" (Detraz and Betsill 2009, 311). At a 2007 African Union summit, Ugandan president Yoweri Museveni similarly called climate change an "act of aggression by the rich against the poor" (Clark 2007). In this scenario, the threat is more clearly attributed to industrialized countries; CO_2 emissions are analogous to weapons and developing countries are the targets. Thus, shifting the discussion from CC as an environmental or "low politics" issue area to a "high politics" conflict issue beneficially refocuses attention on those with the most at risk and places blame on those most culpable.

This state-centric perspective is not ubiquitously held by other developing or developed nations, however. There are a number of concerns about adopting such a conventional conflict framework. While the increased attention and policy-relevance of such a perspective is appreciated, these benefits are outweighed by potential costs. To begin, this type of frame or "scaremongering" with "dire predictions of wars" both risks creating climate change fatigue and a sense of hopelessness as well as diverts attention away from more immediate threats and cost-effective solutions (Brown, Hammill, and McLeman 2007). Desecuritizing climate change and thereby declassifying it as an urgent threat would facilitate greater debate and discussion wherein said policy solutions have a greater chance of being discovered. In other words, framing climate change as "normal politics" may be better suited for such a complex issue (McDonald 2013; Waever 1995).

Additionally, and subsequently, military solutions are not the appropriate means to address the CC problem. First, given that CC is a threat multiplier and that the sources of insecurity are multiple and complex, a one-size-fits-all, top-down military solution oversimplifies the root sources of conflict, likely overlooking crucial variables and interactions, and acts like a band-aid merely attacking the symptom and not those multi-faceted causes. Military interventions also bring their own pathologies. Without a broader understanding and equally multifaceted tactics, conflict will likely reemerge. Similar to critiques of realism's prioritization of a short-term time horizon, military responses to environmental threats are also a short-term solution to a long-term problem. Second, many have criticized a militarized, state-centric discourse arguing that related venues, like the UNSC, are not appropriate spaces for deliberation or authorizing action (Brown, Hammill, and McLeman 2007; Clark 2007; Detraz and Betsill 2009). This is especially true of developing nations fearful that these venues tend to favor industrialized countries with larger, more sophisticated militaries and that these countries may be willing to send troops their way. Preventing or stopping climate change-induced violence could be employed as a rationale to violate weaker states' sovereignty. Such decisions could be a slippery slope to greater military interventions. Approving military action in the name of CC would also be over-stepping the mandates of collective security or military alliance agreements.

Despite such fears, however, the international community has yet to fully concede to a climate change-conflict discourse. Good evidence to this is found in the text of international climate treaties and the subjects of UNFCCC climate negotiations. No treaties or agreements have explicitly connected CC with violent conflict or substantially emphasize state-centric security-related concerns. Additionally, while developing countries, especially the most vulnerable, have worked to integrate security concerns into Conferences of the Parties (COPs) and other international discussions, industrialized countries historically have been successful at redirecting such debates. Detraz and Betsill (2009) also found that, even though CC was the focus of the prominent 2007 UNSC meeting and some states framed it as a threat to physical/state security (employing an environmental conflict discourse), the dominant discourse focused on threats to human security (an environmental security discourse). The discourses competed, but the latter prevailed.

Liberalism

Moving from a realist to a neoliberal institutionalist perspective on the climate change–security nexus expands the scope of key actors, though not radically. Herein, states remain central actors, but as they are part of the larger international community. The referent object of the threat is now international peace and security. Due to existing political, social, and environmental vulnerabilities, the region most under threat is Africa (Brown, Hammill, and McLeman 2007). Institutions are, thus, deemed vital agents in providing security, thereby reflecting the acknowledgment that this international threat requires collection solutions. Though not much remediate action has been taken, such a conceptualization has become a common focus of security discussions. The fact that it is not just states alone that are tackling climate-related security threats, but states in concert, suggests that existing institutions, be they the UN, NATO, or the G7, are being asked to broaden their own definitions of security.

The reality, however, is that not much headway has been made. UNFCCC summits wherein delegates represent their home states, for example, are riddled with acrimony, distrust, and delay. Given the complexity of climate-related security threats and the range of perspectives on the matter (including but not limited to those regarding culpability and responsibility), unanimity may be unattainable. Especially for global institutions like those associated with the UN, agreeing on military-related national or international security solutions is difficult. Regional or smaller institutions may be more successful. Nevertheless, such a state-centric conceptualization, even when expanded to include multilateral institutions they are a part of, may not yield the kind of attention needed.

Another possible explanation for the lack of necessary headway can be found in **public goods** theory. In short, a stable climate is a public good. It is non-rivalrous (one's use or enjoyment does not preclude another's) and non-excludable (actors cannot be easily prevented from enjoying or using the good). The opposite of a private good that the market provides for efficiently, public goods are seen as the purview of governments to provide (when market imperfections cannot provide the good efficiently). Herein, governments work collectively to provide the good for the international community. The difficulty lies in the temptation to free-ride or benefit from the contributions of others without contributing to the provision of the good themselves. Thus, the difficulty in coming to a consensus on culpability and responsibility is compounded by the ease with which countries can decide not to contribute to the mitigation of GHGs or provide adaptation funds, for example, as other states are likely to do so regardless. For countries not immediately experiencing insecurities from CC, there is little incentive to spend time and money providing security.

An alternative liberal perspective is to move beyond states and institutions and look "inside" the state. This allows us to expand our conceptualization of security to include that of individuals. The threat is now to human security or as Khagram and Ali describe it "freedom from both violent conflict and physical want" (2006, 396) or as the IPCC defines it "a condition that exists when the vital core of human lives is protected, and when people have the freedom and capacity to live with dignity" (2014, 759). Here, the referent object is individual people or a collective (on a community level, for example), but could be in specific reference to their food, shelter, livelihood, or culture, for example. The threats, then, are multiple and diffuse, in line with the cascading tiers of consequences. Responses need to be equally comprehensive, both in terms of what is addressed and who addresses it. As for the latter, even though the referent object is now on the individual or community level, responsibility remains with the international community. Members of the international community, in the form of institutions, coordinate efforts, but industrialized countries (Annex I countries) are recognized as having a unique responsibility to implement security.

Over time, the UNFCCC has increasingly incorporated human security concerns into its agenda and policy prescriptions. It has, at the behest of many nations, especially developing nations (non-Annex I), done so by expanding the original focus almost exclusive to mitigation efforts to include vulnerability, resilience, and adaptation. Though not exclusively or explicitly aimed at reducing security threats, discussions have increasingly emphasized the need to support the most vulnerable countries, financially and otherwise, prepare for and minimize the impacts of climate change. Efforts such as the

Cancún Adaptation Framework, Warsaw International Mechanism for Loss and Damage, and the Nairobi Work Programme (each named after the country hosting the COP), were expressly created to adopt a more expansive, integrative and, ideally, thorough approach to climate policymaking that is also more attentive to equity concerns. With these and other efforts, expert groups, task forces and funding mechanisms have been created to facilitate the transfer of information and financial support from Annex I to non-Annex I countries and between non-Annex I countries. In 2016, the UNFCCC formally incorporated migration, displacement, and human mobility into its agenda, thereby casting an even wider net over behaviors affecting and affected by climate change (see Campbell's chapter herein).

Climate-related threats to human security similarly include threats to development and have been incorporated into the charges of many UN agencies and their directives. The UN Development Programme and Environmental Programme as well as the Sustainable Development Goals (SDGs) explicitly link CC and development arguing that climate change is, as former UN Secretary General Ban Ki Moon called it, "the single greatest threat to sustainable development" (UN Regional Information Center for Western Europe 2013). Article 7 of the Paris Climate Accord similarly acknowledges the relationship by establishing a goal of "enhancing adaptive capacity, strengthening resilience and reducing vulnerability to climate change, with a view to contributing to sustainable development" (UNFCCC 2016).

Text box 1.3: The Sustainable Development Goals

Created in 2015, the 17 SDGs "are a universal call to action to end poverty, protect the planet and ensure that all people enjoy peace and prosperity" (UNDP n.d.). They are interconnected international goals to attain, notably, zero hunger, quality education, gender equality, reduced inequalities, and sustainable communities by 2030 (hence its other name: Agenda 2030). Goal number 13 deals explicitly with climate action. Each goal has its own set of measurable indicators. The goals apply to all nations, with no distinctions between developed and developing countries. Though extremely lofty goals, UN agencies and other organizations continue to promote these universal goals globally. The SDGs replaced the eight Millennium Development Goals that unfolded from 2000 to 2015.

Benefits of this conceptualization directly counter the weaknesses of a state-centric model. Most obviously, the focus on human security facilitates bottom-up (as opposed to top-down) strategies that can be better tailored to specific realities and contingencies, better address the fundamental causes of insecurity (as opposed to the symptoms) and, potentially, help slow or prevent contagion effects that result in the greatest insecurities. Each "node" in the cascade is now in play and, thus, there are more opportunities to prevent positive feedback loops and intensifying interactions. Focusing on human security also awards more individual agency and acknowledges groups typically marginalized in state-centric thinking. Examples include women (see Quie's chapter and Gerring's chapter herein), indigenous groups, displaced people or climate migrants/refugees (see Campbell's chapter herein) and poorer communities. In fact, human security discourses often highlight how these actors can be instrumental in reducing insecurity because of the role they play in society and family structures or their use of traditional environmental knowledge, for example (Dankelman 2002; Denton 2002; Eriksen and Brown 2011).

Conclusion

The overarching constructivist framework applied above highlights the variability in how climate security is conceptualized and how that informs different international behavior. It emphasizes the subjectivity inherent in questioning the threat CC poses to security. An emphasis on violent conflict and national security (viewing the threat through a realist lens) prioritizes a state-centric, top-down response that likely addresses symptoms of insecurity rather than root causes. It bypasses the cascading tiers of consequences, focusing instead on selective, terminal consequences. Emphasizing international security and collective responses (from a neoliberal institutionalist approach) suggests institutions like the UNFCCC should protect the security of the international community as a whole, but points to industrialized countries as being the most culpable and most responsible for ensuring the security of the most vulnerable. A human security discourse (constructivist perspective) centers the discussion on individuals and communities, gives them agency, and helps make marginalized groups more visible. It also acknowledges each stage of cascading tiers, including existing vulnerabilities and tensions, thereby potentially best being able to minimize the threats CC may generate. Perhaps it can best curtail the threat multiplier. Overall, then, constructivism serves as a form of meta-theory in its ability to underscore the significance of different applications of international relations theory and, thus, of discourse, varying constructions of security and resulting policy prescriptions.

While originally paying sparse attention to security risks, recent IPCC reports, COPs, and climate agreements have adopted increasingly explicit human security frameworks. What began with a focus on greenhouse gas mitigation has evolved to include climate adaptation and evolved further to consider vulnerability, resilience, compensation and displacement. This evolution was not organic or spontaneous, however. It was the result of decades of scientific study, contentious debate, and public pressure. It is, thus, likely that the *who, what,* and *how* of climate security will continue to evolve as well, leading to new priorities and strategies to provide greater national, international, and human security in the face of inevitable climate change.

Questions for discussion

1   What does it mean to say that CC is a "threat multiplier"? How does it relate to the "cascading tiers of consequences" concept?
2   What is the difference between conceptualizations of CC as a threat to national security, international security, and human security?
3   In what ways has the CC regime (with actors such as the IPCC, UNFCCC, and climate summits) acknowledged and/or addressed contemporary and future threats to security?
4   Are there dangers in adopting a conceptualization of security that is too broad? Is there a point at which accepting too many variables, interactions, contingencies and action/decision nodes becomes unhelpful and overwhelming? Or is the complexity an unavoidable reality?
5   How well do the different conceptualizations of climate insecurity address equity and justice concerns? Would a different conceptualization address them better?
6   Who is the most capable of ensuring security in the face of CC? States? Institutions? Individuals? Who has the greatest responsibility to do so?

References

Barnett, Jon. October 2001. "Security and Climate Change." Working Paper 7. Tyndall Centre Working Paper. Tyndall Centre for Climate Change Research, United Kingdom.

Bernauer, Thomas, and Tobias Siegfried. January 2012. "Climate Change and International Water Conflict in Central Asia." *Journal of Peace Research* 49(1): 227–239.

Bozzo, Sam. 2008. *Blue Gold: World Water Wars.*

Brown, Lester. 1977. *Redefining National Security.* Washington, DC: WorldWatch Institute.

Brown, Oli, Anne Hammill, and Robert McLeman. 2007. "Climate Change as the 'New' Security Threat: Implications for Africa." *International Affairs* 83(6): 1141–1154.

Buhaug, Halvard. September 21, 2010. "Climate Not to Blame for African Civil Wars." *Proceedings of the National Academy of Sciences* 107(38): 16477–16482.

Clark, Andrew. April 18, 2007. "Climate Change Threatens Security, UK Tell UN." *The Guardian.* https://www.theguardian.com/environment/2007/apr/18/greenpolitics.climatechange

Dabelko, Geoffrey D., and David D. Dabelko. Spring 1995. "Environmental Security: Issues of Conflict and Redefinition." Washington, DC: Wilson Center. *Environmental Change and Security Project Report* 1: 3–13.

Dankelman, Irene. July 2002. "Climate Change: Learning from Gender Analysis and Women's Experiences of Organising for Sustainable Development." *Gender and Development* 10(2): 21–29.

Denton, Fatma. July 2002. "Climate Change Vulnerability, Impacts, and Adaptation: Why Does Gender Matter?" *Gender and Development* 10(2): 10–20.

Detraz, Nicole, and Michele M. Betsill. August 2009. "Climate Change and Environmental Security: For Whom the Discourse Shifts." *International Studies Perspectives* 10(3): 303–320.

Deudney, Daniel. December 1990. "The Case Against Linking Environmental Degradation and National Security." *Millennium* 19(3): 461–476.

Dinar, Shlomi, Lucia De Stefano, James Duncan, Kerstin Stahl, Kenneth M. Strzepek, and Aaron T. Wolf. October 18, 2012. "No Wars for Water: Why Climate Change Has Not Led to Conflict." *Foreign Affairs.* https://www.foreignaffairs.com/articles/global-commons/2012-10-18/no-wars-water

Emmerich, Roland. 2004. *The Day After Tomorrow.*

Eriksen, Siri, and Katrina Brown. 2011. "Sustainable Adaptation to Climate Change." *Climate and Development* 3(1): 3–6.

Frolich, Christiana J. 2016. "Climate Migrants as Protesters? Dispelling Misconceptions about Global Environmental Change in Pre-Revolutionary Syria." *Contemporary Levant* 1(1): 38–50.

Galtung, Johan. 1982. *Environment, Development and Military Activity: Towards Alternative Security Doctrines.* Olso: Norwegian University Press.

Gleditsch, Nils Petter, ed. 1997. *Conflict and the Environment.* Dordrecht: Kluwer.

Gleditsch, Nils Petter, ed. January 2012. "Whither the Weather? Climate Change and Conflict." *Journal of Peace Research* 49(1): 3–9.

Goldstone, Jack. 1996. "Debate." Washington, DC: Wilson Center. *Environmental Change and Security Project Report*, no. 2: 66–71.

Goodell, Jeff. 2018. "Welcome to the Age of Climate Migration." *Rolling Stone Magazine*, February 25, 2018. https://www.rollingstone.com/politics/news/welcome-to-the-age-of-climate-migration-w516974

Grundmann, Reiner. July 2016. "Climate Change as a Wicked Social Problem." *Nature Geoscience* 9(8): 562–563. https://doi.org/10.1038/ngeo2780

Hanjra, Munir A., and M. Ejaz Qureshi. October 2010. "Global Water Crisis and Future Food Security in an Era of Climate Change." *Food Policy* 35(5): 365–377.

Hater, Maarten A. 1997. *The Politics of Environmental Discourse: Ecological Modernization and the Policy Process.* Oxford, UK: Oxford University Press.

Head, Brian W. January 2008. "Wicked Problems in Public Policy." *Public Policy* 3(2): 101–118.

Heaton, Laura and Nichole Sobecki. 2017. "Climate for Conflict: Fighting to Survive in Somalia, Once Vibrant and Green, now Plagued by Intense Drought." ABC News and The Ground-Truth Project. https://abcnews.go.com/International/deepdive/nightline-special-report-climate-for-conflict-47435725

Holdren, John P. November 6, 2007. "Global Climate Disruption: What Do We Know? What Should We Do?" John F. Kennedy Jr. Forum. Belfer Center for Science and International Affairs. Harvard University, Cambridge: John F. Kennedy School of Government.

Homer-Dixon, Thomas F. Summer 1994. "Environmental Scarcities and Violent Conflict: Evidence from Cases." *International Security* 19(1): 5–40.

Homer-Dixon, Thomas F. and Marc A. Levy. Winter 1995. "Correspondence: Environment and Security." *International Security* 20(3): 189–198.

Institute for the Study of Diplomacy. 2017. "New Challenges to Human Security: Environmental Change and Human Mobility." Working Group Report. Washington, DC: Walsh School of Foreign Service. Georgetown University.

IPCC. 2007. "Climate Change 2007: Impacts, Adaptation and Vulnerability." Contribution of Working Group II to the Fourth Assessment Report of the Intergovernmental Panel on Climate Change. Cambridge, United Kingdom: Cambridge University Press.

IPCC. 2014. "Climate Change 2014: Impacts, Adaptation and Vulnerability. Part A: Global and Sectoral Aspects." Contribution of Working Group II to the Fifth Assessment Report of the Intergovernmental Panel on Climate Change. Cambridge, United Kingdom: Cambridge University Press.

Kamanzi, Adalbertus. 2014. *Connectedness in Evolution: The Discourse of Modernity on the Ecosophy of the Haya People in Tanzani*. Pretoria (South Africa): Africa Institute of South Africa.

Khagram, Sanjeev, and Saleem Ali. July 2006. "Environment and Security." *Annual Review of Environment and Resources* 31: 395–411.

Lafferty, Kevin D. April 2009. "The Ecology of Climate Change and Infectious Diseases." *Ecology* 90(4): 888–900.

Lazarus, Richard J. 2009. "Super Wicked Problems and Climate Change: Restraining the Present to Liberate the Future." *Cornell Law Review* 94: 1153–1233.

Levin, Kelly, Benjamin Cashore, Steven Bernstein, and Graeme Auld. June 2012. "Overcoming the Tragedy of Super Wicked Problems: Constraining Our Future Selves to Ameliorate Global Climate Change." *Policy Sciences* 45(2): 123–152.

Lobell, David B., Marshall B. Burke, Claudia Tebaldi, Michael D. Mastrandrea, Walter P. Falcon, and Rosamond L. Naylor. February 2008. "Prioritizing Climate Change Adaptation Needs for Food Security in 2030." *Science* 319(5863): 607–610.

McDonald, Matt. March 2013. "Discourses of Climate Security." *Political Geography* 33: 42–51.

McMichael, Anthony J., Rosalie E. Woodruff, and Simon Hales. March 2006. "Climate Change and Human Health: Present and Future Risks." *The Lancet* 367(9513): 859–869.

Paterson, Matthew. 1996. *Global Warming and Global Politics*. New York, NY: Routledge.

Patz, Jonathan A., Diarmid Campbell-Lendrum, Tracey Holloway, and Jonathan A. Foley. November 2005. "Impact of Regional Climate Change on Human Health." *Nature* 438(17): 310–317. https://doi.org/10.1038/nature04188.

Reynolds, Kevin. 1995. *Waterworld*.

Ronnfeldt, Carsten F. November 1997. "Three Generations of Environment and Security Research." *Journal of Peace Research* 34(4): 473–482.

Salehyan, Idean. 2008. "From Climate Change to Conflict? No Consensus Yet." *Journal of Peace Research* 45(3): 315–326.

Scheffran, Jurgen, and Antonella Battaglini. 2011. "Climate and Conflict: The Security Risks of Global Warming." *Regional Environmental Change* 11(1): 27–39.

Scheffran, Jürgen, Michael Brzoska, Jasmin Kominek, P. Michael Link, and Janpeter Schilling. May 18, 2012. "Climate Change and Violent Conflict." *Science* 336(6083): 869–871. https://doi.org/10.1126/science.1221339.

Starr, Joyce R. 1991. "Water Wars." *Foreign Policy* 82 (Spring): 17–36.

Termeer, Catrien, Art Dewulf, and Gerard Breeman. 2013. "Governance of Wicked Climate Adaptation Problems." In *Climate Change Governance*, edited by Jorg Knieling and Walter Leal Filho, 27–39. Heidelbert, Berlin: Springer.

Trombetta, Maria Julia. 2009. "Environmental Security and Climate Change: Analysing the Discourse." *Cambridge Review of International Affairs* 21(4): 585–602.

Ullman, Richard H. Summer 1983. "Redefining Security." *International Security* 8(1): 129–153.

UN Regional Information Center for Western Europe. 2013. "UN Secretary-General: Climate Change Biggest Theat to Sustainable Development." October 22, 2013. https://www.unric.org/en/latest-un-buzz/28783-un-secretary-general-climate-change-biggest-threat-to-sustainable-development-

UNDP. 1994. *Human Development Report*. New York: Oxford University Press.

UNFCCC. 2016. "The Paris Agreement." New York, NY: United Nations. https://unfccc.int/files/meetings/paris_nov_2015/application/pdf/paris_agreement_english_.pdf

UNFCCC. 2017. "Patricia Espinosa: 'The Climate Change Story Is a Security Story.'" 2017. https://unfccc.int/news/patricia-espinosa-the-climate-change-story-is-a-security-story

Vidal, John, Adam Vaughan, Suzanne Goldenberg, et al. December 12, 2015. "World Leaders Hail Paris Climate Deal as 'Major Leap for Mankind.'" *The Guardian*. https://www.theguardian.com/environment/2015/dec/13/world-leaders-hail-paris-climate-deal

Waever, Ole. 1995. "Securitization and Desecuritization." In Ronnie D. Lipschutz ed. *On Security*, 46–86. New York, NY: Columbia University Press.

Wheeler, Tim, and Joachim von Braun. August 2, 2013. "Climate Change Impacts on Global Food Security." *Science* 341(6145): 508–513.

Wolf, Aaron T. 1999. "'Water Wars' and Water Reality: Water Conflict and Cooperation along International Waterways." 251–265 in S. C. Lonergan, ed. *Environmental Change, Adaptation, and Security*. Dordrecht: Springer.

Chapter 2

Geoengineering
A new and emerging security threat?

Michael D. Beevers

Introduction

Climate change (CC) is happening (see Below's chapter herein). Global temperatures increased by 0.85 degrees Celsius during the 20th century, and are projected to rise another two degrees, and potentially five degrees, by 2100 (IPCC 2014). The last 30 year period was the warmest in the last 1400 years, and 2014, 2015 and 2016 broke global temperature records three years in a row (IPCC 2014; Gillis 2017). Temperature is only one of the phenomena that will be affected as precipitation, humidity, soil moisture, atmospheric circulation patterns, storms, snow and ice cover and ocean currents are expected to change dramatically. Declines in food production, water scarcity, human health epidemics, increases in the intensity and frequency of natural disasters, sea level rise and coastal inundation will undermine the ability of people to sustain their livelihoods, intensify poverty, increase migration, and weaken the capacity of states to provide basic services to their citizens (IPCC 2014). The effects of CC could even exacerbate social instability and increase the risk of armed conflict (Barnett and Adger 2007)

Overwhelming scientific evidence concludes that the main cause of CC are **anthropogenic** greenhouse gases (GHG), the largest being carbon dioxide, a heat-trapping gas released into the atmosphere through, mostly, the combustion of fossil fuels. To avoid the most destructive impacts of CC, global GHG emissions would need to be reduced by 50–80 percent by mid-century (IPCC 2014). Because climate change is a global problem, international agreements have been negotiated to mitigate it. The 1992 UN Framework Convention on Climate Change, acknowledged that climate change was a "common concern of humanity", and made clear that industrialized countries (as opposed to less industrialized countries) were responsible, and thus, obligated to take the lead in addressing it. The 1997 Kyoto Protocol went further by mandating specific emissions reductions by industrialized countries. Unfortunately, reducing emissions has proven technically difficult and politically contentious. The United States, which accounted for a substantial share of the world's emissions, failed to ratify the Kyoto Protocol, and although emissions from some industrialized countries were reduced, many others had trouble meeting targets. Moreover, any total GHG emissions reductions set out in the Kyoto Protocol were offset by countries like China and India, which were undergoing rapid economic growth. In fact, global emissions increased by almost 50 percent since 1990 when international attempts to address CC began (IPCC 2014).

Following the 2016 Paris Agreement, all countries agreed to put in place "ambitious" emissions reductions to keep global warming below two degrees Celsius. There is considerable uncertainty whether the Paris Agreement will achieve its aims. The US withdrew from the agreement in 2017, and studies show that commitments to cut emissions are not sufficient given growing global consumption habits and fossil fuel use (Rogelj et al. 2016). Even if emissions were stabilized immediately, we are still "committed" to CC because increases in GHG emission are essentially irreversible (Solomon et al. 2009). In short, getting GHG concentrations down to pre-industrial levels would take hundreds, if not thousands, of years.

Given the inconvenient truths regarding CC, new approaches are required. International agreements are essential, but argue that climate governance needs to take place at a variety of scales, and incorporate a diverse set of initiatives and actors (Bulkeley and Newell 2010). Others argue that only a full-scale transformation of the world's energy system will suffice (Geller 2003). Either way, fewer people now believe we will limit climate change significantly enough in the years ahead. It is within this context that **geoengineering** has emerged as a gradually more plausible alternative or complement to address climate change. *Geoengineering refers to deliberately altering the Earth's climate in response to climate change by capturing and storing excess carbon or altering the amount of solar radiation that hits the Earth.* In other words, humans would intentionally deploy new-fangled technologies and techniques to get the planet back to its "pre-industrial" condition, and thereby reverse the detrimental effects of anthopogenic climate change. But, although geoengineering might help mitigate climate change, it might also endanger the global environment and human life. Little is known, or understood, about how geoengineering would interact with the planet's complex ecosystems. Significant moral and ethical questions would need to be addressed if geoengineering were to be deployed.

Since geoengineering seeks to change the Earth's climate, it has the potential to be a new international, national, and human security threat. This chapter highlights these issues. It begins with an overview of current geoengineering techniques. Next it details the direct and indirect security implications of geoengineering. After that, it discusses how geoengineering could weaken poor and vulnerable states, and make people more insecure if regional weather patterns are affected. Given the security implications of geoengineering, the chapter explains potential options for global governance. The conclusion argues that how geoengineering is framed in the years ahead will ultimately shape not only perceptions of the security threat, but also how geoengineering is governed at the international level.

What is geoengineering?

Over the last dozen years, interest in geoengineering has vastly increased. A handful of books have been published on the topic (Goodell 2010; Kintisch 2010; Hamilton 2013), and articles are appearing more frequently in the mainstream press (Wood 2009; Porter 2017). Discussions about the benefits and pitfalls of geoengineering have started to appear as a serious topic in academic journals (Crutzen 2006; MacCracken 2006; Virgoe 2009; Wannier et al. 2011), and scholarly titles (Burns and Strauss 2013; Keith 2013). Reports by the Royal Society (2009), US GAO (General Accountability Office) (2010), and National Academy of Sciences (National Research Council 2015), among others, have focused on geoengineering, and conferences and symposiums have been organized on the topic. The IPCC even reported openly about geoengineering in its fifth Assessment Report (IPCC 2014; Parker and Geden 2016).

The prospect of intentionally altering the climate (or weather) is not new (Victor et al., 2009; Goodell 2010; Hamilton 2013). Geoengineering was first proposed as a response to climate change as early as 1965 (Revelle et al. 1965). Nevertheless, the world's inability to address CC has led many to take geoengineering seriously. At least 50 novel geoengineering schemes have been identified, with a focus on carbon dioxide removal (CDR) and solar radiation management (SRM) (Parson and Keith 2013).

Text box 2.1: Geoengineering

Geoengineering is the deliberate large-scale intervention in the Earth's climate system, in order to moderate global warming. CDR refers to the removal carbon dioxide from the atmosphere and the storing of it underground, in the oceans or on land. One CDR technique would use an industrial process to "scrub" the atmosphere, and in doing so, mechanically extract carbon dioxide. Another would "fertilize" oceans with iron sulfate to stimulate vast algal blooms that could sequester carbon from the atmosphere. Similar schemes would spread huge amounts of lime in the oceans to increase the acidification process, enhance weathering of rock, or use artificial trees to capture carbon dioxide. CDR techniques remain untested and speculative, especially in terms of deployment on a global scale. However, with the exception of ocean fertilization, CDR would act on the climate in a slow and expensive manner, and the risks would be localized and controllable (Royal Society 2009; Humphreys 2011). SRM, by contrast, refers to the manipulation of the Earth's inbound solar radiation. SRM technologies would reflect sunlight away from the Earth to offset the warming caused by climate change. An often-discussed technique would inject salt particles into the atmosphere to whiten clouds to increase reflectivity (Vaughan and Lenton 2011). Another scheme would inject sulfur particles into the stratosphere, thereby mimicking volcanic eruptions, to deflect sunlight back into space (Crutzen 2006). Yet another would be the deployment of thousands of mirrors or other reflective surfaces into outer space to create a massive "sunshade" that would cool the planet. Little is known about the consequences and effectiveness of SRM, but estimates suggest that if deployed results could be achieved relatively rapidly, at reasonably low cost, using available technologies, and requiring minimal resources or territory (Kravitz et al. 2013). The downside is that SRM could drastically alter regional precipitation patterns and deplete the ozone layer (Bodansky 2011). For these reasons, SRM is the geoengineering technology believed to be the biggest threat to security and require international governance (Lloyd and Oppenheimer 2014).

Unless otherwise noted, geoengineering herein focuses on SRM.

Geoengineering: An emerging threat to security?

Entrepreneurs and scientists continue to speculate about geoengineering, but such technologies have not been fully designed, let alone tested or deployed. Governments have not dismissed the idea, yet none is actively encouraging or seriously researching geoengineering. As such, the security implications and international governance futures are impossible to comprehend (Corry 2017, 299). Regardless, the idea that geoengineering will pose a serious threat to the security of states and people has started to appear as a topic of discussion (Ricke et al. 2008; Victor et al. 2009; Horton 2011; Cairns 2014; Nightingale and Cairns 2014; Horton and Reynolds 2016; Corry 2017).

The emergence of geoengineering raises the specter that it could serve the interests of state power or be deployed as a weapon of war. Military planners have long considered how weather could be controlled and modified to gain an advantage on the battlefield (Fleming 2012). In the late 1940s, the US funded "Project Cirrus" to increase rainfall through "cloud seeding," and during the Cold War there were substantial efforts to "weaponize" the environment in preparation for a possible World War III (Hamblin 2013). In the Vietnam War, "Operation Popeye" was introduced to increase monsoon rains and disrupt enemy supply lines (Hersh 1972). These revelations led to the Convention on the Prohibition of Military or Any Other Hostile Use of Environmental Modification Techniques (ENMOD) that prohibited the "military or any other hostile use of environmental modification techniques having widespread, long lasting or severe effects as the means of destruction, damage or injury" (ENMOD 1978, Article I). The treaty was not tested due to perceptions that modifying the weather was laden with too many uncertainties coupled with a lack of renewed funding in the 1980s and 1990s (Ricke et al. 2008). Nevertheless, modifying the weather and climate for military purposes has not disappeared altogether (National Research Council 2003). House et al. (1996, 6) identified weather as a "force multiplier", and suggested that weather modification "offers the war fighter a wide range of possible options to defeat and coerce an adversary."

Given the development and spread of nuclear weapons, one can well imagine a world in which controlling the weather and climate becomes a viable political and military strategy. Powerful states (or a group of them) with the ability to develop and deploy geoengineering could see fit to alter environmental conditions to weaken an adversary. Faced with a security threat, states could also develop geoengineering technologies to serve as a defensive weapon or deterrent. Or, a "rogue" state could pursue geoengineering in order to threaten powerful states or gain international attention. Regardless, trying to leverage geoengineering for military purposes could backfire. First, "weaponizing" climate could produce collateral damage due to its vast unpredictability. Any state that deploys geoengineering offensively could be the target of unintended impacts, including changing precipitation or temperature patterns that could undermine its power. Second, compared to economic tools or military tactics, modifying the climate could be of comparatively little strategic value. For example, today's precision weapons, use of surveillance, or targeted sanctions might effectively modify a state's behavior without the collateral damage of geoengineering (Nightingale and Cairns 2014). Third, there is the likelihood that any military use would result in **counterbalancing** by other state actors. In such a scenario, a country might deploy geoengineering countermeasures to balance, or offset, the military advantages of geoengineering, or wage war to neutralize any geoengineering threat.

There is no evidence to date that powerful states are unilaterally developing geoengineering as a weapon. However, military and intelligence agencies are likely to be important funders of geoengineering technologies, which can create mistrust about intentions. Conspiracy theorists already claim that temperature spikes around the world are the result of the US deliberately interfering in the climate to produce instability (Cleek 2010). If geoengineering research should lead to major advances in knowledge and techniques relevant for weather control, it is hard to imagine that knowledge not being put to use. Geoengineering, if it develops, will be a dual use technology. In other words, if deployed for the peaceful purpose of addressing CC, geoengineering could quickly and cheaply be converted for hostile purposes with few modifications, creating an "arms race" among powerful states that could lead to proliferation of these technologies.

The likelihood that geoengineering be used as an instrument of state power is plausible. But a more likely scenario is that states unilaterally develop and deploy geoengineering to address the implications of CC itself. Imagine that an unprecedented drought has gripped the US for years leading it to declare a "climate emergency" and prompting US authorities to inject sulfur particles to cool the planet. Or, perhaps, faced with rising seas that threaten virtually all of its population, Bangladesh decides to do the same thing. The problem is that one state's response to a climate emergency will have uncertain consequences for all and could be regarded as a security threat to other states.

The point is that if geoengineering is used unilaterally by a state to address CC, it could disrupt precipitation patterns and impact food systems globally. The risk exists that geoengineering, even if deployed for "non-hostile" CC mitigation, could imperil another state's security by altering their environment. Picture the reaction of the European Union, Russia, or China if the US decided to conduct geoengineering experiments to address a massive drought. The US might view it as a global **public good** that provides benefits to the world (Virgoe 2009, 116). Research suggests, however, that SRM technologies would adversely affect monsoon rains throughout Asia and lead to more droughts in Africa (Tilmes et al. 2013; Jones et al. 2017). The possibility of negative consequences would likely trigger a response of "sanctions, trade war or worse" from states, or a coalition of states, fearful of negative geoengineering consequences (Horton 2011, 57). In other words, the unilateral decision by the US to respond to climate change with geoengineering might be counterproductive for security if it weakens allies or elicits a hostile response from adversaries. In addition, once unleashed on a large scale, virtually every extreme weather event would be linked to geoengineering, causing a series of security challenges that could threaten international instability, or even lead to war.

The idea that geoengineering deployed by a state or group of states is a threat to the security of other states is consistent with realist theories of international relations. From this perspective, the international system resembles an anarchic "self-help" world where states—the only actors that matter in world affairs—have no choice but to perpetually enhance military and economic power to at a minimum guarantee their own survival, and maximum, seek domination (Waltz 1979; Keohane 1986). Suspicion, tensions, and aggression are the normal state of affairs and states must look after their security needs at all costs. Given this logic, states might use, or threaten to use, geoengineering as an instrument of power, and to advance their national interests. This suggests that if one state monopolizes geoengineering technologies it is likely that other states will move to either eliminate any geoengineering threat by military means, or "balance out" any perceived strategic advantage. This dynamic reflects the so-called **security dilemma** in which one country's quest for security ends up as another state's source of insecurity. Efforts to address this dilemma would lead to balancing behavior, and likely result in a geoengineering arms race. For realists, then, geoengineering likely presents a direct challenge to state security and power.

States are the most likely to deploy geoengineering unilaterally, but there is the possibility that private, non-state actors could leverage the technology to forward their interests, and thereby threaten security. Victor et al. note that "some geoengineering options are cheap enough to be deployed by wealthy and capable individuals or corporations" (2009, 66). On the one hand, so-called "greenfingers" could single-handedly finance the deployment of geoengineering technologies in an attempt to reverse CC (Victor 2008). On the other hand, corporations could create and research novel technologies as business ventures. Finally, rogue engineers might want to "save the world and make a little cash on the side" (Hamilton 2015). There have been small-scale experiments carried out by private entities, including one that dumped iron into the Pacific Ocean, and it is apparent that as geoengineering becomes more acceptable the likelihood of additional research, sanctioned by governments or not, will increase.

This perspective diverges from realism by suggesting that non-state actors, and not simply states, are key factors that influence national security (Mathews 1989). New transboundary threats (disease, terrorism, civil wars, cyber-attacks) are central features of globalization and undermine the security of states, but non-state actors (non-governmental organizations, terrorist groups, international organizations, private businesses) are also sources of insecurity. The global diffusion of ideas and technologies makes it easier for non-state actors, be they terrorists, entrepreneurs or activists, to gain access to and deploy dangerous or risky technologies, including geoengineering. In addition, there is a growing perception non-state actors play an increasing role in addressing new threats (Keck and Sikkink 1998; Krahmann 2005). As power and authority in the international system is becoming more diffuse, 21st century security threats will not likely be addressed unilaterally. While states remain the key actors in international relations, addressing future threats and actors will require active cooperation and coordination with non-state actors like NGOs, multinational corporations, and organizations like the United Nations.

The likelihood exists that poor and vulnerable states without the resources to adapt to the negative effects of geoengineering will suffer. Geoengineering could become a threat multiplier that rather than simply reversing CC would adversely disrupt the environment, including the provision of food and water. Environmental degradation and resource scarcity have been linked to instability and even the onset of armed conflict (Homer-Dixon 1994). The picture is complex as poverty, inequality, governance, state legitimacy and capacity, and ethnic tensions are all factors. Nevertheless, it is conceivable that the consequences of geoengineering "gone wrong" could indirectly foment social instability, political crises, and civil strife. The negative consequences of geoengineering would reverberate globally, since weather and climate events affect other parts of the world. For instance, massive declines in wheat production in China would likely reverberate in the Middle East and beyond where people rely on imports of Chinese wheat. Therefore, like climate change, geoengineering poses a potential threat not only to the security of states, but also to the security of individuals (Barnett and Adger 2007). If geoengineering does alter the environment negatively, it would disproportionately affect the poorest states and most marginalized people around the world. This could trigger social and political instability that would be calamitous for human security.

International governance of geoengineering

The perception that geoengineering may cause more harm than good, and that it could be deployed in ways that have serious security implications has opened up discussions about ways to govern geoengineering at the international level (Virgoe 2009; Bodansky 2011; Horton 2011; Dilling and Hauser 2013; Lloyd and Oppenheimer 2014). As Keith notes, "stable control of geoengineering may require new forms of global governance" in the 21st century at a level comparable to nuclear weapons the century before (2013, x–xi). The US and the United Kingdom have both supported an international governance framework for geoengineering (US House Committee on Science and Technology 2010; UK House of Commons 2010).

Calls for international governance largely reject realism, and instead reflect institutionalist theories of international relations. Institutionalism argues that although states are the preeminent actors in world politics and anarchy is the central feature of the international system, institutions (with the influence of non-state actors) play a key part in fostering greater cooperation among states and thereby reducing the prospect of unilateralism and rivalry that often threaten security. Institutions, including organizations, agencies, treaties and agreements help create rules and practices over time become accepted as binding (Haas, Keohane, and Levy 1993). An important result of institutions is the establishment of regimes that would constrain the behavior of states, and shape expectations among states in ways that build trust and provide mutual benefits (Krasner 1983). In theory, a geoengineering regime would provide agreed upon institutions, rules, principles, norms and procedures that would govern its use and deployment, enhance cooperation and coordination, and reduce uncertainties that often underpin security dilemmas.

Since current international institutions fall short of addressing geoengineering, a growing discussion develops around how geoengineering governance should be designed that considers the nature of the problem, amount of uncertainty involved, and variability of state interests. One potential approach suggests that any governance arrangement be led by economic and technologically advanced states such as the US, China, Russia, Brazil, India, Australia, South Africa and European states that are capable of deploying geoengineering technology. The rationale for incorporating a reduced membership of countries is that smaller groups tend to be more coherent in their interests (i.e., collective vulnerability), have a desire to share technical capacity and financial obligations, and reduce uncertainty (Lloyd and Oppenheimer 2014). More importantly, a small group of capable states increases the likelihood of them joining any regime, which at the early stage of regime formation is critical. Such an arrangement would also ensure that decisions are made quicker in the event that any decision about geoengineering research or deployment needed to be made.

Of course, such a model would be criticized by the less financially and technologically powerful, and more vulnerable, states. For one, it would leave conventional power relations intact, and give the vast responsibility for geoengineering to the states that caused CC in the first place. Given that CC and geoengineering would both have global impacts (both positive and negative), the legitimacy of any governance regime would be enhanced by broad public participation and open dialogue among all states (Lloyd and Oppenheimer 2014). Therefore, another governing arrangement would make decisions about geoengineering by consensus where all signatories to any regime would have an equal vote. The benefits of such an arrangement are that decisions that affect the world would need to have wide approval from the international community. The potential downside is that such arrangements, based on the full membership of 197 states, are a hard sell to those that want to restrict power of decision-making. The idea that a small group of states could block "time-sensitive" geoengineering decisions in the face of a climate emergency would likely deter the participation of the advanced states and even increase the likelihood of unilateralism.

A potential hybrid arrangement proposes a small group of states, perhaps 30 or fewer, but one that includes states that are vulnerable, and not capable of geoengineering. According to Lloyd and Oppenheimer (2014), this arrangement would allow for quicker decision-making and implementation, but also add legitimacy if states or regional organizations were included; perhaps on a rotating basis like the UN Security Council. Another possibility would be to allow larger membership to be part of the regime, but weight the votes. More advanced states would receive more voting power, although if vulnerable states voted as a bloc they could influence decision-making. Victor (2008) argues that moving too fast to establish a governance arrangement might result in poor coordination, a counterproductive ban, or political stalemate. As a result, next steps might be to develop norms from the bottom up that will inform international governance. Such bottom up norms would spread not only from states, but also from non-state actors such as researchers, businesses, and activists. In fact, proposals like the Oxford Principles that touch all actors have so far been influential.

Text box 2.2: The Oxford Principles

The Oxford Principles are a proposed set of initial guiding principles for the governance of geoengineering (Oxford Geoengineering Programme, 2018).

Principle 1. Geoengineering to be regulated as a public good
Principle 2. Public participation in geoengineering decision-making
Principle 3: Disclosure of geoengineering research and open publication of results
Principle 4: Independent assessment of impacts
Principle 5: Governance before deployment

Another suggestion is to create a World Commission on Geoengineering that would debate geoengineering principles, create a dialogue for geoengineering research, and investigate various governance structures (Parson 2017). Perhaps annual joint conferences of the parties, or a scientific body comparable to the IPCC, would be developed to share scientific knowledge and research on geoengineering. Any international governance arrangement for geoengineering must be durable. Schneider argued that it must "be maintained without interruption by wars and ideological disputes for the next two centuries" (1996, 299). This is easier said than done. International environmental agreements have increased dramatically over the last 40 years, but efforts to govern the contentious and wicked phenomenon of CC have been difficult. Geoengineering governance will be similar in many respects. Nonetheless, as Humphreys put it, "geoengineering governance is possible and necessary if international conflict is to be avoided and the risks of unintended consequences are to be minimized" (2011, 99).

Conclusion

Geoengineering is emerging on the global scene given growing concerns about runaway CC and our inability to rein in emissions. However, two notions stand out. First, the uncertainties and ramifications inherent in intentionally manipulating the Earth's climate will make developing and deploying geoengineering both contentious and controversial. Indeed, how geoengineering comes to be framed in the human consciousness through ideas, images, and categorizations will ultimately shape its future (Litfin 1994). For example, geoengineering is frequently framed in reference to a future "climate emergency", or as a less risky and cheaper alternative to CC mitigation options (Bellamy

2013; Huttunen and Hildén 2014). Such framings create incentives to develop and deploy geoengineering. Alternatively, geoengineering is framed as a "band aid" that does nothing to address the root cause of climate change and could possibly create new-fangled and irreversible problems (Corner and Pidgeon 2010; Jamieson 2013). These framings advocate extreme precaution in the use of geoengineering, and potentially even a ban on the technology. Moreover, perceptions of the security threat will inform state behavior and how geoengineering is governed at the international level (Wendt 1992). As Horton and Reynolds note, "whether relations among states (and other actors) would be conflictual, cooperative or something else would be a function of the prevailing cultural logic" (2016, 455).

Second, geoengineering is not an "easy option" (Corry 2017, 309). Reining in GHG emissions and addressing climate change have been challenging to date, but at least the technology and knowledge to address the problem exist in abundance. The major constraint is political will. Geoengineering, on the other hand, embraces technologies that do not yet fully exist, and will likely be just as politically difficult to implement. What's more, while CC threatens the security of states and people alike, geoengineering would most certainly introduce a wholly new security paradigm that would rewrite world politics. The question before all of us is whether it is worth it.

Questions for discussion

1   What is geoengineering? What are the two most prominent interventions?
2   How might geoengineering development and/or deployment affect the security of different states? How might it rewrite world politics?
3   Why is international governance of geoengineering potentially important? How would you design geoengineering governance? Why?
4   Compared to other security challenges in the book, how serious is geoengineering? Is it something we should address now or in the future?
5   What are some of the ethical and moral questions surrounding geoengineering? Do you support geoengineering?

References

Barkham, Patrick. February 16, 2015. "Can the CIA Weaponize the Weather?" *The Guardian*.
Barnett, Jon and W. Neil Adger. August 2007. "Climate Change, Human Security and Violent Conflict." *Political Geography* 26(6): 639–655. https://doi.org/10.1016/j.polgeo.2007.03.003
Bellamy, Rob. December 10, 2013. "Framing Geoengineering Assessment." https://www.clima te-engineering.eu/single/bellamy-rob-2013-framing-geoengineering-assessment.html
Bodansky, Daniel. November 2011. "Governing Climate Engineering: Scenarios for Analysis." *Cambridge MA: Harvard Kennedy School: Harvard Project on Climate Agreements, Discussion Paper* 11–47.
Bulkeley, Harriet A. and Peter Newell. 2010. *Governing Climate Change*. New York, NY: Routledge.
Burns, Wil C.G. and Andrew L. Strauss, eds. 2013. *Climate Change Geoengineering: Philosophical Perspectives, Legal Issues and Governance Frameworks*. Cambridge: Cambridge University Press.
Cairns, Rose. November 12, 2014. "Will Solar Radiation Management Enhance Global Security in a Changing Climate?" Climate Geoengineering Governance Working Paper Series: 016. http://www.geoengineering-governance-research.org/perch/resources/workingpaper16ca irnssrmandsecurity.pdf

Cleek, Ashley. July 30, 2010. "Russian Scholar Warns of 'Secret' US Climate Change Weapon." *Radio Free Europe.* https://www.rferl.org/a/Russian_Scholar_Warns_Of_Secret_US_Climate_Change_Weapon/2114381.html

Corner, Adam and Nick Pidgeon. September 2010. "Geoengineering the Climate: The Social and Ethical Implications." *Environment* 52(1): 24–37. https://doi.org/10.1080/00139150903479563

Corry, Olaf. July 10, 2017. "The International Politics of Geoengineering: The Feasibility of Plan B for Tackling Climate Change." *Security Dialogue* 48(4): 297–315.

Crutzen, Paul. August 2006. "Albedo Enhancement by Stratospheric Sulfur Injections: A Contribution to Resolve a Policy Dilemma?" *Climatic Change* 77: 211–220.

Dilling, Lisa and Rachel Hauser. December 2013. "Governing Geoengineering Research: Why, When and How?" *Climatic Change* 121(3): 553–565.

ENMOD. 1978. Convention on the Prohibition of Military and Any Other Hostile Use of Environmental Modification Techniques. https://treaties.un.org/doc/source/docs/A_RES_31_72-E.pdf

Fleming, James Rodger. 2012. *Fixing the Sky: The Checkered History of Weather and Climate Control.* New York, NY: Columbia University Press.

Geller. Howard. 2003. *Energy Revolution: Policies for a Sustainable Future.* Washington DC: Island Press.

Gillis, Justin. 2017. "Earth Sets a Temperature Record for the Third Straight Year." *New York Times,* January 18.

Goodell, Jeff. 2010. *How to Cool the Planet: Geoengineering and the Audacious Quest to Fix the World's Climate.* New York, NY: Houghton Mifflin Harcourt.

Haas, Peter M., Robert O. Keohane and Marc A. Levy, eds. 1993. *Institutions for the Earth: Sources of Effective International Environmental Protection.* Cambridge, MA: MIT Press.

Hamblin, Jacob Darwin. 2013. *Arming Mother Nature: The Birth of Catastrophic Environmentalism.* Oxford: Oxford University Press.

Hamilton, Clive. 2013. *Earthmasters: The Dawn of the Age of Climate Engineering.* New Haven: Yale University Press.

Hamilton, Clive. February 17, 2015. "Geoengineering is No Place for Corporate Profit Making." *The Guardian.*

Hersh, Seymour M. July 3, 1972. "Rainmaking is Used as Weapon by US." *New York Times.*

Homer-Dixon, Thomas F. Summer 1994. "Environment Scarcities and Violent Conflict: Evidence from Cases." *International Security* 19(1): 5–40.

Horton, Joshua B. January 2011. "Geoengineering and the Myth of Unilateralism: Pressure and Prospects for International Cooperation." *Stanford Journal of Law, Science and Policy* 4(1): 56–69.

Horton, Joshua B. and Jesse L. Reynolds. September 2016. "The International Politics of Climate Engineering: A Review and Prospects for International Relations." *International Studies Review* 18(3): 438–461.

House, Tamzy J. et al. June 17, 1996. "Weather as a Force Multiplier: Owning the Weather in 2025." Research paper presented at Air Force 2025. https://www.researchgate.net/publication/2574862_Weather_as_a_Force_Multiplier_Owning_the_Weather_in_2025

Humphreys, David. June 2011. "Smoke and Mirrors: Some Reflections on the Science and Politics of Geoengineering." *Journal of Environment and Development* 20(2): 99–120. https://doi.org/10.1177/1070496511405302

Huttunen, Suvi and Mikael Hildén. February 2014. "Framing the Controversial: Geoengineering in Academic Literature." *Science Communication* 36(1): 3–29. https://doi.org/10.1177/1075547013492435

IPCC (Intergovernmental Panel on Climate Change). 2014. *Climate Change 2014: Synthesis Report.* Geneva: IPCC.

Jamieson, Dale. December 2013. "Some Whats, Whys and Worries of Geoengineering." *Climatic Change* 121(3): 527–537.

Jones, Anthony C., James H. Hawood, Nick Dunstone et al. 2017. "Impacts of Hemispheric Geoengineering on Tropical Cyclone Frequency." *Nature Communication* 8(1382).

Keck, Margaret E. and Kathryn Sikkink. 1998. *Activists Beyond Borders: Advocacy Networks in International Politics.* Ithaca, NY: Cornell University Press.

Keith, David. 2013. *A Case for Climate Engineering.* Cambridge, MA: MIT Press.

Keohane, Robert O., ed. 1986. *Neorealism and its Critics.* New York, NY: Columbia University Press.

Kintisch, Eli. 2010. *Hack the Planet: Science's Best Hope—or Worst Nightmare—for Averting Climate Catastrophe.* Hoboken, NJ: John Wiley.

Krahmann, Elke, ed. 2005. *New Threats and New Actors in International Security.* New York, NY: Palgrave-MacMillan.

Krasner, Stephen D., ed. 1983. *International Regimes.* Ithaca, NY: Cornell University Press.

Kravitz, Ben et al. July 16, 2013. "Climate Model Response from the Geoengineering Model Intercomparison Project (GeoMIP)." *Journal of Geophysical Research* 118(15): 8320–8332.

Litfin, Karen T. 1994. *Ozone Discourses: Science and Politics in Global Environmental Cooperation.* New York, NY: Columbia University Press.

Lloyd, Ian D. and Michael Oppenheimer. May 2014. "On the Design of an International Governance Framework for Geoengineering." *Global Environmental Politics* 14(2): 45–63.

MacCracken, Michael C. August 2006. "Geoengineering: Worthy of Cautious Evaluation?" *Climatic Change* 77(3–4): 235–243.

Mathews, Jessica Tuchman. Spring 1989. "Redefining Security." *Foreign Affairs* 68(2): 162–177.

Nightingale, Paul and Rose Cairns. November 12, 2014. "The Security Implications of Geoengineering: Blame, Imposed Agreement and the Security of Critical Infrastructure." Climate Geoengineering Governance Working Paper Series: 018. http://www.geoengineering-governance-research.org/perch/resources/workingpaper18nightingalecairnssecurityimplications.pdf

National Research Council. 2003. *Critical Issues in Weather Modification Research.* Washington DC: National Academies Press.

National Research Council. 2015. *Climate Intervention: Reflecting Sunlight to Cool Earth.* Washington DC: National Academies Press.

Olson, Robert L. November 2011. "Geoengineering for Decision Makers." Washington DC: Woodrow Wilson Center, Science and Technology Innovation Program Report 2.

Oxford Geoengineering Programme. 2018. "Oxford Principles." http://www.geoengineering.ox.ac.uk/oxford-principles/principles/?

Parker, Andy and Oliver Geden. November 21, 2016. "No Fudging on Geoengineering." *Nature Geoscience* 9: 859–860.

Parson, Edward A. August 15, 2017. "Starting a Dialogue on Climate Engineering Governance: A World Commission." Waterloon, Ont.: Centre for International Governance Innovation: Fixing Climate Governance Series Policy Brief 8.

Parson, Edward A. and David Keith. March 15, 2013. "End the Deadlock on Governance of Geoengineering Research." *Science* 339(6125): 1278–1279.

Porter, Eduardo. April 4, 2017. "To Curb Global Warming, Science Fiction May Become Fact." *New York Times.*

Rayner, Steve et al. December 2013. "The Oxford Principles." *Climatic Change* 121(3): 499–512.

Revelle, Roger. 1965. "Atmospheric Carbon Dioxide." Washington, DC: The White House. Restoring the Quality of our Environment, Report of the Environ Pollut Panel, President's Science Advisory Committee (Appendix Y4).

Ricke, Katharine M. et al. May 5, 2008. "Unilateral Geoengineering." Washington DC. Non-technical briefing notes for workshop at the Council on Foreign Relations.

Rogelj, Joeri et al. 2016. "Paris Agreement Climate Proposals Need a Boost to Keep Warming Well Below 2°C." *Nature* 534: 631–639.

Royal Society. September 2009. *Geoengineering the Climate: Science, Governance and Uncertainty.* London: Science Policy Centre Report.

Schneider, Stephen. July 1996. "Geoengineering: Could or Should We Do It?" *Climatic Change* 33 (3): 291–302.

Solomon, Susan et al. February 2009. "Irreversible Climate Due to Carbon Dioxide Emissions." *Proceedings of the National Academies of Science* 106(6): 1704–1709.

Tilmes, Simone et al. October 3, 2013. "The Hydrological Impact of Geoengineering in the Geoengineering Model Intercomparison Project." *Journal of Geophysical Research Atmospheres* 118 (19): 11036–11058.

UK House of Commons. March 10, 2010. *The Regulation of Geoengineering*. Science and Technology Committee, Fifth Report of Session 2009–2010.

US GAO (US Government Accountability Office). 2010. *Climate Change: A Coordinated Strategy Could Focus Federal Geoengineering Research and Inform Governance Efforts*. GAO-10-903. October 26.

US House Committee on Science and Technology. 2010. *Geoengineering: Parts I, II, and III*. Hearing Before the Science and Technology, US House of Representatives.

Vaughan, Naomi E. and Timothy M. Lenton. December 2011. "A Review of Climate Geoengineering Proposals." *Climatic Change* 109(3–4): 745–790.

Victor, David G. July 2008. "On the Regulation of Geoengineering." *Oxford Review of Economic Policy* 24(2): 322–336. https://doi.org/10.1093/oxrep/grn018

Victor, David G. et al. March–April 2009. "The Geoengineering Option: A Last Resort Against Global Warming?" *Foreign Affairs* 88(2): 64–76.

Virgoe, John. July 2009. "International Governance of a Possible Geoengineering Intervention to Combat Climate Change." *Climatic Change* 95(1–2): 103–119.

Waltz, Kenneth N. 1979. *Theory of International Politics*. Reading, MA: Addison-Wesley.

Wannier, Gregory E. et al. May 2011. "Editor's Note: Geoengineering Governance Systems." *Stanford Journal of Law, Science and Policy* 4(1): v–viii.

Wendt, Alexander. Spring 1992. "Anarchy is What States Make of It: The Social Construction of Power Politics." *International Organization* 46(2): 391–425. http://www.jstor.org/stable/2706858

Wood, Graeme. July/August 2009. "Re-Engineering the Earth." *The Atlantic*.

Chapter 3

The intersecting dimensions of water security

Neda A. Zawahri and Erika Weinthal

Introduction

Climate change, population growth, rapid urbanization, and mismanagement of supplies are challenging states' ability to meet growing demands for water across the world. Approximately 25 percent of the world's population lives under physical water scarcity (World Bank 2016, 1). Hundreds of millions in China, India and throughout the Middle East, especially in Gaza, Somalia, and Yemen, are already experiencing water scarcity.

Water scarcity not only threatens human security and welfare, it also contributes to domestic tension and political instability, as crowds demonstrate against ineffective water management. In September 2016, for example, protests erupted in Bengaluru, India, after the Indian Supreme Court ordered the Indian state of Karnataka to release additional water from the Cauvery River to the neighboring state of Tamil Nadu (Safi and Doshi 2016). The increasing threats to the available supply of water globally can disrupt food and energy security in both exporting and importing states. Water shortages and increasing dependence on transboundary resources can also contribute to regional tension as states increase their demand on shared resources—for instance, in the Nile Basin with Ethiopia exerting control over its main source, the Blue Nile. The Global Risks Report 2016 placed water security among its top threats to economies and societies across the world over the next ten years, and almost all the other threats it lists are directly related to effective water resources management (World Economic Forum 2016). Figure 3.1 illustrates that connection between water security and other forms of security.

To demonstrate how water security is intimately linked to security issues across multiple issue areas, this chapter shows that the concept of water security in the 21st century moved beyond narrow conceptions that securitized water as an existential threat. Over time, both academics' and practitioners' understandings of water security have broadened to account for the ways in which water permeates security concerns across different levels of analysis from the individual to the state to the transboundary, and across multiple issues areas that include human security, food security, and energy security. First, we review the theoretical literature on environmental security, which provided an early challenge to the military-centric field of security studies. Next we consider the relevance of fresh water to human security, food security, and energy security, along with the challenges presented by the reliance on transboundary resources. Our conclusion presents possible solutions to the impending water crisis across the world.

Figure 3.1 Intersecting dimensions of water security

Challenging traditional conceptions of security

During the Cold War, the field of security studies was predominantly focused on military and nuclear weapons in its consideration of issues threats to national security. As the Cold War declined, the intellectual space for considering nonmilitary threats to national security opened up. The environmental security literature entered this new debate positing a direct relationship between natural resources (water, oil, etc.) or global environmental degradation (e.g., climate change) and national security threats that can ultimately contribute to domestic or international conflict (Homer–Dixon 1994; Diehl and Gleditsch 2001; Ross 2004; Le Billon 2001). Peter Gleick's 1993 article "Water and Conflict" helped frame the field of water security. He defined threats to security as including "resource and environmental problems that reduce the quality of life and result in increased competition and tensions among subnational or national groups" (81–82). In terms of measuring water scarcity, Gleick posited four factors in a water basin that would affect access to water: degree of scarcity, extent to which a water supply is shared by more than one region or state, relative power of the basin states, and the ease of access to alternative freshwater resources (84–85). Combined, these would affect the extent to which water might lead to conflict. Zeitoun and Warner (2006) have pointed out that not only does water scarcity affect understandings of water security, but the structural and bargaining power of riparians also affects whether states will engage in conflict or cooperation—what they refer to as "hydro-hegemony."

Policymakers concerned with national security also often emphasize water scarcity. For example, in order to understand the political implications of increasing water scarcity for national security, the US Defense Intelligence Agency identified water basins at risk for political conflict owing to "inadequate" river basin management capacity in the Amu Darya in Central Asia and the Brahmaputra in South Asia (Defense Intelligence Agency 2012). Other scholars and policymakers have sought to identify areas where the United States, in particular, could take steps to cope with water scarcity through prioritizing linkages between water and security in its foreign policy (Busby 2017; Reed 2017).

This chapter takes a broader perspective on water security as "the availability of an acceptable quantity and quality of water for health, livelihoods, ecosystems, and production, coupled with an acceptable level of water-related risks to people, environments, and economies" (Grey and Sadoff 2007, 547–548). Water insecurity tends to disproportionately impact the poor within the developing world and within conflict-torn societies. The developed world has generally built the institutional structure for water security, and resource-rich states such as the oil-rich Persian Gulf states are able to use their financial resources to secure water security. Given the challenges of building effective institutions and financing construction of hydrological infrastructure to store and deliver water, developing nations are highly vulnerable to water insecurity.

There is sufficient fresh water in the world to meet basic human needs, but it is unevenly distributed, which results in many regions containing large populations—such as the Middle East, North Africa, and the western portion of the United States—being arid or semi-arid. Likewise, in China, the heavily populated north is water scarce, unlike its southern and eastern parts. Water is also often temporally distributed unequally, so that in South Asia, the monsoons only occur in the summer months, resulting in extensive flooding followed by periods of limited rain. Furthermore, in regions such as sub-Saharan Africa and parts of South Asia, countries not only face physical scarcity, but also confront water shortages due to insufficient investment in hydrological infrastructure and poor management policies. Given this dynamic, sub-Saharan Africa and parts of South Asia experience what is referred to as *economic water scarcity*, while the former areas experience physical shortages. Thus, at the same time that physical water scarcity impacts 1.2 billion people across the world, economic water scarcity impacts 1.6 billion people (FAO 2007).

Population growth, rapid urbanization, and socioeconomic development are putting higher demand on existing water supplies globally. In the 20th century the world's population tripled and is expected to reach eight billion by 2025. Concomitant with this population growth is the rapid rate of urbanization and associated migration from villages to cities, as people search for better livelihoods. In 2014, 54 percent of the world's population lived in urban areas, and this figure is expected to increase to 66 percent by 2050 (United Nations

2014). Moreover, the one billion people currently living in urban slums is expected to double by 2030 due to the increase in rural to urban migration (USAID 2016). Population growth, along with added migration from rural to urban areas, will increase pressure on all cities—and especially megacities such as Jakarta, Cairo, and Dhaka.

Kuwait, China, India, South Africa, and other countries are experiencing socio-economic developments that increase the consumption of water for food, energy, and livelihoods. As a result, there will be added pressure from the growing middle class everywhere on water and demands on the agricultural, energy, and industrial sectors. Water is furthermore an important input in the economy and is thus needed directly or indirectly (**virtual water**) for countless industrial processes and services, as well as for creating and maintaining employment. Approximately 42 percent of the global workforce is employed in a sector that is water-dependent (United Nations 2016).

Text box 3.1: Virtual water

Virtual water (embedded water, embodied water) is a concept created by John Anthony Allan, King's College London and the School of Oriental and African Studies. It refers to the direct use of water for foodstuff production, since agriculture uses 70–90% of the global water use, depending on regions and products. It also refers to the invisible water used in industrial processes to create goods and services throughout their life-cycle, from extraction to transportation to production to recycling or destruction, etc. For instance, the garment industry is very water intensive because of the many chemicals and multiple processes mobilized to produce clothing. The virtual water concept is connected to the virtual water trade (when country A imports foodstuff, clothing, or cement from country B, it is also importing the water used in country B), and the global water footprint.

The combination of increasing demand and decreasing supplies means that many states will confront severe water shortages in the near future. China, Mexico, Pakistan, South Africa, Jordan, Saudi Arabia, Morocco, and Yemen already confront acute water scarcity that is only expected to worsen. Combining climate models with socioeconomic scenarios, the World Resources Institute (WRI) ranked countries according to their expected water stress in 2040. The most water-stressed countries in 2040 are located in the Middle East—states such as Bahrain, Kuwait, Palestine, Israel, Saudi Arabia, Qatar, Oman, Jordan, and Lebanon (Maddocks et al. 2015).

As demand for water increases, climate change and mismanagement are combining to decrease supplies throughout the world, which will also reduce opportunities for states to cooperate over shared water resources. Various climate change models expect increases in intense floods and prolonged droughts, variability in precipitation, and shifts in precipitation patterns (see Below's chapter and Beevers's chapter herein). There is also an expectation of increase in **evapotranspiration**, an overall deterioration in water quality, and an increase in the melting of glaciers that will challenge the capacity of states to meet domestic water demand. Arid and semi-arid regions are expected to experience a decrease in overall water supplies, while humid regions are expected to see an increase in precipitation. Due to the impact of climate change on water resources, by 2050 more than 40 percent of the global population will be living under severe water stress (OECD 2013).

Worldwide, governments are mismanaging their water supplies, resulting in contamination and waste. Water infrastructure is aging and poorly functioning, resulting in leakages in water distribution systems and contamination of water networks by sewage systems. Groundwater aquifers, such as the Almeria in Spain or Azraq in Jordan, are being extracted at unsustainable rates, leading to their contamination. Transboundary rivers, such as the Ganges, Jordan, and Indus, are assaulted by industrial effluent, agricultural runoff, and untreated wastewater. In the developing world, 90 percent of wastewater remains untreated and is dumped into rivers and streams (Hameeteman 2013). Governments tend to focus on expanding existing water supplies by building hydrological infrastructure to meet immediate needs, instead of undertaking policy changes to increase efficiency in water use. Notably, Jordan has pushed for projects such as the Red Sea–Dead Sea Water Conveyance Project to provide additional drinking water for its population (Zawahri and Weinthal 2014).

Human security

Not only is access to water vital for economic well-being, but access to safe and sufficient water is essential for ensuring human health, nutrition, and welfare, as well as poverty reduction and human security. Across the developing world, 663 million people do not have access to sufficient safe water (JMP 2017). In sub-Saharan Africa, over 300 million people do not have access to clean water (Hameeteman 2013). To gain access to safe water, the poor typically pay five to ten times more than those with access to piped water. As the poor struggle to secure and pay for safe water, they can divert resources away from healthcare and education, harm their future earnings, and perpetuate a cycle of poverty. Poor water and sanitation services contributed to $260 billion in economic loss globally (Sadoff et al. 2017).

In many places in the developing world, infrastructure is so underdeveloped that people lack access to a secure and safe water supply and sanitation system. In 2015, 2.4 billion people did not have access to an improved sanitation facility (JMP 2017). In sub-Saharan Africa, over 500 million people lack access to safe sanitation (Hameeteman 2013). Today more people die from poor water quality than from war or other forms of violence (Sadoff et al. 2017). Poor water quality contributes to waterborne diseases, infant mortality, and reduced family income, while placing an inordinate work and health burden on girls and women in the developing world. About 80 percent of diseases in developing countries can be connected directly to poor water quality and sanitation problems (Hameeteman 2013, Formentos' and Gokcek's chapter herein). Annually, water pollution contributes to illness that plagues five million people; many are children under five years of age (Hameeteman 2013), and 2.2 million people die from diarrhea (UNICEF 2017).

Across the developing world, women and girls have the predominant responsibility of securing household water supplies. It is estimated that females walk about 6 kilometers each day to collect household water (Wahaj 2012). In sub-Saharan Africa, girls and women spend a total of 40 billion hours annually collecting water, which decreases the time they spend in school or working to increase household income (United Nations 2017). Due to the lack of safe public washing facilities and private toilets, girls reaching the age of puberty tend to drop out of school (UNICEF 2017). The lack of education only serves to perpetuate the cycle of poverty, inequality, and gender violence throughout the developing world (see Gerring's chapter herein).

Thus, as countries strive to meet **Sustainable Development Goal** (SDG) 6, which calls for universal and equitable access to water and sanitation, it is critical for states to take a broader approach to understanding water. In particular, SDG 6, unlike Millennium Development Goal 7, not only focuses on expanding quantitative access to improved water and sanitation, but also incorporates water quality, encouraging international cooperation, and protecting water-related ecosystems (Weinthal et al. 2017a). In emphasizing a human right to water, the SDG for water and sanitation accentuates the universality of access to water and sanitation as well as the role of women, all of which are essential for examining water security through a human security lens.

Food security

Water is a critical resource for food security (see Abnedur's and Resende's chapter herein). Unless a state imports all its domestic food, which would mean that it imports food products with "virtual water" (Allan 2011), the agriculture sector is essential to achieving national and individual food security. While on average, 70 percent of the domestic water budget globally is consumed by the agricultural sector, in the arid MENA, agriculture consumes up to 90 percent of the water. Within traditional security studies, scholars have examined food both as a tool for foreign policy and a vital resource for human security; and increasingly, studies of food security emphasize the connections between population growth, globalization, and climate change and their effect on the global food system (McDonald 2010).

States such as Israel, India, and Egypt that are located in conflict-ridden regions perceive access to sufficient supplies of food as integral to national security. Without sufficient food, a state's ability to endure trade disruptions, economic crises, or warfare can be compromised by its vulnerability to external supplies. Leaders are also concerned that dependence on the international market leaves them economically, politically, and militarily vulnerable. This vulnerability increases exponentially during regional or international wars. During regional wars, a state must possess sufficient foodstuff to feed its population and protect itself against an embargo or a disruption in food supplies. Without sufficient reserves, a state's ability to fight a war is hampered by its inability to feed its soldiers and citizens (Morgenthau 1948). Furthermore, in post-conflict countries, 60–80 percent of livelihoods rely on agriculture and natural resources (Bruch et al. 2009). Therefore, a robust agricultural sector is key for securing domestic food security.

Many families across the developing world rely on rainfed farming for individual food security in times of need, which leaves them highly vulnerable to weather extremes. In June 2017, over 100 million people across 48 countries were experiencing acute food insecurity (FAO and World Food Programme 2017). Globally, 800 million people are hungry, while one in ten people confront chronic hunger (Kim 2015). In the developing world, over 12 percent of the population are undernourished (FAO 2015), with the majority being children. Malnutrition and food insecurity stunt growth, slow down cognitive development, increase illness, and perpetuate a cycle of poverty. Consequently, food insecurity has a negative impact on the economic and social well-being of the family unit, society, and country.

Climate change is expected to threaten food security. The World Bank noted that "[u]nder high emissions scenarios, changes in rainfall patterns are projected to negatively affect crop yields globally, reducing them by up to 10 percent by 2030, and up to nearly

35 percent by 2080" (2016, 16). Thus, owing to the potential effects of droughts, floods, and rising temperatures on crop yields, the international food market is expected to be more volatile with less available food supplies. Prices are expected to fluctuate as food-exporting states experience weather extremes. Subsistence farmers are increasingly expected to face challenges in meeting their *own* food security. As populations and consumption patterns of the middle class increase globally, pressure on limited international agricultural commodities is expected to grow, worsening the competition for scarce resources among food importers. It has been estimated that by 2050, the agricultural sector will need to expand production by 60 percent in order to meet the increasing global demand for food (World Bank 2016, 2017), notably in sub-Saharan Africa, South Asia, and East Asia.

Food insecurity impacts conflict-torn states such as Haiti, Sudan, Somalia, Nigeria, Syria, Libya, and Yemen. Due to the prolonged conflict and drought in Yemen, severe food insecurity is affecting 17 million people (about 60 percent of the population). Two governorates, Taiz and Al Hudaydah, are on the verge of a severe famine outbreak (FAO 2017). South Sudan, Somalia, and northeastern Nigeria are also at risk of famine (Gettleman 2017; FAO and World Food Programme 2017). In South Sudan, conflict has contributed to acute food insecurity for almost 5 million people—over 40 percent of the population—and 100,000 people are confronting famine (FAO and World Food Programme 2017). In Iraq, over three million people confront acute food insecurity, and 50 percent of families face food insecurity (FAO and World Food Programme 2017).

The linkages between food, water, and health become clearer in these conflicts affected by famine, as families flee to refugee camps that greatly need clean water. As a UNICEF specialist on water, sanitation, and hygiene underscored, "We underestimated the role of water and its contribution to mortality in the last famine [Somalia]. It gets overshadowed by the food" (Gettleman 2017).

Energy security

Water is key for food security. It is also a vital input for the production of energy, and water and energy often cannot be compartmentalized (Weinthal et al. 2017b). Scholars refer to these connections as the **water–energy nexus** (Siddiqi and Anadon 2011). Water is necessary for the production of hydropower, oil and gas, coal, and nuclear power. Water is required for cooling coal combustion and for cooling processes in nuclear power plants. Increasingly, the production of unconventional energy that reshaped the energy security in the United States—helping to turn an energy importer into an energy exporter—requires water for hydraulic fracturing (Kondash and Vengosh 2015).

Likewise, the provision of clean water depends on energy for treating water and for desalination. As countries find their water resources diminishing or contaminated, they often turn to new technologies for the production of water. For wealthier or energy-rich countries, reliance upon desalination can provide water for its citizenry, as is the case in the Persian Gulf. Thus, research that looks at the energy–water nexus in the Middle East has focused on the amount of energy that will be required to produce new water (Siddiqi and Anadon 2011) such that water security broadly conceived is constrained by the availability of energy.

Energy is further needed to move water, which becomes important in countries where water resources are unevenly distributed or where population centers are far removed from abundant water sources. Thus, in water-poor Jordan, the government has invested in a conveyance system to move water from the Disi aquifer in the south to the heavily populated capital city of Amman. Likewise, the Chinese government is investing heavily in the South–North Water Transfer Project to bring water from the Yangtze River. Energy is also necessary to move water to support the agricultural sector, which scholars refer to as the **water–energy–food nexus** (Keulertz et al. 2016).

Transboundary water

Approximately 60 percent of the world's fresh water supply is located in 276 transboundary rivers, such as the Euphrates, Jordan, Nile, Indus, Columbia, and Mekong. Transboundary river basins cover 45 percent of the earth's land surface and are home to 40 percent of the world's population (Wolf et al. 1999). About 90 percent of the rivers and lakes in Africa are transboundary (Hameeteman 2013), and over 60 percent of the domestic water resources in the Middle East come from transboundary basins (United Nations 2015). Across the world, 300 transboundary aquifers provide water for two billion people (United Nations Water 2017).

Transboundary waters impose complex relations on riparian states, which can challenge states' ability to meet domestic needs for water, food, and energy. It can also challenge states' ability to respond to floods and droughts. A state's failure to meet these domestic demands can contribute to regional tension and domestic insecurity. While some have argued that shared water resources can contribute to "water wars," there has never been an international war fought solely over water (Wolf 1998). However, shared water resources can result in tension and conflict between states that fall short of war (Mitchell and Zawahri 2015).

Because water basins are often shared and users are mutually dependent upon one another to effectively manage a water basin, international relations theory would thus expect states to demand water regimes to mitigate conflicts of interests among the different users (Krasner 1983; Keohane 1982). Yet, only 43 percent of the world's transboundary basins are governed by transnational institutional commitments (Giordano et al. 2014). When considering these existing treaties, protocols, and agreements, 86 percent are bilateral arrangements and only 13 percent of multilateral basins are governed by formal basin-wide commitments. An examination of the interaction between riparian states reveals that institutionalized mechanisms for addressing water disputes are essential for helping states to avert conflict. In fact, conflict is most likely to occur in basins that are shared between countries with a history of conflict, where the states confront water quantity disputes and lack institutionalized mechanisms to manage disputes (De Stefano et al. 2010).

A database analysis of transboundary water treaties, protocols, and agreements reveals several factors that can contribute to their rise and effectiveness (Zawahri 2016). Accords are more likely to be present in basins whose riparians are heavily dependent on water to meet their domestic needs, and power distribution seems to be an important factor contributing to treaty formation. But the literature tends to disagree about whether it is power asymmetry or symmetry that contributes to treaty formation (Tir and Ackerman 2009; Zawahri and Mitchell 2011). Treaty design appears to be significant in facilitating cooperation among riparian states. Enforcement mechanisms are an important treaty design feature that facilitates cooperation among these states (Tir and Stinnett 2012; Mitchell and Zawahri 2015). Other studies point to the impact of monitoring, conflict resolution mechanisms, information exchange, and river commissions as effective design features (Dinar et al. 2015). Effective governance/management of transboundary systems is vital for cooperation and conflict prevention, and it provides the framework for ensuring that countries can meet their energy, food, and human security needs. For countries emerging from conflict, building security/governance regimes for managing water is inextricably linked to helping countries provide for basic human needs, rebuild livelihoods, and assist with economic recovery (Weinthal et al. 2014).

Conclusion

In sum, water is critical for many sectors across society, yet many regions across the world experience water scarcity. To feed a growing global population and middle class, the global food supply system will need close to 50 percent more water by 2050. Other sectors of the economy, such as municipal and industrial sectors, will need respectively 50–70 percent more water each. To meet its growing energy needs, this sector will demand 85 percent more water by 2050 (World Bank 2016). Yet, climate change models and mismanagement of existing supplies indicate that water supplies are expected to decrease, especially in arid regions. To avert domestic instability and regional tension over decreasing water supplies, states must adapt their strategies, broaden their definition of water security, and think across issue areas. To achieve water security at the individual, state, and regional levels requires focusing on issues of governance, institution building, and the challenges of state–society relations.

Given the impending water shortages, state actors will increasingly confront significant challenges as they attempt to maintain existing domestic allocations of the domestic water budget whereby the agricultural sector remains the predominant consumer, and where wealthy domestic consumers continue to benefit from cheap water that they overconsume. To avert the increasing internal pressures on society, policymakers will need to undertake difficult changes: improving water allocation across competing sectors of society, targeting subsidies to the poor, and increasing the efficiency by which water is being used domestically. Domestic water allocation is inherently a political process whereby powerful constituents in urban and rural areas benefit from high water subsidies, especially in the developing world. As a result, it is important to consider state–society relations and the political economy of domestic water resource management—whereby wealthy domestic constituents capture and use the majority of domestic water supplies and pay little for their consumption. On the other hand, the poor tend to pay a higher price for water, which often tends to be of lower quality. And national decision-makers are often hesitant to increase water prices to powerful constituents for fear of upsetting the status quo (World Bank 2016; Zawahri 2012).

It is essential to build institutions to improve the governance of domestic water resources. In sub-Saharan Africa, for example, the World Bank (2016) identifies a low institutional capacity to govern domestic water supplies and adapt to climatic variability. Approximately 70 percent of the population is dependent on the agricultural sector, which is predominately subsistence and rainfed (World Bank 2016). This combination means that sub-Saharan Africa is the most at-risk region in the world because of its weak capacity to adapt to climate change's impact on water supplies (World Bank 2016).

Questions for discussion

1   How does water impact human, food, and energy security?
2   How does population growth, climate change, and socio-economic development impact the available supply of water throughout the world?
3   How can secure access to fresh water challenge future economic, political, and social stability?
4   What are transboundary water resources and how do they present potential threats to regional and national stability?
5   Should the concept of national security be expanded to include environmental security? How has the concept of water security evolved over the past decades?
6   How is water related to the welfare of girls and women in the developing world?

References

Allan, Tony. 2011. *Virtual Water: Tackling the Threat to Our Planet's Most Precious Resource*. London: I.B. Tauris.

Bruch, Carl, David Jensen, Mikiyasu Nakayama, et al., ed. January 2009. "Post-Conflict Peace Building and Natural Resources." *Yearbook of International Environmental Law* 19(1): 58–96.

Busby, Joshua W. 2017. "Water and U.S. National Security." January 18, 2017. New York, NY: Council on Foreign Relations. Discussion Paper. https://www.cfr.org/sites/default/files/pdf/2017/01/Discussion_Paper_Busby_Water_and_US_Security_OR.pdf

Defense Intelligence Agency. February 2, 2012. *Global Water Security*. Washington DC: Office of the Director of National Intelligence. www.dni.gov/files/documents/Special%20Report_ICA%20Global%20Water%20Security.pdf

De Stefano, Lucia, Paris Edwards, Lynette de Silva, et al. 2010. "Tracking Cooperation and Conflict in International Basins: Historic and Recent Trends." *Water Policy* 12(6): 871–884.

Diehl, Paul, and Nils Petter Gleditsch. 2001. *Environmental Conflict*. Boulder, CO: Westview Press.

Dinar, Shlomi, David Katz, Lucia De Stefano, et al. March 2015. "Climate Change, Conflict and Cooperation." *Political Geography* 45(1): 55–66.

FAO (Food and Agriculture Organization of the United Nations). 2007. *Coping with Water Scarcity*. http://www.fao.org/3/a-aq444e.pdf

FAO (Food and Agriculture Organization of the United Nations). 2015. *The State of Food Insecurity in the World*. http://www.fao.org/3/a-i4646e.pdf

FAO (Food and Agriculture Organization of the United Nations). 2017. *Yemen*. Situation Report. April 2017. http://www.fao.org/fileadmin/user_upload/emergencies/docs/FAOYemen_SitRep -April2017.pdf

FAO (Food and Agriculture Organization of the United Nations) and World Food Programme. 2017. *Monitoring Food Security in Countries with Conflict Situations*. http://www.fao.org/3/a -i7490e.pdf

Gettleman, Jeffrey. March 27, 2017. "Drought and War Heighten Threat of Not Just 1 Famine, but 4." *New York Times*.

Giordano, Mark, Alena Drieschova, James A. Duncan, et al. September 2014. "A Review of the Evolution and State of Transboundary Freshwater Treaties." *International Environmental Agreements: Politics, Law and Economics* 14(3): 245–264.

Gleick, Peter H.Summer 1993. "Water and Conflict." *International Security* 18(1): 79–112.

Grey, David, and Claudia W. Sadoff. "Sink of Swim? Water Security for Growth and Development." 2007. *Water Policy* 9: 545–571.

Hameeteman, Elizabeth. 2013. "Future Water (In)security: Facts, Figures, and Predictions." Global Water Institute. http://www.academia.edu/36012370/Future_Water_In_security_Facts_Figur

es_and_Predictions_Global_Water_Institute_Future_Water_In_Security_Facts_Figures_and_Pre
dictions_Acknowledgments

Homer-Dixon, Thomas F. Summer 1994. "Environmental Scarcities and Violent Conflict: Evidence from Cases." *International Security* 19(1): 5–40.

JMP (Joint Monitoring Programme for Water Supply and Sanitation). 2017. Country Reports.
https://www.wssinfo.org/documents/?tx_displaycontroller[type]=country_files.demand

Keohane, Robert O. Spring 1982. "The Demand for International Regimes." *International Organization* 36(2): 325–355.

Keulertz, Martin, Jeannie Sowers, Eckart Woertz, and Rabi Mohtar. 2016 (online version). "The
Water-Energy-Food Nexus in Arid Regions: The Politics of Problemsheds." In *The Oxford
Handbook of Water Politics and Policy*, Ken Conca and Erika Weinthal, eds. Oxford: Oxford
University Press.

Kim, Jim Yong. 2015. *Future of Food*. Washington, DC: World Bank. http://documents.worldba
nk.org/curated/en/645981468189237140/pdf/100046-WP-PUBLIC-dislcose-7am
-10-8-15-Box393216B.pdf

Kondash, Andrew, and Avner Vengosh. 2015. "Water Footprint of Hydraulic Fracturing." *Environmental Science & Technology Letters* 2(10), 276–280.

Krasner, Stephen D., ed. 1983. *International Regimes*. Ithaca, NY: Cornell University Press.

Le Billon, Philippe. June 2001. "The Political Ecology of War: Natural Resources and Armed
Conflicts." *Political Geography* 20(5): 561–584.

Maddocks, Andrew, Robert Samuel Young, and Paul Reig. August 26, 2015. "Ranking the
World's Most Water-Stressed Countries in 2040." World Resources Institute. http://www.wri.
org/blog/2015/08/ranking-world's-most-water-stressed-countries-2040

McDonald, Bryan. 2010. *Food Security*. Cambridge: Polity Press.

Mitchell, Sara McLaughlin, and Neda A. Zawahri. February 2015. "The Effectiveness of Treaty
Design in Addressing Water Disputes." *Journal of Peace Research* 52(2): 187–200.

Morgenthau, Hans J. 1948. *Politics Among Nations*. New York: Knopf.

OECD. September 2, 2013. *Water and Climate Change Adaptation: Policies to Navigate Uncharted
Waters*. OECD Studies on Water, OECD Publishing. http://dx.doi.org/10.1787/
9789264200449-en

Reed, David, ed. 2017. *Water, Security and U.S. Foreign Policy*. New York, NY: Routledge.

Ross, Michael L. May 2004. "What Do We Know about Natural Resources and Civil War?"
Journal of Peace Research 41(3): 337–356.

Sadoff, Claudia W., Edoardo Borgomeo, and Dominick Revell de Waal. March 14, 2017. *Turbulent Waters: Pursuing Water Security in Fragile Contexts*. Washington, DC: World Group. https://
openknowledge.worldbank.org/handle/10986/26207 License: CC BY 3.0 IGO

Safi, Michael, and Vidhi Doshi. September 15, 2016. "Angry Clashes in Karnataka as India's Water
Wars Run Deep." *The Guardian*.

Siddiqi, Afreen, and Laura Diaz Anadon. August 2011. "The Water-Energy Nexus in Middle East
and North Africa." *Energy Policy* 39(8): 4529–4540.

Tir, Jaroslav, and John T. Ackerman. 2009. "Politics of Formalized River Cooperation." *Journal of
Peace Research* 46(5): 623–640.

Tir, Jaroslav, and Douglas M. Stinnett. January 2012. "Weathering Climate Change: Can Institutions Mitigate International Water Conflict?" *Journal of Peace Research* 49(1): 211–225.

UNICEF. 2017. *Gender and Water, Sanitation and Hygiene*. 2017. https://www.unicef.org/esaro/
7310_Gender_and_WASH.html

United Nations. 2014. *World Urbanization Prospects*. https://esa.un.org/unpd/wup/publications/
files/wup2014-highlights.Pdf

United Nations. 2015. *United Nations World Water Development Report 2015: Water for a Sustainable
World*. Paris: United Nations Educational, Scientific, and Cultural Organization (UNESCO).
http://unesdoc.unesco.org/images/0023/002318/231823E.pdf

United Nations 2016. *United Nations World Water Development Report 2016: Water and Jobs.* http://unesdoc.unesco.org/images/0024/002440/244041e.pdf

United Nations 2017. *International Decade for Action "Water for Life" 2005–2015.* http://www.un.org/waterforlifedecade/scarcity.shtml

United Nations Water. 2017. *Transboundary Waters.* http://www.unwater.org/water-facts/transboundary-waters/

USAID (US Agency for International Development). 2016. *2016–2025 Food Assistance and Food Security Strategy.* https://www.usaid.gov/sites/default/files/documents/1867/FFP-Strategy-FINAL%2010.5.16.pdf

Wahaj, Robina. 2012. "Gender and Water. International Fund for Agricultural Development." https://www.ifad.org/documents/10180/2ffa1e63-8a8e-47ed-a4aa-cbf249fafab2

Weinthal, Erika, Farah F. Hegazi, and Lesha Witmer. 2017a. "Development and Diplomacy: Water, the SDGs, and U.S. Foreign Policy." 69–96 in David Reed ed., *Water, Security and U.S. Foreign Policy.* New York, NY: Routledge.

Weinthal, Erika, Jessica Troell, and Mikiyasu Nakayama, eds. 2014. *Water and Post-Conflict Peacebuilding.* New York: Routledge/Earthscan Press.

Weinthal, Erika, Avner Vengosh, and Kate Neville. 2017b (online version). "The Nexus of Energy and Water Quality." 197–225 in *Oxford Handbook of Water Politics and Policy*, edited by Ken Conca and Erika Weinthal. Oxford: Oxford University Press.

Wolf, Aaron. April 1998. "Conflict and Cooperation along International Waterways." *Water Policy* 1(2): 251–265.

Wolf, Aaron Jeffrey Natharius, Jeffrey Danielson, et al. December 1999. "International River Basins of the World." *International Journal of Water Resources Development* 15(4): 387–427. http://dx.doi.org/10.1080/07900629948682

World Bank. 2016. *High and Dry: Climate Change, Water, and the Economy.* Washington, DC: World Bank.

World Bank 2017. *Water.* Last updated September 20, 2017. http://www.worldbank.org/en/topic/water/overview

World Economic Forum. 2016. *The Global Risks Report 2016.* http://www3.weforum.org/docs/GRR/WEF_GRR16.pdf

Zawahri, Neda. 2012. "Popular Protests and the Governance of Scarce Freshwater in Jordan." *Arab World Geographer* 15(4): 265–299.

Zawahri, Neda 2016. "Managing Transboundary Rivers to Avert Conflict and Facilitate Cooperation." In *The Oxford Handbook of Water Politics and Policy*, edited by Ken Conca and Erika Weinthal. Oxford: Oxford University Press.

Zawahri, Neda and Sara McLaughlin Mitchell. 2011. "Fragmented Governance of International Rivers: Negotiating Bilateral versus Multilateral Treaties." *International Studies Quarterly* 55(3): 835–858. http://dx.doi.org/10.1111/j.1468-2478.2011.00673.x

Zawahri, Neda and Erika Weinthal. 2014. "The World Bank and Negotiating the Red Sea and Dead Sea Water Conveyance Project." *Global Environmental Politics* 14(4): 55–74.

Zeitoun, Mark, and Jeroen Warner. 2006. "Hydro-Hegemony—a Framework for Analysis of Trans-Boundary Water Conflicts." *Water Policy* 8(5): 435–460.

Chapter 4

Competition and cooperation in energy policies
Dilemmas for national security and influence

Michael A. Davis and Jonathan Drake

Note: The opinions expressed in this article are the authors' own and do not reflect the views of the North Atlantic Treaty Organization, the US Department of Defense, or the United States government.

Introduction: The blood of modern life

Energy is the lifeblood of our civilization. From the moment humans mastered fire, societies have sought and protected sources of energy, and relied upon energy for economic activity and growth. Since the industrial revolution, energy has either limited or enabled states to realize their strategic goals, and their relative energy security—real or perceived—has fueled rivalries, alliances, and conflicts. As E. F. Schumacher said, "There is no substitute for energy. The whole edifice of modern society is built upon it (…) It is not 'just another commodity' but the precondition of all commodities" (Kirk 1983, 1).

> **Text box 4.1: Energy security**
>
> The International Energy Agency (IEA) defines energy security as "the uninterrupted availability of energy sources at an affordable price" (IEA website).

States' approaches to energy security range from laissez-faire economics to cooperation, collectivism, and lethal competition. They reflect the values and ambitions of their societies and leaders, and especially their evolving beliefs about economic freedom, private/public ownership, the role of government in society, and the use of natural endowments. Whereas most nations seek to acquire and deliver sufficient energy to meet their needs, many energy-rich nations treat energy as both currency and power—a component in a new **Great Game**.

We examine these different national approaches with a focus on oil and natural gas. First, we analyze the energy diplomacy of Russia and China as authoritarian states. Next, we study the internationalist strategies of the European Union (EU) as a net importer. Finally, we conclude with an exploration of Canada as a resource-abundant democracy and lead democratic energy exporter. These case studies show the value of coupling pragmatic, short-term energy policies with an overarching long-term energy strategy to ensure continual access to energy and long-term protection of interests, including the protection of the global commons. Our case studies demonstrate that energy security is a

Gordian knot, that realism best explains the geopolitical quest for energy, and that—just as in the **security dilemma**—perceptions of energy security matter.

Integrated energy systems: Both Gordian knot and Achilles' heel

Ensuring energy security is no simple task and can be a nation's **Achille's heel**. Nations perceive differently the opportunities and risks inherent to energy, and tailor their strategies accordingly. With global interdependence, a secure energy supply relies upon stable, complex networks of energy systems. Infrastructure deficiencies, pipeline disruptions, natural disasters, civil unrest, price disputes, labor strikes, war: all these affect these multilayered, imbricated systems. Within that energy architecture, oil retains primacy as the world's largest energy source due to its centrality to ground and air transport. Demand for oil is increasing, especially in the developing world, and will globally increase by 30 percent by 2047 (Yergin 2012, 219; Exxon Mobil Corporate 2017). Given the unique importance of fossil fuels to security and development, their unequal distribution, and the geopolitical competition they provoke, this chapter will be partly a departure from the majority of this book. When it comes to energy, realism still dominates international relations.

Assessing the impact of these challenges on state actors helps us understand relative national security interests. Many nations perceive the stability and viability of the overall global energy system as a vital national security interest. Other nations, such as Russia, give priority to their relative standing in energy politics, which often leads to destabilizing policies. Some nations—e.g., Saddam Hussein's Iraq—develop(ed) such a reliance on petroleum income that undesirable market conditions, such as rival production by neighboring states, violate their perceptions of energy security and overall regime stability. The very centrality of energy as a means to provide for other forms of security (economic, strategic, and human) demonstrates that energy, and especially oil, is a critical commodity for our civilization and an essential precondition for security writ large.

Since the Industrial Revolution, economists have studied our growing reliance on finite resources, noting the paradox (the **Jevons paradox**) that increased technological efficiency did not slow demand, but rather led to increased consumption. Technologies and machines have become more energy- and resource-efficient, and while resource intensity may diminish at the unit level (micro-level), it augments at the aggregate level (the **rebound effect**) because of rising aggregate demand. Today, natural scientists and environmentalists further explain the risk inherent in dependence on non-renewables. With the oil shock of 1973, resource pessimists or "Doomers" such as M. King Hubbert suggested that resources have an ultimate depletion point, coining the term "**peak oil**," also known as **Hubbert's peak**. Today, a sharpening, widening, and deepening globalization leads to the aggressive pursuit of untapped reserves as "a concerted drive by governments and resource firms to gain control over whatever remains" (Klare 2010, 12). Therefore, resource realists highlight that states act to secure their interests because these dwindling resources spur leaders "to ensure that *their* country or *their* company will have sufficient supplies to survive" (Klare 2010, 14–15).

In contrast, the "Boomers" point out that innovation always followed scarcity and defend the idea of a "Bottomless Well." For instance, Simon saw human ingenuity as the "ultimate resource" (1983; 1998), able to maximize existing resources and even expand the earth's carrying capacity. Others highlight the critical value of fossil fuels in reducing poverty (Epstein 2014). This Boomer/Doomer debate is best illustrated by the famous **Ehrlich/Simon bet** (Sabin 2013; Tierney 1990). Despite the long-term implications of their positions, it would appear that technology, conservation, and innovation seem to be winning the Doomer/Boomer argument in the short term.

Text box 4.2: The Ehrlich/Simon bet

In 1980, two antagonists in the Doomer/Boomer debate decided to make a bet based on their predictions. Julian Simon, a relatively unknown economist, wagered $1,000 to Robert Ehrlich, a well-known and media-savvy Malthusian, that innovation would prevent runaway mineral prices. The bet rested on the future price of five metals. Simon won the bitter bet; over the time considered, technology had overcome the challenges of scarcity and rising prices.

Russia's authoritarian antics to win a zero-sum game

When Vladimir Putin succeeded Boris Yeltsin on May 7, 2000, the Russian economy and political system were in crisis. After nearly a decade of transition, the reformers of the 1990s had failed to transform the Soviet command economy into a market democracy. Their flawed privatization process led to the wholesale collapse of Russian industries, the enrichment of the oligarchs, and a collapse of ordinary Russians' standards of living. Putin thought that Russia's abundant natural resources, if appropriately managed, would eventually play a role in "all vital state functions" (Putin 2008). He believed that Russia's weakness was the result of state impotence and set out to restore the *vertikal vlasti* (power vertical), in which all industries and civil society yield to the will of, and show loyalty to, the state. Putin would then wield them as tools and weapons in his effort to restore the prestige and power of a reinvigorated Russia to compete in the great geopolitical struggles ahead.

The Russian approach to energy differs fundamentally from that of Western nations. Rather than let market forces direct energy exchanges, Russia recognized that energy resources could be wielded for strategic political effect—a new component of high politics. Russia is one of Earth's mineral and hydrocarbon behemoths, holding the world's fourth largest natural gas reserves (CIA 2017) and third in global petroleum production (EIA 2016). Its geographic location between the hydrocarbon-rich Caspian Sea and Central Asian countries and the consumers of Europe also ensures it can control energy transit. By controlling pipelines between Asian producers and European consumers, Russia has sought to control the Eurasian energy market itself (Rutland 2008, 203). Russia exploits this new energy power as a weapon—using national control of energy to influence, coerce, and exploit its neighbors. By monopolizing supplies and using energy rents, Russia has dominated nations in its "near abroad"— states in Russia's periphery (Blank 2011, 174). Indeed, with 90 percent of its natural gas bound for European markets (EIA 2016), Russia is Europe's leading oil and gas supplier (BP Global 2015).

Russian energy companies, especially Gazprom, are key actors in the energy game. Created from the Soviet Gas Ministry in 1989, Gazprom inherited all natural-gas-related projects and infrastructure in the Russian Federation. Today, it is the world's largest gas exploration and production company, controlling 90 percent of Russian production and 100 percent of gas exports (BBC 2006). This company is majority government-owned, and while the Kremlin does not direct daily operations, Gazprom often acts as an arm of the state, earning Putin's praise for prioritizing state interests over profits.

Moscow's use of coercive techniques and energy power is evident in former Soviet states seeking to escape Russian hegemony, such as Ukraine, Georgia, and the Baltic countries. In December 2005, during parliamentary elections following Ukraine's Orange Revolution, Russia hiked gas prices by over 400 percent. While price negotiations were underway, Russia accused Ukraine of stealing EU-bound gas, effectively claiming that Ukraine was violating its international agreements. In January 2006, with Ukraine unable to pay the increase, Russia stopped gas flows to a frozen Ukraine. Ukraine was forced to either surrender or steal Europe-bound fuel. To avoid losing Western support, Ukraine negotiated a 95 percent price increase (Nygren 2008, 6). By contrast, Belarus continued to pay Ukraine's former rate, signaling that political alignment with Moscow pays off (Radio Free Europe Radio Liberty 2005). Additional disputes over gas delivery to Ukraine occurred in 2008–2009, when Western-leaning political parties held both the Premiership and Presidency of Ukraine. These crises served to discredit Ukrainian reformists, highlighting Ukraine's inability to solve problems without Russia's consent. Today, with staunchly pro-European leaders in Kyiv, Gazprom maintains a website devoted to discrediting Ukraine's reliability as an energy transit state.

In Georgia, a similar saga played out after the Rose Revolution, when Russia raised prices by 200 percent after pro-Western forces came to power. When Georgia refused to pay, pipelines were sabotaged in Russia during the coldest winter in decades (Allen 2006). But Georgian supply diversification—from the Caspian basin and the Baku–Tbilisi–Erzurum Pipeline—demonstrated resilience against Russia's geopolitical blackmail (Sahakyan 2016; Saakashvili 2006).

In Estonia, Latvia, and Lithuania, Russia consistently leveraged their 90 percent dependence on Russian oil and nearly 100 percent dependence on Russian gas, punishing these Baltic governments for policies at odds with Russia's (Grigas 2012). On different occasions, Latvia and Lithuania both rejected offers for Russian companies to acquire oil terminals. Immediately following these rejections, Russian oil completely ceased to flow to those very terminals (Trenin 2008, 23). In Estonia, the relocation of a Soviet-era statue, which Moscow protested vigorously, caused a complete cessation of oil and gasoline deliveries (officially because of railway track repairs) (Grigas 2012).

Russia's energy policies reflect its *Realpolitik* approach in other ways. When Russia invaded and annexed Ukraine's Crimean Peninsula in 2014, it gained a massive maritime zone with the best deep-water energy potential of the Black Sea—the same maritime energy prospects Russia attempted to acquire legally a few years prior—worth potentially trillions of dollars (Broad 2014). The annexation also shortened the likely route for a proposed pipeline across the Black Sea, reducing potential construction costs. By seizing these energy resources, Russia denied their use to a new anti-Moscow government in Kyiv, clearly demonstrating Moscow's zero-sum perspective.

Russia defends a historical narrative and worldview in which it is in a permanent state of competition with the West (Zwack 2017, 228). Whereas in the past this struggle was represented by competing ideologies (Marxism vs. capitalism), future conflicts will be resource-driven. This explains why, despite having an inordinate share of the world's yet-untapped hydrocarbon potential, Russia continues to aggregate more of the supply and distribution market, denying these resources to future adversaries.

China's great game

China's energy policy offers insights into how another authoritarian nation attempts to achieve energy and internal security. Though far from energy-deficient, China imports tremendous amounts of energy. Like Russia, the Chinese Communist leadership has devised a comprehensive approach, combining short- and long-term aims. China's explosive growth of 7–10 percent annually since its opening in 1979 has required a steady stream of imported energy (Shambaugh 2013). As Gueldry and Liang highlight, "the scarcity of domestic energy (with the exception of domestic coal) to support its 1.37 billion people and rapid economic growth is an increasingly serious problem for China" (2016, 2).

Since Mao Zedong's proclamation of the People's Republic of China in 1949, the Chinese Communist Party (CCP) Central Committee has shaped domestic and foreign policy through successive 5-year plans. While early 5-year plans focused on growth, production, and agriculture, the 2010 plan shifted toward a more sustainable economy (Ma 2015). The latest 2015 plan continues this approach: economic growth, increased social advancement, the development of a world-class environmental technology industry, plus ecological living and culture (National People's Congress 2016, 6, 30–31).

The CCP provides economic growth to its citizenry as a *quid pro quo* for its retention of power. The cohesion of China's massive population and disparate communities requires continued economic growth for security. Separatist elements have little popular support when economic conditions and living standards are improving. The middle class, which has seen 700 million people lifted out of poverty since the early 1980s, relies on colossal—and still growing—use of natural resources for continuous growth. Chinese leadership considers economic development its most urgent task, thus requiring increased energy resources (*People's Daily* 2005). In 2014, China accounted for 45 percent of global coal consumption and 30 percent of global oil consumption, and it will remain the world's largest aggregate energy consumer for the coming two to three decades (EIA 2015).

As the world's largest economy, China's efforts to increase sustainability are focused on replacing coal with "cleaner" fossil fuels, while developing alternative energy systems. Therefore, China conducts a *global energy diplomacy* to preserve economic growth and internal security without destroying its environment (Gueldry and Liang 2016, 4–5).

Tapping into Africa's under-developed energy resources is one key effort. Economist Dambisa Moyo (2012, 150–170) pinpoints the key weapons in China's energy trade arsenal: "no strings attached" development aid infrastructure projects (no political conditionality, no attention paid to social standards, human rights, etc.), colossal loans to state providers, and a *laissez faire* approach to business ethics. The elements combined form the **Beijing consensus**. This approach demonstrates *Realpolitik*, a readiness to enter into economic arrangements with any nation, regardless of its standing on international indexes of human rights, good governance, or corruption. Government-controlled national oil companies (NOCs) explore and extract in remote or politically dangerous regions of Africa at the beckoning of their government. While the conventional wisdom on China's three NOCs—China National Petroleum Corporation (CNPC), China National Offshore Oil Corporation (CNOOC), and China Petroleum and Chemical Corporation (Sinopec)—suggests that these three entities are merely state tools seizing global assets, some authors hypothesize that their linkages to the CCP only serve to provide them a competitive advantage (Pascual and Elkind 2010, 23–24). By focusing on these problematic regions, China is developing energy relationships whereby African nations become dependent on China as the only buyer who will ignore their internal affairs.

China's expansionism in the East and South China Seas, where underlying historical and territorial grievances are exacerbated by energy politics, causes great concern. China's unilateral declaration of the 9-dash line (or 11-dash) asserting sovereignty over the South China Sea reflects a desire to control maritime riches and transit (United Nations 2009). The ocean floor is rich in hydrocarbons, and the maritime space provides passage for more than half of the world's annual merchant fleet tonnage, including oil. The sea is also a vital energy transportation lane for all East Asian economies and provides strategic depth for all, making it a geostrategic "cauldron" (Kaplan 2015). Like Russia's control of Central Asian energy transport, control of these waterways is paramount to Chinese energy security, as well as influence over regional markets and potential competitors (Steven, O'Brien, and Jones 2015, 28, 35–36).

We now examine European responses to Russian efforts to control distribution of trans-continental energy and solidify leverage over its European customers.

Europe: Market multilateralism crashes into a wall of realism

The EU continues to struggle between Negawatts and Megawatts. Is energy security achieved via efficiency or supply? Since the fall of the Berlin Wall in 1989, the European Union has trumpeted ambitious objectives for European collective defense and security policy. In 2006, Brussels crafted a holistic, optimistic, and trend-setting energy policy focusing on three pillars: an internal energy market, security of supply, and sustainable energy production and use (Commission of the European Communities 2006). Other EU energy policy literature reveals a nearly myopic focus on the desire for efficiency, reduction in demand, and development of alternative energy sources as key components of Europe's long-term energy outlook. The spread of democracy to the former Eastern Bloc and subsequent EU enlargement led to unbridled optimism that multilateralism and economic interdependence would replace old-time realism and state competition.

Confidence in renewable energy abounded, and concerns about irreparable environmental damage demanded action. Public opinion on energy issues was cohesive by European standards: in 2007 nearly two-thirds of EU citizens believed that the EU itself (rather than national governments) should tackle energy-related issues. Almost 90 percent expressed concern about climate change and carbon dioxide emissions, and 98 percent of EU citizens said that governments should institute energy efficiency initiatives (Commission of the European Communities 2007). However, the call for collective action to develop and support cleaner energy alternatives disregarded Europe's massive dependence on fossil fuels—primarily Russian oil and gas.

In the early 2000s, Russia's improving relations with the West seemed to indicate their reliability as Europe's eastern partner. Long-term energy contracts (LTCs) were deemed desirable, as they fixed the demand and supply for both consuming and supplying countries. However, LTCs hampered the emergence of a true market. Meanwhile, EU energy policy continued to focus on promoting renewables and efficiency as a means to address energy-related pollution (Commission of the European Communities 2007). EC experts developed phased benchmarks for improving energy efficiency and for the share of renewable energy in overall consumption (Van Efferink 2010). Meanwhile, contracts with Gazprom increased, and the risks associated with pipeline arrangements were cast aside.

A pipeline signifies more than the value of liquids passing through it; the physical link also creates political-economic forces among conjoined countries. In a true market economy, market rules might dictate outcomes, but Russia is using its energy institutions to tilt the geopolitical calculus in its favor. Early signs of Europe's political vulnerabilities emerged in 2006–2008, when Europe noted its inability to broker peace during the Russia–Georgia war. By 2009, European gas pipeline arrangements were more extensive than other imports: 85 percent of natural gas imports were from pipelines, compared to 20 percent of oil (European Parliament 2009, 3). Eastern Europe's reliance was overwhelming; six nations relied on Russia for 100 percent of their gas needs, and many had given operational control of energy infrastructure to Russian companies.

Following Russian gas shutdowns to eastern and southeastern Europe, European institutions realized their dependence on transit states. By 2008, 80 percent of all Russian gas destined for Europe transited through Ukraine, and Russia–Ukraine disputes led to a boycott of gas to Ukraine and shortages in Europe (BBC 2009). The inflexibility of Europe's gas infrastructure—especially pipelines—underscored the absence of true market conditions. In response, Europe started to diversify suppliers, increase import infrastructure, build a more flexible and integrated gas market that included all the EU regions, and establish market norms facilitating energy contract negotiations (European Parliament 2009). Therefore, the 2014 European Energy Security Strategy attempted to simultaneously advance energy security, environmental objectives, and socio-cultural energy preferences, while recognizing that Europe's chief energy supplier is a champion of realism. Recognizing that Europe's "prosperity and security hinges on a stable and abundant supply of energy," the strategy established a few pillars and implementing mechanisms. It created additional flexibility by mandating 120-day energy reserves and the installation of reverse flow switches at national junctions. It also promoted indigenous deposits, new suppliers and transit routes, boosting efficiency, and an integrated internal market. Emphasis is on the Southern Gas Corridor, the only path by which Caspian and Central Asian resources reach Europe while bypassing Russia (Commission of the European Communities 2014). This policy clearly reflects greater concern for potential energy crises, attempts at forging a durable collective approach, and balancing environmental objectives and socio-cultural energy preferences.

The impact of this apparent recognition of realist concerns has not yet been seen; however, as the EU energy policy shows, dependence on natural resources brings multiple threats to national and regional security.

Conclusion: Knot frustrated, keep tugging!

The case of resource-abundant Russia shows the linkage between authoritarian domestic politics and realist foreign policies. The case of resource-deficient China shows a mixture of participating in international energy markets on normal terms with mature providers, special relationships with Africa (Bejing Consensus), and in the East and especially South China Seas, state-sanctioned energy adventurism, intractable nationalism, and power projection. The case of the European Union demonstrates the risks associated with collective policy, resource dependency, and asymmetrical interdependence toward Russia, the poster child for old-time realism.

In response to the experiences highlighted earlier in this chapter, some nations again are leveraging technology and innovation to change the game. Canadians now market their vast energy reserves (via bitumen or oil sands) to the European market and beyond. Canada appears prepared to serve as a new "benevolent" provider in the Great Game of energy "based on competitive market principles, not self-serving monopolistic political strategies" (Canada–UK Chamber of Commerce 2006). The growth of Canada's oil sands has significantly diversified global energy supply. The rapid exploitation and growth of this previously unattainable resource has recently made Canada the United States' largest source of oil imports, recently exceeding the combined volumes of the OPEC exporters (IHS Energy 2015).

In conclusion, innovation continues to be humankind's "ultimate resource." In the short term, diversification and the use of "benevolent" providers are crucial factors for a coherent European energy security strategy. Any reader or leader should look toward a blend of "energy doom and boom"—short-term abundance via diversification *and* the "race for what is left"—as well as recognize the dangers, notably power politics and climate change, associated with fossil fuels.

Questions for discussion

1   Most developing nations seek to acquire and deliver sufficient energy to meet the needs of their populace and growing economies. At the same time, resource-abundant nations such as Nigeria and Venezuela cannot fully leverage their energy supplies. Is the logic flawed or are these two nations examples of the **resource curse**?

2   Europe's reliance on Russian energy seems tempered by the fact that Russia is reliant on Europe as a customer. Is this a stable relationship?

3   There is a crucial water/energy interface: nations use water to refine, frack, cool plants, and energy to extract, transport and purify water, etc. (See Zawhari's and Weinthal's chapter herein.) Will our appetite for energy limit our water options in the future, creating or worsening another wicked problem?

4   "Resource imperialism" is the idea that developed countries forbid developing countries to use coal due to its harmful effects on the environment, denying these nascent developers the ability to exploit cheap energy options. Given the reality of climate change (see Below's chapter and Beevers' chapter herein), should developing nations have the right to utilize inexpensive, yet dirty, options to fuel their growth?

References

Allen, Nick. January 23, 2006. "Attack on Gas Pipeline is 'Sabotage by Russia.'" *The Telegraph*.

Blank, Stephen. Winter/Spring/Winter/Spring 2011. "Russian Energy and Russian Security." *The Whitehead Journal of Diplomacy and International Relations* XII(1): 173–193.

BP Global. 2015. "Country Insight – Russia 2015." www.bp.com/en/global/corporate/energy-economics/statistical-review-of-world-energy/country-and-regional-insights/russia.html

British Broadcasting Corporation, BBC News. July 5, 2006. "Duma Approves Gazprom Export Bill." http://news.bbc.co.uk/2/hi/business/5159042.stm

British Broadcasting Corporation, BBC News August 1, 2009. "EU Reaches Gas Deal with Ukraine." http://news.bbc.co.uk/2/hi/europe/8179461.stm

Broad, William J. May 17, 2014. "In Taking Crimea, Putin Gains a Sea of Fuel Reserves." *New York Times*.

Canada–United Kingdom Chamber of Commerce. July 14, 2006. "Speeches: Stephen Harper, Remarks to the Canada-UK Chamber of Commerce." http://www.canada-uk.org/event/speeches

Central Intelligence Agency (CIA). 2017. *The World Factbook*. www.cia.gov/library/publications/the-world-factbook/rankorder/2253rank.html

Commission of the European Communities. August 3, 2006. "Green Paper: A European Strategy for Sustainable, Competitive and Secure Energy." http://europa.eu/documents/comm/green_papers/pdf/com2006_105_en.pdf

Commission of the European Communities. April 2007. "Attitudes on Issues Related to EU Energy Policy—Analytical Report." http://ec.europa.eu/commfrontoffice/publicopinion/flash/fl206a_en.pdf

Commission of the European Communities. January 31, 2007. "Stricter Fuel Standards to Combat Climate Change and Reduce Air Pollution." http://europa.eu/rapid/press-release_IP-07-120_en.htm?locale=en

Commission of the European Communities. May 28, 2014. "Communication from the Commission to the European Parliament and the Council: European Energy Security Strategy." http://eur-lex.europa.eu/legal-content/EN/TXT/PDF/?uri=CELEX:52014DC0330&from=EN

Energy Information Administration (EIA). February 7, 2013. "South China Sea." https://www.eia.gov/beta/international/regions-topics.cfm?RegionTopicID=SCS

Energy Information Administration (EIA). 2015. "China International Analysis." May 14, 2015. https://energy.gov/sites/prod/files/2016/04/f30/China_International_Analysis_US.pdf

Energy Information Administration (EIA). 2016. "Country Analysis Brief: Russia." October 25, 2016. www.eia.gov/beta/international/analysis.cfm?iso=RUS

Epstein, Alex. 2014. *The Moral Case for Fossil Fuels*. New York, NY: Portfolio/Penguin.

European Parliament, Directorate-General for Internal Policies. 2009. "An Assessment of the Gas and Oil Pipelines in Europe." November 2009. http://www.europarl.europa.eu/RegData/etudes/note/join/2009/416239/IPOL-ITRE_NT(2009)416239_EN.pdf

Exxon Mobil Corporate. 2017. "Canadian Oil Sands." http://corporate.exxonmobil.com/en/current-issues/oil-sands/canadian-oil-sands/overview

Gazprom. 2016. "Gazprom Ukraine Facts, 2016." www.gazpromukrainefacts.com/ukraine-natural-gas-facts/ukraine-gazprom-and-transit-issues-%E2%80%93-factsheet

Grigas, Agnia. August 2012. "Legacies, Coercion and Soft Power: Russian Influence in the Baltic States." Chatham House. https://www.chathamhouse.org/sites/files/chathamhouse/public/Research/Russia%20and%20Eurasia/0812bp_grigas.pdf

Gueldry, Michel, and Wei Liang. June 2016. "China's Global Energy Diplomacy: Behavior Normalization through Economic Interdependence or Resource Neo-Mercantilism and Power Politics?" *Journal of Chinese Political Science* 21(2): 217–240.

Hubbert, M. King. 1969. *The Theory of Groundwater Motion: And Related Papers*. New York, NY: Haffner.

IEA (International Energy Agency). www.iea.org/

IHS Energy. July 2015. "Why the Oil Sands? How a Remote, Complex Resource Became a Pillar of Global Supply Growth." https://letstalkroyalties.ca/wp-content/uploads/2015/11/10-30-2015_Why-the-oil-sands.pdf

Kaplan, Robert D. 2015. *Asia's Cauldron: The South China Sea and the End of a Stable Pacific*. New York, NY: Random House.

Kirk, Geoffrey, ed. 1983. *Schumacher on Energy*. London: Jonathan Cape.

Klare, Michael T. 2010. *The Race for What's Left*. New York, NY: Picador.

Klare, Michael T. March 3, 2015. "Hard Power, Soft Power, and Energy Power: The New Foreign Policy Tool." *Foreign Affairs*. www.foreignaffairs.com/articles/united-states/2015-03-03/hard-power-soft-power-and-energy-power

Ma, Damien. January 6, 2015. "Rebalancing China's Energy Strategy." *Paulson Papers on Energy and Environment.* http://www.paulsoninstitute.org/think-tank/2015/01/06/rebalancing-chinas-energy-strategy/

Moroney, John R., ed. 1994. "Bias and Theoretical Error in Long-Term Oil Market Forecasting." *Advances in the Economics of Energy and Natural Resources.* JAI Press.

Moyo, Dambisi. 2012. *Winner Take All: China's Race for Resources and What It Means for the World.* New York, NY: Perseus.

National People's Congress. 2016. "China's National People's Congress Approves Thirteenth 5-Year Plan." *The People's Congresses Journal.* www.npc.gov.cn/npc/zgrdzz/site1/20160429/0021861a bd66188d449902.pdf

Nygren, Bertil. July–August 2008. "Putin's Use of Natural Gas to Reintegrate the CIS Region." *Problems of Post-Communism*, 55(4): 3–15.

Pascual, Carlos, and Jonathan Elkind, eds. 2010. *Energy Security: Economics, Strategies, and Implications.* Washington, DC: The Brookings Institution.

People's Daily. July 8, 2005. "Chinese President Calls for International Cooperation in Climate Change." http://english.people.com.cn/200507/08/print20050708_194812.html

Putin, Vladimir. August 20, 2008. "Putin's Thesis Raw Text." *The Daily Dish; The Atlantic.* www.theatlantic.com/daily-dish/archive/2008/08/putins-thesis-raw-text/212739/

Radio Free Europe Radio Liberty. December 14, 2005. "Gazprom to Raise Ukraine Gas Price." www.rferl.org/a/1063827.html

Russian Federation Ministry of Energy. 2010. "Energy Strategy of the Russia for the Period Up to 2030."www.energystrategy.ru/projects/docs/ES-2030_(Eng).pdf, p. 10.

Rutland, Peter. June 2008. "Russia as an Energy Superpower." *New Political Economy*, 13(02): 203–210.

Saakashvili, Mikheil. January 9, 2006. "The Path to Energy Security." *Washington Post.*

Sabin, Paul. 2013. *The Bet. Paul Ehrlich, Julian Simon, and Our Gamble Over Earth's Future.* Yale University Press.

Sahakyan, Armine. March 11, 2016. "How Georgia's Public Foiled Gazprom and Russia." *Huffington Post.*

Simon, Julian L. 1983. *The Ultimate Resource.* Princeton, NJ: Princeton University Press.

Simon, Julian L. 1998. *The Ultimate Resource 2.* Princeton, NJ: Princeton University Press.

Shambaugh, David. 2013. *China Goes Global: The Partial Power.* Oxford: Oxford University Press.

Steven, David, Emily O'Brien, and Bruce Jones, eds. 2015. *The New Politics of Strategic Resources: Energy and Food Security Challenges in the 21st Century.* Washington, DC: Brookings Institution.

Tierney, John. December 2, 1990. "Betting on the Planet." *New York Times.*

Trenin, Dmitri. 2008. "Energy Geopolitics in Russia-EU Relations." In Katinka Barysch, ed. *Pipelines, Politics and Power: The Future of EU–Russia Energy Relations.* Centre for European Reform.

United Nations. May 7, 2009. "Submission by the PRC to the UN Commission on the Limits of the Continental Shelf." www.un.org/depts/los/clcs_new/submissions_files/mysvnm33_09/chn_2009re_mys_vnm_e.pdf

Van Efferink, Leonhardt. October 2010. "EU-Russian Gas Trade: Nord Stream, South Stream and Nabucco Pipelines." *Exploring Geopolitics.* http://www.exploringgeopolitics.org/publication_efferink_van_leonhardt_russian_gas_nordsouthstream_nabucco_pipelines_eni_edf_eon_ruhrgas_wintershall_gasunie_azerbaijan_uzbekiturkmenikazakhstan/

Yergin, Daniel. 2012. *The Quest: Energy, Security, and the Remaking of the Modern World.* New York, NY: Penguin.

Zwack, Peter B. 2017. "Russia." 225–248. In R.D. Hooker, Jr., ed. *Charting a Course: Strategic Choices for a New Administration.* Washington, DC: National Defense University Press.

Part II

Human security, community and gender issues

Chapter 5

The body politics of security
Sexual and reproductive health rights

Marissa Quie

Introduction

Margaret Atwood's *The Handmaid's Tale* (1985) discloses what happens when bodily autonomy is lost. A Christian theocracy controls a global population crisis, enslaving fertile women and raping them to "reproduce" the fictional nation of Gilead. Following the 2017 television adaptation, women dressed as handmaids to express anger over the state of **sexual reproductive health rights** (SRHR) in the United States (Oates, 2006). Sometimes, dystopian fiction reflects brutal realities. Despite constituting half the world's population, women are often marginalized in discussions of security. Gender and sexuality remain an addendum to "hard" security challenges—to be addressed only once "real" conflict is eradicated and stability achieved. Therefore, this chapter connects gender, sexuality, and security, examines why they matter and why policymakers deny their significance, and develops a composite perspective for the **biopolitical security nexus** (BPSN).

We draw on critical approaches from human and ecological security discourses, Foucault's notion of **biopower**, and feminisms to expose the limitations of conventional security thinking. First, we explore how and why traditional definitions and theories of security—particularly realism—fall short for women. Next, we focus on gendered insecurities, showing how **gender-based violence** (GBV)—incorporating multiple forms of violence against women (VAW)—reinforces the dangers females face as females. The BPSN forces us to recognize the linkages between seemingly disparate forms of violence—from intimate partner to interstate. SRHR demonstrate the need for expanding mainstream human rights discourses to include sexuality-related issues. Subsequently, we explore the use of **neo-Malthusian** conceptualizations of "overpopulation" as instruments of male, state, and first-world hegemony. Finally, we discuss potential solutions working toward **reproductive justice** (RJ), which links reproductive rights with social justice.

Text box 5.1: Acronyms

BPSN	biopolitical security nexus
CEDAW	Convention on the Elimination of All Forms of Discrimination against Women
GBV	gender-based violence
LGBTQI	lesbian, gay, bisexual, transgender, queer, and intersex
RH	reproductive health
RJ	reproductive justice

SRH	sexual reproductive health
SRHR	sexual reproductive health rights
STI	sexually transmitted infection
VAW	violence against women

Shortfalls of traditional definitions of security

Traditional definitions of security are characterized by a triple denial of gender, the mechanics of gender hegemony, and social domination. Realist theory utilizes "scientific" legitimizations that create artificial separations between territories, populations, and knowledge, and between the private and public spheres. Classical realism is rooted in negative assumptions about humans as egoistic; these segue into a theory of state power and the struggle for survival in an anarchic world. It argues that "moral judgments have no place in discussions of international affairs or foreign policy" (Beitz 1979, 15).

But beyond realism, **critical security studies**—including constructivism, feminisms, ecological theory, and postmodernism—flourish, decentering the state as the principal security **referent** and specifying more expansive objectives such as emancipation. The meanings of peace, equality, and justice are deepened. Peaceful relations exist in the realist worldview but are usually understood in temporary, negative terms, as simply the absence of violent conflict, rather than a positive condition incorporating individual and communal well-being. Realists claim to recognize an "objective reality," as opposed to the subjective, value-laden perspectives of rival theories. Critical security theories deconstruct realist metanarratives, revealing their subjective, male-oriented roots, and argue that there is no "truth" beyond acts of interpretation; rather, the "knowledges" that emerge are a function of power within an existing social structure.

Weaknesses in the realist view of power become obvious when thinking about population. Realists assume that large populations and sizable militaries are critical elements of state power. In making the state the key referent, gender is significant only insofar as it impacts state capacities; the structural inequalities women confront are simply epiphenomena. In comparison, Foucault's (1984) notion of biopower reminds us that the body itself is a site of politics—of intervention, discipline, regulation, and resistance. Beyond realist parameters, competing moral and religious authorities fortify state power; women are configured as duty-bound vessels of family, social, and religious values; and many forms of male hegemony intertwine, leading to oppression, inequality, violence, and insecurity.

Critical theories expose gaps in traditional international relations theory by interrogating its fundamental assumptions, units of analysis, and implicit values. The challenges posed by the BPSN are embedded within this wider framework of ecological security. In our **Anthropocene** epoch, humans form the most potent transformative force. The global population more than quadrupled over the twentieth century, and resource consumption has accelerated. Countless women and men are powerless to make genuine choices about having children because of gender discrimination or cultural and financial constraints. In contrast with realism, critical security studies call for the inclusion of women and nonmilitary security sectors and issues. Feminists highlight gender as a central hierarchical principle to understand global distributions of power, status, and resources. Gender is a fundamental component of individual identity, shaped by the cultural representations of men and women. Recognition of its significance entails considering previously unexamined security issues like reproduction, sexuality, and gender-based violence.

Multidimensional violences and gendered insecurities

Women experience gendered inequalities internationally and in all spheres of life. They are underrepresented in political decision-making bodies; only 22.8 percent of national parliamentarians were women in 2016 (UN Women 2017). They do not receive equal pay for equal work, leading to the lifetime penalty of the gender wage gap—particularly for women of color and women in the Global South—and the "feminization of poverty" (Pearce 1978; Holmes and Corley 2017). These multidimensional violences hinder women's potential, creating gendered insecurities. Violences permeate women's lives on almost every level, as expressed by the violence against women/gender-based violence and sexual reproductive health challenges that are critical to the BPSN.

VAW and GBV

VAW is one of the most prevalent human rights violations worldwide. Globally, it is estimated that one in three women will experience physical and/or sexual violence in her lifetime (WHO 2016). Gender-based violence clearly correlates with health, autonomy, and security, yet it is persistently masked by cultures of silence. Victims may suffer SRH consequences, including unwanted pregnancies, unsafe abortions, STIs, and even death. Multiple UN treaties have been passed to tackle VAW, including the Convention on the Elimination of All Forms of Discrimination against Women (UN 1979), yet a blatant gap between rhetoric and implementation persists.

Geography, culture, economy, and religion can intermesh in generating gendered threats. Sierra Leone, for example, is one of the worst places in the world to be a girl, having been destabilized by a violent civil war and the devastating spread of Ebola. The majority of Sierra Leone's women have suffered female genital mutilation—their initiation into adulthood, which traditionally improves their marital chances. Almost 50 percent of girls marry before they are 18. Many endure pregnancies before their first period, and rape often goes unpunished. In 2013, more than 25 percent of girls ages 15 to 19 were pregnant or had children—one of the highest global rates (Amnesty International UK 2016). Pregnant girls are banned from attending school and struggle to re-enroll.

Femicide and sex-selective abortions are further forms of GBV. The famous Indian economist Amartya Sen (1990) coined the phrase "missing women" to refer to the 100-million-strong disparity in sex ratios in Asian countries' populations in particular. The number of missing women is measured by contrasting actual population numbers with expected numbers if there were no sex-selective abortions or female infanticide, and equal levels of health care and nutrition. In countries like China and India, gender imbalances have proven difficult to correct (Hudson and den Boer 2005).

Sexual and reproductive health

Globally, gender is a central determinant of health. According to recent estimates, 215 million women want to avoid getting pregnant but have no access to contraception, and 23 million 15- to 19-year-old women in developing regions have an unmet need for contraception (Gribble and Bremner 2016). The greatest obstacle to reproductive choice is not simply access to contraceptives but the deeper challenge of gender inequality (Population Institute 2011). When contraception is unavailable, the probable consequence is not less sex, but more unwanted pregnancies. Pregnancy and childbirth remain the leading causes of death for women in Africa and South Asia. In the world's poorest states, the most dangerous thing a woman can do is to get pregnant. One in every 90 women in the Global South dies from pregnancy or childbirth, compared to one in 3,600 in developed nations (Population Reference Bureau 2011). In countries where women's health is a low priority, expectant mothers lack adequate nourishment and are susceptible to severe childbirth complications (see Abnedur's and Resende's chapter herein). Girls who marry before their bodies have fully developed suffer further risks.

The unintended pregnancy rate is an important indicator of reproductive health, demonstrating the degree to which women and couples are able to plan their families. Unplanned pregnancy rates in the United States have remained essentially unchanged for decades, resulting in substantial public health, personal, financial, and emotional costs. Marginalized populations, especially women of color, are more vulnerable; African American women die in pregnancy or childbirth at a rate of three to four times that of white women. No single factor in itself explains this racial disparity, but access to prenatal care can reduce maternal mortality and other negative pregnancy outcomes. Most pregnancy-related deaths occur following childbirth, and women who do not receive prenatal care are three to four times more likely to die after a live birth than women who attend even one prenatal appointment (Center for Reproductive Rights, n.d.). In addition, in the early 2010s, 45 % (or 2.8 million) of all pregnancies in the United States were unintended, with the highest rates found among minorities. Almost one-third of US girls become pregnant as teenagers, and 42% percent of these pregnancies end in abortion (Guttmacher Institute 2016). Unequal health provision means that the United States has the highest rate of maternal mortality in the developed world; women in Texas are ten times as likely to die from pregnancy as women in Spain or Sweden (Kristof 2011).

Meanwhile, HIV currently afflicts 17.8 million women in the United States; power imbalances, harmful social norms, violence, and marginalization correlate with HIV diffusion. Education, ethnicity, and race also have an impact. Together, African American women and Latinas comprise 25 percent of the US female population, but account for 80 percent of reported female HIV/AIDS diagnoses. Older men generally pose the greatest threat to younger women, who lack the knowledge to negotiate safe sex (see Fromentos' and Gokcek's chapter herein).

Text box 5.2: Sexual and reproductive health: The continuing challenge

1   In some parts of the world, especially Africa, total fertility rates and the unmet need for contraception remain high.
2   Hundreds of millions of women annually suffer disability because of pregnancy complications, and more than half a million die in pregnancy and childbirth, or following unsafe abortion. Almost all of these deaths are preventable.
3   STIs are the second most significant cause of poor health, particularly for young women, and an important cause of morbidity in men.

4   Adolescents are especially vulnerable to SR ill health, and services are often inaccessible or denied to them.

5   VAW is a major cause of ill health, and a consequence (and cause) of gender inequality.

6   FGM is associated with obstetric morbidity and an increased risk of stillbirth and early neonatal death.

7   Obstetric fistula, pelvic pain, and fecal and urinary incontinence cause widespread morbidity.

8   Despite the above, SRH has been neglected. Increasing conservative political, religious, and cultural forces threaten to undermine progress.

Expanding the net: The BPSN

The BPSN forces us to expand the security net to encompass sex and reproduction—subjects conventionally considered private and apolitical. Casting the net wider creates space to question traditional tropes, and feminist theories help delineate the connections between different forms of violence, from intimate partner violence to interstate violence.

The BPSN and feminisms

Feminist theories scrutinize genders and gender relations, examine previously unacknowledged conditions, and call for change, since reproduction and sexuality are central. How can sex be about fulfillment of desire, and not a risk to social status and health? When, how, and why do women want to become mothers? Can they fully participate in the political and economic spheres after having children?

Although a contested proposition, the BPSN draws on feminism to understand "the social role of women in relation to men (…) animated by a conviction that women suffer and have suffered injustices because of their sex" (Bethke Elshtain 2000, 151). Many strands of feminism focus on women as sexual objects and mothers, underscoring their differences from men and male dominance through control of their bodies, sexuality reproduction, and labor. For Judith Butler (1990), gender is a performance, produced through repetitive actions like dressing. This makes gender flexible. While avoiding essentialism, Simone de Beauvoir (2010) analyzes how women are differently situated, investigating experiences pertaining to wives, mothers, and young and old women. In refining the BPSN toolbox, **intersectionality** provides a way of conceptualizing the relations between forms of oppression and violence that construct multiple identities, including sexuality, "race," social class, and nationality. Kimberlé Crenshaw (1989) charts the insecurities of those on the margins, helping to penetrate the "private domain" to capture issues like domestic abuse.

The BPSN also utilizes transnational feminism, focusing on how globalization and capitalism impact gender and sexuality, and how colonial legacies shape oppression. It shows that economic forces are a primary health determinant—and that such forces are intimately linked with the actions of powerful institutions (World Bank, IMF), which implement top-down economic policies throughout the Global South. Incorporating transnational feminism creates space for resistance, enabling women in diverse local contexts to develop empowering solutions that transcend national borders.

In contrast to realist scholarship, feminists like Mary Caprioli (2005) investigate whether democracy and human rights ensure women's security, defined through measures of fertility rates, rape, conditions of childbirth, education, and political and economic inequalities. Caprioli contends that countries with higher fertility rates are nearly twice as likely to experience intrastate conflict as those with lower rates, and that countries with fewer women in the labor force are more likely to experience conflict. She confirms the fundamental link between gender inequality and intrastate conflict—a key measure of security. To uncover the real consequences of the patriarchal state, a shift in emphasis is required from realism's abstract state to feminism's focus on women's lived experiences.

Feminism is incorrectly assumed to be concerned only with women. It is actually "the pursuit of deep, deep justice for women in ways that change the behaviors of both women and men, and really change our notions of what justice looks like" (Van Hook 2012). To reach this goal, we cannot simply reproduce the model of men as protectors and women as victims of physical violence. We need to investigate masculinities. Different conceptualizations of patriarchy have highlighted men's social and structural relations to women in terms of sexuality, reproduction, family, culture, politics, and economy. Since the late 1970s, critiques of the notion of "patriarchy" as ahistorical, culturally insensitive, and biologically determined have developed. The BPSN understands masculinities as signs and practices that obscure unequal power relations (Connell 1995).

Connecting different forms of violence

New security studies (Buzan and Hansen 2004, 2007) call for greater inclusion of views from women, minorities, and the South, connecting with widening understanding of the meanings of violence—particularly GBV. Innovative research (Walby 2013) exposes hidden violences. Although democracy appears to blunt physical violence, even developed states are unable to guarantee safety (for a discussion of GBV violence in Germany, see Reiling's chapter herein). Johan Galtung (1996) expands the notion of violence to include social inequalities that may lead to unnecessary death, labeling this structural violence. The field of human (in)security analyzes a broad range of variables conducive to premature death. GBV research further extends this research, moving away from pure physicality to capture the psychological, social, emotional, symbolic, and bodily dimensions of violence.

Links between different forms of violence disrupt conventional divisions between private and public spheres, and connect local, national, and international processes. There is a close correspondence between macro level state security and micro level GBV, and VAW correlates with public violence linked to intra and interstate insecurity. For example, almost one-third of mass shootings in the United States in 2015 were related to domestic violence (LaFraniere et al. 2016). Domestic abuse could be a predictor for terrorism. A rapist leads ISIS; both the 2013 Boston Marathon bombers and the 2016 Nice (France) truck terrorist had been arrested previously for domestic violence.

Gender inequalities, asymmetrical practices such as polygamy, and unequal family law adversely affect state security. A state's treatment of its female citizens is a critical predictor of peace. Such treatment also affects the state's security, stability, wealth, bellicosity, corruption, health, regime type, and relative power. Democracies with higher levels of VAW are as insecure and unstable as nondemocratic regimes (Hudson et al. 2014). The wider the gender disparity, the likelier it is that a nation is involved—and the first to use force—in intra and interstate conflict.

SRHR and human rights

Reproductive health is the cornerstone of sexual health, women's rights, and security. The 1948 Universal Declaration of Human Rights outlines rights to life, liberty, and the security of the individual. Yet in many countries, including the United States, women are not in control of their lives, liberty, or bodies. Rape is often used as a weapon of war. In refugee camps, girls are vulnerable to trafficking. In cities everywhere, fear disempowers women on public transport and in the streets, compromising their fundamental human rights. Inequality is entrenched without "security of the person," imprisoning women in vicious cycles of poverty and unfulfilled potential (for the situation in Syria and among Syrian refugees, see Reiling's chapter herein).

The inclusion of sexual rights within mainstream human rights discourse links widened traditional human rights covenants to include sexuality-related issues, including sexual autonomy and the right to pleasure (Shalev 1998). When SRHR are unmet, individuals are deprived of the right to make choices about their own bodies and lives, with a cascading impact on their security and that of their families and future generations. Denial of SRHR undermines development and the environment, exacerbating poverty and gender inequality. But a growing body of evidence suggests that female leadership improves decision-making in politics. Women often champion gender equality, and work to combat gender-based violence and gender disparities in legal and political reform. They also enhance the effectiveness of peace processes in the violent context of war; post-conflict agreements negotiated without women erode faster than agreements that include them (UNFPA, n.d.).

Gender dynamics do not tell the whole story. But given the concentration of violent practices among men, they appear significant. Viable strategies for peace must include challenging forms of masculinity that value violence, and supplanting them with forms more open to negotiation, cooperation, and equality.

Rethinking the "overpopulation" narrative

The politics of reproduction seeps into the socioeconomic and political arenas, emerging as an important index of security. Demographers regularly speculate about fertility, mortality, and migration, imagining levels of earth's habitation in the future. This section explores the **Malthusian** origin of these concerns and their contemporary manifestations in transnational attempts to regulate fertility. It also discusses the demographic storm facing Europe and connects low fertility with gender, arguing that SRHR investment is essential to unlock the **demographic dividend**.

The origins of population regulation

In 1798, English cleric and scholar Thomas Robert Malthus (1766–1834) predicted that the human population would increase more rapidly than its ability to grow food; eventually, many would starve. Although over 800 million people are undernourished today, mass starvation has not occurred, but the debate Malthus initiated continues (Ehrlich 1968). Neo-Malthusian tropes have translated into national and international policies to regulate population, encouraging reproductive "quality" over "quantity." Having "too many children" has been described as a "crime," and interventions as "disaster measures" against a "disease" attacking the body politic (Connelly 2008, 201). The idea that population is outstripping the earth's capacities remains powerful—and both authoritarian experiments (China) and "lighter touch" efforts (Europe) ultimately falter on the battleground of women's bodies. Without the multilayered security of BPSN, state interventions go awry.

In the context of population control, biopower is not neutral. In 1974, a US National Security Council classified study (NSSM 200) falsely claimed that population growth in developing countries was a grave threat to national security. The study outlined a covert plan to reduce population growth in specified countries through birth control—and, implicitly, war and famine. Washington then became intricately involved in international family planning, and contraception became a condition of foreign aid.

Transnational attempts to regulate fertility

Despite its imperialist and eugenicist implications, biopower is transnational. Diverse strands of the family planning movement were attracted to **eugenics**. William Vogt (1948), for example, described tropical diseases as "advantages" because they reduced population growth. He criticized doctors for believing they had "a duty to keep alive as many people as possible"—racist code for disempowering non-white populations (Krenn 1999, 252). The significance of population-control activists in paving the way for some strands of contemporary authoritarian environmentalism (e.g., Garrett Harding) is now concealed through new "green" discourses.

China's controversial one-child policy was introduced in 1979 to slow population growth, and is estimated to have prevented about 400 million births. The policy led to forced abortions, female infanticides, and underreporting of female births. China now has a problematic gender imbalance. In 2015, the policy was revised as demographers raised concerns about social costs, including a shrinking workforce and aging population. Continued state surveillance and quotas clearly undermine SRHR and subjective security. Yet curiously, many countries with high birth rates (e.g., sub-Saharan Africa) have the least impact on environmental problems like climate change (see Below's chapter herein). Between 1950 and 2000, Africa was responsible for only 2.5 percent of global carbon dioxide emissions (Friedrich and Damassa 2014). Therefore, BPSN issues cannot be reduced to population size.

How these problems are addressed can determine fundamental issues of security: whether states survive and their well-being. Entire regions can be propelled to greater prosperity and stability, or state fragility can be exacerbated. Over 25 percent of Japan's population is over 65; a proportion projected to reach 40 percent within a generation. This creates a huge demographic challenge for a state struggling with zero growth. Nations across the Middle East, Africa, and South Asia, meanwhile, confront a youth bulge. More than 50 percent of Egypt's workforce is under 30. Half of Nigeria's population of 167 million is aged 15 to 34; and the population of 26 African nations is predicted to at least double by 2050 (UN 2017). Some experts worry that this increase will not only exacerbate the current migration crisis (see Campbell's chapter herein) but could also reinforce terror groups across the Sahel, which often recruit from large, impoverished families (see Joshi's chapter herein).

Europe's demographic storm

In stark contrast to Malthus's warnings, 21st century Europe now faces a sub-replacement fertility dilemma: birth rates are substantially below the rate (2.1) necessary to keep a population steady. This fortifies populist parties, which frame immigration as an existential threat known as "the great replacement" (of white natives by dark-skinned immigrants). In 1963, Europe represented 12.5 percent of the world population; today, it represents 7.2 percent, and is predicted to hit 5 percent by 2050 (see Garrett's chapter herein).

What might this mean for biopolitical security? Some of the European Union's weakest countries have the least favorable demographics. Lower birth rates in southern Europe could mean weaker growth and productivity, generating ever-deepening fiscal problems. Inequalities between northern and southern Europe may become structural rather than cyclical, creating entrenched conflict. A key component in this equation is lifespan. Demographers project that 30 million working-age Europeans could "disappear" by 2050 (Eurostat, n.d.), and the number of those aged over 80 could increase in tandem with retirement spans. The subsequent demographic storm could intensify demands on welfare states and health-care systems, undermining resilience through decreased tax contributions from a shrinking workforce.

Paths to reproductive justice

Reproductive justice

The litmus test for SRHR is reproductive justice (RJ), which interrogates the control of oppressed groups—particularly women of color and trans- and gender-nonconforming people. The regulation of reproduction and exploitation of women's bodies and labor derives from oppression engrained in gender, sexuality, "race," ethnicity, and class. RJ addresses issues of population control, bodily self-determination, immigrant rights, economic and environmental justice, sovereignty, militarism, and criminal injustices—all of which limit individual human rights.

When considering new directions for the BPSN, we might ask: How can identity politics grasp the "thickness" of reproductive questions? For Lorde (1982), "There is no such thing as a single-issue struggle because we do not live single-issue lives." If RJ means control over when and how we have children, the question of whether we have the resources to raise children is equally important. Reproductive politics is founded on gendered, sexualized, and racialized forms of dominance that are integral to daily life. RJ provides an evaluative lens to gauge and challenge these power relations.

Free reproductive health care

A more serious commitment to free and comprehensive reproductive health (RH) care is a critical step toward meeting the needs of low-income women. Many women realize that birth control enables them to support themselves financially (56 percent), complete their education (51 percent), and get or keep a job (50 percent) (Frost et al. 2012). Providing family planning services at no cost—including routine and emergency contraception—results in more effective contraceptive use, decreased rates of unintended pregnancy, and significant declines in abortion rates (WHO 2017).

International frameworks and national implementation

International human rights instruments define reproductive freedom and public provision of voluntary family planning as a fundamental human right of women, and a foundation of human security. Multiple interventions are required to alleviate poverty, but none can work if women lack the agency to make—and act on—well-informed decisions about their own bodies. SRHR push us beyond "right to life" debates that center on abortion. The right to life does not end with birth. It is also about parenting with dignity, continuing access to education and well-paid work, and realizing desires connected with the types of relationships and families individuals want (Fuentes et al. 2010).

At least 119 nations have passed legislation on domestic violence, 125 on sexual harassment, and 52 on marital rape. SRHR have been recognized in a range of international frameworks, including CEDAW and the Beijing Platform for Action. The UN Security Council recognizes sexual violence as both a tactic of war and terrorism. Unfortunately, this "progress" does not always equate with effective implementation or compliance with international recommendations. Basic international commitments like Responsibility to Protect (R2P) are gender-blind.

Substantive mitigation of humanitarian crises requires states to adopt a feminist, human rights-based approach. Canada's *Feminist International Assistance Policy* (2017) demonstrates this: 90 percent of its aid budget is targeted toward achieving gender equality by 2022. If subjective security means feeling safe according to one's own norms, devising an authentic foreign policy entails eradicating all forms of inequality within the aid-industrial complex.

The case for integrating state and human security

The BPSN ties with a "thick" notion of security, intertwining protection from harm with freedom and well-being. Women in the Global South are especially likely to experience their lives as subordinated to others, including the demands of patriarchal cultures and fragile environments. The BPSN expands the net on security. It entails mental, spiritual, and bodily health, including reproductive health, food security, and sustainable shelter.

From Malthus to some contemporary environmental campaigns, violence is sometimes shrouded in "emancipatory" discourses of population control. Masquerading as "objective knowledge," these often translate into detrimental policy interventions. Yet differing interpretations of subjective security frequently frustrate policy objectives. Subjective security pivots on gender disparities. Security is inherently connected to struggles for social justice and human rights. Feminisms provide an aperture through which we can excavate pervasive inequalities in power, status, and resources.

A drawback of the RH framework is its focus on service delivery to address inequalities via low- or no-cost care. It presumes effective political participation within democratic political systems. Yet this assumption conceals multiple violences. Similarly, a deepened vision of security requires sensitive policies, public dialog on sexualities, and protections for marginalized groups. Social norms and cultural values are dynamic and discursively constructed. Differences that appear immutable can be negotiated in the name of more equitable lives and deepened security. The challenge, both domestically and internationally, is to create spaces in which viable strategies that engender a greater measure of safety can evolve.

Security, then, is *always* more than survival. It involves both freedom from life-determining threats and the "emancipatory space" in which to make choices (Booth 2007, 102). Such emancipation is "the freeing of people (as individuals and groups) from the physical and human constraints which stop them carrying out what they would freely choose to do (...) Security and emancipation are two sides of the same coin. Emancipation, not power, or order, produces true security. Emancipation, theoretically, is security" (Booth 1991, 319).

Questions for discussion

1   How do critical security studies contribute to integrative views of human security?
2   How are nations (in)secured through the BPSN?
3   What are some key connections between violence in the domestic sphere and public insecurity?
4   What kinds of solutions does the BPSN suggest?
5   Why should security studies incorporate gender and SRHR? Why is there resistance to the idea that SRHR matter for (in)security?

References

Amnesty International UK. November 8, 2016. "Sierra Leone: Pregnancy Ban in Schools Threatening Teenage Girls' Futures." https://www.amnesty.org.uk/press-releases/sierra-leone-pregnancy-ban-schools-threatening-teenage-girls-futures.
Beitz, Charles R. 1979. *Political Theory and International Relations*. Princeton, NJ: Princeton University Press.
Bethke Elshtain, Jean. 2000. *Real Politics: At the Center of Everyday Life*. Baltimore, MD: Johns Hopkins University Press.
Booth, Ken. October 1991. "Security and Emancipation." *Review of International Studies* 17(4): 313–326.
Booth, Ken. 2007. *Theory of World Security*. Cambridge: Cambridge University Press.
Butler, Judith. 1990. *Gender Trouble: Feminism and the Subversion of Identity*. London: Routledge.
Buzan, Barry, and Lene Hansen, eds. 2004. *The Evolution of International Security Studies*. Cambridge: Cambridge University Press.
Buzan, Barry, and Lene Hansen, eds. 2007. *International Security*. London: Sage.
Caprioli, M. June 2005. "Primed for Violence: The Role of Gender Inequality in Predicting Internal Conflict." *International Studies Quarterly*. 49(2): 161–178.
Center for Reproductive Rights. n.d. "Addressing Disparities in Reproductive and Sexual Health Care in the US." https://www.reproductiverights.org/node/861
Connell, Raewyn W. 1995. *Masculinities*. Berkeley, CA: University of California Press.
Connelly, Matthew. 2008. *Fatal Misconception: The Struggle to Control World Population*. Boston, MA: Harvard University Press.
Crenshaw, Kimberlé W. 1989. "Demarginalizing the Intersection of Race and Sex: A Black Feminist Critique of Antidiscrimination Doctrine, Feminist Theory and Antiracist Politics." *University of Chicago Legal Forum* Issue 140(1): 139–167.
de Beauvoir, Simone. 2010 (1947). *The Second Sex*. New York, NY: Alfred A Knopf.
Ehrlich, Paul R. 1968. *The Population Bomb*. New York, NY: Ballantine.
Eurostat. n.d. "Theme 4: Demographic Changes." http://ec.europa.eu/eurostat/web/sdi/indicators/demographic-changes
Foucault, Michel. 1984 (1976). *The History of Sexuality*. London: Allen Lane/Penguin.

Friedrich, Johannes, and Thomas Damassa. May 21, 2014. "The History of Carbon Dioxide Emissions." *World Resources Institute*. http://www.wri.org/blog/2014/05/history-carbon-dioxide-emissions

Frost, Jennifer J., Laura D. Lindberg, and Lawrence B. Finer. June 2012. "Young Adults' Contraceptive Knowledge, Norms and Attitudes: Associations with Risk of Unintended Pregnancy." *Perspectives on Sexual & Reproductive Health* 44(2): 107–116.

Fuentes, Liza, Verónica Bayetti Flores, and Jessica Gonzalez-Rojas. 2010. *Removing Stigma: Towards a Complete Understanding of Young Latinas' Sexual Health*. New York, NY: National Latina Institute for Reproductive Health.

Galtung, Johan. 1996. *Peace by Peaceful Means: Peace and Conflict, Development and Civilization*. London: Sage; Oslo: PRIO.

Gribble, James N., and Jason Bremner. 2016. *2016 Annual Report: Fact and Impact*. https://www.guttmacher.org/annual-report-2016

Guttmacher Institute. September 2016. Fact Sheet: *Unintended Pregnancy in the United States*. https://www.guttmacher.org/fact-sheet/unintended-pregnancy-united-states#8-12a

Holmes, Kaitlin, and Danielle Corley. April 4, 2017. "International Approaches to Closing the Gender Wage Gap." Center for American Progress https://www.americanprogress.org/issues/women/reports/2017/04/04/429825/international-approaches-closing-gender-wage-gap/

Hudson, Valerie M., and Andrea M. den Boer. 2005. "Missing Women and Bare Branches: Gender Balance and Conflict." *Environmental Change and Security Program Report* 11: 20–24.

Hudson, Valerie M., Bonnie Ballif-Spanvill, Mary Caprioli, et al. 2014. *Sex & World Peace*. New York, NY: Columbia University Press.

Krenn, Michael L., ed. 1999. *The Impact of Race on US Foreign Policy: A Reader*. New York, NY: Garland.

Kristof, Nicholas. November 2, 2011. "The Birth Control Solution." *New York Times*.

LaFraniere, Sharon, Daniela Porat, and Agustin Armedariz. May 22, 2016. "Shootings, But America Isn't Listening." *New York Times*.

Lorde, Audre. 1982. "Learning From the 60s." Speech delivered February 1982 at Malcolm X Weekend, Harvard University, Cambridge, MA. BlackPast.org. http://www.blackpast.org/1982-audre-lorde-learning-60s

Malthus, Thomas R. 1798. *An Essay on the Principle of Population*. London: J. Johnson in St Paul's Church-Yard. http://www.econlib.org/library/Malthus/malPop.html

Oates, Joyce C. November 2, 2006. "Margaret Atwood's Tale." *New York Review of Books*.

Pearce, Diana. January 1978. "The Feminization of Poverty: Women, Work and Welfare." *Urban and Social Change Review*, special issue: "Women and Work," 11(1): 1–2, 28–36, 78.

Population Institute. 2011. "From 6 Billion to 7 Billion: How Population Growth Is Changing and Challenging Our World." https://www.populationinstitute.org/external/files/reports/from-6b-to-7b.pdf

Population Reference Bureau 2011. *Annual Report*. http://www.prb.org/pdf12/annualreport-2011.pdf

Sen, Amartya. December 2, 1990. "More Than 100 Million Women Are Missing." *New York Review of Books*. http://www.nybooks.com/articles/1990/12/20/more-than-100-million-women-are-missing/?pagination=false

Shalev, Carmel. March 18, 1998. "Rights to Sexual and Reproductive Health: The ICPD and the Convention on the Elimination of All Forms of Discrimination against Women." Paper presented at the International Conference on Reproductive Health, Mumbai, India. http://www.un.org/womenwatch/daw/csw/shalev.htm

UN (United Nations). 1979. "Convention on the Elimination of All Forms of Discrimination against Women." *Treaty Series* 1249: 13. http://www.un.org/womenwatch/daw/cedaw/cedaw.htm

UN (United Nations). 2017. "World Population Projected to Reach 9.8 Billion in 2050, and 11.2 Billion in 2100—Says UN." http://www.un.org/sustainabledevelopment/blog/2017/06/world-population-projected-to-reach-9-8-billion-in-2050-and-11-2-billion-in-2100-says-un/

UN (United Nations). *Sustainable Development Goals*, June 21, 2017.

UN Women. July 2017. "Facts and Figures: Leadership and Political Participation." http://www. unwomen.org/en/what-we-do/leadership-and-political-participation/facts-and-figures

UNFPA. n.d. "Gender-Based Violence." http://www.unfpa.org/gender-based-violence

US National Security Council. 1974. "National Security Study Memorandum 200: Implications of Worldwide Population Growth for US Security and Overseas Interests (NSSM 200)." December 10, 1974. https://pdf.usaid.gov/pdf_docs/PCAAB500.pdf

Van Hook, Stephanie. September 13, 2012. "Taking Women's Lives Seriously: An Interview with Cynthia Enloe." Waging Nonviolence. https://wagingnonviolence.org/feature/taking-womens-lives-seriously-an-interview-with-cynthia-enloe/

Vogt, William. 1948. *Road to Survival*. New York, NY: Sloane Associates.

Walby, Sylvia. March 2013. "Violence and Society: Introduction to an Emerging Field of Sociology." *Current Sociology* 61(2): 95–111.

WHO (World Health Organization). 2016. "Violence against Women: Intimate Partner and Sexual Violence against Women Fact Sheet." http://www.who.int/mediacentre/factsheets/fs239/en/

WHO (World Health Organization). 2017. "Family Planning/Contraception." http://www.who. int/mediacentre/factsheets/fs351/en/

Chapter 6

Gender-based violence
A threat to human security in the Global North and Global South

Nicole Gerring

Gender-based violence (GBV) is not a new form of insecurity, yet it has long been ignored or marginalized within International Relations. Scholars working in the two major paradigms of International Relations, realism and liberalism, have not considered GBV as a serious security threat (see Quie's chapter herein). For instance, *The Real World Order: Zones of Peace, Zones of Turmoil* (Singer and Wildavsky 1996) exemplifies the ways that IR has neglected alternative security threats such as gender-based violence. Singer and Wildavsky argue that the post-Cold War world is comprised of two distinct geographic areas. War is unlikely in the "zones of peace," characterized by democracy, wealth, and security (Western Europe, the United States, Canada, Japan, Australia, and New Zealand). The rest of the world comprises "zones of turmoil," wherein one finds most of the world's violence and instability. The authors contend that this violence will not spread to the zones of peace.

Examining the extent and variation in GBV across the globe helps us understand that security threats cannot be limited to certain geographic regions. GBV brings turmoil for people around the world, even in the so-called "zones of peace." While mindful of the particularized nature of conflict-related gender-based violence, this chapter seeks to emphasize the extent of GBV across contexts in both war and peace. GBV creates interpersonal "zones of turmoil" at home, in the workplace, and in neighborhoods, as evidenced by its extent even in wealthy, democratic Germany. And as illustrated by the Syrian refugee crisis, GBV may contribute to the diffusion of conflict to "zones of peace." In examining the political, cultural, legal, and economic aspects of GBV in Germany and Syria, this chapter illustrates the importance of including it in any analysis of security threats.

Text box 6.1: WHO Definition of gender-based violence

In this chapter, we adopt the World Health Organization definition for gender-based violence: any kind of violence that targets women because they are women or that affects women disproportionately. Gender-based violence can include physical, sexual, and psychological violence, and involve intimidation, suffering, coercion or deprivation of liberty within the family or within the community. It can be perpetrated by a stranger, an intimate partner, or the state.

Freedom from GBV is a critical part of human security, an approach that emphasizes the protection of individuals, and critiques traditional, state-centric approaches. Two theories shape the following analysis of GBV as a global security threat. Galtung's structural violence theory suggests that in studying peace and security, we should consider both personal violence, which involves direct violence committed by an actor such as a person or the state, and indirect violence, which can occur due to social structures and repressive systems such as patriarchy (1996, 40–48). Personal and structural violence, alone or in concert, prevent individuals from achieving their full potential in life (Galtung 1969, 168). Galtung also observed an important distinction between two kinds of peace: negative and positive. Negative peace is characterized by an absence of direct violence, whereas positive peace includes social justice. GBV occurs in direct and structural forms, and prevents societies from achieving positive peace.

The second theoretical perspective that informs this chapter is feminist international relations theory. Feminist IR theory considers the ways that a social construction of gender contributes to women's subordination. Feminist IR scholars argue that gender binaries built on sex differences tend to privilege male/masculine over female/feminine. In subordinating women/the feminine, the social construction of gender thus provides the grounds for further hierarchies of power within society, the state, and world. The creation of gendered hierarchies thus contributes to a culture of militarization and violence. We draw upon the work of Cynthia Cockburn (1998), who introduced the notion of a continuum of violence against women. Cockburn observed that although wartime violence has distinct properties and forms, this violence—like intimate partner violence and harassment—reflects underlying social inequalities between men and women. A continuum of GBV suggests that wartime violence is an escalation of the "everyday" violence that women face in their homes, work, and public places. This continuum exists in countries "at peace" and countries at war.

Galtung's structural violence theory and Cockburn's continuum of violence theory enable us to explore the ways that GBV appears as both a form of structural violence—caused by patriarchy and unequal gender relations—and direct violence that can be attributed to individuals or groups of perpetrators. The varied, multiple forms of GBV present major barriers to achieving human security and positive peace. We define and examine the political, cultural, legal and economic dimensions of GBV before discussing the application of these concepts in Syria and Germany.

Four key aspects of gender-based violence

First, we turn to the ways that gender-based violence intersects with women's political power and political participation. Feminist IR theorists have argued that GBV reflects hierarchies of power within the home, community, and state. As feminists from the 1970s argued, "the personal is political." Despite the persistence of GBV and patriarchal cultures, women's rights activists have worked at the local, state and international levels to increase women's political power. Yet, women who enter the political arena may face harassment, intimidation, and risks to their physical security as those who have traditionally held power resist women's entry into the political realm (Eckert et al. 2017). This backlash—such as sexual assaults of women voters and political activists in Kenya in 2007–2008 and in Zimbabwe—has the potential to suppress women's political participation (Huber and Kammerud 2016). However, some women who have suffered GBV cite these experiences as motivation to participate. For example, Colombian journalist Jineth Bedoya Lima became an advocate for survivors of sexual violence after she was kidnapped and raped in retaliation for reporting state and paramilitary group violence (IFEX 2017). Lima founded a campaign, "It's Not Time to Be Silent" to advocate for survivors of sexual violence in Colombia. Later, we discuss the ways that GBV in Germany and Syria interacts with political participation.

GBV has cultural aspects, as well. These may be based in religion, traditional practices, or other local, regional, or national belief systems. As Quie describes herein, certain cultures practice female genital cutting (FGC) to prepare girls for marriage. The World Health Organization estimates that more than 200 million girls and women alive today have undergone FGC. This procedure is practiced in many countries in Africa as well as parts of the Middle East and Asia. In Africa for example, UNICEF found that more than 80% of girls and women, ages 15–49, had undergone FGC in Guinea, Mali, Sierra Leone, Egypt, Sudan, Somalia, Ethiopia, Eritrea, and Djibouti (United Nations Children's Fund 2013). However, aspects of culture may also be leveraged to reduce GBV. The NGO Tostan, based in Dakar, Senegal, has implemented community-based dialogue and human rights education programs at the grassroots level in countries such as Guinea, Senegal, Mali, and Somalia. So far, 8,000 communities have come together to publicly declare they will abandon the practice of FGC in favor of protecting girls' human rights (Tostan 2017). Research suggests that FGC and other forms of gender-based violence are less prevalent in villages that have participated in these interventions (Diop and Askew 2009).

Another important cultural aspect of GBV is the way that survivors of certain forms of GBV—such as wartime rape—are perceived by their families and communities. Although intimate partner violence may be prevalent within families, the use of GBV by an outsider is often considered an attack on the cultural values of a community. GBV against a woman or girl may be perceived as an attack on the honor of the family—places that Hudson et al. (2012) characterize as honor/shame societies. Honor killings—which occur in both the Global South and Global North—are illegal in places such as Afghanistan, Pakistan, and Turkey but happen nonetheless. Cultural acceptance of honor killings allows individuals to retaliate against perceived threats to their family's honor. In conflict, the family members of women who are targeted by sexual and other forms of GBV may perceive an attack on their female relatives as an attack on their masculinity. As Julia Brooks states, "violence against women serves as tactic to symbolically 'emasculate' enemy men by demonstrating their failure to protect the physical and moral integrity of 'their' females, and by extension, their communities" (Brooks 2016). The use of GBV in wartime can have ripple effects on families and communities by furthering the cycle of violence.

Additional considerations are important when men and boys, as well as women and girls, are the targets of sexual and other forms of GBV, as has been the case in the Syrian civil war. Male civilians and combatants have been targeted. In wartime just as in peace, GBV also may be committed against men because they are men—as a way of emasculating and weakening them. Examining situations in which men are targeted by sexual violence challenges our conception of what constitutes GBV.

The legal aspects of GBV are important for understanding its prevalence and persistence despite a decades-long, global movement in favor of gender equality. We highlight two legal dimensions of GBV: 1) domestic prohibitions on forms of GBV including for example child marriage, marital rape, female genital cutting, and infanticide, and 2) the domestic and international legal remedies available to survivors.

Finally, GBV has economic implications and may contribute to women's poverty. Galtung classified economic violence as a form of structural violence where, "The violence is built into the structure and shows up as unequal power and consequently as unequal life chances" (1969, 171). A political economy approach to GBV suggests that we need to examine the structural causes—such as gender inequality and economic deprivation—that may drive the use of sexual and GBV (True 2012). GBV threatens the security of citizens and workers in every sector. However, it poses a particularly acute threat to vulnerable populations such as migrant or undocumented workers, low-income workers, and workers in illicit trades such as sex work. Economic insecurity can put women at risk of GBV, such as women in conflict zones who engage in transactional or survival sex with members of the military and aid workers.

Gender-based violence in war and peace

To illustrate the ways GBV poses a threat in the Global North and Global South, we examine gender-based violence in Germany and Syria. The Syrian civil war (2011 to present) and accompanying refugee crisis has had a major impact on German and European politics. The point is that women experience GBV in war and peace, in the advanced industrialized world as well as developing world, and in a European context as well as a Middle Eastern one. The analysis may at first glance emphasize contextual dichotomies. Instead, an examination of GBV in Syria and Germany shows us that GBV occurs in varied forms in both "zones of peace," and "zones of turmoil." Structural forces such as patriarchy and unequal gender relations exist everywhere, and act in tandem with social, cultural, economic and other factors to produce distinct forms of GBV.

Syria

GBV perpetrated by government forces, militias, and combatants including the Islamic State has contributed to massive insecurity of persons inside of Syria and to the refugee flows from Syria to Europe. Refugees have cited the fear of sexual violence as a primary factor for leaving Syria and seeking asylum in other countries (Brosnan and Winkler 2013, 6–7). GBV—including sexual torture, sexual violence of children, wartime rape by government and nonstate actors and rape in government detention—is among the horrors of war inflicted on Syrian women, men, boys and girls. Yet, the danger does not end for these refugees as they cross the borders of Syria. Refugees in Europe face sexual and other types of GBV—perpetrated by partners, aid workers, security forces, other refugees and migrants—at every stage of their journey and after arrival in Europe (European Union Agency for Fundamental Rights 2016a, 2016b).

The use of GBV and specifically sexual violence during the Syrian Civil War has had a regional as well as global impact, as refugees seek protection from persecution in neighboring states such as Jordan, but also in Europe and the United States (see Campbell's chapter herein). In addition to wartime violence, women and girls in Syria also face "everyday" violence including intimate partner violence. Women and girls experience GBV across contexts—in peacetime, in wartime, as refugees, and when resettled in their destination country.

When we examine the political aspects of GBV during the Syrian civil war, two important themes emerge. One is the continued prevalence of "everyday" violence such as intimate partner violence, which reflects gendered hierarchies of power in which men have more social, political and economic power than women. Reports from the United Nations and humanitarian agencies suggest that intimate partner violence and violence against women and girls may have increased during the war due to economic insecurity, the normalization of violence, an environment of legal impunity, and other factors. Research suggests that in emergency contexts such as conflicts, intimate partner violence may be more common than violence perpetrated by strangers (Stark and Ager 2011).

The second observation is that GBV—including sexual violence—has been used by multiple parties to the conflict in pursuit of military or political objectives. The Syrian government has detained thousands of political prisoners, including women lawyers, journalists, and human rights defenders, and relatives of opposition supporters or militia members (Independent International Commission of Inquiry on the Syrian Arab Republic 2018, 9). The government has been implicated in the sexual and GBV of political prisoners. The Islamic State in Iraq and Syria committed violations such as forced marriage and rape of Yazidi girls and women, using the promise of marriage or sex as a recruitment tool for its fighters. ISIS kidnapped Yazidi women and girls from their homelands in Sinjar, northern Iraq, and took thousands of them to Syria (Commission of Inquiry on the Syrian Arab Republic 2016). As of 2016, ISIS had retained at least 3,200 Yazidi women and girls as captives inside of Syria.

Given the culture of shame surrounding sexual violence and a fear of honor killings, many women survivors of sexual violence fear stigmatization. GBV has a particularly destructive effect in communities in which the honor of the family is tied to the honor of the women. Sexual violence is particularly destructive because it violates a woman's sense of modesty, honor, and reputation. Cultures such as that of the Yazidis have prohibitions against premarital sex. Women who survive sexual abuse may be viewed as spoils of war and face harsh stigma from their family, friends, and neighbors. And due to the war, many shelters and support services that survivors had used are now unavailable.

The ongoing war and the government's acts of sexual violence and other war crimes has meant continued impunity for the perpetrators of conflict-related GBV. Even if the Syrian government had the political will to prosecute the perpetrators of GBV, there is little government capacity to do so. The UN Security Council could establish an international tribunal for Syria. However, such efforts would likely be stymied by Russia and China, which vetoed a resolution to refer Syria to the International Criminal Court. Legal scholars have suggested alternatives to the ICC or an international criminal tribunal; these include the possibility of a hybrid court that combines features of domestic and international law (Van Schaack 2014) or a domestic court willing to prosecute Syrian war crimes. Sweden, Germany, Finland and Switzerland have taken legal action against Syrian migrants accused of war crimes (Chadwick 2017). NGOs have been actively documenting the massive extent of human rights violations, including various forms of sexual violence and sexual torture, to provide grounds for future legal action.

In addition to the cultural, political, and legal challenges, survivors of GBV face a host of economic challenges. They may face stigmatization from peers and difficulty finding work or seeking employment (Raistick 2014). Economic concerns have pushed families to seek protection for their girls through early marriage, which exposes them to rape and other forms of GBV. Some women and girls exchange sex for food or money in a context of sexual abuse and exploitation by aid workers. The war has meant more women have taken on financial responsibilities, but the bread-winner status may put them at risk to backlash from male relatives (Buecher and Rwampigi Aniyamuzaala 2016, 28). Thus, the lack of economic security during war contributes to the prevalence of GBV.

Despite the grave risks that women in Syria have faced, many women have emerged as leaders of pro-democracy movements, human rights organizations, and humanitarian efforts. And after multiple rounds of peace talks excluded women, finally in 2016 women were included as third-party observers and in official negotiating teams.

Germany

Although a peacetime country with a strong economy and vibrant democratic institutions, Germany faces its own challenges with respect to GBV. Further, its government and economy have been impacted by the forced migration of Syrians seeking asylum from GBV and other types of wartime violence. More than half a million Syrian refugees have sought asylum in Germany since the beginning of conflict in 2011 (Connor 2018). The Syrian refugee crisis thus shows us one way that GBV in a "zone of turmoil" can have profound effects on stability and security in a so-called "zone of peace."

Chancellor Angela Merkel promoted politics to support asylum seekers, and has faced massive backlash from far-right parties including the PEGIDA movement and the Alternative for Germany party (Alternative für Deutschland—AfD). The AfD, which gained 13 percent of the vote in the 2017 elections, has warned of an "Islamization" of Europe associated with Muslim migration. Far-right parties portray immigrants from the Middle East, including Syria, as threats due in part to their Muslim religion (see Camp-bell's chapter and Garrett's chapter herein). Some of the objections to Islam include references to practices described as harmful to women, including dress codes and mar-riage and divorce practices.

Along with their xenophobic ideas, the AfD opposes gender equality measures. The party fails to address harmful practices, including sexism, gender inequality, and GBV, in Germany. The party has characterized gender quotas and gender-neutral language cam-paigns as anti-constitutional and a threat. The AfD criticizes Islam's treatment of women, yet does not appear concerned with the mistreatment and abuse of German women, including the estimated 100,000 German women who are subject to intimate partner violence (DPA 2016).

GBV is widespread in Europe; a 2014 study of 42,000 women from each of the EU member states found that one in three women said they had experienced some form of physical, sexual, or psychological violence since the age of 15. One in 20 women reported that they had been raped. And despite the high gender equality in states such as Sweden, Finland, and Norway, higher percentages of women in these states say they have been victims of intimate partner violence than in other European countries (European Union Agency for Fundamental Rights 2014). This phenomenon is referred to as the "Nordic Paradox" (Gracia and Merlo 2016), and poses an interesting puzzle for understanding the root causes of GBV.

Text box 6.2: The Nordic Paradox

Denmark, Finland, Iceland, Sweden, and Norway are considered among the world's most gender equitable states. They rank highly on cross-national indices such as the United Nations Development Program Gender Inequality Index, which considers reproductive health, empowerment, and labor market participation, and the World Economic Forum Global Gender Gap Index, which considers national gender gaps in economic participation and opportunity, political participation, education, and health. Yet, women in these countries report higher rates of intimate partner violence than in other European countries.

In Germany, 35% of women said they had experienced some type of physical or sexual violence. Of those, 22% said they had experienced violence from an intimate partner, while 24% said they were attacked by a person who was not their partner, such as a stranger or an acquaintance (European Union Agency for Fundamental Rights 2014). A national study by the German Federal Ministry for Family Affairs, Senior Citizens, Women and Youth found that among the 10,000 randomly sampled women interviewed, 37 percent said they had experienced an attack or threat of violence by a partner or non-partner (Müller and Schröttle 2004). Another study found that women who had experienced physical abuse cited an intimate partner as the most common perpetrator (50%), followed by family members (30%). In discussing GBV in Germany, we understand the contours of the problem in developed, wealthy, and well-educated societies.

Women politicians in Germany are subject to harassment and intimidation from the general public and from their colleagues. Online harassment and other forms of intimidation are common in the Global North and in the Global South. Women politicians frequently receive online and verbal threats and experience sexual harassment within political parties and institutions. Members of parties including Merkel's Christian Democratic Union and the Social Democratic Party of Germany say they have been harassed by party members and colleagues, and have criticized the sexism, sexual harassment, and machoism within national politics.

Women's rights activists in Germany have pressured the government to implement legal reforms to strengthen protections for victims of GBV. Prior to a legal reform in 2016, German rape laws had required proof that the victim physically resisted assault (Connolly 2016). This meant that many cases were not prosecuted. However, after approximately 1,000 women reported sexual assaults (committed by groups of migrant men) during New Year's celebrations in Cologne, a massive outcry put the country's rape laws squarely on the national political agenda. The AfD and others demanded that Merkel spearhead a change to the country's rape laws that would better protect German women. Critics were quick to point out the xenophobic nature of the far-right's concern, given their opposition to gender equality measures. The change to German law reflects a societal bias about who is deserving of protection and which members of society are the worst perpetrators (Boulila and Carri 2017). The legal reform, which passed in 2016, now means that the standard for rape is lack of consent or, "no means no." It also makes it easier to deport migrants who are convicted of sex crimes, and makes groping a criminal offense.

Public opinion data provides us with a way of gauging the cultural aspects of GBV in Germany. Although Germany scores well on gender equality when compared to the rest of the world, it lags behind other states in Europe. For example, German respondents were twice as likely to strongly agree that "men make better political leaders than women," (6.7%) as opposed to Sweden (where 3.3% said they strongly agreed with that statement). Eurobarometer surveys indicate that fewer Germans agree with the statement "domestic violence is unacceptable and should always be punished by law" (80%) compared to an EU average of 84%. And as other states in Europe and North America have grappled with the fallout from the #MeToo movement, Germany has not had a major national conversation related to abuse of power and sexual violence (Jennen 2018).

An intersectional analysis shows that not all women in Germany face the same risk of GBV. **Intersectionality** (Crenshaw 1991, 1244–1250) incorporates economic, racial, or other social identities to understand the ways that various types of discrimination can make women more vulnerable to violence. Women from discriminated groups have a lower social status, and perpetrators know that these women face more obstacles when reporting the violence or seeking help (United Nations 2005, 11). In Germany, surveys suggest that certain groups of women are most at risk of GBV; these include prostitutes, prisoners, and refugee women (Müller and Schröttle 2004, 23). These women experience intersecting forms of discrimination that limit their educational and work opportunities. Although a national study did not find a relationship between social class and experience with GBV, it did note that a woman's reliance on a partner's financial support created conditions of dependence that made it difficult for women to divorce or leave abusive partners (Müller and Schröttle 2004, 21).

Text box 6.3: Intersectionality

"Intersectionality" refers to how multiple aspects of a person's identity (such as race, class, sex/gender, and sexual orientation) intersect to influence life experiences and discrimination. Critical race scholar Kimberlé Crenshaw introduced the term in 1989 in writing about black feminism.

Conclusion

IR scholars tend to emphasize the problems of GBV in the Global South, as reflected by the studies of extensive sexual violence during the civil wars in Liberia and Sierra Leone. Yet, stories of sexual abuse and harassment that have come to light in association with the #MeToo movement suggest that sexual and GBV is a pervasive phenomenon that happens even in wealthy, more gender-equitable societies. GBV creates insecurity for women from Lagos to Los Angeles, as demonstrated by national discussions of sexual assaults in government, entertainment, the media, and major corporations spurred by the #MeToo movement in the United States and the "BalanceTonPorc" ("Expose your pig") movement in France.

In examining the extent of GBV in Syria and Germany, we see that GBV occurs due to the direct/personal violence of individuals and groups who are living in a world characterized by structural factors such as patriarchy, gender inequality, and economic deprivation. Common forms of GBV in Germany are intimate partner violence, sexual harassment, human trafficking of prostitutes, and abuse of migrant women. This GBV, along with political conflict related to Syrian refugees who have fled a state with extreme levels of sexual and gender-based violence, prevents Germany from achieving positive peace. Patriarchy, gender inequality, and cultural factors mean that Syrian women and girls live with the possibility of intimate partner violence, forced marriage, and sexual exploitation. They face these "everyday" forms of violence as well as GBV perpetrated by armed actors. Conflict-related GBV promotes cycles of violence and retribution, making it more and more difficult to achieve negative peace. In Syria and Germany, we see how the four dimensions of GBV—political, cultural, legal, and economic—work together and often reinforce a state of insecurity for women and girls.

GBV is a threat to human security that often spurs additional types of insecurity. Discussing the problem of GBV in both contexts shows us that although it may vary in its nature and forms in war and peace, it is a legitimate security threat in both contexts. The prevalence and consequences of GBV in the Global North and Global South should cause us to reconsider IR's emphasis on civil and interstate wars often fought in "zones of turmoil" as the supposedly dominant forms of global insecurity.

Questions for discussion

1   How does studying the global problem of GBV challenge your understanding of the distinction between "peacetime" and "wartime?" Does violence against women constitute an ongoing "war" against women and people who identify as female?
2   In what ways does GBV against civilians and combatants in Syria perpetuate the civil war there?
3   Should the World Health Organization definition of GBV (Text box 6.1) include violence against men and boys? Why or why not?
4   Visit the web sites of Amnesty International (www.amnesty.org) and Human Rights Watch (www.hrw.org) to learn about recent cases of GBV. Write an op-ed letter to your local newspaper identifying actions that your national government could take to address the problem.
5   The problem of violence against women politicians has been recognized in recent years. Research the case of a woman politician who has been the subject of online abuse or other harassment. How did the legislative body respond to the abuse/harassment? How can violence against women in politics undermine democratic norms and processes?

References

Boulila, Stefanie C, and Christiane Carri. August 2017. "On Cologne: Gender, Migration and Unacknowledged Racisms in Germany." *European Journal of Women's Studies* 24(3): 286–293.

Brooks, Julia. August 4, 2016. "The Gendering of Genocide: ISIS's Crimes Against the Yazidis." *ATHA: Advanced Training Program on Humanitarian Action* (blog). Harvard Humanitarian Initiative. http://atha.se/blog/gendering-genocide-isis's-crimes-against-yazidis

Brosnan, Alexandra, and Melissa Winkler. January 2013. *Syria: A Regional Crisis*. London: International Rescue Committee UK. https://www.rescue-uk.org/sites/default/files/document/991/finalsyriareportanglicised.pdf

Buecher, Beatrix, and James Rwampigi Aniyamuzaala. 2016. *Women, Work & War: Syrian Women and the Struggle to Survive Five Years of Conflict*. Amman, Jordan: CARE International. https://www.careinternational.org.uk/sites/default/files/CARE%20Women%20Work%20War%20report%20FINAL%20WEB%2013032016.pdf

Chadwick, Mark. 2017. "Justice in Syria: Five Ways to Prosecute International Crime." *The Conversation* (blog). Last modified July 10, 2017. https://theconversation.com/justice-in-syria-five-ways-to-prosecute-international-crime-75908

Cockburn, Cynthia. 1998. *The Space between Us: Negotiating Gender and National Identities in Conflict*. New York, NY: Zed.

Commission of Inquiry on the Syrian Arab Republic. 2016. *"They Came to Destroy": ISIS Crimes Against the Yazidis*. A/HRC/32/CRP.2. Geneva: Office of the High Commissioner for Human Rights. http://www.ohchr.org/Documents/HRBodies/HRCouncil/CoISyria/A_HRC_32_CRP.2_en.pdf

Connolly, Kate. July 7, 2016. "Germany Toughens Rape Laws after New Year's Eve Attacks in Cologne." *The Guardian*.

Connor, Phillip. January 29, 2018. "Most Displaced Syrians are in the Middle East, and about a Million are in Europe." Washington, DC: Pew Research Center. http://www.pewresearch.org/fact-tank/2018/01/29/where-displaced-syrians-have-resettled/

Crenshaw, Kimberlé. July 1991. "Mapping the Margins: Intersectionality, Identity Politics, and Violence Against Women of Color." *Stanford Law Review* 43(6):1241–1299.

Diop, Nafissatou J., and Ian Askew. December 2009. "The Effectiveness of a Community-Based Education Program on Abandoning Female Genital Mutilation/Cutting in Senegal." *Studies in Family Planning* 40(4):307–318.

DPA. November 22, 2016. "Domestic Violence Affects over 100,000 Women in Germany." *Deutsche Welle*. http://www.dw.com/en/domestic-violence-affects-over-100000-women-in-germany/a-36482282

Eckert, Stine, Nicole Gerring, Kyu-Nahm Jun, et al. 2017. *Strengthening Women's Civic and Political Participation: A Synthesis of the Scholarly Literature*. Research and Innovation Grants Working Papers Series. Washington, DC: USAID. https://www.iie.org/Research-and-Insights/Publications/DFG-WSU-Publication

European Union Agency for Fundamental Rights. 2014. *Violence against Women: an EU-wide Survey*. Luxembourg: Publications Office of the European Union. http://fra.europa.eu/en/publication/2014/vaw-survey-main-results

European Union Agency for Fundamental Rights. 2016a. "Thematic Focus: Gender-based Violence. Vienna." http://fra.europa.eu/en/theme/asylum-migration-borders/overviews/focus-gender-based-violence

European Union Agency for Fundamental Rights. 2016b. "Women Refugees at High Risk of Being Victims of Gender-based Violence." http://fra.europa.eu/en/press-release/2016/women-refugees-highrisk-being-victims-gender-based-violence

Galtung, Johan. 1969. "Violence, Peace and Peace Research." *Journal of Peace Research* 6(3):167–191.

Galtung, Johan. 1996. "Woman: Man = Peace: Violence?" 40–48. In *Peace by Peaceful Means: Peace and Conflict, Development and Civilization*. London: Sage.

Gracia, Enrique, and Juan Merlo. May 2016. "Intimate Partner Violence against Women and the Nordic Paradox." *Social Science & Medicine* 157: 27–30.

Huber, Jessica, and Lisa Kammerud. 2016. *Violence Against Women in Elections: A Framework for Assessment, Monitoring, and Response*. Arlington, VA: International Foundation for Electoral Systems. http://www.ifes.org/publications/violence-against-women-elections

Hudson, Valerie, Bonnie Ballif-Spanvill, Mary Caprioli, et al. 2012. *Sex & World Peace*. New York, NY: Columbia University Press.

IFEX. October 19, 2017. "Jineth Bedoya Lima: A Chronicle of Justice Delayed." https://www.ifex.org/noimpunity/cases/jineth/

Independent International Commission of Inquiry on the Syrian Arab Republic. March 8, 2018. "I Lost my Dignity: Sexual and Gender-Based Violence in the Syrian Arab Republic." Geneva: UN Human Rights Council. https://www.ohchr.org/Documents/HRBodies/HRCouncil/CoISyria/A-HRC-37-CRP-3.pdf

Jennen, Birgit. March 6, 2018. "German Laws Protect Women. German Culture Does Not." Bloomberg. https://www.bloomberg.com/news/articles/2018-03-07/german-laws-protect-women-german-culture-does-not

Müller, Ursula, and Monika Schröttle. 2004. *Health, Well-Being and Personal Safety of Women in Germany–A Representative Study of Violence against Women in Germany*. Berlin: Federal Ministry for Families, Senior Citizens, Women and Youth.

Raistick, Nick. 2014. *Reporting on Gender-Based Violence in the Syria Crisis: A Journalist's Handbook*. Ruba Hikmat and Jennifer Miquel, eds. United Nations Population Fund. https://www.unfpa.org/sites/default/files/resource-pdf/UNFPA%20Journalsits%27s%20Handbook%20Small%5B6%5D.pdf

Singer, Max, and Aaron Wildavsky. 1996. *The Real World Order: Zones of Peace, Zones of Turmoil*. Chatham, NJ: Chatham House Publishers.

Stark, Lindsay, and Alastair Ager. July 2011. "A Systematic Review of Prevalence Studies of Gender-Based Violence in Complex Emergencies." *Trauma Violence Abuse* 12(3):127–134.

Tostan. 2017. "Cross-Cutting Issues: Female Genital Cutting" https://www.tostan.org/areas-of-impact/cross-cutting-gender-social-norms/female-genital-cutting/

True, Jacqui. 2012. *The Political Economy of Violence Against Women*. New York, NY: Oxford University Press.

United Nations. May 2005. *Good Practices in Combating and Eliminating Violence against Women*. Vienna, Austria. http://www.un.org/womenwatch/daw/egm/vaw-gp-2005/docs/FINALREPORT.goodpractices.pdf

United Nations Children's Fund. 2013. "Female Genital Mutilation/Cutting: A Statistical Overview and Exploration of the Dynamics of Change." https://data.unicef.org/wp-content/uploads/2015/12/FGMC_Lo_res_Final_26.pdf

Van Schaack, Beth. May 29, 2014. "Alternative Jurisdictional Bases for a Hybrid Tribunal for Syria." New York University School of Law. https://www.justsecurity.org/10968/alternative-jurisdictional-bases-hybrid-tribunal-syria/

Chapter 7

Food security governance
Lessons from the Global South

Erica Resende and Adriana Erthal Abdenur

Introduction

According to the **Food and Agriculture Organization** of the United Nations (**FAO**), malnutrition is the main cause of disease in the world. Food insecurity affects around 20 million children of preschool age (WHO 2013)—a particularly significant fact because an adequate diet, especially in childhood and adolescence, is key to preventing diseases and ensuring the full physical and mental development of individuals. Therefore, it is important for national and international institutions to develop adequate policies to deal with hunger and malnutrition. The growing uncertainty around securing access to food is also why food security has become a core issue in the international agenda and a pivotal area of global governance change within a multipolar world order—one in which the Global South is becoming increasingly influential.

> **Text box 7.1: Global governance for food security**
>
> Not to be confused with global government, global governance is based on inter-subjective meanings derived from shared knowledge that needs to be supported by a certain majority of the actors involved. In other words, it can still be of a messy nature, but it is certainly not anarchic (Rosenau 1992, 4, 7–8). The production of global governance involves multiple structures of powers, featuring both state and non-state actors. In the case of food security, these include not only international organizations like FAO, World Bank, International Monetary Fund, and the International Fund for Agricultural Development, but civil society actors as well, such as the Bill & Melinda Gates Foundation, ActionAid, Oxfam, and Save the Children.

There have been some important landmarks on the policy framework for global food security in the last decades. In 1996, heads of state and government met at the World Food Summit in Rome, which established the goal of reducing by 50 percent the number of undernourished people by 2015. In 2000, the UN Millennium Development Goals set a similar target and led to the establishment of a UN Special Rapporteur on the Right to Food to monitor world hunger. Between 2002 and 2004, FAO member states negotiated a set of voluntary guidelines to contribute to the progressive realization of the right to adequate food. In September 2015, the Sustainable Development Goals incorporated the concept of food security, proposing nothing less than "a profound change of the global food and agriculture system."[1]

Text box 7.2: The UN Millennium Development Goals and Sustainable Development Goals

In September 2000 representatives and delegates from all UN member states as well as from key international organizations met at the Millennium Conference in New York to discuss and agree on a joint international agenda in human development for the twenty-first century. The resulting document is the UN Millennium Declaration, which expresses a global commitment to achieve eight goals by 2015: 1) to eradicate extreme poverty and hunger; 2) to achieve universal primary education; 3) to promote gender equality and empower women; 4) to reduce child mortality; 5) to improve maternal health; 6) to combat HIV/AIDS, malaria, and other diseases; 7) to ensure environmental sustainability; and 8) to create a global partnership for development. See http://www.un.org/millenniumgoals/.

Officially known as "Transforming Our World: The 2030 Agenda for Sustainable Development," the Sustainable Development Goals (SDGs) are a set of 17 goals negotiated and agreed upon by UN member states as well as non-state actors from global civil society. The declaration was signed as a result of the Rio+20 Conference held in 2012 in Rio de Janeiro, Brazil. UN Resolution A/RES/70/1 of September 25, 2015, lists the goals set in Rio, which will guide national policies and initiatives of international cooperation as a follow-up to the 2000 UN Millennium Declaration. See http://www.un.org/sustainabledevelopment/sustainable-development-goals/.

These policy landmarks have contributed toward some notable successes. The number of people living in a situation of food insecurity around the world decreased from around 995 million in 1990 to 842 million in 2013 (FAO, IFAD, and WFP 2014). The number of people starving also decreased from 23.6 percent to 14.3 percent (FAO, IFAD, and WFP 2014). Notwithstanding these timid improvements, hunger remains one of the most serious challenges of our time, especially in developing countries.

Changes in the global governance structure bring solutions, as both state and non-state actors work to tackle food insecurity and hunger. Although FAO remains at the center of these multilateral governance structures, many other non-state entities, as well as traditional state actors, are engaged in this fight. This chapter demonstrates how Brazil, India, and China contribute to global governance in the area of food security. Our aim is twofold: to understand how their particular challenges shape their approaches to food security governance, and to ascertain how non–core states are able to influence international norms regarding this issue.

The interest in the so-called emerging powers arises from a fundamental theoretical and empirical puzzle in the transformation of the international system. One unique element of social change in the last decade has been the rise of new hubs of power, partly due to high rates of economic and trade growth. This economic rise has also been accompanied by the political rise of these nation-states, including challenging and disrupting parts of the global governance system. The **BRICS (Brazil, Russia, India, China, South Africa)** coalition is a notable example and, increasingly, an important driver of change.

Although it remains to be seen if and how this coalition will acquire greater geopolitical weight, there has been a considerable degree of institutionalization (Abdenur and Folly 2015). By expanding their collaboration and policy coordination, they send a message to the world that they want to have a greater say in matters of global governance, including climate change, trade, health, and hunger. In this chapter, we adopt comparative lenses to examine the food security experiences and policies of three BRICS members: Brazil, India, and China.

We argue that these countries' growing stature in multilateral fora indicates that the Global South has a role to play in the legitimization of the multiple "spheres of authority" (Rosenau 2006, 149) through which power is exercised for the production of governance. One of the most relevant spheres of authority today for this kind of power projection by the BRICS is that of food security.

This chapter first discusses one of this book's main *problématiques*, i.e., the characterization of inadequate access to natural resources such as food—especially fresh food and seeds—as a new form of insecurity in our contemporary globalized world. Next, we discuss some of the key national experiences of Brazil, India, and China regarding food security. Finally, we analyze how the individual experiences of these countries contribute to the production of new norms in this specific issue.

Global governance and human security as theories for food security

"We live in a messy world" (Rosenau 2002, 70) increasingly dominated by "disaggregated rather than unitary state actors" (Slaughter 2004, 5–6), and whose main underlying process has been globalization (Held and McGrew 2002). Globalization has triggered a wide range of fundamental changes that have brought about some unprecedented challenges to the global order (Hurrel 2008), especially with respect to the need to produce some level of global governance. In recent years, the appearance of new nodes of political power, such as the BRICS and other influential Global South actors, has made this landscape more complex, including in the field of food security.

The concept of food security emerged from the field of human security studies, marking a departure from the traditional understanding of what international security means. The UN's expanding security agenda has incorporated issues such as human rights, poverty and hunger, children's education, racial discrimination, women's rights, and global health, which moved the individual to the forefront of the international agenda. Hence, both in scholarly and policy debates, the term "human security" began to appear as the basis for a number of proposals targeting the protection of people from severe and widespread threats and situations that are not necessarily derived from classical state-centric forms of insecurity.

Text box 7.3: Human security: An alternative theory of security

Since the end of the Cold War, concern about individuals has become essential for the study of international relations, given that states, which are the primary analytical unit of traditional theories in the field, do not explain many phenomena. This represents something of a departure from mainstream issues such as nuclear proliferation or terrorism. The concept of human security described in the *United Nations Human Development Report 1994* remains the most widely accepted definition. This definition stresses the importance of taking individuals into account in their quest for security in their daily lives: "In the final analysis, human security is a child who did not die, a disease that did not spread, a job that was not cut, an ethnic tension that did not explode in violence, a dissident who was not silenced." Human security focuses not on weapons but rather on human life and dignity (UNDP 1994, 22).

The United Nations Development Programme's conception also diverges from the traditional view of security in that it sees security as being assured not through weapons, but through sustainable human development in other areas such as economic, food, health, environmental, personal, community, and political security. In this perspective, human security displays four dimensions: universality (threats common to all people), interdependence (not constrained by national borders), early prevention, and a people-centric approach (UNDP 1994, 22–23).

This concept of human security has been adopted by the International Monetary Fund (IMF), the World Bank, Japan, and Canada (Smith 2005, 53). In 2003, the Commission on Human Security submitted a report to the UN calling for a new people-centered concept of security, which it argued should be understood as an interlinked phenomenon because of today's global flow of goods, services, finances, and people (Commission on Human Security 2013).

Given this expanded conception of security, what particular conditions represent a threat to the survival of groups or individuals? From a policy perspective, the answer involves safeguarding against chronic threats like hunger, disease, and repression, and against sudden, painful interruptions to patterns of daily life. Roland Paris (2011, 71–79) offers a similar breakdown as the UNDP of the different dimensions of human security, which, taken together, would provide a world where individuals may enjoy security, freedom, dignity, and equal opportunities to fulfill their maximum human potential. Here we have opted for a broad definition of human security, which includes economic, social, environmental, and other concerns that impact individual well-being. Following this rationale, order and security are not taken from the perspective of sovereign states but the individual (Hampson 2008, 234). In this sense, poverty and human insecurity are in many ways synonymous "because they relate to a human condition marked by the absence of basic rights like adequate food, health, housing, and education, and the expectation that this situation will remain unchanged" (Thomas 2008, 244).

Today, food security does not refer narrowly to the supply of food, but to the reliable supply of good quality, healthy food (free of harmful chemicals) produced in a way that does not jeopardize future food production and that develops the capacities of the local people so that they cease to be dependent on external food aid. For Maluf and Menezes (2000, 4), "food and nutritional security is the assurance of the right of everybody to have access to quality foods in sufficient quality on an ongoing basis, based on healthy eating habits and respecting the cultural features of each people, manifested in the act of eating." Public policies for food security, therefore, must seek to integrate the urban and rural environments so as to take advantage of local production/crops and ensure access to, and availability of, foodstuffs.

Besides being supported through national policies, food security has also been targeted in assistance initiatives and South–South cooperation. Successful domestic policies often serve as sources of inspiration for international cooperation initiatives related to food and agriculture. Moreover, because so many challenges to food security are transnational, food security has become a core concern in the international agenda, as reflected in the fact that FAO has the largest budget among the UN specialized agencies. A discussion that was once cloistered inside institutional walls has finally attracted the attention of leading international actors.

Lessons from the Global South

Growing interest in the BRICS has yielded a large literature (Kwang 2013). Although these five states are diverse, the coalition has both expanded and deepened its cooperation agenda across sectors, from development financing to international security. The following section of the chapter analyzes how three of those countries—Brazil, India, and China—draw inspiration from their domestic experiences as increasingly active players in the changing landscape of global food security governance (Ashley 2016).

Brazil: Traditional focus on school feeding

Created in the 1940s, Brazil's National School Feeding Program (NSFP) is one of the oldest of its kind in the world. It was originally devised when the Brazilian Institute of Nutrition advocated for free school meals by the federal government. Its impact, however, was limited due to a shortage of funds. In the 1950s, the Brazilian government initiated a broad-based plan for the nationwide provision of school meals under public responsibility (FNDE 2014). Most effective was the School Feeding Program, which enabled the distribution of surplus milk powder for mothers and children, and the National School Feeding Campaign, which distributed meals to public primary schools. In 1965, the United States Agency for International Development (USAID) teamed with Brazil to create a series of food distribution programs directed to developing nations, including the Food for Peace project, which targeted the distribution of food for school-age children in poor population groups. After 1979, the Brazilian part of the program began to be funded exclusively by Brazil and was rebranded as the National School Feeding Program (NSFP), an important food policy that still exists today.

The principles behind NSFP are: the human right to adequate, nutritious, and fresh food as a means for assuring food security for the population; and the provision, sustainability, and continuity of universally free meals in public schools. The program is designed to respect local eating habits—regarded as the traditional practices and dietary preferences of the local culture—and involves community participation in overseeing the execution of the program by state entities (Brazil 2009). The aims are to contribute to the growth and development of students, to improve school performance, and to address dietary and nutritional issues as an integral part of the education process. The decentralization of such policies has been achieved through coordination among different levels of government and local school communities.

Key features of the program include: support for sustainable development; the acquisition of locally produced foodstuffs, preferably by family farms and businesses; the fostering of healthy eating habits that respect the local culture, traditions, and dietary preferences; and the prioritization of indigenous and African-Brazilian communities (Brazil 2009). One of its guidelines—the acquisition of food from local family farms—is considered key to the success of this policy as it combines nutrition needs, respect for local eating habits, and the consolidation of a market for local farmers.

The 2014 budget for the NSFP was $1.15 million, designed to provide 42 million schoolchildren, youths, and adults with 130 million meals (the program covers around 190,000 schools in 5,565 municipalities) (FNDE 2014). Another improvement is the formation, within each municipality, of a School Feeding Board, a deliberative body responsible for overseeing and assisting in the execution of the program. These boards include representatives from civil society organizations, education professionals, students, parents of students, and representatives of the executive branch. In 2006, it was decided that a nutritionist would be technically responsible for the program and that all the executive entities must have nutritionists on staff (FNDE 2014).

To date, the NSFP has proved successful in reducing school dropout rates; reducing impaired learning and educational performance because of hunger and malnutrition; reducing nutritional (micronutrient) deficiencies; contributing to household budgets (free school meals are understood as a financial benefit for more vulnerable families); and reducing food and nutrition insecurity in situations of financial, political, and environmental instability (FAO 2012a and 2012b).

The relative success of the Brazilian food security policies has inspired a set of international agreements between Brazil, FAO, and the World Food Programme (FNDE 2014) to promote the NSFP in other developing countries, most notably in Latin America and Africa (Tokarnia 2013). The NSFP guidelines are similar to the 1996 World Food Summit regarding all four dimensions of the fight against food insecurity (FAO, IFAD, WFP 2014).

Text box 7.4: World Food Summits

FAO has convened four World Food Summits (1974, 1996, 2002, and 2009). The 1996 summit produced the Rome Declaration on World Food Security, which reaffirms the right of everyone to have access to safe and nutritious food consistent with the right to adequate food, as well as the fundamental right of everyone to be free from hunger. As a result, it focuses on the so-called four dimensions of food security: availability (sufficient food of appropriate quality to ensure an adequate diet), access (the physical infrastructure needed to transport food), stability (factors that need to be controlled for food security to be maintained in the long run), and utilization (determinants for the adequate utilization of foodstuffs, such as water and sanitation, as well as the handling and cooking of food to ensure its nutrients are maintained). See http://www.fao.org/WFS/ and http://www.fao.org/docrep/013/al936e/al936e00.pdf.

According to the director-general of FAO, Brazilian José Graziano da Silva, "the relationship between school feeding programs and family agriculture can make an important contribution to food security and complement other efforts that are already underway, such as the Food Acquisition Program for Africa" (FAO 2013, 1). The FAO–Brazil partnership for food security has incorporated a range of good practices from the Brazilian experience into school feeding programs targeting poor nations. José Carlos Wanderley Dias de Freitas, former chairman of FNDE (2011–2013), noted that the most important aspect of this cooperation is the recognition of Brazil as a world reference in school feeding: "Concepts such as family farming and food security make the country a model. This challenges us to guarantee this efficiency and to seek out means and instruments to do so more and better, because we believe that whenever we teach, we learn" (FAO 2013).

The two projects based on the Brazilian school feeding program (regional cooperation in Latin America and the Caribbean, since 2009, and a more recently launched project in Africa) are part of a total of 17 projects implemented through the FAO–Brazil Program for International Cooperation. The agreement has given Brazil a more active role in world politics by acknowledging Brazil's contribution to food security and the fight against hunger and poverty (FAO 2013). In governmental documents produced by countries that have benefited from FAO's Strengthening School Feeding Programs, Brazil's policies to tackle food insecurity, like Zero Hunger and the NSFP, are cited as examples (Nicaragua 2013).

Although Brazil is not a system-determining state (Keohane 1969), it has joined forces with regional neighbors that share its social proposals to tackle inequalities and the lack of representativeness in the current international system, thereby improving the lives of its citizens. Its increased influence in the world order has brought both social gains (food security and the fight against poverty), and political gains (seats on important international organizations) giving its priority agendas a stronger voice. Balaban et al. (2012) argue that Brazil has been instrumental in spreading the norms of food security, especially through means of international cooperation programs. One might conclude that Brazil enjoys influence on the international agenda thanks to its recognition by other states, international organisms, and non-governmental organizations. Brazil is increasingly achieving recognition as a benchmark "in public policies for hunger eradication and the tackling of poverty [which have been] expressed in international awards received by President Lula, in official documents from international organizations like FAO and the World Bank, and also with non-governmental organizations" (Maluf et al. 2014, 19).

India: Closing the gap

In 1945, when India became one of the founding members of FAO, it was a low-income country with grave deficiencies in food. In some respects, the country has come a long way: India is now self-sufficient in grains, in part due to the **Green Revolution** that led to increased yields, especially of wheat and rice. Other gains were due to the public distribution system introduced during World War II and expanded in the following decades. Despite these advances and the present context of relative economic growth, India still faces significant food security challenges, which center not on the availability of food, but on its distribution (Hoda and Gulati 2013).

With more than 1.3 billion inhabitants, India has the second largest population in the world, after China. Its agriculture sector accounts for an estimated 18 percent of its GDP and provides employment to over 46 percent of its population across a vast and highly heterogeneous agricultural system. At the same time, food insecurity persists, especially with regard to malnutrition. This gap is closely linked to India's poverty issue, which is reflected in the fact that 21 percent of the population lives on less than $1 a day. These facts suggest that, despite years of steady economic growth, inequality and exclusion have not yet been adequately addressed, with serious implications for food security.

Since the 1990s, income per capita in India has risen more than threefold, yet socio-economic inequality has expanded. During the same period, dietary minimum in the country has fallen. India faces the "triple paradox of malnutrition": While a large swath of the population still suffers from malnutrition, among another section of the population, obesity is emerging. At the same time, there are serious deficiencies in micronutrients (Narayanan 2015). This inequality is associated with social class and other cleavages in Indian society shaping the patterns of hunger and malnutrition. For instance, Indian policy discourse and policies around food and nutrition are not gender-sensitive. Likewise, children are arguably the largest group affected by malnutrition. Deficiencies in food security, and how best to address them, have become the focus of heated policy debates.

Contributing toward this problem are surging food prices. Some of the government's responses—such as export controls and a highly restrictive import regime, especially in agriculture—are meant to address the impact of trade. While this approach was effective in the past in curbing food price inflation, more recently it has not yielded the same results, with inflation persisting even as the government holds considerable grain stocks.

Domestically, the government has expanded support through food security schemes, including the Midday Meal Scheme and the Integrated Child Development Services. There have also been initiatives by individual states, such as the Amma Canteen, a food subsidy program implemented by the government of Tamil Nadu. Despite some local successes, these schemes are often beset by grave inefficiencies and corruption. In response, some economists have called for an overhaul of the system toward the use of cash transfers, including a replacement of the Public Distribution System (PDS).

There have been some advances on the legal front. In 2014, India promulgated its National Food Security Act, which was designed to ensure access to adequate food at affordable prices by affirming the right to food and paving the way for highly subsidized food grains to targeted households, especially in rural areas. The progressive law legally binds both the national and state governments to extend social protection to the population (Kishore et al. 2014). The law, however, has largely gone unimplemented despite requests from the Supreme Court that India's states implement key aspects of the law due to political inertia (Mander 2015).

This changing landscape has also transformed the way India interacts with external actors in food security. The WFP has been active in India since 1963 and now supports India in improving its food distribution systems. FAO has transitioned from grain provision to providing technical assistance. Since India achieved self-sufficiency in cereal production, FAO now works to facilitate India's multilateral cooperation in areas such as trans-boundary pests and diseases, livestock production, fisheries management, food safety, and climate change.

India is also a key knowledge partner for FAO, in that it offers technical expertise to other countries from its wide gamut of lessons learned over time, some of which are now applied in other parts of the world, especially through South–South cooperation. In part due to its food security concerns, India is also an influential player in the agricultural trade system. Faced with calls to defend its policies (especially with respect to agricultural trade) to the international food trade community even as it seeks to maintain food sovereignty, India has been a frequent critic of the global trade regime for reducing developing countries' capacity to strengthen their own food security.

China: Venturing abroad

For China, food security has become a core domestic concern and, increasingly, a key topic in its international agenda. Since the early 1990s, reforms and economic growth have lifted some 138 million Chinese out of poverty and hunger. Yet China's rapidly expanding middle class has altered consumption habits, making food security a question of political legitimacy and even survival for the Chinese leadership. China's progress in this area in the past two decades encompassed all components: availability, utilization, access, and stability (Zhou 2016). However, several challenges remain, leading China to alter its goals from food self-reliance to securing complementary supplies from abroad through trade.[2]

China pursues its food security goals through a variety of strategies to modernize food production—measures undertaken at multiple levels, from individual farmers to large corporations, through institutional reforms. On one hand, the government has supported scientific and technological innovation to increase yield and diversify production. On the other, it has also provided incentives to family farmers to boost their productive potential. There are now over one million farmer cooperatives in China, allowing small-scale producers to join forces and scale up.

Even as economic reforms have raised living standards, the deep social changes taking place in China have created new demands and challenges for food security. In response, China has developed a policy framework to guide related initiatives. In 1996, the government released a white paper, "The Grain Issue in China," which underscored the need for self-reliance. The government established targets for self-sufficiency in terms of arable land and grain production and began holding some of the world's largest grain stockpiles. In 2004, however, China became a net food importer, and its dependence on the global market is unlikely to abate given the gap between its limited agricultural resources and growing food demands (Ghose 2014).

In 2013, China announced a revamped food security strategy at the Central Economic World Conference, recognizing for the first time that imports would henceforth constitute an important component of its strategy. The following year, another white paper focused on ensuring long-term supply, including through Chinese agricultural investments abroad, such as acquisitions of foreign firms. This reorientation to expand China's influence in the world's food supply has paved the way for some major corporate acquisitions and attempts, such as repeated efforts by China National Chemical Corporation to take over Syngenta, the Swiss farm chemical and seed company—one of three proposed major mergers.[3]

However, China still faces challenges. Domestic food distribution remains highly uneven. Food safety also encounters significant challenges, with several cases of food poisoning causing alarm. Sustainability is yet another issue. China's previously heavy focus on grain output contributed to widespread environmental degradation—a problem also impacted by climate change. The changing dietary consumption patterns of China's expanding middle classes continue to have a major environmental footprint. An estimated one-fifth of Chinese soil is fallow due to exposure to heavy metal contaminants (especially from industrial pollution, chemicals, and coal-fired power industries) (Patel 2014).

As a result, China recognizes that ecological security is needed alongside food security. In China's thirteenth five-year plan, environmental protection appears among the government's main objectives. The plan establishes ten binding targets and generally pushes for a new development paradigm that makes sustainability a priority. China now tries to balance its previous heavy focus on grain output with efforts to mitigate and even reverse environmental degradation, so as to make its food security policies more sustainable. Results so far are mixed (Lam et al. 2013).

In part due to the size of its economy and expanding food demands, China has become a highly influential player in global food markets. For instance, China accounts for 60 percent of the global market for soybeans, with most of its imports used for animal feed. In order to boost its food security, the Chinese government will have to seek new markets and sign new cooperation agreements to help ensure a reliable and safe food supply through imports.

China has increased its role in multilateral organizations working on food security—both established institutions and emerging ones. China and FAO have built up a strong partnership in areas such as innovative intensification of agricultural production, revitalization of ecosystems, and biodiversity.[4] Since 2008, China has built on an FAO initiative, backed by a $30 million trust fund, to support technical field missions with Chinese agricultural experts in developing countries—an initiative that has encompassed 100 countries. In 2015, China signed a $50 million cooperation agreement with FAO to support developing countries in building sustainable food systems and inclusive agricultural value chains.[5] China also participates more actively in normative debates about global food security, in particular, advocating for South–South cooperation. At the G20, it has also worked to put the topic on the G20 agenda, in the process helping to shift the group's agenda from a more narrow economic focus to encompass food security.[6] Finally, since Donald Trump's decision to back out of the Paris climate agreement in fall 2017, China has chosen to take on a more visible leadership position in climate change, which also indicates its evolving role in global food security governance.

Conclusion: What can we expect from the Global South?

Brazil, India, and China have drawn on their domestic experiences to promote (and sometimes, reshape) international initiatives in both multilateral and bilateral arrangements in food security. At the same time, these countries' interests and positions are far from homogeneous. Most notably, their agendas in global agricultural trade and their patterns of South–South agricultural cooperation have often diverged considerably. Brazil, for example, has promoted more open agricultural trade and rapidly expanded its official South–South cooperation in Latin America and Africa through Embrapa, the Brazilian agency for agricultural development. India's quest for self-sufficiency, on the other hand, has prompted agricultural subsidy policies that often clash with Brazil's trade positions. China, in the meantime, has become a vital pillar of agricultural commodities trade and, more recently, an open champion of globalization.

However, these countries also have some converging interests. In addition to believing that global mechanisms for ensuring food security are more necessary than ever, all three countries have become strong proponents of, and practitioners of, South–South cooperation for food security. At the same time, principles such as the centrality of school feeding programs and the importance of national seed reserves indicate that the Global South has a role to play in shaping the future of global governance in this area. In fact, since the first BRIC summit, held in Yekaterinburg in 2009, BRICS meetings have always yielded a separate, specific statement on food security.[7]

As a result of this diversity, there is a multiplicity of strategies for promoting food security. They work simultaneously with established organizations such as FAO, as well as within loose coalitions such as BRICS, the IBSA Dialogue Forum (India, Brazil, South Africa), and G20. Rising powers have become legitimate players in global governance, allowing them to exercise global power. Brazil, China, and India have each harnessed their own understanding of food security to meet national demands for development, and also found ways to coordinate some positions, thereby magnifying their voices in global politics.

Questions for discussion

1   Does the ultimate responsibility for guaranteeing basic entitlements as well as food and livelihood security rest with the state?
2   How can the right to be free from hunger and malnutrition be implemented and fulfilled?
3   FAO estimates that enough food is being produced in the world today to feed the globe's current population. Is the problem of food security then mainly about access and distribution?
4   The common FAO definition cited earlier pitches food security as about three As: accessibility, affordability, and availability. Rocha (2008) suggests that the meaning of food security needs to be widened to 5 As: availability, adequacy, accessibility, acceptability, and agency. The last term refers to the need for policy actors to "own" and deliver the goods. Do you agree?
5   Could new technologies help us grow food more effectively? Or do we need to stop wasting so much food and try to be more efficient in how we consume? And what role does population control play in food security?

Notes

1   UN (2015) "Goal 2: End hunger, achieve food security and improved nutrition and promote sustainable agriculture": http://www.un.org/sustainabledevelopment/hunger/.
2   This shift is mostly due because while China has 19 percent of the global population it has only 7 percent of the planet's arable land and freshwater resources.
3   https://www.nytimes.com/2017/04/05/business/syngenta-chemchina-takeover.html.
4   http://www.fao.org/3/a-au075e.pdf.
5   http://www.fao.org/news/story/en/item/289386/icode/.
6   http://www.tandfonline.com/doi/abs/10.1080/10670564.2015.1013381?journalCode=cjcc20.
7   Agriculture ministers from the five states continue to discuss the negative effects of climate change on world food security and possible solutions. See http://thebricspost.com/brics-vow-to-meet-food-security-challenges/#.Wcf5uGWYc9c.

References

Abdenur, Adriana Erthal, and Maiara Folly. 2015. "The New Development Bank and the Institutionalization of the BRICS." *R/evolutions: Global Trends & Regional Issues* 3(1): 66–92.

Ashley, John M. 2016. *Food Security in the Developing World*. London/Cambridge: Academic Press/ Elsevier.

Balaban, Daniel et al. 2012. *Programas de Alimentação Escolar Sustentáveis: a criação do Centro de Excelência contra a Fome. Relatório Anual*. Available at: http://documents.wfp.org/stellent/group s/public/documents/special_initiatives/wfp253795.pdf

Brazil. 2009. Ministério da Educação. *Resolução/CD/FNDE n. 38*. Available at: http://portal.mec. gov.br/index.php?option=com_content&view=article&id=16691&Itemid=1115

Commission on Human Security. 2013. *Final Report*. Available at: http://www.unocha.org/huma nsecurity/chs/finalreport/Outlines/outline.html

FAO. 2012a. *Fortalecimiento de los Programas de Alimentación Escolar en el ámbito de la Iniciativa América Latina y Caribe Sin Hambre 2025*. Available at: http://www.rlc.fao.org/es/programabrasilfao/p royectos/alimentacion-escolar/

FAO. 2012b. *Sustainable Nutrition Security: Restoring the Bridge between Agriculture and Health*. Roma: Food and Agriculture Organization of the United Nations. Available at: http://www.fao.org/ docrep/017/me785e/me785e.pdf

FAO. 2013. *FAO e Brasil levam experiência da alimentação escolar para a África*. Available at: http://www.rlc.fao.org/es/paises/brasil/noticias/fao-e-brasil-levam-experiencia-da-alimentacao-escolar-para-africa/

FAO, IFAD, and WFP. 2014. *State of Food Insecurity in the World 2014*. Available at: http://www.fao.org/publications/sofi/en/

FNDE. 2014. Fundo Nacional de Desenvolvimento da Educação. *Apresentação*. Available at: http://www.fnde.gov.br/programas/alimentacao-escolar/alimentacao-escolar-apresentacao. *Histórico*. Available at: http://www.fnde.gov.br/programas/alimentacao-escolar/alimentacao-escolar-historico

Ghose, Bishwajit. 2014. "Food Security and Food Self-sufficiency in China: From Past to 2050." *Food and Energy Security* 3:2: 86–95.

Hampson, Osler. 2008. "Human Security." In: *Security Studies: An Introduction*, ed. Paul Williams. Abingdon: Routledge, pp. 229–243.

Held, David, and Anthony McGrew (eds). 2002. *Governing Globalization: Power, Authority and Global Governance*. Oxford: Blackwell.

Hoda, Anwarul, and Ashok Gulati. 2013. *India's Agricultural Trade Policy and Sustainable Development*; ICTSD Programme on Agricultural Trade and Sustainable Development; Issue Paper No. 49; International Centre for Trade and Sustainable Development, Geneva, Switzerland.

Hurrel, Andrew. 2008. *On Global Order*. Oxford: Oxford University Press.

Keohane, Robert. 1969. "'Lilliputians' Dilemmas: Small States in the International Politics." *International Organization*, 23, 2.

Kishore, Avinash, Pramod Kumar Joshi, John F. Hoddinott. 2014 "India's Right to Food Act: A Novel Approach to Food Security." IFRI Book chapter: http://www.ifpri.org/publication/india's-right-food-act-novel-approach-food-security

Kwang, Ho Chun. 2013. *The BRICs Superpower Challenge: Foreign and Security Policy Analysis*. London: Ashgate.

Lam, H.-M., Remais, J., Fung, M.-C., Xu, L., Sun, S. S.-M. 2013. "Food Supply and Food Safety Issues in China." *Lancet*, 381 (9882).

Maluf, Renato, and Francisco Menezes. *Caderno Segurança Alimentar*. 2000. Available at: http://www.forumsocialmundial.org.br/download/tconferencias_Maluf_Menezes_2000_por.pdf

Maluf, R., M. Santarelli, and V. Prado. 2014. "A Cooperação Brasileira em Segurança Alimentar e Nutricional: determinantes e desafios presentes na construção da agenda internacional." *Textos para Discussão* nº 3. Available at: http://r1.ufrrj.br/cpda/ceresan/docs/Cooperacao_Brasileira_em_SAN.pdf

Mander, Harsh. 2015. *State Food Provisioning as Social Protection*. FAO. http://www.fao.org/3/a-i4957e.pdf

Narayanan, Sudha. 2015. "Food Security in India: The Imperative and Its Challenges." *Asia & The Pacific Policy Studies* 2:1: 197–209.

Nicaragua. 2013. Gobierno de Reconciliación y Unidad Nacional. *Manual de Compras Locales de la Agricultura Familiar para la Alimentación Escolar*. Matagalpa.

Patel, Keshar. 2014. "China's Food Security Dilemma." *World Policy Journal* blog, June 4. Available at: http://www.worldpolicy.org/blog/2014/06/04/chinas-food-security-dilemma

Paris, Roland. 2011. "Human Security." In Christopher W. Hughes and Lai Yew Meng (eds.) *Security Studies*. Abingdon: Routledge, pp. 71–79.

Rocha, C. 2008. *Brazil–Canada Partnership: Building Capacity in Food Security*. Center for Studies in Food Security, Ryerson University, Toronto.

Rosenau, James N. 1992. *Governance without Government: Order and Change in World Politics*. Cambridge University Press.

Rosenau, James N. 2002. "Governance in a New Global Order." In David Held and Anthony McGrew (eds.) *Governing Globalization: Power, Authority and Global Governance*. Oxford: Blackwell, pp. 70–86.

Rosenau, James N. 2006. *The Study of World Politics. Volume 2: Globalization and Governance*. New York: Routledge.

Slaughter, Anne-Marie. 2004. *A New World Order*. Princeton, NJ: Princeton University Press.

Smith, Steve. 2005. "The Contested Concept of Security." In Ken Booth (ed.) *Critical Security Studies and World Politics*. Boulder, CO: Lynne Rienner Publishers, pp. 27–62.

Thomas, Caroline. 2008. "Poverty." In Paul Williams (ed.) *Security Studies: An Introduction*. Abingdon: Routledge, pp. 244–259.

Tokarnia, M. 2013. *ONU leva experiência brasileira com merenda escolar para América Latina e África*. EBC. Available at: http://www.ebc.com.br/noticias/internacional/2013/08/onu-leva-experien cia-brasileira-com-merenda-escolar-para-america

UNDP (United Nations Development Programme). 1994. *Human Development Report 1994*. New York: Oxford University Press. http://hdr.undp.org/sites/default/files/reports/255/hdr_1994_ en_complete_nostats.pdf

WHO. 2013. *Guideline: Updates on the Management of Severe Acute Malnutrition in Infants and Children*. Geneva: World Health Organization. Available at: http://apps.who.int/iris/bitstream/ha ndle/10665/95584/9789241506328_eng.pdf;jsessionid=0AAFC1FA6392346E966654 CABC75B4FE?sequence=1

Zhou, Jiayi. 2016. "China and (World) Food Security." SIPRI blog 16 October. Available at: https:// www.sipri.org/commentary/blog/2016/china-and-world-food-security

Chapter 8

Invisible foes and micro-enemies
Pathogens, diseases, and global health security

Adrienne Formentos and Gigi Gokcek

Introduction

A family follows traditional burial practices and washes the corpse of a deceased parent; a woman displaced by an earthquake collects water from a stream; a businessman returns home and is admitted to a shared hospital room and is visited by his children. Within 24–48 hours these people are seriously ill or dying, a consequence of microscopic bacterial or viral organisms that cause diseases. Within a week their community experiences rapid infections, and within months an outbreak begins to overwhelm a city, a region, a country. Such epidemics begin with seemingly inconsequential actions as illustrated in the Ebola virus disease (EVD), cholera in Haiti outbreak, and Middle Eastern Respiratory Syndrome (MERS) emergencies in the last few years. Epidemics of diseases that are new or evolved, or highly fatal, can decimate rural communities by killing or disabling working adults or vulnerable groups like children. Emerging infectious disease (EID) and even centuries old virulent strains of illnesses can cripple urban centers of commerce, trade, and government. Increasingly porous borders have transformed the world into a global community, which means that the burden of disease is no longer confined to one geographical region, but is now a burden borne by all.

Health security is a function of both public health and national security. It depends on detecting, preventing, and responding to outbreaks in order to protect the health and safety of a population. Illnesses caused by pathogens are as old as life on planet earth. But in an era of globalized physical and digital interconnection, the urgency to prevent, treat and address, and recover from the biological impacts of disease proves an elevated threat. Sovereign states are responsible for the management of threats to human health because outbreaks, small or large, are very disruptive. The challenge requires finding a delicate balance of scientific and material evidence and appropriate governance.

Given the seriousness of such threats, this chapter first examines the core tenants of epidemiology, notably the terminology used in public and global health fields that defines how science and decision making occurs. It then analyzes public health measures that local and state governments implemented since outbreaks from ancient Greece to the 19th-century plague in Hong Kong. Next, we focus on international cooperation through intergovernmental organizations (IGOs), most notably the United Nations (UN) and the World Health Organization (WHO), in response to global health crises and emergencies since World War II. This third section discusses the emergence of transnational governance for disease prevention and management through the theory of neoliberal institutionalism, which focuses on IGOs as facilitators of cooperation among sovereign states to overcome a **public** or collective goods problem. Good health is a **collective good** because it is a common interest, shared among human beings everywhere. Halting the spread of deadly disease beyond borders requires states to forsake their national interests for the common good. The risk to human life can be reduced only through the cooperation of the international community. Finally, we illustrate the emergence and severity of new infectious and non-communicable chronic diseases and problems such as antimicrobial resistance (AMR), and their connections to related issues of climate change and urban misgovernance or lack of public health infrastructure.

Epidemiology and basics of public health

Epidemiology studies the occurrence of disease in a group, how it occurs, and why. Strategies within epidemiology include using observation and surveillance of diseases within a population. These strategies are used to screen, mobilize resources, uncover transmission, and treat diseases (Rose and Barker 1978). One of the core tenants of epidemiology and public health efforts is understanding how diseases move within populations. Diseases that are communicable or infectious such as the common cold or Human Immunodeficiency Virus (HIV) are passed between hosts, or living beings like humans or birds, that contain the agent, which is the actual virus, bacteria, fungus.

A disease that is **endemic**, or routinely occurring in a geographical area, varies widely from **epidemics**, which are rapid spikes in an illness that exceeds normal trends and is from a common source. The Yellow Fever outbreak in Angola and the Democratic Republic of Congo (DRC) in 2015–2016 (WHO 2017a) is an example of an epidemic, in contrast with endemic seasonal influenza in, say, North America. When an epidemic reaches global levels, it is categorized as a **pandemic** though tracking cases of relatively new diseases are challenging with people on the move (Dehner 2010). **Pathogens** survive in a number of surfaces and **reservoirs** or breeding ground, such as stagnant water where mosquito larvae grow. Animals can also serve as reservoirs for specific strains of viruses. Between 2015 and 2017 there have been studies of bats and camels as reservoirs for Middle Eastern Respiratory Virus Corona Virus (MERS-CoV) that show animal carriers do not necessarily have to be ill to transmit the virus (Vergara-Alert et al. 2017).

Transmission occurs through a number of means including objects, animals, and humans. A **fomite** is a contaminated object such as a doorknob, used needles, or cookware. A **vector** such as a mosquito or tick is an organism that carries the pathogen that is transmitted. Mosquitos worldwide are responsible for carrying many fatal and debilitating diseases such as Dengue Fever, Yellow Fever, Zika virus, malaria, Japanese Encephalitis, and West Nile Virus (WHO 2018b) as they carry the agent and proceed to bite humans and animals, which transmits the pathogen. Transference of a microorganism can also occur between the infected host and uninfected persons. Other vectors include other insects such as ticks, Tsetse flies, and fleas. According to the WHO, up to 17% of all infectious diseases are vector-borne and are the cause of about one million deaths per year (WHO 2017b).

Text box 8.1: What is it an outbreak?

In every city, region, state in the world, common illnesses are considered natural to that population, or **endemic**. In many parts of Sub-Saharan Africa malaria is common. This also can be applied to parts of the U.S. where workers in specific industries commonly experience illnesses attributed to their occupation, such as with respiratory illnesses among miners. When the number of cases of a particular illness bypass the normal prevalence in one particular period of time and are attributed to one particular cause, this is known as an **epidemic** or an **outbreak**. In this instance, the use of "epidemic" can applied to the U.S. wide spike in cases of HIV among specific communities, such as the gay, lesbian, bisexual communities, in the 1980s. Outbreaks can also be applied to event-specific situations where large amounts of people fall ill, such as diseases among passengers on cruise ships. Once an outbreak reaches a level that surpasses a state's borders, it is often considered **pandemic**. Though there is no specific number of cases needed to be considered a pandemic, generally outbreaks are considered worldwide once a disease has reached another state. This is not to say that once a disease is a pandemic, all persons are susceptible or at risk. Disease transmission still has its own rules—if a disease is transmitted only by exposure to a sick person's blood, then wearing a face mask is unlikely to stop contamination. Understanding these basic tenants of epidemiology strengthens competency in times of crisis.

Diseases can and are transmitted from person to person, often among members of the same household, workplaces, travelers, and medical care workers (Rosenberger et al. 2012).

The rapidly changing nature of microbes and their response to the environment compounds the difficulty of keeping a population totally free of disease. For instance, the seasonal influenza is made up of two subtypes of influenza virus, Influenza A and Influenza B (Grohskopf et al. 2016).

Antigen variation—the process in which the surface proteins of the virus change—causes slight changes that allow re-entry and infection in hosts (Cox and Subbarao 1999). Changing surface antigens offer little to no protection against influenza through the vaccinations offered to most people as they cannot always be effective against all strains. However, vaccination against the seasonal variant can offer some protection. Other changes in microorganisms include a growing resistance to drugs used to combat bacterial infection and overall antimicrobial resistance (WHO 2018b).

Text box 8.2: Micro-organisms

Micro-organisms are part of the natural environment and exist outside of and within the human body. **Microbes** or **pathogens** are microscopic organisms that in the right conditions can cause disease. Despite the negative connotations associated with bacteria, viruses, fungi, and protozoa these are all naturally occurring and coexisting micro-organisms that help to make up normal human functions. Pathogens become an issue when the colonization of a human host presents with symptoms that bypass normal immune system response and successfully replicate within the human host's body. The most common types of microbes that can cause disease are bacteria, viruses, fungi, and protozoan parasites. Prions are a type of folded protein that have the ability to replicate and most commonly cause Mad Cow Disease.

Bacteria are responsible for causing diseases such as shigella, food poisoning due to Salmonella contamination, and cholera.

Viruses are responsible for causing diseases such as the Human Immunodeficiency Virus, smallpox, and herpes.

Fungal pathogens cause diseases such as ringworm.

Protozoan parasites are responsible for causing diseases such as malaria.

Source: Alberts et al. 2002

The mere presence of disease alone in the human body does not itself suffice as a quantifiable measure of illness. Diseases must be precisely defined by characteristics or symptoms (e.g., blood in the stool, weakness in lower limbs, or shortness of breath) and measured within an individual (e.g., blood test, x-ray scans, or lowered heart beats per minute). If and when these requirements are met, an individual with a disease becomes a case (Coggan et al. 1997). Non-cases—individuals without a disease—become part of the population at risk. Defining persons as cases versus non-cases assists in identifying whether a disease becomes a threat. For instance, a university will require a specific policy or protocol if an outbreak of bed bugs occurs on several floors of a dorm. Similarly, a refugee camp may need to scale up medical services if a third of its population is infected with cholera.

Quantifying disease frequency is contingent upon the population in which it occurs or the population at risk. Prevalence is the proportion of disease cases in a given population (Coggan et al. 1997). Prevalence can be used to describe the number of cases at any given point, or point prevalence, or can be used to describe the number of cases over a period of time or period prevalence. Counting the number of cases of neonatal births with congenital abnormalities exactly 24 months after the atomic bombings in Japan is an example of point prevalence. Counting the number of neonatal births with congenital abnormalities in the 20 years following the bombings is an example of period prevalence.

Contracting a disease, however common or transmissible, depends on many factors that one cannot control, including genetics which determines much of one's physical and mental health. Some diseases will inevitably present themselves in a person's life if one of their parents had the condition or is a carrier of a gene that is passed onto the child, such as sickle cell disease (Bender and Douthitt Seibel 1993). Other conditions develop over time due to individual behavior and lifestyle choice, environmental exposure, and social determinants of health, such as lead exposure from contaminated water in poor communities.

Only about 10–15 percent of overall health is determined by the quality of medical care that one receives (McGinnis et al. 2002). Social determinants of health are considered largely impactful and are defined by the WHO as conditions into "which people are born, grow, live, work and age" (WHO 2018a). Circumstances beyond anyone's control can affect health in minuscule or important ways. Poverty and level of education are large determinants, in association with an increased likelihood for mortality (McGinnis et al. 2002) and disability from non-fatal illnesses such as mental disorders (Tampubolon and Hannadita 2014). Poverty and lack of education contribute to illness and lack of access to care or resources compounded over a lifetime may increase the risk of chronic disease (Mercado et al. 2007; Guerrero et al. 1998). Studies have also found correlated data between medical care adding to the financial burden on poor households in the US (Cohen and Kirzinger 2014).

The degree to which disease and sickness impact an individual or population is defined through the use of measures such as healthy years of life and deducting time "lost" from illness or disabilities associated with that illness. These indicators combine specific measures like mortality and morbidity for comparisons within and across populations (Hyder et al. 2012). **Mortality** is the number of deaths from all causes over the total number of the population in which the deaths occurred. This rate is then multiplied by 100,000. To determine the mortality from a specific cause, the total number of deaths from one cause is divided over the total number of deaths from all causes over the population from which it occurred and multiplied by 100,000. Comparing two countries' rates creates a standard value to determine the overall health of a nation. The **maternal mortality rate** is a standard measurement in global health that identifies areas that need resources to improve the quality of antenatal and postnatal care. These measurements and resulting data are used to identify the causes and conditions of death. For example, a decrease in the maternal mortality rate following a pilot program that deploys skilled midwives to rural areas allows health authorities and partner organizations to assess the benefits of the program. Though health indicators are sometimes difficult to measure, these data give public health scientists, epidemiologists, ministries of health and finance, partner states and NGOs the information needed to make informed decisions about funding, resource allocation, and advocacy.

Public health policy and disease management history

Humans have had to manage disease and infection control since time immemorial. Elementary understandings of disease transmission were illustrated in the Bible, where persons with visible skin conditions were treated as mythical punishments, and society would initiate isolation and quarantine practices, requiring an infected person to eventually "abandon his family and his relatives" (Grzybowski and Nita 2016). Moreover, early outbreaks of highly fatal unidentified illnesses spread rapidly in ancient Greece, disrupting military campaigns and social stability. Thucydides (c. 460–400 BCE) observed a breakdown of morality and law in Athens during the epidemic that also coincided with the Peloponnesian War in 430–427 BCE (Hays 2005, 7). The ensuing panic and chaos in Athens serve as an early albeit common example of the responsibility by states to address the dual disasters of mass illness and war. Subsequent centuries experienced recurring periods of disease outbreaks, domestic and regional wars, the ending and founding of new countries, and increasing international trade and travel. Newly created regional governments were forced to reckon with managing urban populations and their health, and more mobile masses. These management strategies included screening, isolation, quarantine. Advances in scientific discoveries, such as mass vaccination, and adoption of better sanitation processes in medical practice also changed in the mid-20th century in much of Western Europe and the US.

The use of quarantine began in 1374 and is derived from the Italian word "quaranta," a reference to the 40 days required waiting period for ships. Quarantine typically included inspection of a ship's goods, crew, sailors and captain before all were allowed to reach land. Maritime travel, trade, and migration in effect circumvented expansive land area, mountains, and other difficult terrain that had originally served as natural barriers and defenses. This was also the case in Western Europe as the Bubonic plague (1347–1351) killed close to 30–40% of the population, after the disease was brought by ships from the Ottoman

Empire to ports in Venice, Italy, and France. In the case of the several waves of the plague in Hong Kong in the 1870s and 1890s, port access and the ability for smaller boats and junks to travel upriver, coupled with ignored warnings to remain indoors, and lack of quarantine enforcement spread the disease among the densely populated streets (Harrison 2012, 175).

There are recorded instances of the use of weaponized diseases, or early biological warfare, for instance in present-day Ukraine in the 14th century (Wheelis 2002) that illustrated crude but effective military tactics. A historical account by a notary within Caffa (modern-day Ukraine) during the 1346 siege described the Tartar army as using catapult-like devices to hurl infected cadavers over the city walls (Wheelis 2002). Later examples of the deliberate use of disease to wipe out populations included the decimation of native tribes in the Americas following European colonization. States historically struggled to contain both infections and panic among at-risk populations as local municipalities mishandled containment efforts or whose violent approaches created fear and mistrust among locals.

In reaction to such transnational problems, public authorities, private organizations, and scientists began organizing regional efforts beginning with the first international conference of physicians and health experts from 12 European countries in 1851 in Paris to discuss cholera outbreaks. Nine international sanitary conventions were held between 1859 and 1897 in Europe, the US, and Istanbul. They offered competing ideas and theories among state delegations and led to no clear outcomes or goals (Markel 2014, 125). These conventions served as a foundation for future global cooperation in the realm of health and disease management and led to the establishment of IGOs such as the WHO, which was created in 1948.

Public health transnational governance and public goods theory

Delegates from 50 states created the United Nations charter in October 1945. The creation of this historic institution heralded a shift in global attitudes toward conflict and peace, freedom from fear, and power distribution. In essence, this was the genesis for neoliberal institutionalism. The lack of a world authority compels sovereign states to provide protection of their national interests in an environment of global anarchy. Some international problems require that states place global interests above national ones when the two may be at odds. Neoliberal institutionalism explains why and how sovereign states can overcome their national interests to address a common or shared goal: cooperation is facilitated through international or intergovernmental organizations to deal with a collective goods dilemma, which benefits all, irrespective of individual contributions to its production. Global health security is a public good because disease prevention and management are beneficial to all humans. IGOs like the UN and WHO provide the setting where sovereign states are incentivized to cooperate in thwarting the spread of dangerous and fatal diseases. Incentives may be in the form of rewards for cooperation, or punishment for those states that cheat the collective effort (zero cost for benefit).

As President Harry Truman stated, institutions are only as strong as their members: "All member nations, large and small, are represented here as equals. Wisdom is not the monopoly of strength or size. Small nations can contribute equally with the large nations toward bringing constructive thought and wise judgment to bear upon the formation of collective policy" (Truman 1946). The collective idealism led to form several specialized bodies of the UN in the following years and to develop new approaches to human equality in the form of health. The creation of an international governing health agency would be "a vehicle to facilitate the basic and fundamental right of health for every human inhabitant on the planet... [Further, it was] inspired by the devastation of both world wars, along with the social and political maelstroms that led to them, the proto-WHO insisted that an international health agency signified far more than traditional bulwarks against contagion" (Markel 2014, 124).

The WHO constitution finally came into force in 1948. Its early functions, still prioritized today, include control of and eradication of infectious diseases. Officially, the 11th General Programme of Work for the WHO from 2006–2015 focused on six core functions (Shi 2013): (1) Providing leadership and partnership on worldwide health issues; (2) Setting research priorities and information sharing; (3) Establishing, supporting, and monitoring standards of practice; (4) Advancing health policy options based on evidence and ethical principles; (5) Offering technical assistance and support toward health program implementation and capacity building; (6) Monitoring health issues, identifying patterns and trends.

The WHO has to maintain ever-expanding responsibilities while balancing its member states' political and economic agendas, including stewardship of resources. As such, the WHO was never intended to be the sole solution to a plethora of health problems. This returns to the inherent issues of upholding member states to obligatory mechanisms that in practice were voluntary or ignored. In 1951, the International Sanitary Regulations were adopted and later renamed the International Health Regulations (IHR). They created reporting mechanisms for member states to WHO for outbreaks of smallpox, cholera, plague, and yellow fever (Davies et al. 2015). However, many states failed to comply with the IHR, rendering ineffective the basic function and purpose of disease surveillance. States' management of global health policies also became more complex because of the diffusion of power and stakeholders.

Global health governance connects a multitude of actors ranging from ministries of health, public development agencies, non-governmental organizations (NGOs) and non-profit organizations, foundations, donors, large financing institutions, religious groups, corporations, medical groups, and international organizations. These stakeholders, along with targeted populations in developing countries, exert influence in policy-making and implementation, practice, as well as popular opinion. Stakeholders also include patients and consumers, healthcare providers and workforce, health care organizations, insurers, educational institutions and teaching schools, and private medical equipment and pharmaceutical companies.

NGOs, multilateral and financing institutions

NGOs can perform missions specific to a population (e.g., Save the Children) or in times of conflict and disaster (e.g., Doctors Without Borders). Often embedded within and partnered closely with communities, NGOs can carry out work funded internally or externally, and serve as technical assistance in states or regions where governance and institutions are weak. Sometimes they serve as the primary actor in delivering goods and services, for instance, religious organizations managing primary health facilities. This leverage is often because these organizations fall outside of the state-based constraining framework (Tulchinsky and Varavikova 2000).

International financing institutions can also direct efforts toward specific diseases such as the Global Fund to Fight AIDS, Tuberculosis, and Malaria. Others, such as the World Bank that provides funding and technical assistance in development to address poverty, and the International Monetary Fund (IMF) that offers technical assistance in developing sustainable economic policies, can, directly and indirectly, support health policies and outcomes. Both have large impacts on health and development, including the successful campaign against Onchocerciasis, or river blindness. Onchocerciasis is a disease caused by a parasitic worm transmitted by flies that breed in rivers; following a blackfly bite these worms breed and multiply causing itchy lesions in the skin and eyes that can lead to blindness over the long term (WHO 2017b) In 1974, a campaign was launched by the World Bank, the UN Development Program (UNDP), the FAO, and the WHO in partnership with 11 countries in West Africa (World Bank 2014). The campaign spanned at least 20 years, halted transmission, and averted 600,000 new cases, guaranteeing that now 22 million children are born in this region without risk of infection (Center for Global Development 2004). Effectiveness in this instance came from equal buy-in and cooperation from donors, implementing partners, and recipient countries. Recreating efforts of this scale and cost over the span of 20 years is rare and runs against issues of control, funding, and sustainability.

There are several private foundations with specific missions such as Accordia Global Health Foundation working to strengthen health systems in Africa, the Wellcome Trust, and the Rockefeller Foundation that has influenced the movement toward selective primary health care (National Institute of Health n.d.). The Bill and Melinda Gates Foundation is built on the premise that all lives are equal. One of its major cornerstones is the investment in the prevention of communicable disease such as HIV/AIDS, malaria, and in ongoing campaigns toward long-term health progress such as maternal and child health, and nutrition (Gates Foundation n.d.). Gates profoundly impacted the field of global health as it has given almost $9 billion in grants from 1998 to 2007 (McCoy et al. 2009). Such movements of funds and grants that can be larger than the operating costs of some ministries of health shape their action: "The Gates Foundation is also involved in setting the research agenda of several public health priorities…[The] Gates Foundation is not a passive donor. The foundation actively engages in policy making and agenda setting activities" (McCoy et al. 2009, 1650). Therefore, in recent years the Gates Foundation has become a major player in the research, development, service delivery and implementation of global health programs traditionally associated with the WHO.

Financial institutions and private foundations offer tangible packages of aid, funding, and technical assistance, broken down into quantifiable objectives, indicators, and targets. Transparency and accountability are easily monitored throughout the lifetime of programs. Securing health is a dynamic, evolving state within individuals, groups, populations, and ecosystems, and channeling large grants into specific disease research and treatment is often more palatable to donors and economists seeking measurable and immediate outcomes. This, however, offers only a partial solution to much larger problems where external circumstances cannot be predicted or accounted for in contracts. Such is the case within global health security, which relies on states to self-monitor and self-report, requiring appropriate surveillance and tracking of outbreaks, and the ability for states to respond effectively.

Global health systems reflect the high health care spending in rich countries like the US, as well as the lack of health workers and essential medicines in countries recently ravaged by war, such as Sierra Leone and Liberia (Vandi et al. 2017; Jones et al. 2016). States that cling to isolationist policies today must still reckon with trans-border issues such as poverty, migrations, and such (see Campbell's chapter herein). Adequately addressing the future of global health security thus requires a multilateral and multi-sectoral approach to ensure healthy, safe, and sustainable communities. Landmark decisions such as the United Nations Security Council Resolution 1308 (2000) addressed HIV/AIDS as a health security issue and further legitimized the need for cooperation (UNSC 2000). A unilateral or state-centric, realist approach will only impede efforts to combat the global spread of disease. Overcoming the public goods problem is difficult as each state weighs the costs and benefits of eradicating a disease that may not have reached its borders. Global health experts face this challenge to convince policymakers to take action now against a disease that has the potential to strike populations in the future.

The future of global health security

A disease is unpredictable as pathogens change rapidly. Furthermore, other factors contribute to and worsen the risk for disease transmission and burden. They include: antibiotic resistance and AMR, armed conflict and refugees, climate change, and natural disasters (see Below's chapter and Campbell's chapter herein).

The rise of AMR is a problem that goes beyond the medical sector as antibiotics are used in commercial agriculture, animals, and crops, and are often over-prescribed by medical providers to treat minor ailments (WHO 2015). Resistant strains of bacteria including methicillin-resistant staphylococcus aureus (MRSA) already are common in hospitals and other healthcare settings where patients are vulnerable to infections. Cost and length of treating even common infections will likely increase in all countries, including in low- and middle-income countries where people may rely first on drugs before seeking professional treatment. In 2017, the WHO made recommendations to reduce the use of antibiotics in food animals based on a systemic analysis (Tang et al. 2017), and format reference as a way to stem AMR. A more promising approach may be through poverty reduction in regions that are prone to disease resistance and spread borne out of climate change.

Global health governance hinges on the cooperation of sovereign states to maximize education, income levels, and gender equality (see Quie's chapter herein) in areas vulnerable to conflict and natural disasters borne out of climate change (see Below's chapter herein). In an anarchic world, the only way to better manage the spread of diseases and prevent mass loss of life to illness is through international institutions (neoliberalism) and not with isolationist or unilateral policies (realism). No state exists in a vacuum as long as microscopic pathogens have the power to cross man-made borders.

Questions for discussion

1   Which actors are given designated powers to carry out global health security missions, and which is best suited to fulfill these missions?
2   Is there a way to punish non-compliant actors in failure to report disease epidemics? Is this any one agency's responsibility?

3   Why is disease likely to spread more easily in poverty-stricken regions of the world? How might maximizing standard of living, income level, and gender equality facilitate the management of disease in areas most prone to conflict and natural disasters borne out of climate change?

4   How do states effectively resolve the conflict between citizens' rights (e.g., religious and personal beliefs) regarding medical care or treatment and the safety of the population? How is this reflected in the international arena?

5   Are international pressure and diplomacy (soft power) effective tools in upholding global health security?

6   How do intergovernmental or international organizations provide the context in which cooperation is more likely among sovereign states?

References

Alberts, B., Johnson, A., Lewis, J., et al. 2002. *Molecular Biology of the Cell: Introduction to Pathogens*. 4th edition. New York: Garland Science.

Bender, Michael A., and Douthitt Siebel, Gabrielle. 1993. *Sickle Cell Disease*. GeneReviews®. Seattle: University of Washington.

Center for Global Development (CGD). 2004. "Case 7: Controlling Onchocerciasis (River Blindness) in Sub-Saharan Africa." *Millions Saved*. https://www.cgdev.org/doc/millions/MS_case_7.pdf

Coggan, David, Rose, Geoffrey, and Barker, David. 1997. *Epidemiology for the Uninitiated*. 4th edition. Oxford: Wiley-Blackwell.

Cohen, Robin A., and Kirzinger, Whitney K. January 2014. "Financial Burden of Medical Care: A Family Perspective." *NCHS Data Brief* 142:1–8. https://www.ncbi.nlm.nih.gov/pubmed/24472320

Cox, Nancy J., and Subbarao, Kanta. October 9, 1999. "Influenza." July 30, 2017. *The Lancet*. 354.9186: 1277–1282. DOI: doi:10.1016/S0140-6736(99)01241-01246.

Davies, Sara, Kamradt-Scott, Adam, and Rushton, Simon. January 2015. *Disease Diplomacy: International Norms and Global Health Security*. Baltimore, MD: Johns Hopkins University Press.

Dehner, George. October 15, 2010. "WHO Knows Best? National and International Responses to Pandemic Threats and the 'Lessons' of 1976." *Journal of the History of Medicine and Allied Sciences* 64(4): 478–513. doi:10.1093/jhmas/jrq002

Gates Foundation. n.d. "What We Do." Retrieved December 11, 2017. https://www.gatesfoundation.org/

Grohskopf, Lisa, Sokolow, Leslie, Broden, Karen, et al. August 26, 2016. "Prevention and Control of Seasonal Influenza with Vaccines: Recommendations of the Advisory Committee on Immunization Practices – United State, 2016–2017 Influenza Season." Retrieved July 30, 2017. *MMWR Recommendations and Reports* 65(5):1–54. doi:10.15585/mmwr.rr6505a1

Grzybowski, Andrzej, and Nita, Małgorzata. February 2016. "Leprosy in the Bible." Retrieved October 15, 2017. *Clinics in Dermatology* 34:3–7. doi:10.1016/j.clindermatol.2015.10.003.

Guerrero, Rodrigo, Michael Jancloes, John D. Martin et al. May 9, 1998. "How the Cycle of Poverty and Ill Health can be Broken." Retrieved June 11, 2018. *British Medical Journal* 316. 7142: 1456. https://www.ncbi.nlm.nih.gov/pmc/articles/PMC1113124/

Harrison, Mark. 2012. *Contagion*. New Haven, CT: Yale University Press.

Hays, J. N. 2005. *Epidemics and Pandemics: Their Impacts on Human History*. Santa Barbara, CA: ABC-CLIO.

Hyder, Adnan A., Puvanachandra, Prasanthi, and Morrow, Richard H. December 28, 2012. "Measuring the Health of Populations: Explaining Composite Indicators." Retrieved July 6, 2017. *Journal of Public Health Research* 1.e35: 222–228. doi:10.4081/jphr.2012.e35.

Jones, Susan A., Gopalakrishnan, Somasundari, Ameh, Charles A. et al. 2016. "'Women and Babies are Dying but Not of Ebola': The Effect of the Ebola Virus Epidemic on the Availability,

Uptake, and Outcomes of Maternal and Newborn Health Services in Sierra Leone." Retrieved November 19, 2017. *BMJ of Global Health* 1(3): e000065. doi:10.1136/bmjgh-2016-000065.

Markel, Howard. February 2014. "Worldly Approaches to Global Health: 1851 to the Present." Retrieved September 15, 2016. *Public Health* 128(2):124–128. doi:10.1016/j.puhe.2013.08.004.

McCoy, David, Gayatri Kembhavi, Jinesh Patel et al. May 9, 2009. "The Bill & Melinda Gates Foundation's Grant-Making Programme for Global Health." *The Lancet* 373. 9675: 1645–1653. https://www.thelancet.com/journals/lancet/article/PIIS0140-6736(09)60571-60577/abstract?code=lancet-site

McGinnis, J. Michael, Williams-Russo, Pamela, and Knickman, James R. March/April 2002. "Health Promotion." Retrieved June 15, 2017. *Health Affairs* 21(2): 78–93. doi:10.1377/hlthaff.21.1.78.

Mercado, Susan, Kristen Havemann, Mojgan Sami et al. May 2007. "Urban Poverty: An Urgent Public Health Issue." Retrieved June 11, 2018. *Journal of Urban Health* 84. Suppl 1: 7–15. https://www.ncbi.nlm.nih.gov/pmc/articles/PMC1891652/

National Institute of Health, Fogarty International Center. n.d. "Nongovernmental Organizations (NGOs) Working in Global Health Research." https://www.fic.nih.gov/Global/Pages/NGOs.aspx

Rose, Geoffrey and Barker, DJ. December 16, 1978. "Epidemiology for the Uninitiated: Experimental Studies." Retrieved August 27, 2017. *British Medical Journal* 2 (6153): 1687–1688. https://www.ncbi.nlm.nih.gov/pmc/articles/PMC1608967

Rosenberger, Laura, Riccio, Lin, Campbell, Kristin Turza, et al. April 3, 2012. "Quarantine, Isolation, and Cohorting: From Cholera to Klebsiella." Retrieved August 27, 2017. *Surgical Infections* 13(2): 69–73. doi:10.1089/sur.2011.067.

Shi, Leiyu. 2013. *Introduction to Health Policy*. First Edition. Health Administration Press.

Tampubolon, Gindo, and Hanandita, Wulung. April 2014. "Poverty and Mental Health in Indonesia." Retrieved September 1, 2017. *Social Science and Medicine*106:20–27. doi:10.1016.j.socscimed.2014.01.012.

Tang, Karen L., Caffrey, Niamh P., Nóbrega, Diego B. et al. November 2017. "Restricting the Use of Antibiotics in Food-Producing Animals and Its Associations with Antibiotic Resistance in Food-Producing Animals and Human Beigns: A Systematic Review and Meta-Analysis." Retrieved August 25, 2017. *The Lancet Planetary Health* 1(8):e316–327. doi:10.1016/S2542-5196(17)30141-30149.

Truman, Harry S. October 24, 1946. "Address in New York City at the Opening Session of the United Nations General Assembly." Retrieved June 9, 2018. Independence, MS: Truman Presidential Library. https://trumanlibrary.org/publicpapers/index.php?pid=914

Tulchinsky, Theodore H., Varavikova, Elena A. 2000. *The New Public Health: An Introduction for the 21st Century*. Cambridge, MA: Academic Press.

United Nations (UN). 2015. Sustainable Development Goals. Retrieved August 27, 2017. http://www.un.org/sustainabledevelopment/sustainable-development-goals/

United Nations Security Council. 2000. "Resolution 1308 on the Responsibility of the Security Council in the Maintenance of International Peace and Security: HIV/AIDS and International Peace-Keeping Operations." Retrieved August 8, 2017. New York: UN. http://www.unaids.org/sites/default/files/sub_landing/files/20000717_un_scresolution_1308_en.pdf

Vandi, M. A., van Griensven, J., Chan, A.K. et al. June 21, 2017. "Ebola and Community Health Worker Services in Kenema District, Sierra Leone: Please Mind the Gap!" Retrieved November 19, 2017. *Public Health Action* 7. Suppl 1: S55–S61. doi:10.5588/pha.16.0082.

Vergara-Alert, Julia, Vidal, Enric, Bensaid, Albert, et al. June 2017. "Searching for Animal Models and Potential Target Species for Emerging Pathogens: Experience Gained from Middle East Respiratory Syndrome (MERS) Coronavirus." *One Health* 3: 34–40. doi:10.1016/j.onehlt.2017.03.001.

Wheelis, Mark. September 2002. "Biological Warfare at the 1345 Siege of Caffa." Retrieved September 20, 2016. *Emerging Infectious Disease* 8(9):971–975. doi:10.3201/eid0809.010536.

World Bank. July 3, 2014. "Forty Years Later: The Extraordinary River Blindness Partnership Sets its Sights on New Goals." Retrieved July 8, 2017. http://www.worldbank.org/en/news/fea

ture/2014/07/03/forty-years-later-the-extraordinary-river-blindness-partnership-sets-its-sight
s-on-new-goals

World Health Organization. 2015. *Global Action Plan on Antimicrobial Resistance.* Retrieved June 11, 2017. Geneva, Switzerland: WHO Press. http://www.wpro.who.int/entity/drug_resistance/resources/global_action_plan_eng.pdf

World Health Organization. 2017a. "Vector-borne Diseases." Retrieved June 11, 2018. http://www.who.int/mediacentre/factsheets/fs387/en/

World Health Organization. 2017b. Onchocerciasis (river blindness) – disease information. Retrieved July 8, 2017. http://www.who.int/blindness/partnerships/onchocerciasis_disease_information/en/

World Health Organization. 2018a. "About Social Determinants of Health." Retrieved June 26, 2018. http://www.who.int/social_determinants/sdh_definition/en/

World Health Organization. February 15, 2018b. "Antimicrobial Resistance." Retrieved June 11, 2018. http://www.who.int/mediacentre/factsheets/fs194/en/

Chapter 9

Push, pull and politics

The international migration issue after the Syrian Civil War, Brexit and Trump

Joel R. Campbell

Introduction

Migration has become a major political issue—notably in Europe, the United States, and Australia—as conservative anti-immigrant sentiment has greatly increased and xenophobic politicians find greater success. This chapter examines the major issues involving refugees and displaced persons, illegal and legal migration, and the implications for policy and political development in both the developed and developing worlds. It suggests several analytical lenses for analyzing these sensitive issues. It also examines the similarities and differences in the use of migration issues in the pro-Brexit campaign in the United Kingdom and the Donald Trump campaign in the United States.

The migration crisis: The size of the issue

The international refugee crisis has spotlighted migration issues. In recent years, refugee migration has reached unprecedented levels: There are 65.3 million forcibly displaced persons in the world, including 21.3 million refugees and 10 million stateless persons. This is larger than the population of the United Kingdom, or greater than Canada, Australia, and New Zealand combined. About 54 percent of refugees come from three countries: Syria, Afghanistan, and Somalia. The top host countries for refugees are Turkey (2.9 million), Pakistan (1.6 million), Lebanon (1.1 million), Iran (979,000), Ethiopia (736,000), and Jordan (664,000). Roughly 39 percent of displaced persons are from the Middle East and North Africa, 29 percent are from Africa, 14 percent are from Asia and the Pacific, and 12 percent from the Americas. The United Nations refugee agency UNHCR noted in 2015 that one in every 113 persons worldwide is either seeking asylum, displaced internally, or a refugee (UNHCR 2015; Edwards 2016).

Conflict is the major source of most forced migration. This includes long-term conflicts such as those in Afghanistan and Somalia, and renewed conflicts such as in South Sudan, Yemen, Burundi, and the Central African Republic. Conflicts begun in the post-Cold War era have been less amenable to solution in recent years. Europe has served as a magnet for refugees from most of these recent or renewed conflicts, due to its relative wealth, stability, and proximity. Over one million migrants fled to Europe in 2015, and over 136,000 came to Europe in the first quarter of 2016. The top three sources of migrants to Europe were, unsurprisingly, Syria, Afghanistan, and Iraq, with other conflicted countries such as Pakistan, Eritrea, Nigeria, and Ukraine in the top ten. Germany took in the highest number of arrivals in 2015 due to its "easy" process for asylum applications. Over 1.2 million people applied for asylum within the European Union in 2015.

Most of these migrants to Europe (1,011,700) came by sea—mostly through the Aegean—while another 34,900 arrived by land, generally through the Balkans. Nearly 3,800 migrants died on the way to Europe, mostly while crossing from North Africa, although over 800 died in the Aegean. This included Aylan Kurdi, a Syrian three-year-old who drowned after his family's dinghy sank while making a treacherous journey across Turkey to Europe. The photograph of his drowned body on an Aegean beach on September 2, 2015, became an international heartbreak (BBC News 2016; Rankin 2016). Syria, immersed in civil war since 2011, is the epicenter of the current crisis. In addition to the one million who have applied for asylum in Europe, 4.7 million Syrians are refugees in neighboring countries, and 6.6 million are internally displaced. Five million have registered with the UNHCR, the UN refugee agency. Most refugees who have entered Europe have done so through Turkey. Some Syrian refugees have in turn become trapped in Iraq's own civil war (Mercy Corps 2016).

In Southeast Asia, the plight of Burma/Myanmar's Rohingya people echoed ethnic conflicts of the 1990s—such as in Bosnia, Rwanda, or Darfur—as a perceived foreign ethnic group was persecuted and forced to leave the country, first in small groups on boats to other Southeast Asian nations, and later, en masse as whole-scale killing and rape drove them out to neighboring Bangladesh. At first, much of the violence against them was carried out by local groups, but then the military began systematically burning Rohingya villages in August 2017. Ethnic Burmese and Buddhist nationalists had long claimed that the ethnically Bengali Rohingya were not truly Burmese, even though most of them had lived in the country for many decades. UN officials labeled it as a clear case of ethnic cleansing the next month. Over 600,000 Rohingya ultimately fled across the border, where they were temporarily housed in large refugee settlements near the border city of Cox's Bazar (Albert 2017).

Despite dire figures, observers note that most of the world's population stays put. About 99.5 percent of all people are non-refugees or non-migrants, and the number migrating in the 2010–2015 period was actually lower than in the previous five years. However, it is the unprecedented 2015–2016 numbers that are striking (Mingels 2016).

Theories of migration

Why is migration important? Scholarship refers to a migration paradox, which suggests that despite the key role of migrants in building the modern world economy, most persons stay at home and do not migrate. The total number of current migrants is in dispute and may be as high as 214 million. The numbers of illegal, undocumented, or "irregular" migrants is also debated, and the role of "illegal aliens" is a key political and economic issue in all developed countries. There are at least three major groups of migrants: labor migrants, settler-migrants, and refugees. Theoretical debates among various disciplines make forging an interdisciplinary consensus difficult, and many observers suggest that the domination of economic theories means that the field is weakly theorized (King 2012).

Traditional migration theories were built on the work on Ernest Georg Ravenstein's notion of a **push–pull** process, in which poor conditions in one country tend to push people away from their countries of origin, and good conditions in the recipient countries attract people. The most important factors driving people, Ravenstein suggested, are economic, while volumes of migration depend on the distances involved: Greater distance means less migration. Various theories since have sought to update Ravenstein (1834–1913). Everett Lee, for instance, put greater stress on push issues and possible intervening variables in migration. Economic theories since the 1960s have emphasized supply and demand for labor, differences in income between sending and receiving countries, and segmented labor markets in developed countries that need greater amounts of labor than developing economies (JRank 2016). Additional economic-related theories include the new suggestion that networks involving families are key to decisions to migrate. Network theories similarly look at diasporas, families, and communities (Kurekova 2011).

Wilbur Zelinsky's "mobility transition" examines the supposed stages of labor mobilization in developing countries and its relationship to migration. World systems approaches focus on international migration as an outcome of the development and expansion of the global capitalist system since the 16th century (King 2012). Recent theorizing also draws attention to the difficulties inherent in economically focused theories, it emphasizes the need for interdisciplinary studies and for combining various existing theoretical approaches. Kurekova notes that post-accession Eastern European EU countries with similar economic conditions were expected to have similar rates of outward migration, but these often varied greatly. She argues for a more nuanced approach examining a variety of "institutional and structural variables," including the process of transition from state-owned to private-led economies, and the nature of the welfare system in sending and receiving countries (Kurekova 2011, 17, 28–31).

In fact, current major theories, while useful in understanding economic migration, are of only limited value in explaining the recent global migration crisis, which has blended with existing immigration issues in Western Europe and the United States. Building on Kurekova, a more explicitly political theory involving conflict and war would be more useful. It suggests that mass-migration, defined as more than 1,000 persons per month, occurs when domestic conflicts become irresolvable, i.e., they are of a long-term nature, there is little prospect of resolution, or there are major external interventions. Syria and Afghanistan are paradigmatic irresolvable conflicts, as they meet all three criteria. Receiving nations then react politically, in large part out of fear of loss of jobs or diminishment of culture, as happened in both Britain and America.

Brexit and Donald Trump

On June 23, 2016, the United Kingdom held a referendum on continued membership in the European Union, with the two sides labeled as "Leave" and "Remain." The vote had been promised by conservative Prime Minister David Cameron as a way to head off growing support for the anti-EU UK Independence Party (UKIP) and rally his own Conservative troops. As often happens in referenda, voters view the vote as a proxy for other issues and for expressing popular frustrations with the government. Immigration into the UK, especially movement of EU citizens from Eastern Europe but also including migration from the Middle East, became perhaps the most important issue in the campaign. With immigration at record levels, British voters linked this issue to earlier anti-EU concerns about perceived loss of economic control and erosion of sovereignty within a united Europe. Fear of immigration, rather than actual immigration, drove popular thinking. Unsurprisingly, areas with high levels of immigration voted for the Remain option, while the north and west, with consistently low levels of immigration, opted for Leave. Polls indicate the Leavers felt that exiting the EU would be the best way to control immigration (*The Economist* 2016; Bennett 2016; Travis 2016).

The Trump phenomenon in the United States shares with the **Brexit** campaign a concern for high levels of immigration and negative perceptions of immigration among Donald Trump's supporters that may not match reality. Trump's candidacy differed from the Brexit campaign in that it harkened back to long-held American traditions of populism and nativism. Trump decided to use immigration as the central issue of his primary campaign. He used the immigration issue at critical junctures during the primaries and revised his stance on immigration to court the general electorate while holding onto his base. Whereas British Leavers were worried about immigration from other European countries, Trump focused on long-standing fears of Mexican illegal aliens and migrant Muslim terrorists from the Middle East. Promises to build a wall to keep out Mexican illegals helped fortify his appeal to white workers who have suffered since the **Great Recession**. Proposing a temporary ban on Muslims entering the United States allowed Trump to pose as the defender of American security (Agbale 2016).

No single theory can account for both the Brexit vote and the success of the Trump candidacy. The particular constellation of factors that fueled both campaigns differed greatly. Building on approaches developed by Stephen Castles et al. (2013), we examine the "local dimensions of global change," i.e., how local factors in both sending and receiving countries influence migration decisions, while a "range of political, economic, and social factors and processes [affect] the agency of migrants..." (Kurekova 2011, 28–31). Specifically, perceptions of immigration and its consequences within the political cultures of Great Britain and the United States shaped the development of the Brexit and Trump campaigns. This aligns with constructivist International Relations theories, which suggest that perceptions of reality and changing values, norms, and institutional processes shape political outcomes.

Brexit and immigration/migration

Text box 9.1: Europe's migration crisis

The facts of the recent European migrant crisis are relatively simple. Large numbers started arriving from Africa about 2012, and continued to arrive through the Central Mediterranean, but their numbers were under 200,000. The vast majority of migrants come from three countries: Syria, Afghanistan, and Iraq. Over one million refugees arrived by sea, principally through Greece, while only 34,000 came by land. More have gone to Germany than any other country: 476,000 asylum claims out of over 1 million migrants in 2015. Hungary was second with 177,000 asylum applications, and Sweden was not far behind. With their smaller populations, the latter two states accepted between 1,667 and 1,800 asylum applications for refugees per 100,000 populations. By 2016, only 292,000 applications were approved.

(BBC News 2016)

Immigration and migration as issues in the Brexit outcome were less clear-cut than in America. Various media outlets noted clear similarities between Trump's campaign and the "Leave" effort in Britain led by UKIP leader Nigel Farage: a feeling that immigration was out of control, political institutions were out of touch, and the negative consequences of an anti-immigration crackdown were "overrated" (Cillizza 2016). White identity politics and populist appeals also played background roles. UKIP's rising support in the years leading up to Brexit was built on the perceived British loss of sovereignty and fear of being swamped by immigrants from Europe and the Muslim world. Of the two, the more immediate concern was the large number of EU citizens who had immigrated to the UK, although fears of Muslim migrants gained prominence each time a terrorist incident occurred.

The most fundamental concerns among Leave voters were the loss of self-determination, the feeling that EU governance had become too intrusive and caused the UK to lose control of its own borders. However, the Remain campaign was widely considered to be lackluster; the Labour Party failed to strongly back membership in the EU; and the Leave campaign successfully put across the notion that withdrawal from the EU would be relatively painless while boosting resources for the National Health Service, the United Kingdom's much-beloved public health care system. Many in the UK felt that too many Europeans were flooding into the country, taking jobs and burdening social and medical services.

Ironically, UKIP gained almost no advantage from Brexit and, due to Britain's first-past-the-post electoral system, in the 2017 parliamentary election attained no seats in the House of Commons. UKIP's founding leader, Nigel Farage, lost his leadership post and, ironically, held only a seat in the EU Parliament. The effects of immigration on the UK were hotly debated. According to one estimate, as many as five million net immigrants came to the UK from 1990 to 2014, and almost half of the net inflow came from other EU countries (Siegel 2016). This added to preexisting immigration from outside Europe, which had been intensely debated for the three decades before 1990.

The Conservatives, who had generally opposed liberal immigration, have tried to rebrand themselves in recent years. Proponents of immigration believe that immigration helps economic growth, while opponents argue that it draws down public welfare resources and alters underlying British values and culture. In fact, the economic effects probably are muted at best. A key source of anger for opponents is that there never was a full-blown debate on changing immigration to Britain, the public was never consulted, and politicians' promises to confront immigration issues were never followed through. Others wanted Britain to shift to a more skills-based immigration system. However, even with Brexit, immigration patterns will not change quickly, and low-skilled migrants will continue to seek low-wage UK jobs.

Polls indicated that immigration affected Leave votes in four major ways. First, voters were not necessarily affected personally by immigration but had strong opinions anyway. Therefore, it was fear of immigration—not immigration itself—that drove opinions. Second, gaining control of immigration mattered more than access to the European Single Market, and the Remain camp was not able to get across the supposed benefits of staying in the EU. Third, Leave voters were more set in their opinions than Remainers. Finally, older voters were more intense in their support for Leave than younger voters for Remain, and more mobilized to show up and vote at polling stations (Siegel 2016; Khan 2016; Travis 2016).

Once Brexit negotiations commenced in 2017, EU authorities made it clear that guaranteeing rights for EU citizens residing in Britain, along with UK financial obligations and the Northern Ireland/Republic of Ireland border, would be the key issues to be addressed before any agreement on future EU–British relations could be decided. In the end, if those rights were fully protected, opting for Brexit might not appreciably lessen the number of Europeans living in the United Kingdom.

The EU and migration

A much different and more obvious set of migration concerns were front and center for most other EU members. Migration has been a long-term trend that has intensified in recent years. Since 2012, large numbers of migrants from Africa escaping conflict have entered Mediterranean countries, especially Italy and Greece, and have been held in refugee camps. The outbreak of the Syrian civil war in 2011 sparked an exodus of at least two million people, most of whom have fled to neighboring countries or Europe. The Syrian refugee crisis peaked in 2015, as over one million migrants flooded into Greece and made their way through the Balkans to Germany (and some to Scandinavia) after Chancellor Angela Merkel decided to open German borders and indicated that Germany would not send back migrants.

At first, Germans warmly welcomed the migrants, and communities throughout the country worked hard to accommodate the arrivals. Then, problems began to surface. Many of the migrants lacked German language skills and seemed difficult to train; migrants became frustrated at living in temporary housing; some were accused of sexually assaulting German women at New Year's celebrations in 2016 (especially in Cologne); and a few terrorist incidents throughout the continent were linked to militants who had entered Europe along with migrants. Growing disquiet about the large migrant presence in Germany fueled the growth of the anti-immigrant Pegida movement and the subsequent rise of the right-wing Alternative for Germany (AfD) Party. With close to 13 percent of the popular vote in the September 2017 elections, AfD was the first post-World War II far-right party to gain a bloc of seats at the Bundestag (see Garrett's chapter herein).

Trump and immigration

Text box 9.2: US immigration policy

The politics of American immigration and migration has always been contentious. Observers note the continuous interplay between those accepting the notion of the United States as a "nation of immigrants" and those calling for great "immigration restrictions." Refugees were often allowed into the country after major wars or humanitarian disasters, especially in the wake of World War II and the Vietnam War, and immigrants from strategic allies such as South Korea were liberally allowed into the country. For much of the 19th century, immigration was unrestricted until the Chinese Exclusion Act of 1882 prohibited Chinese immigration due to fear that Chinese migrants could not be assimilated into American society. The 1924 Immigration Act extended the idea of immigration bans to much of the world beyond northern Europe and set national quotas for various groups.

President Lyndon Johnson pushed for the Immigration and Nationality Act of 1965, which eliminated the quota system and allowed more liberal immigration from much of the world. It also allowed family members of US citizens and permanent residents to immigrate. Legislation in 1990 created an employment category for immigration. Attempts by Congress in 2005 and 2006 to address the ongoing issue of mass illegal migration from Mexico and Central America to the United States ended in a legislative stalemate, as both anti-immigrant and pro-migrant communities mobilized major demonstrations across the country. Attempts to reform immigration policy became stuck for the next decade, as it became an untouchable issue for many politicians in both political parties.

Going into the 2016 election, conventional wisdom held that the Republicans would avoid immigration and migration issues due to their bad experiences with these issues in previous presidential and congressional elections. In the 2012 election, candidate Mitt Romney called for "self-deportation" of illegal aliens, which attracted much negative comment from Latino communities. The GOP "autopsy" report after Romney's loss to Barack Obama asserted that the Republican ticket lost the Latino vote because of its perceived anti-Hispanic stance, and recommended that candidates take centrist positions in 2016.

Though the American political culture had been changing since the 1990s, the global financial crisis and the Great Recession greatly polarized it, and Americans became far less forgiving of illegal immigration and migration. America's great white middle class had been the basis of centrist politics for both parties from the 1930s to 1980s, but stagnating wages and lack of upward mobility made them more susceptible to increasingly rightist and leftist appeals. Identity politics replaced partisan politics for many Americans, crystallizing issues of class, culture, and gender for many voters. Many whites felt beleaguered as if they had become "the new minority," suffering just as much as other ethnic minorities of the past.

The first major post-Great Recession movement was the Tea Party, which emerged in opposition to Obama's Affordable Care Act (ACA, or Obamacare). The Tea Party dethroned a number of centrist Republicans in the 2010 and 2012 primaries while pushing conventional conservative politicians rightward. Tea Party ideas informed much of Donald Trump's program in his abortive presidential run in 2012, and again in his 2016 victory. Meanwhile, the Occupy movement, with its calls for ending privileges for the rich, the one percenters, and large corporations, galvanized millennials and much of the American left. While the movement gained few tangible accomplishments for its long-running protests in 2011–2012, it helped push the Democratic Party leftward and fueled Senator Bernie Sanders's insurgent candidacy for president in 2016 (Gest 2016, vii–viii, 20–38, 134–148).

Text box 9.3: Populism

Populism, or support for the concerns of the common people, reinforced the appeal of Donald Trump and Bernie Sanders in the 2016 presidential campaign. Political leaders who embrace populism pledge to work on behalf of ordinary people and in opposition to the ruling political and economic elites that supposedly are oppressing them. Populism has a long history in America, dating back to the People's (or Populist) Party of the 1890s and encompassing such later figures as Huey Long in the 1930s and George Wallace in the 1960s and 1970s. Long's appeal was mostly economic, while Wallace also leveraged fears of white diminishment. In most cases, populist movements were co-opted and their leaders defanged by skillful maneuvering of the major parties. Neoliberalism and globalization became obvious targets of populists, beginning with Ross Perot's independent candidacy and Pat Buchanan's insurgent presidential campaigns in the 1990s. After the Great Recession, populist-like appeals helped feed the Tea Party and the Occupy movement. By campaigning as populists, Sanders and especially Trump were more successful in winning the ideological battles within their parties in 2016.

Polls indicated widespread disquiet over the immigration issue within working-class, middle-class, and white voters. In fact, white concern over displacement by foreign immigrants and migrants ranked as high among white working-class voters as fear of job loss due to globalization and economic restructuring. Real estate developer and reality TV personality Donald Trump's political innovation was to grasp that an anti-immigration position was a winning cudgel against most of the other GOP candidates, who were likely to stay circumspect on the immigration issue. Such conservative candidates as Senator Ted Cruz (Texas), former Hewlett-Packard CEO Carly Fiorina, and former Governor Mike Huckabee (Arkansas) might have been expected to use stronger rhetoric on immigration but did not, and others such as former Governor Jeb Bush (Florida), Governor Chris Christie (New Jersey), and Senator Marco Rubio (Florida) ignored the issue or promoted merely enhanced border security. All of them thus ceded the issue to Trump, hoping that his luster would fade over time and his voters would come their way. Among Democrats, all announced candidates called for protecting the rights of immigrants and migrants, while providing a path to citizenship for migrants who have lived in the country for extended periods (Stein 2016; Pew Research Center 2016).

Trump began his presidential campaign with an emphasis on immigration issues. In his June 2015 announcement speech, he accused Mexican migrants of being criminals, rapists, and drug dealers. His call to build a new border wall that somehow would be paid for by Mexico became one of his most popular lines at his public rallies. The notion of an impenetrable barrier that would keep out illegal migrants seemed like a simple solution that had been ignored for decades by multiple administrations. The fact that most illegal immigrants arrive by air, drive through border checkpoints, or overstay their visas was not discussed. Walls have often served as last resorts, but results are often dubious, from South Africa to Israel/Palestine.

As the Syrian refugee issue seized the news in Europe, Trump accused the Obama administration and Hillary Clinton of allowing large numbers of dangerous migrants into the country. He called for much stricter controls on the entry of migrants into the United States, along with an unspecified "extreme vetting" process. Many American Latinos viewed the Trump campaign as anti-Hispanic, as Trump's anti-immigrant rhetoric was aimed primarily at Mexican migrants. Trump moved to bar Latino journalists from some of his press conferences, and in June 2016 he suggested that Judge Gonzalo Curiel—in charge of a case brought against Trump University's real estate training program—could not be objective because of his Mexican heritage.

The eventual Republican nominee also targeted Muslim migrants, insisting that they pose risks as potential terrorists. In truth, no terrorists had entered the United States that way, but instead had either come on training visas or were homegrown lone wolves—radicalized but not directly recruited by terrorist organizations. Trump's harsh comments about migrants fit with his overall reputation for blunt remarks, unfiltered Twitter posts, and frequent personal attacks on his opponents. The more Trump insulted other candidates and violated supposed political norms, the more support he gained with white Republican voters. Within three months into his announced candidacy, Trump led in the polls and went on to win most of the primaries and caucuses.

In his acceptance speech at the Republican National Convention in July 2016, Trump painted a dark picture of an America being overwhelmed by crime, crumbling infrastructure, and unfettered immigration. Throughout the fall campaign, he insisted that Democratic nominee Hillary Clinton was out of touch and planned to let hundreds of thousands of Syrian refugees into the country if elected. The election results shocked political experts and the pundit class, particularly Trump's seizure of such previously solid Democratic states as Michigan, Pennsylvania, and Wisconsin. While immigration was only one of several issues cited by white working-class voters who jumped on the "Trump train," it was one of the most popular issues for Trump voters in the swing states of the Upper Midwest (Jones 2016).

Trump's emphasis on immigration issues appealed not only to ordinary white working-class and middle-class voters, along with (mostly white) evangelical Christians, but also to an assortment of right-wing forces that traditionally have not fit within the mainstream of the Republican Party: white nationalists and white supremacists, neo-Nazis, the Ku Klux Klan and its sympathizers, and the "alt-right"—those who reject traditional conservatism, free trade, and liberal immigration policies, and who espouse isolationism, protectionism, anti-Semitism, and white supremacy. Trump never explicitly embraced the alt-right movement, but on January 27, 2016, he appointed Steve Bannon—one of its key spokesmen and editor of the leading alt-right website Breitbart News—as one of his campaign managers and then as White House chief strategist. (Bannon was subsequently fired on August 18, 2017.)

Trump brought into his administration a number of figures who had campaigned for tougher immigration policies. Most notably, he appointed Senator Jeff Sessions (Alabama) as Attorney General, and Steven Miller as one of his White House assistants. Sessions vowed to get tough on illegal immigrants. As Sessions' assistant, Miller had tried to get the senator to run for president on a strong anti-immigration platform and had later gone to work for Trump's campaign. Once in office, Trump immediately issued an executive order to curb the entry of immigrants from six Middle Eastern countries: Libya, Sudan, Yemen, Syria, Iraq, and Iran. Such US allies as Egypt and Saudi Arabia—the sources of most of the 9/11 hijackers—were not included. Though Trump's people insisted that it was not a Muslim ban, Christians and other minorities from those countries were exempted from the order.

Neither the Justice Department nor the Homeland Security Department was given advanced warning of the ban, and Acting Attorney General Sally Yates was fired for refusing to enforce the order after she decided it was unconstitutional. Airports around the country were unsure how to implement the new policy, and chaos ensued for several days at American entry points. Several states and the American Civil Liberties Union (ACLU) sued to overturn the order, and stays were granted by two federal courts, and later upheld in appeals courts. The Supreme Court agreed to hear the government's appeal and issued a decision on the ban in the fall of 2017 (Kulish et al. 2017; Quigley 2017).

Arguably, the most significant changes in immigration policy were bureaucratic. The Department of Homeland Security under General John Kelly made a major push to strictly enforce immigration controls, arresting and deporting illegal immigrants at much higher rates than the Obama administration (Obama had been called "the deportation president"). The Trump administration sought to cut off federal funding for "sanctuary cities"—cities that refused to prioritize immigration enforcement over criminal law enforcement in order to allow immigrant communities to cooperate with local police. Trump also called for a preliminary study of his proposed border wall but was unable to obtain funding for construction from Congress. In September 2017, he claimed that existing walls were being strengthened, and demonstration projects to test types of prospective walls were underway.

Trump did not state clearly during the campaign whether he intended to scrap Obama's Deferred Action for Childhood Arrivals (DACA) program, which gave temporary legal status in the United States to as many as 800,000 illegal migrants who had come to America as children and subsequently had not lived in their parents' home countries. Many of these young people were students or were working full-time jobs, and would have great difficulty adjusting to the countries of their births. In September 2017, Attorney General Sessions ruled that DACA was unconstitutional, and should have been enacted by Congress rather than being promulgated in a presidential executive order. Later that month, Democratic congressional leaders claimed they had reached a deal with Trump to save DACA in return for enhanced border security funding; but, perhaps fearing a backlash from his conservative and working-class "base," Trump quickly disavowed the deal but insisted a bipartisan compromise would ultimately be struck.

Conclusion

Immigration and migration issues have become linked in public opinion as never before. The confluence of unprecedented, conflict-induced migration and rising working-class and middle-class anger at perceived high levels of immigration to Europe and America has partly fueled populist movements in both the United States and the United Kingdom, as well as in continental Europe. The Brexit vote for Britain to leave the EU and the election of Donald Trump as president of the United States might not have been possible without widespread fears of both migration and immigration.

Recent events in both America and Britain undermine traditional migration theories, which emphasize the rational forces of push-and-pull compelling large numbers of people to look for better opportunities. Recent migrants begin their journeys in conflict zones, hoping for better lives in the West. The Brexit vote and the rise of Trump illustrate the value of nuanced migration theories, especially those of Kurekova and Castles. Both Brexit and Trump's campaign were the culmination of populist political movements that took advantage of migration and immigration issues to gain control of the national discussion and markedly shift the political landscape. Brexit was the result of a more diffuse movement than the candidate-directed Trump campaign, but the consequences were no less profound for Britain's political future.

Questions for discussion

1   What are the most important causes of migration in the contemporary world?
2   Is the current form of migration different from migration during the 20th century?
3   What are the similarities and differences between Syrian and Rohingya refugees/ migrants?
4   What was the most important issue in the Brexit referendum?
5   Can populism explain the rising anti-immigration sentiment in Europe and America?
6   Is the current US immigration policy fair and just? Please substantiate your analyses.
7   What are some major differences between European and American immigration debates?

References

Agbale, Victor. 2016. "Immigration and the 2016 Election." *Harvard Political Review*, January 18, 2016, pp. 1–2. http://harvardpolitics.com/united-states/immigration-2016-election/ (retrieved 8/23/16).
Albert, Eleanor. 2017. "The Rohingya Migrant Crisis." Council on Foreign Relations *Backgrounder*, September 13, 2017, pp. 1–12. https://www.cfr.org/backgrounder/rohingya-migrant-crisis (retrieved 9/21/17).
BBC News. 2016. "Migrant Crisis: Migration to Europe Explained in Seven Charts." *BBC online*, March 4, 2016, pp. 1–14. http://www.bbc.com/news/world-europe-34131911 (retrieved 9/19/16).
Bennett, Asa. 2016. "Did Britain Really Vote Brexit to Cut Immigration?" *Daily Telegraph*, June 29, 2016, pp. 1–12.
Castles, Stephen, Hein de Haas, and Mark J. Miller. 2013. *The Age of Migration: International Population Movements in the Modern World*. New York: The Guilford Press.
Cillizza, Chris. 2016. "The Remarkable Parallels between the Brexit Vote and the Rise of Donald Trump." *The Washington Post*, June 24, 2016, pp. 1–8.
The Economist. 2016. "Explaining the Brexit Vote." July 16, 2016, pp. 1–2.
Edwards, Adrian. 2016. "Global Forced Displacement Hits Record High." New York: UNHCR, June 20, 2016, pp. 1–7. http://www.unhcr.org/news/latest/2016/6/5763b65a4/global-forced-displacement-hits-record-high.html (retrieved 9/19/16).
Gest, Justin. 2016. *The New Minority: White Working Class Politics in an Age of Immigration and Inequality*. New York: Oxford University Press, pp. vii–viii, 20–38, 134–148.
Jones, Robert P. 2016. "How Immigration and Concerns About Cultural Change Are Shaping the 2016 Election—Findings from the 2016 PRRI/Brookings Immigration Survey." Brookings Institution report. https://www.brookings.edu/wp-content/uploads/2016/06/20160623_prri_jones_presentation.pdf (retrieved 11/20/16).
JRank. 2016. "Migration–Theories of Migration." n.d., pp. 1–2. http://family.jrank.org/pages/1170/Migration-Theories-Migration.html (retrieved 9/19/16).
Khan, Aalia. 2016. "Four Ways the Anti-Immigration Vote Won the Referendum for Brexit." *New Statesman*, July 7, pp. 1–6.
King, Russell. 2012. "Theories and Typologies of Migration: An Overview and a Primer." *Willy Brandt Series of Working Papers in International Migration and Ethnic Relations*. Malmo: Malmo University Institute for Studies of Migration, Diversity and Welfare, March 2012, pp. 1–31. https://www.researchgate.net/publication/260096281_Theories_and_Typologies_of_Migration_An_Overview_and_A_Primer (retrieved 9/19/16).
Kulish, Nicholas, et al. 2017. "Trump's Immigration Policies Explained." *The New York Times*, February 21, pp. 1–8.

Kurekova, Lucia. 2011. "Theories of Migration: Conceptual Review and Empirical Testing in the Context of the EU East-West Flows." Presentation, April 6, 2011, pp. 1–15 (University College London). https://cream.conference-services.net/resources/952/2371/pdf/MECSC2011_0139_paper.pdf (retrieved 9/19/16).

Mercy Corps. 2016. "Quick Facts: What You Need to Know About the Syria Crisis." Mercy Corps, June 18, 2016, pp. 1–10. https://www.mercycorps.org/articles/iraq-jordan-lebanon-syria -turkey/quick-facts-what-you-need-know-about-syria-crisis (retrieved 9/19/16).

Mingels, Guido. 2016. "Global Migration? Actually, the World Is Staying Home." Der Spiegel, May 17, 2016, pp. 1–12. http://www.spiegel.de/international/world/why-global-migration-sta tistics-do-not-add-up-a-1090736.html (retrieved 9/19/16).

Pew Research Center. 2016. "Top Voting Issues in 2016 Election." July 7, 2016. http://www. people-press.org/2016/07/07/4-top-voting-issues-in-2016-election/ (retrieved 9/21/16).

Quigley, Aidan. 2017. "What's Happening with Trump's Immigration Laws? The Latest on Who Is Safe and Who Isn't." Newsweek, June 18, 2017, pp. 1–8.

Rankin, Jennifer. 2016. "EU Refugee Crisis: Asylum Seeker Numbers Double to 1.2m in 2015." BBC online, March 4, 2016, pp. 1–6.

Siegel, Josh. 2016. "How Immigration Fueled the Brexit Result." The Daily Signal, June 23, 2016, pp. 1–5.

Stein, Dan. 2016. "Why Immigration Is Shaking Up the 2016 Election." Voices Magazine, April 2016, pp. 1–2.

Travis, Alan. 2016. "Fear of Immigration Drove the Leave Victory—Not Immigration Itself." The Guardian, June 24, 2016, pp. 1–4.

UNHCR. 2015. "UNHCR—Figures at a Glance." New York: UNHCR, pp. 1–4. http://www. unhcr.org/figures-at-a-glance.html (retrieved 9/19/16).

Part III

Sub- and trans-state actors and forces: Disruptions and violence

Chapter 10

Sub-state actors' threats to international security
Religious extremists and terrorist groups

Sharad Joshi

Introduction

A significant development in world politics has been the emergence of non-state actors as major participants and forces—both positive and negative—in the system. Trans-state actors include multinational corporations, non-governmental organizations, **epistemic communities**, international organizations, insurgent groups, terrorist groups, etc. This chapter examines non-state threats from religious extremists and terrorist groups. This is not to suggest that non-state actors are always autonomous, independent of states—there are numerous instances of states creating, and/or supporting terrorist groups as their proxies. Nevertheless, terrorist groups have their own identity even if they are substantially or wholly dependent on a state entity. Terrorism is also a tactic used in pursuit of a political objective. This implies that terrorism and extremism are not exclusively the domain of non-state actors. State entities can and have engaged in terrorism.

This chapter shows the global diffusion of terrorism and describes the various motivating factors driving terrorist individuals and groups and their recruits, as well as enabling factors such as state-sponsorship. This chapter also embraces multiple theoretical approaches and uses examples from multiple regions to illustrate its points.

Today's global diffusion of terrorism

For most of recorded history, international security threats and conflict primarily involved state actors, including empires, kingdoms, nation-states, with the use of conflict and violence as a strategy toward territorial conquest, balance of power, rivalry, ideology, etc. Sub-state threats to international security have become prominent in recent decades, as the attacks of September 11, 2001, made the international community more aware of threats from terrorist groups. Present-day terrorist groups are frequently driven by an extremist ideology based on an immoderate interpretation of a religious identity.

Contemporary terrorism is said to have begun in the late 1960s and early 1970s with the rise of groups like the Palestinian Liberation Organization (PLO) and Black September, Marxist groups such as the Baader–Meinhof Gang, Kurdistan Workers Party (PKK), the Red Army Faction, and separatist groups such as the provisional Irish Republican Army (IRA), and the Euskadi Ta Askatasuna (ETA). During the 1980s, terrorist groups had emerged in different parts of the world, including the Khalistani groups in India and the Liberation Tigers of Tamil Eelam (LTTE) in

Sri Lanka. The number of groups also increased in the Middle East, including the Abu Nidal group, Hezbollah, Hamas, and Islamic Jihad. By the 1990s, South Asia had become one of the key areas of terrorist activities due to the Kashmiri terrorist movement, and the rise of the Taliban and Al Qaeda in Afghanistan after the end of the anti-Soviet **mujahideen** campaign there (1979–1989). During this period, global jihadist ideology influenced terrorism in many parts of the world, with Al Qaeda spearheading this terrorist alliance, which included regional terrorist groups like Jemaah Islamiyah (Indonesia), Abu Sayyaf (Philippines), Harkat-ul Jihad al-Islami (Pakistan, Bangladesh), al-Jamaah al-Islamiyah (Egypt). Ethno-religious movements such as Buddhist extremist groups in Myanmar and Sri Lanka also sprang into action. An important turning point was the 9/11 attacks in the United States, which pre-cipitated the 2002 US-led campaign in Afghanistan against Al Qaeda and the Taliban and their affiliated jihadist groups. The Islamic State of Iraq and Syria (ISIS) captured large territories in Iraq and Syria (2013–2017) and sought to take over the leadership of the global jihadist movement from Al Qaeda. The advent of ISIS demonstrates how international terrorism has evolved—i.e., recruitment and radicalization (use of social media), changes in organizational behavior, targeting strategies, tactics, etc.

Defining and theorizing terrorism and extremist violence

Terrorism manifests itself through numerous kinds of violent attacks, such as assassina-tions, suicide bombings, car bombings, hijackings, executions, vehicular terrorism, attacks on facilities, chemical/biological/radiological/nuclear (CBRN) attacks. The underlying political message that terrorist groups send to a wider audience is as important as the operational success in carrying out the attack.

Scholars, governments, and international organizations have defined terrorism exten-sively. There is a common thread in these definitions, especially those from an academic perspective. These commonalities include a political objective, and the use or the threat of violence to terrorize and send a message to a wider audience.

Text box 10.1: Definitions of terrorism

Two such academic definitions are instructive. According to Bruce Hoffman:

> We may therefore now attempt to define terrorism as the deliberate creation and exploitation of fear through violence or the threat of violence in the pursuit of political change. All terrorist acts involve violence or the threat of violence. Terrorism is specifi-cally designed to have far-reaching psychological effects beyond the immediate victim(s) or object of the terrorist attack. It is meant to instill fear within, and thereby intimidate, a wider 'target audience' that might include a rival ethnic or religious group, an entire country, a national government or political party, or public opinion in general. Terrorism is designed to create power where there is none or to consolidate power where there is very little. Through the publicity generated by their violence, terrorists seek to obtain the leverage, influence and power they otherwise lack to effect political change on either a local or an international scale.
>
> (2006, 40–41)

And according to Alex Schmid and Albert Jongman:

> Terrorism is an anxiety-inspiring method of repeated violent action, employed by (semi-) clandestine individual, group or state actors, for idiosyncratic, criminal or political reasons, whereby—in contrast to assassination—the direct targets of violence are not the main targets. The immediate human victims of violence are generally chosen randomly (targets of opportunity) or selectively (representative or symbolic targets) from a target population, and serve as message generators. Threat- and violence-based communication processes between terrorist (organization), (imperiled) victims, and main targets are used to manipulate the main target (audience(s)), turning it into a target of terror, a target of demands, or a target of attention, depending on whether intimidation, coercion, or propaganda is primarily sought.
>
> (1998, 28)

These definitions show how terrorism differs from other kinds of conflict and violence, such as traditional state-to-state warfare, which involves regular militaries in battle (Williams 2008). Terrorism also differs from organized crime, where the primary rationale is criminal profit. At the same time, these kinds of violence are not mutually exclusive (see Clarke's chapter and Simoni's chapter herein). There are instances of terrorist groups cooperating with organized crime entities and in some cases, taking on hybrid characteristics involving both criminal and terrorist characteristics, one example being the Dawood Ibrahim organized crime network operating from Pakistan (Joshi, Peters, and Williams 2015). The Haqqani Network in Pakistan and Afghanistan, and the Revolutionary Armed Forces of Colombia (FARC) are examples of groups that are regarded as terrorist/insurgent but are (or have been) also substantially involved in drug trafficking.

Terrorist violence is a form of **asymmetric warfare**, in which there is an imbalance of forces, strategies of violence are used on different levels, and where the militarily weaker side seeks to capitalize on the imbalance through different sets of violent strategies. Terrorism is premeditated and seeks to coerce the political views and policies of governments and populations that are its audience (Wilkinson 2011, 4). Targets carry important symbolism: they might be important representations of a state's political identity (such as a national legislature), its economic, religious, or historical identity. Attacking such targets would not only be an important blow to the adversary, it would also generate substantial publicity for the terrorist cause. Some definitions of terrorism also consider the identity of the targets and victims and state that non-combatants and civilians are the primary targets of terrorism.

Text box 10.2: Terrorism, insurgency, and guerrilla warfare

Terrorism is frequently conflated with "insurgency", which is also a form of non-state armed violence in pursuit of political objectives, but which differs from terrorism despite overlapping tactics and goals. An insurgency generally includes an armed revolt against the government, which prioritizes the objective of capturing substantial territory and portraying themselves as equivalent to a government through formation of military forces, judicial court system, currency, and other basic identifying features of a sovereign state. Insurgent groups also seek popular support to a much higher degree and use a combination of strategies, which can be both violent and non-violent (Moghadam 2017, 3).

Relatedly, terrorism is frequently confused with guerrilla warfare. Various scholars have described guerrilla warfare as a prolonged war of attrition that guerrilla forces resemble regular military forces, while according to Samuel Huntington, "guerrilla warfare is a form of warfare by which the strategically weaker side assumes the tactical offensive in selected forms, times and places" (qtd. in Kalyanaraman 2003, 172). Apart from resistance to stronger authorities and forces, guerrilla operations can also be driven by ideological and extremist zeal and also be used by weaker countries against stronger military powers (Kalyanaraman 2003, 182–183). Guerrilla fighters, who carry out mobile hit-and-run attacks, assassinations, and sabotage, generally target elements of the state, including the military, police, and administrative and economic targets (Moghadam 2017, 4). Examples of guerrilla warfare include Maoist revolutionary strategy in China in the 1920s to 1950s, as well as Che Guevara's tactics in Cuba and Latin America from the late 1950s to the late 1960s.

Numerous groups can be classified as insurgent, guerrilla, and terrorist, depending on the area of operations, time period, tactics used, and the objectives behind the specific operations. Terrorism can be one of several tactics used by an insurgent group. For instance, the LTTE which operated in Sri Lanka from the late 1970s to 2009 can be considered to have been both an insurgent and terrorist group. Similarly, the separatist insurgency that commenced in Chechnya from 1994 morphed over time to be dominated by jihadist terrorism, through groups such as the Caucasus Emirate, which was officially formed in 2007, and through secessionist jihadi leaders such as Shamil Basayev and Doku Umarov.

Providing a clear definition of terrorism is also important because of the politically charged nature of the term. A neutral, academic, analytical definition that does not pre-judge the designees is thus essential for understanding the problem. Ideally, definitions of terrorism should try to remove all subjectivity from the term, although in practice such definitions are likely to be open to charges of political bias. Moreover, there are numerous instances of governments around the world labeling opposition elements as "terrorist" despite such entities not fulfilling the commonly accepted academic definitions of the term. Governments frequently misuse the term "terrorism" in order to put international pressure on opposition entities, since the international community is less tolerant of the "freedom fighter versus terrorist" equivalence than it used to be.

From the perspective of international relations theory, non-state actors such as terrorist, insurgent, and extremist groups are relative newcomers. Until recently, the realist paradigm paid little attention to how non-state actors and threats fit into the international system. Realism focuses primarily on states as the main participants in the international system and major players in interstate conflict and rivalries. But with terrorist groups emerging as non-state actors posing important security threats, International Relations (IR) theory should account for their role in the international system. Understanding the role and influence of sub-state groups is crucial to be able to formulate effective counter-terrorism and counter-insurgency policies. Existing theoretical concepts can be applied to terrorist groups as well. For instance, the concept of **security dilemma** (Liff and Ikenberry 2014, 58) helps to explain rivalry and conflict at the sub-state level. When ethnic groups seek to enhance their security through increased military capabilities and alliances, this leads to insecurity and similar buildups among other rival ethnic groups, which would then make conflict among these groups more likely (Wilkinson 2011, 13–14). (In a number of cases, ethno-nationalist groups have adopted terrorism as a primary tactic.)

From the liberal theory perspective, terrorism is a violent ideology that is the antithesis of liberal principles of tolerance and peace, and one influential view is that Western countries are justified in militarily combating terrorism and terrorist supporters (Dunne 2009, 107). Within the constructivist paradigm, definitions of terrorism and designations of terrorists are not regarded as an objective exercise, but one that is meant to label as terrorists those entities and states that are regarded as challengers to the hegemony of major powers (Butko 2009, 190–92).

Motivations of terrorist individuals and groups

If terrorism is based on underlying political objectives, what are those political goals founded upon? What makes individuals join terrorist groups and commit heinous acts of violence? In any case of terrorism, there is never just one factor that exclusively determines the emergence of a terrorist individual or group. Rather, it is frequently a combination of factors—a "perfect storm," ideology, state support, local support, capabilities, provocations, leadership, and organizational characteristics. The exact causal linkage between a set of factors and terrorist violence might not be obvious: What causes terrorism in a specific case might be a matter of vigorous debate, rather than a unanimously accepted explanation. Moreover, the causal factors behind ter-rorism in one case might not be applicable—at least in the same combination—in other instances. Explanations of the causes of terrorist violence might also be colored by the analyst's pre-conceived notions and political leanings.

Religious and ethnic identities are also used by terrorist groups to radicalize and recruit individuals into carrying out acts of violence. Terrorist ideologues can portray the ethnic and/or religious community under threat from other communities and/or the state—an important recruitment and radicalizing message based on community identity. Thus, terrorist leaders portray ethnic and religious diversity and differences as a violent faultline, on the basis of which they advocate violent tactics in pursuit of these identity and ideology-based political objectives. These identity markers are used to recruit individuals through visual imagery, including posters, videos, audio messages, and extremist ideolo-gues' sermons and manifestos.

Causes of terrorism can be categorized under individual-level and group-level expla-nations. Individual-level factors focus on motivations within the individual's psyche that propel them toward terrorism while group-level motivations are driven by ethnic, reli-gious, and political ideology.

Psychological factors

What sort of psychological factors make an individual more likely to join a terrorist group and act? There are major challenges in constructing a terrorist profile, but "predisposing risk factors" are useful to consider, which would include emotional vulnerability and feelings of anger, hopelessness, alienation, **anomie**, and disen-franchisement. Additionally, feelings of dissatisfaction with current political strategies in the face of adversaries regarded as bent on humiliating the individual's community and its identity, making terrorism appear to be a defensive strategy for the individual; a belief that involvement in terrorist violence would bring rewards to the individual, including increased respect and status for the recruit and his/her family; and role models within the group that influence the continued involvement of the recruit within the group (Horgan 2008, 80, 84–85, 88). Such motivations, especially the sense of posthumous respect within the group and the larger support base, have been demonstrated in the case of suicide bombers in different terrorist groups who are venerated as martyrs and whose families are treated with respect within the group. Although the LTTE, an ethno-nationalist group, was one of the first terrorist groups to push suicide bombings as a major tactic from the late 1980s, a number of jihadist groups have since incorporated this tactic.

Psychological factors help explain why some individuals become terrorists and others in similar circumstances do not; other factors influence the process, including (but not limited to) ideological indoctrination, influence of the group's leadership, and the strength and control of the group itself (Horgan 2008, 85). Thus, external psychological factors such as group and organizational psychology and collective identity shape the decisions and actions of potential terrorist recruits, even more so than an individual's internal psychological makeup (Post 2005, 617). This involves charismatic leaders and ideologues who are able to manipulate, indoctrinate, and radicalize emotionally vulnerable and alienated individuals. Mechanisms for such radicalization processes have increased in recent decades including compact discs, digital video discs, and online videos of speeches of ideologues and suffering of the potential recruit's religious community in different parts of the world. Such materials are used to provoke anger and radicalize and indoctrinate potential recruits. Psychological factors can also be influenced by material, "root cause"-related factors, such as poverty, deprivation, and underdevelopment, to create an environment in which vulnerable individuals would be more susceptible to being swayed by religious extremists.

Especially in the case of religious extremism and terrorism, inflammatory speeches of leaders and ideologues, including those with clerical and theological standing (such as Anwar al-Awlaki who radicalized and recruited jihadist terrorists before being killed by a drone strike in Yemen in 2011) are frequently regarded as representative of divine pronouncements and guidance (Post 2005, 620; Shane 2015). The charismatic leader and ideologue explain to impressionable recruits the identity of the external enemy, and how their personal deprivation and grievances fit into a broader collective identity narrative, which helps subsume the individual's psychological problems into the group's collective social identity (Post 2005, 622). For these recruits, becoming part of a terrorist group and carrying out violent attacks becomes a mechanism for striking back against perceived oppressors, not just for their own sake, but for the sake of their community, thereby providing the individual with a sense of broader purpose in their hitherto meaningless lives. Religious indoctrination also provides the theological justification for specific kinds of attacks, for instance, suicide bombings, which are described as martyrdom within jihadist ideology (Post 2005, 627). With religious extremism (and especially jihadism), indoctrination becomes a transnational process, with potential recruits made aware of the suffering of their co-religionists in different parts of the world. But such psychological imperatives have to be viewed as a complement to group-level causal mechanisms.

Ethno-nationalist separatist objectives

One of the key motivations driving terrorist groups are goals driven by ethno-nationalist objectives. An ethnic community can be defined as a "named human population with a myth of a common ancestry, shared memories, and cultural elements; a link with a historic territory or homeland; and a measure of solidarity" (Smith qtd. in Brown 2010, 93). Ethno-nationalism remains a crucial basis for terrorism in part because ethnicity remains an enduring source of identity for communities around the world. Crucially, there are numerous multi-ethnic countries whose national boundaries have not been accepted by ethnic communities within and remain beset by irredentism, secessionism, historical grievances, and animosities, which then lead to insurgent and terrorist violence in some cases (Wilkinson 2011, 13). Among such groups, terrorist violence is used to achieve and consolidate political power for a specific ethnic community, including especially the goal of a sovereign state. These groups portray their community, its interests, and identity as under threat from the state and/or other communities, and through terrorist violence seek to instill fear in rival communities, leading to ethnic cleansing and the intensification of the ethnic divide, which further consolidates support for the terrorist group in question within its community. Similarly, ethnic terrorist groups also want to provoke a violent backlash from the state in the belief that it might lead to greater publicity and support for their cause, both domestically and internationally (Byman 1998).

Important examples of ethno-nationalist groups include the LTTE, which used terrorism as part of a broader set of insurgent tactics over three decades in Sri Lanka to wrest an independent Tamil state until it was comprehensively defeated militarily in 2009. In Spain (primarily), the Basque separatist group Euskadi Ta Askatasuna adopted terrorist tactics in its quest for an independent Basque country before permanently renouncing violence and announcing disarmament in 2017. The Moro separatist movement (Southern Philippines) can also be classified as an ethno-nationalist movement, although some of the constituent groups also acquired a strong jihadist identity as well.

Examples such as the Moro separatist-terrorist groups and the Kashmiri terrorist groups in India show that ethno-nationalist terrorism and religiously motivated terrorism are not mutually exclusive. Terrorism groups can frequently be driven by both ethno-nationalist and religious extremist ideology, and encompass political objectives that reflect this dual influence. This reflects different strands of a community and terrorist group's identity. Over time, a separatist terrorist movement might move from an ethno-nationalist character to a religious extremist influence (or a combination of both), especially if the ethnic identity of the community coincides with a religious identity. Such a shift toward religious extremism within the same movement might also come about through interactions with external forces, whether a state sponsor or increased receptivity to a religious ideology.

Religious extremism

Perhaps the predominant motivation for contemporary terrorist groups is religious extremism. Examples include Al Qaeda, ISIS, and various regional jihadist groups such as the Afghan and Pakistani Taliban, Lashkar-e-Taiba (India), Boko Haram (Nigeria), Jemaah Islamiyah (Indonesia), Abu Sayyaf (Philippines), Hezbollah (Lebanon), and Al Shabaab (Somalia). Thus, most religious terrorist groups today are driven by an Islamist and jihadist ideology. Many come from among the Sunni extremist milieu, although Hezbollah is the dominant Shi'a militant group. At the same time, regional jihadist groups are also rooted in local political grievances subsumed under a global extremist ideology.

This is not to suggest that religious terrorism emerges only from extremist interpretations of one religion. Most mainstream religious traditions have included extremist elements, some of whom have descended into terrorist violence. These include extremist Sikh terrorist groups in the Indian state of Punjab from the early 1980s to the mid-1990s, who sought an independent state of Khalistan. More recently, Buddhist extremist groups and mobs in Sri Lanka and Myanmar have carried out violence directed by radical clergy against the minority Muslim communities in the two countries. Buddhist violence in the two countries demonstrates some important characteristics of contemporary extremist violence, including the possibility of attacks carried out by disorganized, but radicalized mobs. In addition, Jewish extremists have carried out violence, including the assassination of Prime Minister Yitzhak Rabin on November 4, 1995, and against Palestinian targets in what has been termed as "settler terrorism" (Juergensmeyer 2003, 45–60; Pedahzur and Perliger 2009). In recent years, Hindutva extremist groups in India have also carried out acts of violence against the Muslim community (Ramachandran, 2017).

Religiously motivated terrorists are driven by an extreme interpretation of their religion that justifies and recommends violence in pursuit of certain political objectives. Religious (and ethnic) identity is used as an instrument to mobilize followers toward a political objective and use such violence as a tactic. The rise of religious terrorism over the last three decades reflects a variety of factors including the awareness and intensification of fault-lines among religious communities in the post–Cold War period, as well as a sense of fear and threat to their identity among religious extremists from other religions, major powers, and secularizing tendencies from external and internal forces. Religious violence is then adopted as a way of combating a corrupt, immoral political system, society, and religious establishment (Ranstorp 1996, 47–48). Religious terrorists are driven by a fundamentalist ideology in which they believe that only their interpretation of the religion is legitimate and that other traditions and sects within the same religion, as well as other religious communities, deserve violence. They justify violence against other sects and communities within the same religion by labeling them as apostates.

Religious fundamentalism regards "religion as a body of 'essential' and unchallengeable principles, which dictate not only personal conduct but also the organization of social, economic, and political life. Religion cannot and should not be confined to the 'private' sphere but finds its highest and proper expression in the politics of popular mobilization and social regeneration" (Heywood 2003, 297). Religious fundamentalists are more likely to view the world in Manichean terms which would hold that other entities, communities, groups that do not hold their extremist world-view are opposing God's will on earth, are evil, and should be actively opposed and punished (Heywood 2003, 303). Such exclusionary thinking makes it more likely for their followers of all religions to engage in extremist violence.

Religiously motivated terrorism sometimes also arises from separatist and freedom movements when the campaign for an independent homeland acquires religious ideological characteristics (as opposed to being exclusively driven by ethno-nationalist separatism) as well as the involvement of fundamentalist clergy and ideologues, and external state parties. Examples include the Palestinian and Kashmiri militant movements, which became more and more Islamist, and jihadist ideology through groups such as Hamas, Islamic Jihad, Lashkar-e-Taiba, and Jaish-e-Muhammad. Since the

1990s, localized political conflict in parts of Indonesia also became imbued with a religious divide with the entry of Al Qaeda and its ideology and network in the region.

Religious extremism as a form of violence is not just in the domain of organized terrorist groups such as ISIS and Al Qaeda. The ideology and violence are also visible in other unorganized entities that carry out lower levels of violence and high-profile, high casualty terrorist attacks. In Pakistan for instance, extremist violence against individuals and communities on charges of committing blasphemy has become prominent in recent years with radicalized Sunni mobs rioting and killing individuals on charges of insulting Islam and the Prophet Muhammad (Engel Rasmussen and Baloch 2017). The January 2015 terrorist attack in Paris at the offices of the satirical weekly *Charlie Hebdo* was carried out by jihadists claiming that the magazine committed blasphemy against Islam when they published cartoons of Prophet Muhammad (although the attack was claimed by Al Qaida in the Arabian Peninsula) (Saiya 2017, 1087; Yuhas 2015).

Finally, one of the most crucial international security threats concerns chemical, biological, radiological, and nuclear (CBRN) terrorism, despite the immense technological, logistical, procurement challenges for terrorist groups toward acquiring such capabilities (Schaper 2003; Bunn and Wier 2006). Nevertheless, religiously motivated terrorist groups have expressed an interest in acquiring such weapons. ISIS carried out chemical weapons attacks against Iraqi soldiers in April 2017 (O'Connor 2017). Al Qaeda expressed a serious interest in acquiring CBRN capability and its ideologues have even provided theological justifications and endorsement for such weapons (Forest 2009, 108–109; Mowatt-Larssen 2010). It is also worth noting that in 1995, the Japanese doomsday cult Aum Shinrikyo carried out a sarin gas attack in the Tokyo subway, killing 13 people. While ethno-nationalist groups like the LTTE have also pursued CBRN weapons capabilities, one can hypothesize that religious extremists are more likely to pursue CBRN capability due to the Manichean nature of their beliefs, without necessarily being constrained by ethno–nationalist territorial objectives.

Extremist political ideology

Terrorist violence frequently occurs on the basis of extremist political ideology, whether from the far-right or the far-left. Unlike ethnic terrorism, such groups (especially those from the far-left) are much more broad-based in terms of their constituency since they are not focusing on the political objectives of just one community.

Far-right terrorism comprises a range of groups and movements in different parts of the world, including Western Europe and the United States. They are frequently driven by an intense belief that their targets are illegitimate, whether in terms of their legal status or even as human beings (Sprinzak 1995, 21). Such targets of violence frequently include religious and ethnic minority communities, immigrants, and leftist groups, who are regarded by right-wing groups as threatening the status quo power structure in the country. Two major attacks by far-right elements in recent decades were the Oklahoma City bombing in 1995 which killed 168 people and the 2011 attack by Anders Breivik in Norway which killed 77. The first was an instance of anti-government right-wing extremism driving the attack (Gumbel 2015). In the second, a lone wolf attack, Brevik was driven by anti-Islamic beliefs and the threat to the West from perceived Islamization, and anger toward political, economic, cultural, academic, media elites whom he regarded as weakening Western society by allowing this Islamization (Berntzen and Sandberg

2014). In recent years, concerns have also been expressed in the United States about the threat from far-right extremist groups, including white supremacists, anti-government extremists, anti-abortion, and anti-immigration groups (Blair 2014). Far-right extremist groups also frequently overlap with religious extremism, as is the case with Hindutva extremists in India. In fact, Anders Breivik, in his manifesto released just before committing the massacres, supported various Hindutva ideas and ideologues (Nanda 2011). On the other hand, left-wing groups are much less likely to overlap with religious extremism given Marxist antipathy towards religion. Leftist terrorist groups have been understood as either utopian, aspiring to global change; or national revolutionary, pushing for revolutionary transformation within specific nation-states (Long 1990, 66–85).

Enabling factors

In addition to the direct factors summarized above, enabling aspects can act as catalysts or even a driving force for religious extremists and terrorist groups. Such factors have to be viewed contextually. To illustrate this connection, we discuss state sponsorship and failed/weak states. They demonstrate that extremist groups frequently require and make use of external assistance or conditions as a catalyst for expanding their terrorist activities and networks.

Over the last five decades, terrorist groups have received considerable state support from a variety of countries. Often terrorist groups depend completely on state sponsors. Instances of groups that received state support at various points include the Palestinian Liberation Organization, terrorist groups in Kashmir, the Taliban, the Irish Republican Army. Countries that supported such groups at various points include Pakistan, Libya, Iran, and Syria. For state sponsors, attacks on the territory of their adversaries is a useful way of striking at their targets while claiming plausible deniability and fulfilling military and political objectives indirectly. Such a strategy exploits any uncertainty within the international community regarding the culpability of the sponsor. The sponsor also does not have to engage in costly direct military strikes. State sponsorship or support takes place through several means—financial support, arms transfers, military training, training camps, diplomatic and political support. Allowing sanctuary to a terrorist group and allowing it to carry out its activities from the sponsor's territory is itself state support even if there is little material support from the state. An important objective for the state is maintaining control over the proxy's agenda: the terrorist client should follow the objectives of the state and not develop an agenda of its own that could contradict the interests of its sponsor.

Extremist religious ideology often becomes part of a state sponsorship strategy. Pakistan's policy of sponsoring Kashmiri militant groups in India has involved supporting the more Islamist and jihadist elements of the movement (such as Lashkar-e-Taiba, Jaish-e-Muhammad, Hizb-ul Mujahideen) as opposed to the more ethno-nationalist groups (which were also Islamist, like the Jammu and Kashmir Liberation Front) in the belief that it would be easier to control the agenda of Islamist groups as opposed to the ethno-nationalist ones. Ethno-nationalist groups were more aligned with the independence option for Kashmir while the primarily Islamist groups were expected to follow the Pakistani state's objective of wresting Kashmir from India and merging it with Pakistan. This illustrates how within a state-sponsorship strategy, religious extremist ideology played an important role in shaping the direction of the policy. Cases like Pakistan's alliance with jihadist groups also demonstrate the violent blowback from a state sponsorship strategy when some terrorist clients turn against the state, angered by a perceived betrayal of the original cause by the regime. After the 9/11 attacks, the Pervez Musharraf regime in Pakistan reluctantly agreed to assist the United States in its counter-terrorism operations against the Taliban and Al Qaeda in Afghanistan. Islamabad's jihadist allies regarded this as a betrayal of the Islamist cause and contributed to the rise of jihadist terrorist attacks within Pakistan.

Second, an important factor often seen in the context of the rise of terrorist and insurgent groups is the phenomena of failed and weak states. Such conditions assist in (and are in turn, reinforced by) the rise of terrorist groups by providing a supportive environment. Weak, failed, or collapsed states, or ungoverned spaces have existed in different parts of the world in recent decades, including in South Asia, the Middle East, and Africa. Current examples include Libya, Somalia, Syria, and Yemen, while Afghanistan is frequently on the brink of failed state status. Failed states provide a base where terrorist groups can set up camps, secure that they are less likely to be expelled due to the lack of adequate security control by the authorities. From these areas, they can export their extremist ideology and violence. This is especially so with respect to jihadist groups and networks. For instance, since the 1980s Afghanistan has been shaky at the best of times with fierce ethnic tribal rivalries, competing warlords, external interference, and the collapse of the internal governance system. Since the anti-Soviet mujahideen campaign (1979–1989), Afghanistan became a major center of militant Islamism attracting volunteers from all parts of the world, and eventually became a safe haven for jihadist groups, especially Al Qaeda (Haqqani 2007). After 2011, ISIS emerged from upheavals and instability in Iraq and the Syria civil war and was able to control substantial territory in both countries while also establishing an important presence in Libya in the midst of the civil war there (Lynch 2016). Additionally, the civil war in Yemen since 2011 has allowed Al Qaeda in the Arabian Peninsula (AQAP) to establish its influence in most of southern Yemen (Horton 2017).

Conclusion

Terrorist and extremist violence, especially that driven by religious ideology, remains one of the most severe threats in many parts of the world. Religious extremism and terrorism operate on a different level than ethno–nationalist terrorism, which often has a more limited constituency. Moreover, on account of their Manichean worldview, religious extremists and terrorists would be much less amenable to a negotiated settlement than ethno–nationalists. From the policy perspective, there is no easy set of prescriptions, given the pervasiveness of religious extremism as an ideology. Mechanisms such as Countering Violent Extremism (CVE) have been adopted in various countries, but those remain a work in progress of uncertain efficacy.

Questions for discussion

1   How is terrorism defined?
2   What is religious fundamentalism? What is ethno–nationalist separatism?
3   Distinguish terrorism from other forms of non–state violence, such as insurgency and organized crime-related violence.
4   What are some cases of religiously motivated terrorism globally? How do they compare and differ?

5   How do issues such as climate change, natural disasters, poverty, mass migrations and refugee flows create enabling conditions for terrorist recruitment and radicalization?
6   How can we address the terrorist threats?

References

Berntzen, Lars Erik, and Sveinung Sandberg. 2014. "The Collective Nature of Lone Wolf Terrorism: Anders Behring Breivik and the Anti-Islamic Social Movement." *Terrorism and Political Violence* 26(5): 759–779.

Blair, Charles P. June 9, 2014. "Looking Clearly at Right-Wing Terrorism." *Bulletin of the Atomic Scientists.* https://thebulletin.org/looking-clearly-right-wing-terrorism7232

Brown, Michael E. 2010 (1997). "Causes and Implications of Ethnic Conflict," 92–109. In Montserrat Guibernau and John Rex, eds. *The Ethnicity Reader: Nationalism, Multiculturalism and Migration.* Cambridge, UK: Polity Press.

Bunn, Matthew, and Anthony Wier. September 2006. "Terrorist Nuclear Weapon Construction: How Difficult?" *The ANNALS of the American Academy of Political and Social Science* 607: 133–149.

Butko, Thomas J. May 2009. "Four Perspectives on Terrorism: Where They Stand Depends on Where You Sit." *Political Studies Review* 7(2):185–194.

Byman, Daniel. 1998. "The Logic of Ethnic Terrorism." *Studies in Conflict and Terrorism* 21(2): 149–169.

Dunne, Tim. March 2009. "Liberalism, International Terrorism, and Democratic Wars." *International Relations* 23(1):107–114.

Engel Rasmussen, Sune, and Kiyya Baloch. April 26, 2017. "Student's Lynching Sparks Rare Uproar in Pakistan over Blasphemy Killings." *The Guardian.* http://bit.ly/2oK4nzM

Forest, James J.F. 2009. "Terrorist Use of WMD," 93–119 in Barry R. Schneider, Jerrold M. Post and Michael T. Kindt, eds. *The World's Most Threatening Terrorist Networks and Criminal Gangs.* New York, NY: Palgrave Macmillan.

Gumbel, Andrew. April 13, 2015. "Oklahoma City Bombing: 20 Years Later, Key Questions Remain Unanswered." *The Guardian.* http://bit.ly/2hdUOLO

Haqqani, Husain. May 23, 2007 "Afghanistan's Islamist Groups." *Current Trends in Islamist Ideology.* Washington, DC: Hudson Institute, https://www.hudson.org/research/9772-afghanistan-s-islamist-groups

Heywood, Andrew. 2003 (1992). *Political Ideologies: An Introduction.* New York, NY: Palgrave MacMillan.

Hoffman, Bruce. 2006 (1998). *Inside Terrorism.* New York: Columbia University Press.

Horgan, John. July 2008. "From Profiles to Pathways and Roots to Routes: Perspectives from Psychology on Radicalization into Terrorism." *The ANNALS of the American Academy of Political and Social Science* 618(1): 80–94.

Horton, Michael. January 2017. "Fighting the Long War: The Evolution of al-Qa'ida in the Arabian Peninsula." Wes Point, NY: *CTC Sentinel* 10(1): 17–22. https://ctc.usma.edu/fighting-the-long-war-the-evolution-of-al-qaida-in-the-arabian-peninsula/

Joshi, Sharad, Gretchen Peters, and Phil Williams. 2015. "The Transnational Security Threat from D-Company," 259–283 in Lawrence E. Cline, and Paul Shemella, eds. *The Future of Counterinsurgency: Contemporary Debates in Security Strategy.* New York, NY: Praeger.

Juergensmeyer, Mark. 2003 (2000). *Terror in the Mind of God: The Global Rise of Religious Violence.* Berkeley, CA: University of California Press.

Kalyanaraman, Balaraman. 2003.

Liff, Adam P., and G. John Ikenberry. Fall 2014. "Racing Toward Tragedy: China's Rise, Military Competition in the Asia-Pacific, and the Security Dilemma," *International Security* 39(2): 52–91.

Long, David E. 1990. *The Anatomy of Terrorism.* New York, NY: The Free Press.

Lynch, Marc. November 2016. "Failed States and Ungoverned Spaces." *The ANNALS of the American Academy of Political and Social Science* 668(1): 24–35.

Moghadam, Assaf. 2017. *Nexus of Global Jihad: Understanding Cooperation Among Terrorist Actors.* New York: Columbia University Press.

Mowatt-Larssen, Rolf. January 2010. "Al Qaeda Weapons of Mass Destruction Threat: Hype or Reality?" Belfer Center for Science and International Affairs, Harvard Kennedy School. http://belfercenter.ksg.harvard.edu/files/al-qaeda-CBRN-threat.pdf

Nanda, Meera. December 31, 2011. "Ideological Convergences: Hindutva and the Norway Massacre." *Economic and Political Weekly.* 46(53): 61–68.

O'Connor, Tom. April 17, 2017. "ISIS Militants Launch Multiple Chemical Weapons Attacks on Iraqi Troops." *Newsweek.*

Pedahzur, Ami, and Arie Perliger. 2009. *Jewish Terrorism in Israel.* New York, NY: Columbia University Press.

Post, Jerrold M. August 2005. "When Hatred is Bred in the Bone: Psycho-cultural Foundations of Contemporary Terrorism," *Political Psychology* 26(4): 615–636.

Ramachandran, Sudha. July 7, 2017. "Hindutva Terrorism in India." *The Diplomat.* http://bit.ly/2hkFg92

Ranstorp, Magnus. Summer 1996. "Terrorism in the Name of Religion." *Journal of International Affairs* 50(1): 41–62.

Saiya, Nilay. 2017. "Blasphemy and Terrorism in the Muslim World," *Terrorism and Political Violence* 29(6): 1087.

Schaper, Annette. 2003. "Nuclear Terrorism: Risk Analysis after 11 September 2001." Frankfurt, Germany: Peace Research Institute. *Disarmament Forum - Nuclear Terrorism* Nbr 2: 7–16.

Schmid, Alex P., and Albert J. Jongman. *Political Terrorism: A New Guide to Actors, Authors, Concepts, Data Bases, Theories and Literature.* New Brunswick: Transaction Publishers.

Shane, Scott. August 27, 2015. "The Lessons of Anwar al-Awlaki." *New York Times Magazine.*

Sprinzak, Ehud. 1995. "Right-Wing Terrorism in a Comparative Perspective: The Case of Split Delegitimization." *Terrorism and Political Violence* 7(1): 17–43.

Wilkinson, Paul. 2011 (2001). *Terrorism Versus Democracy: The Liberal State Response.* London: Routledge.

Williams, Phil. 2008. "Violent Non-State Actors and National and International Security." International Relations and Security Network (ISN), ETH Zurich. https://www.files.ethz.ch/isn/93880/VNSAs.pdf

Yuhas, Alan. January 14, 2015. "How Yemen Spawned the Charlie Hebdo Attacks." *The Guardian.* http://bit.ly/2h7ihu7

Chapter 11

Organized crime and trafficking
Mapping out the threats and actors to find solutions

Colin P. Clarke

Introduction

The July 2011 White House Strategy to Combat Transnational Organized Crime laid out a plan to neutralize the threat posed by the proliferation of criminal networks and markets. Transnational criminal organizations (TCOs) are smart, adaptable, and highly effective at exploiting new criminal opportunities. Effective administrative structures, law enforcement, and customs can inhibit or deter illicit actions, but criminal organizations seek and find opportunities in weak, fragile, and corrupt states by exploiting poor governance and augmenting their power through cooperation with one another, with vulnerable or crooked elites, and with violent extremists.

A global problem with particularly pernicious local, national, and regional manifestations, transnational crime exploits rapid and disruptive change resulting from population growth, shifting migratory patterns, urbanization, technological developments (including highly disruptive technologies—see Manrod's chapter herein), and the ineffective governance that characterizes regions such as the Middle East and Central America. Transnational organized crime is perhaps best understood in terms of criminal hubs, black market routes, and illicit flows, and their interplay with contextual opportunities and constraints. The threats and actors are ubiquitous, but implementing effective solutions has been elusive and short-lived.

This chapter provides a global perspective of transnational organized crime and a systematic overview of the various types of crimes and perpetrators, their *modus operandi*, their organizational structure, and their level of cooperation with each other or other non-state actors. Next, the false promises of neoliberalism as an economic theory for organizing the common good within borders and globally, especially as it relates to TCOs is discussed. Globalization and failed states are other important variables discussed in this analysis. Finally, the chapter argues that despite the praise of neoliberalism from dogmatic elites, not enough attention has been devoted to boosting the contributions that this ideology has provided to our greater understanding of transnational organized crime throughout the world.

What is being trafficked and by whom?

Transnational criminal groups are involved in myriad trafficking and smuggling operations to fund their organizations. Some of the most frequently trafficked commodities include weapons, humans, precious gemstones, and narcotics. With the interconnectedness facilitated by globalization, new market demands have emerged and criminals have rushed in to meet these demands. As these non-state actors have broadened their global reach, the realist mindset focusing on the importance of the state fails to account for this elevated role.

Surplus weaponry flooded the global arms market with the end of the Cold War in the early 1990s. Following the collapse of the Soviet Union, former Eastern Bloc countries inundated the market with everything from small arms to missiles, and mines to nuclear components. As Glenny et al. posit in *McMafia: A Journey Through the Global Criminal Underworld*, "The fall of Communism and the end of superpower proxy regimes in hot spots such as Africa, Southeast Asia, and Latin America generated huge instability for criminals to exploit" (2008, 223). With the closer integration of markets and the broader impact of economic globalization, opportunities expanded for both licit and illicit trade. The growing integration of the European Union and the Schengen Zone agreement also made it easier for criminals to operate within Europe proper, and to link up with smuggling and trafficking networks extending throughout the Balkans and into Turkey, the Caucasus, and beyond.

Different cities throughout the world have become infamous for open-air arms and weapons bazaars: Bangkok, Thailand and Peshawar, Pakistan in the 1970s and 1980s, and the Bakara Market in Mogadishu in the 1990s. Today, weapons are brazenly bought and sold with relative impunity online, including on the Dark Web (Paoli et al. 2017). In Colombia, post-Cold War arms stockpiles, deficient state capacities, and demilitarized zones contributed directly to the development of crime.

Throughout major conflict zones, the AK-47 and AK-57 remain popular assault rifles, valued for their ease of use, low cost, and ready availability (Lal 2007, 157). The surplus of weapons and ammunition in some of the least governed regions of the world helps fuel continued conflict, as witnessed in the Arabian Peninsula, the North Caucasus, the Sahel, and the Levant—and feeds mass migration (see Campbell's chapter herein). During the brutal wars in West Africa in the 1990s (Liberia and Sierra Leone), international arms traffickers from the former Soviet Union, Israel, and South Africa mingled with warlords, diamond merchants, and mercenaries. At the same time, the disintegration of Yugoslavia was driving demand on the global arms market. Reverting to its role as a clearinghouse for trafficked weapons during the Iran–Iraq War (1980–1988), the Balkans once again became a crossroads for a vast array of equipment. Old networks were reinvigorated in an attempt to satisfy market shortages (Bacon 2007, 79–93; Arsovka and Kostakos 2008). This same scenario unfolded over the past several years in Libya, following the violent toppling of longtime dictator Muammar Qaddafi (Estes 2011).

Arms trafficking may soon undergo a major transition, as the advent of additive manufacturing ("3-D printing") could be a disruptor to this industry and its main participants. In 2013, the first 3-D printed gun was successfully created (Morelle 2013). By 2020, the quality of these weapons will improve and it may become easier to produce them on a larger scale, offering opportunities to organized criminals, but also significantly lowering the barrier for entry into this market, which could have lethal second- and third-order effects, while also undercutting the role traditionally enjoyed by traffickers and arms manufacturers.

Each year, hundreds of thousands of women and children are trafficked and forced into prostitution, many of them traveling along the "pipeline of people and contraband" originating from Eastern Europe, Central Asia, the Middle East, Russia, and North Africa destined for Western Europe. Although the global sex trade is a major driver in these operations, humans are trafficked for many reasons, including labor exploitation, which is increasingly common in agriculture, construction, and forced domestic servitude. The trafficking of humans not only provides funding for criminal and terrorist organizations but also fuels worries of lone wolves and sleeper cells infiltrating states undetected and blending into everyday society before attacking. The civil wars in Syria and Libya have fueled human trafficking networks since the **Arab Spring** began in 2011, with Libya now dubbed "the human conveyor belt" for its role at the epicenter of a transcontinental smuggling network of human beings (Micaleff 2017) (see Campbell's chapter herein).

In resource insurgencies, violence entrepreneurs do not seek so much to win control of the state or establish their own government as to eliminate state interference with their exploitation of natural resources (e.g., diamonds, timber). During the brutal civil wars in West Africa throughout the 1990s, the Revolutionary United Front (RUF) acquired weapons either by raiding Sierra Leonean army forward supply posts or by trading diamonds with Liberian warlord Charles Taylor. Where precious gems or stones are unavailable, like in Somalia, non-state actors fighting to control territory throughout the Horn of Africa, including the Al-Qaida linked Al-Shabaab militant group, rely on a range of other criminal activities linked to the exploitation of natural resources, from the illicit ivory trade to the booming market for smuggled charcoal.

The early 2000s have also brought significant diversification in transnational criminal activities. TCOs are now branching out into unorthodox and unconventional categories of goods and products, to include human organs, wildlife, and antiquities.

The crime–terror nexus

In order to properly map out threats and actors to find solutions, it is essential to identify the nature and scope of the threat. Experts roundly disagree over the extent to which a crime-terror nexus exists, and if it does, its strength. This "nexus" debate plays an important role in discerning the organizational structure of the threat posed by organized crime and trafficking syndicates. It also highlights narcotics trafficking, where a nexus is most clearly evident, and which can help provide an analytic framework for the types of responses needed to combat the threat.

> **Text box 11.1: The crime–terror nexus**
>
> The crime-terror nexus includes two independent, but related, components. First, it incorporates the straightforward involvement in criminal activities by terrorists as a source of funding, and second, it refers to the linkages between organized criminal organizations and terrorist groups. Indeed, the criminal and political organizations appear to be learning from each other, adopting each other's tactics and strategies, and frequently partnering with one another.

Despite much debate and research on the nexus between TCOs and terrorism, very little is known about how strong this convergence might be (Reitano 2017). Moreover, the concept of a nexus should not be applied globally. While a nexus may exist among groups in South Asia, and in areas of weak governance and weak rule of law, no such thing may be present in North America, Europe, and comparably managed areas. There is, therefore, no "one size fits all" application of the nexus between TCOs and terrorism. Indeed, there is a markedly different situation between comparable developed countries and regions that are suffering to various degrees from conflict and wider developmental challenges, particularly where there is a dearth of rule-of-law mechanisms and state institutions (see Simoni's chapter herein). The area in which the nexus presents itself most clearly is narcotics trafficking, where a nefarious comingling of criminals, terrorists, and corrupt state officials collude to profit from the sale of illicit drugs.

Due to the high value and the low volume-to-value ratio of illicit narcotics (cocaine, ecstasy, heroin, hashish, marijuana, methamphetamine, opiates, etc.) and the availability of chemical precursors required to manufacture these drugs, this criminal activity is very attractive for criminals and terrorists. The narcotics trade in drug-producing countries may also provide terrorists with recruits and sympathizers among impoverished, neglected, isolated farmers who can help cultivate drug crops while also serving as a bulwark against pro-government groups and anti-drug campaigns. Farmers have also resorted to drug crops for lack of better options.

Involvement in the narcotics trade can bring together terrorist or insurgent groups and drug cartels (Dishman 2005). The demise of the latter could also present opportunities for terrorists or insurgents to fill the void, as in Colombia when the far left guerrilla organization FARC took over some of the territory previously controlled by the Medellin and Cali drug cartels in the 1990s. Other times, as with the Kurdistan Workers' Party (PKK) and its drug trafficking activities in Europe, rather than cooperate with traditional criminal enterprises, insurgent or terrorist groups seek to drive them out of the market in order to supplant them (Williams 2012, 32–33, 46). Finally, as in the case with the relationship between drug traffickers and *Sendero Luminoso* (Shining Path) in Peru, the dominant party in the relationship can change over time. In the 1990s, a powerful and brutal *Sendero* held sway, while beginning in the mid-2000s—especially in the Valley of the Apurimac and Ene River (VRAE)—the insurgents have played a more secondary role (Williams 2012, 32–33, 46).

Narcotics remains the most common and most lucrative form of criminal activity used by terrorist groups, including well-known traffickers like the Kosovo Liberation Army (KLA) (Dishman 2005, 245–246), Basque Homeland and Liberty (ETA) in Spain, and the Islamic Movement of Uzbekistan (IMU). Profits derived from drug trafficking have enabled groups like FARC to obtain sophisticated weapons and communications technology (Sanderson 2004, 51–53). A 2014 investigation in Australia uncovered 40 separate money laundering operations, one of which delivered proceeds from drug trafficking to Hezbollah (McKenzie and Baker 2014). The cultivation of illicit crops like poppy or coca is labor-intensive and provides employment to hundreds of thousands, perhaps even millions, of people in countries such as Afghanistan and Colombia respectively (Felbab-Brown 2012).

The examples of insurgent and terrorist groups relying on criminal activities to fund their organizations, particularly drug trafficking, are abundant in both historical and contemporary cases. From the Cold War era to modern times, the examples span ethno-nationalist groups, separatists, Marxist-oriented organizations, and religious groups alike, making it difficult to predict which groups may be more or less likely to rely on this method of raising funds.

Among the most prolific terrorist organizations to rely on narcotics trafficking to fund its activities was the Liberation Tigers of Tamil Eelam (LTTE) in Sri Lanka. Involvement in the drug trade first became apparent as early as 1984 when Swiss police reported that Tamils were responsible for trafficking approximately 20 percent of the heroin coming into the country (Weiss 2011). The "Tamil connection" in Switzerland was eventually dismantled by the police, although the drug market in Sri Lanka itself expanded, with an estimated 100,000 users by the end of the 1990s (Williams 2012). Sri Lanka's geographic proximity to the **Golden Triangle** of Laos, Myanmar, and Thailand, combined with the LTTE's advanced maritime capabilities made heroin trafficking an obvious racket for the group to pursue. The LTTE also extended operations into Pakistan, where its members used the port city of Karachi to solidify a foothold in South Asia and diversify smuggling activities to include humans, in addition to heroin (Williams 2008, 139).

Two well-known terrorist groups in the Middle East have both been associated with involvement in the drug trade at various points: Hezbollah and Hamas. In 2004, the Federal Bureau of Investigation (FBI) accused known Hezbollah supporters and brothers, Ali and Hassan Farhat, of trafficking in cocaine, heroin, and marijuana, in collaboration with a Nigerian drug dealer in possession of a Canadian immigration document (Levitt 2013). More broadly, Hezbollah has also dealt methamphetamine and in the last several years has been receptive to a burgeoning relationship with Mexican drug cartels. Hezbollah operatives have been accused of trafficking in arms, drugs, and women. Hezbollah operatives have also been tied to drug operations in Poland, Hungary, Moldova, the Balkans, and Romania (Levitt 2013, 227, 320).

Throughout the mid to late 1990s, Hamas took advantage of the Muslim diaspora in South America's semi-lawless **Triple Frontier**, a region known for money laundering, drug trafficking, and a host of other illicit and unsavory activities (Sanderson 2004, 51–53). Hamas—perhaps emulating Hezbollah—established partnerships with various drug trafficking organizations in the infamous Latin American region (Ribando et al. 2011, 6–8). The group has also been involved with drugs in the United States, at least on the margins—a pseudoephedrine smuggling scam in the Midwest in the United States involved bank accounts tied to Hamas (Levitt 2013, 227, 320; Levitt 2015, 10).

As the noose was tightened around charities that funded Al Qaida after the terrorist attacks of 9/11, the group attempted to diversify its revenue sources to include garnering money earned through drug trafficking, particularly through both an alliance with the Islamic Movement of Uzbekistan (IMU) in Central Asia and in North Africa by one of its affiliates. In the latter case, Al Qaida in the Islamic Maghreb (AQIM) has been linked to Colombian cocaine traffickers in a quid pro quo relationship that brings cash to the terrorists while providing the traffickers with unfettered access (and in some cases, heavily armed escorts) across the desert region between Mauritania, Mali, and Algeria, where narcotics transit through on their way to a growing European market. In addition to money obtained through kidnapping, AQIM earns significant sums of money from trafficking untaxed cigarettes and synthetic drugs between Spain and Algeria (del Cid Gomez 2010).

Perhaps the most prolific terrorist organization associated with drug trafficking today is the Afghan Taliban. On narcotics, the Taliban's position has evolved considerably throughout the years, and at different points, the group has knowingly suppressed the cultivation of poppy in Afghanistan in order to manipulate the international market price. At one point, a Taliban ban on poppy cultivation suppressed the supply by 90 percent, thus increasing the value of the group's stocks ten-fold (Felbab-Brown 2006). Once the insurgency began in earnest in late 2001, Taliban fighters maneuvered shrewdly, including through loans to opium farmers in order to obtain their backing while simultaneously ensuring a future source of revenue (Peters 2009). Keeping in line with its renewed offensive to win "hearts and minds," the Taliban now actively promotes the farming of poppy and provides protection to farmers cultivating the crop (Brahimi 2010, 9).

The future of the nexus

The wave of migrants flooding Europe since the onset of the Syrian civil war in 2011 demonstrates the ability of transnational criminal networks to smuggle and traffic migrants with relative ease, even as nation-states struggle to cope with the onslaught (Tinti and Reitano 2017). A common policy refrain has been—in a reversion yet again to the Cold War realist mindset—to erect barriers, build walls, and strengthen porous borders. But in reality, it has proven more difficult to "turn back the clock" and reverse engineer well-entrenched facets of globalization and integration. Moreover, in both the United States and Europe, the issue has proven to be highly divisive and driven by political ideology, and solutions remain elusive (see Campbell's chapter herein). The current wave of migration since the early 2010s has the potential to be far more relevant to future configurations of a TCO–terrorism nexus. Unless new migrants are better integrated than their predecessors, they could become the recruiting pool for tomorrow's transnational criminal (and/or extremist) organizations. Some of the migrants will not be adequately assimilated into their host countries, despite renewed attention to public policies designed specifically to address this immense challenge.

The response to the movement of people from Africa and the Middle East to Europe has been the emergence of a vast, sprawling network of networks that involves different kinds of groups and individuals and, according to the Director of Europol, Rob Wainwright, could number as many as 30,000 people (Deutsch 2015). Although migrants are usually eager to start anew in their adopted countries, some are members of criminal organizations and bring with them illegal skills and knowledge, as well as illicit affiliations and contacts (Clunan and Trinkunas 2010).

For criminals looking to expand their base of operations, recently arrived migrants who are not well integrated into society or the licit economy—who survive on the fringes of the official economy and resort to the black market—are the ideal type of recruits. Diaspora communities can provide cover and logistical functions that facilitate illicit activities, but their reputation for criminality can also inhibit ethnic diasporas' integration and job opportunities. The future of the nexus will also be complicated further by technological advancements, including but not limited to encryption, virtual currencies, the evolution of 3-D printing, and the dark web (see Manrod's chapter herein).

Text box 11.2: The dark web

The dark web is the www content that exists on darknets, overlay networks that use the internet but require specific software, configurations, or authorization to access. It forms a small part of the deep web, the part of the web not indexed by search engines, although sometimes the term *deep web* is mistakenly used to refer specifically to the dark web. Many illicit goods, substances, and services are bought and sold on the dark web, complicating the mission of law enforcement (see Manrod's chapter herein).

The failure of neoliberalism as organizer of common good and security

Just as there is no universally accepted consensus or theory on how best to conduct global counter-terrorism operations or deter rogue states from pursuing nuclear weapons programs, so too is there a dearth of agreement on what role the international community, regional organizations, or the nation-state should play in countering transnational organized crime operations. The matter is complicated by the vast disparity in both capability and political will of individual nations, state governments, and local actors.

In many ways, neoliberalism puts forth an intellectual rationale for the nation-state to cede not only power and authority but also the responsibility for the welfare and security of its citizens. Despite no shortage of lip service paid to the benefits of good governance—repeated *ad nauseam* throughout the early 21st century—globalization and neoliberalism have indeed served to undermine the foundations of the state. This corrosion of authority has contributed to what can only be understood as a pervasive and widespread crisis of governance. Clunan and Trinkunas highlight the irony that "Western liberalism created the criteria for 'good governance' that states are expected to adhere to today, while at the same time undermining the ideological legitimacy and institutional capacity of state authority" (Clunan and Trinkunas 2010, 5). Many entities have failed to recognize the juxtaposition of these competing agendas, which often work at cross-purposes.

By elevating the market and capital accumulation above all else, neoliberalism has helped create conditions that favor transnational criminals (Gilman 2016, 47–60). TCOs are perhaps a representation of neoliberalism in its purest form. These entities respond to market demand, operate beyond traditional notions of ethics and morality (the market is natural and therefore amoral), and focus ruthlessly and single-mindedly on profit maximization. From this orientation, TCOs should be understood as the ultimate expression of unfettered and predatory capitalism. Neoliberalism fails as a security construct precisely because of its excessive focus on profits, its lack of ethical accountability, and the amoral activities often associated with this dogmatic and ruthless approach to markets. Other external negativities of market activity include social and economic polarization, the crisis of representative government, populist backlash, and the general insecurity wrought not only through the fraying of the social fabric but also throughout environmental degradation and climate change.

Another major facet of globalization—global connectivity—also comes with its own baggage. In a highly connected world, contagion is an ever-present possibility. Nation-states have never actually been the impermeable hard shells (the "billiard balls") imagined by realist theory. Border crossings and border transactions have increased exponentially in both volume and speed, while the type and flow of commodities across borders have also expanded. One of the main pillars of sovereignty—a state's capacity to determine who and what enters or exits its borders—has been significantly eroded, in part by the sheer volume of traffic flow and in part from the dominance of the "free-for-all" market ideology of neoliberalism. Other factors that are impossible to ignore include the expansion of smuggling and trafficking flows that governments have proved unable (or in some cases unwilling) to blunt.

Globalization is, in essence, about connectivity and the speed, ease, and low-cost of global interactions (Held 2004). Accordingly, globalization has facilitated vast flows of both goods and information on a level heretofore unseen. The constant movement of people, money, commodities, data, messages, digital signals, and services all combine to form a global "space of flows" (Castells 2004). Game-changing innovations have transformed the way people live, work, travel, and trade. The **intermodal** and the internet are just two contemporary examples. The former led to remarkably low transportation and transaction costs, while the latter, along with mobile communication systems, created seemingly unlimited opportunities for endless types of interactions. Markets have most certainly become truly global and provide unprecedented opportunities to millions throughout the developing world, while also helping to alleviate global poverty. Still, the persistent volatility of market dynamics has numerous disruptive effects, further exacerbated by the constant migration of jobs to countries with the lowest labor costs, and a lack of economic resilience in many developing countries.

As a result, globalization has created many winners and many more losers. Vast swaths of victimized populations have been excluded from the benefits of globalization and are seriously hurt by market dynamics. Instead of being saved by globalization, hundreds of millions of people have been deliberately expelled from the global economy because neoliberalism is intrinsically exploitative (Sassken 2014). These individuals and groups are forced to survive in "zones of social exclusion," a phrase popularized by Manuel Castells (Castells 1998, 71–72). Such zones are economic, social, and political, and are common throughout Central Asia, Sub-Saharan Africa, as well as parts of Latin America and the Caribbean, and in South and Southeast Asia. These negative dynamics have been reinforced and even accelerated by neoliberalism, which has become ingrained as the ideological rationale for economic deregulation, trade liberalization, and privatization (including of security and law enforcement), for the reduction of social welfare provision and the relegation of efforts to pursue "the public good…by enhancing civil society and social justice" (Steger and Roy 2010, 12).

For decades, globalization has facilitated, at least in part, "the retreat of the state" and "the softening of sovereignty," while increasing the porosity of borders (Strange 1996). Furthermore, in many countries, neoliberalism encouraged the state to relinquish power and authority, which in turn led states to forsake their responsibility for the welfare and security of their citizens. Even while promoting the benefits of good governance, reduced corruption, and strengthened rule of law (without offering much advice on how to actually achieve these indicators of progress), globalization and neoliberalism in many ways enervated the foundation of the nation-state. This is especially true for those states that never met the **Westphalian ideal** in the first place and were perennially weak, and lacking the resources to change their status.

In many societies, especially since the **Great Recession**, the result has been the atomization of the public or collective interest, the decline of social capital, and a renewed upsurge in *anomie* (normative and cultural destructuring), or violence for the sake of violence, accompanied by the proliferation of tribalism. As opposed to fostering closer integration, neoliberalism has led many people to revert to familiar social networks and identify more closely with the ethnic, familial, and patronage networks that may have been dormant, or to turn to criminal activities to survive. After all, these networks never really disappeared but were instead covered by the veneer of free-market capitalism and its proponents (Fukuyama 2014; Putnam 2013, 68–76; Ronfeldt 2007). The erosion of the state could very well intensify in the near future if globalization is simply consolidated.

Ironically, transnational criminal networks sometimes also provide a safety net for casualties or losers of globalization who, unless they have the means and wherewithal to migrate to locales where economic opportunities are available, become trapped in poorer nations, where they enjoy no rights of citizenship and are vulnerable to forced servitude, slavery, and—especially for women and children—sexual exploitation. Many have little recourse than migrating from the licit economy through its seams and gaps to its dark and sordid underbelly.

Beginning as a mass global movement in the 1990s, following on the success of populist politicians in Europe, and accelerating with the election of Donald Trump in the United States in 2016, the anti-globalist impulse has encouraged and facilitated the reassertion of state prerogatives. In some other very tangible ways, it has even enjoyed a modicum of success in rolling back key aspects of globalization, such as the 2017 rejection of the Trans-Pacific Partnership (TPP) by the Trump administration. The rejection of neoliberalism in favor of a more balanced and less permissive relationship between the state and the market and a new emphasis on the provision of **collective goods** could limit the opportunities for criminal organizations to provide alternative governance (see Campbell's and Garrett's chapters herein).

Conclusion

States and international organizations need to make greater progress in countering transnational organized crime, especially in developing countries and weak states, where corruption, the weak rule of law, and weak governance remain significant challenges to progress and peace. A mix of educational programs and concerted multinational efforts to degrade and destroy trafficking networks could put the human trafficking business into recession. Continued efforts to slow down global climate change, coupled with an emphasis on consequence mitigation and urban resilience, could go a long way in helping the most vulnerable nations. In short, the solutions to countering transnational organized criminal organizations must be crafted across governments and include a wide range of stakeholders, from NGOs to the private sector. Moving beyond traditional theories of economics and security, and reassessing the conventional wisdom of neoliberalism, can help governments and policymakers approach new and emerging threats with a flexible and responsive framework that is not tied to rigid dogmas, old and new.

Questions for discussion

1   What effect does a terrorist group's involvement in criminal activities have on the organization? Do criminal groups ever engage in terrorism?
2   Describe the impact of globalization on the activities of transnational criminal organizations. Does globalization make it easier or harder for criminals to operate? Why?
3   How does transnational crime exploit rapid and disruptive change resulting from population growth, shifting migratory patterns, urbanization, and technological developments?
4   How have the civil wars in Libya and Syria contributed to an increase in transnational criminal activities?
5   Should countering transnational crime be elevated to a higher priority on the overall agenda of "hard" security issues?
6   What role will "the rise of the right" and broader anti-globalism impulses have on transnational organized crime throughout the world?

References

Arsovka, Jana, and Panos A. Kostakos. 2008. "Illicit Arms Trafficking and the Limits of Rational Choice Theory: The Case of the Balkans." *Trends in Organized Crime* 11(4): 352–378.

Bacon, Esther A. 2007. "Balkan Trafficking in Historical Perspective." In Kimberly L. Thachuk, *Transnational Threats*. Westport, CT: Praeger.

Brahimi, Alia. July 2010. "The Taliban's Evolving Ideology." London School of Economics Global Governance Working Paper WP 02/2010.

Castells, Manuel. 1998. *End of Millennium*. Malden, MA: Blackwell.

Castells, Manuel. 2004. "An Introduction to the Information Age" 138–149. In Frank Webster, Raimo Blom, Erkki Karvonen, Harri Melin, Kaarle Nordenstreng, and Ensio Puoskari, eds. *The Information Society Reader*. London: Routledge.

Clunan, Anne L., and Harold A. Trinkunas, eds. 2010. *Ungoverned Spaces: Alternatives to State Authority in an Era of Softened Sovereignty*. Stanford, CA: Stanford Security Studies.

del Cid Gomez, Juan Miguel. October 2010. "A Financial Profile of the Terrorism of Al-Qaeda and Its Affiliates." *Perspectives on Terrorism* 4(4):12–23.

Deutsch, Anthony. September 16, 2015. "Europol Tracking 30,000 Suspected People Smugglers." *Reuters*.

Dishman, Chris. 2005. "The Leaderless Nexus: When Crime and Terror Converge." *Studies in Conflict & Terrorism* 28(3): 237–252.

Estes, Adam Clark. October 25, 2011. "Libya's Awash in Qaddafi's Golden Guns and Other Weapons." *The Atlantic*.

Felbab-Brown, Vanda. Summer 2006. "Kicking the Opium Habit? Afghanistan's Drug Economy and Politics since the 1980s." *Conflict, Security, and Development* 6(2): 127–149.

Felbab-Brown, Vanda. April 19, 2012. "Fighting the Nexus of Organized Crime and Violent Conflict while Enhancing Human Security." In *Drug Trafficking, Violence, and Instability*. Carlisle Barracks, PA: Strategic Studies Institute of the U.S. Army War College.

Fukuyama, Francis. September–October 2014. "America in Decay: The Sources of Political Dysfunction." *Foreign Affairs*.

Gilman, Nils. 2016. "The Twin Insurgencies: Plutocrats and Criminals Challenge the Westphalian State," 47–60. In Hilary Matfess and Michael Miklaucic, eds., *Beyond Convergence: World Without Order. October 2016*. Washington, DC: Center for Complex Operations, Institute for National Strategic Studies, National Defense University.

Glenny, Misha et al. 2008. *McMafia: A Journey Through the Global Criminal Underworld*. New York: Knopf, 2008.

Held, David, ed. 2004. *A Globalizing World? Culture, Economics, Politics*. London: Routledge.

Lal, Rollie 2007. "South Asian Organized Crime and Linkages to Terrorist Networks." In Kimberly L. Thachuk, *Transnational Threats: Smuggling and Trafficking in Arms, Drugs, and Human Life*. Westport CT: Praeger.

Levitt, Matthew. 2013. *Hezbollah: The Global Footprint of Lebanon's Party of God*. Washington, DC: Georgetown University Press, 320.

Levitt, Matthew. May 25, 2015. "Hezbollah: Financing Terror Through Criminal Enterprise." Testimony presented to United States Senate Committee on Homeland Security and Governmental Affairs.

McKenzie, Nick and Richard Baker. January 23, 2014. "Terrorists Taking Cut of Millions in Drug Money." *The Canberra Times*.

Micaleff, Mark. March 2017. "The Human Conveyor Belt: Trends in Human Trafficking and Smuggling in Post-Revolution Libya." *Global Initiative Against Transnational Organized Crime*.

Morelle, Rebecca. May 6, 2013. "Working Gun Made with 3D Printer." *BBC News*.

Paoli, Giacomo Persi et al. 2017. *Behind the Curtain: The Illicit Trade of Firearms, Explosives and Ammunition on the Dark Web*. Santa Monica, CA: RAND Corporation.

Peters, Gretchen. 2009. *Seeds of Terror: How Drugs, Thugs, and Crime Are Reshaping the Afghan War.* New York: St Martin's.

Putnam, Robert. 2013. "Bowling Alone: America's Declining Social Capital," 68–76. In Jan Lin and Christopher Mele, eds. *The Urban Sociology Reader.* New York: Routledge.

Reitano, Tuesday, et al. April 13, 2017. "Examining the Nexus Between Organized Crime and Terrorism and Its Implications for EU Programming." International Centre for Counter-Terrorism (ICCT)-The Hague.

Ribando Seelke, Clare, Liana Sun Wyler, June S. Beittel, and Mark P. Sullivan. May 12, 2011. "Latin America and the Caribbean: Illicit Drug Trafficking and U.S. Counterdrug Programs." Congressional Research Services Report R41215. Washington, DC: Library of Congress, 6.

Ronfeldt, David. 2007. *In Search of How Societies Work: Tribes—The First and Forever Form.* Santa Monica, CA: RAND Corporation.

Sanderson, Thomas M. Winter–Spring 2004. "Transnational Terror and Organized Crime: Blurring the Lines." *SAIS Review* XXIV(1): 49–61. Project MUSE, doi:10.1353/sais.2004.0020.

Sassken, Sasia. 2014. *Expulsions: Brutality and Complexity in the Global Economy.* Boston, Mass.: Harvard University Press.

Steger, Manfred B., and Ravi K. Roy 2010. *Neoliberalism: A Very Short Introduction.* New York: Oxford University Press.

Strange, Susan. 1996. *The Retreat of the State.* Cambridge University Press.

Tinti, Peter and Tuesday Reitano. 2017. *Migrant, Refugee, Smuggler, Savior.* New York: Oxford University Press.

Weiss, Gordon. 2011. *The Cage: The Fight for Sri Lanka and the Last Days of the Tamil Tigers.* London: Bodley Head, 89.

Williams, Phil. 2008. "Terrorist Financing and Organized Crime: Nexus, Appropriation, or Transformation?" 126–148. In Thomas J. Biersteker, Sue E. Eckert and Nikos Passas, eds. *Countering the Financing of Terrorism.* London: Routledge.

Williams, Phil. April 2012. "Insurgencies and Organized Crime," 27–72. In Phil Williams and Vanda Felbabd-Brown. *Drug Trafficking, Violence, and Instability.* Carlisle Barracks, PA: US Army War College Strategic Studies Institute.

Chapter 12

Transnational organized crime and globalization

Godmothers of the Mafia and the undermining of the Italian state and society

Serena Simoni

Introduction

"I am not a man, I am a woman, but only on the outside (...) Inside, I am more man than you. And here, in Naples, I rule," declared Nunzia D'Amico, one of the highest-profile female bosses of the *Camorra* (Reguly and Tondo 2016). D'Amico ruled her criminal empire until October 10, 2015 when a few yards from her apartment and in broad daylight, a hooded man shot her four times. Blood sprayed the stroller where her baby slept. "The Godmother" was killed like a true godfather. She was 37. Traditionally, mafia women, especially those with young children, were considered off-limits to mafia homicide. Usually, men killed other men. But, since the mid to late 1990s, with the constant imprisonment of male mafia bosses, the wives, sisters, and daughters of these kingpins began to increasingly assume leadership roles. Women bosses rapidly ceased to be a novelty; their numbers rose dramatically within just two decades. These women know the rules of the mafia from the inside, and with the arrests of scores of male relatives, they stepped up to lead the clans. According to the Italian Ministry of Justice, more than 150 women linked to the mafia were in jail in 2017, a record high, and almost all of them had leadership positions in various Italian transnational crime (TNC) organizations including the *Cosa Nostra* in Sicily, the *Camorra* in Naples, the 'Ndrangheta in Calabria, and the *Sacra Corona Unita* in Apulia.

This dramatic story reveals a deeper trend in the feminization of crime and the criminalization of state and society in Italy. This chapter analyzes a seldom-discussed phenomenon, the feminization of crime leadership, and focuses on the Italian case study because it is the most advanced case of feminization of crime, and the most deleterious example of state and society erosion among all developed democracies. The first part sketches the types of threats that mafias pose to the state; the second offers an examination of women in Italian mafia and their emergence; the third details the impact of mafia on global governance; and the fourth suggests some potential advantages of adopting a constructivist approach.

This chapter discusses the origins of various mafias, the process of feminization of leadership, their toll on society and state security, and their functions as counter-state. We explore some of the challenges that nation–states are confronting from within their own borders and how such challenges constitute threats to international security. Furthermore, we analyze how TNC organizations pose a serious threat to both state governance and international security, using the specific example of the Neapolitan *Camorra* vis-à-vis the Italian state. Additionally, we question the framing of masculine hegemonic identities that are commonly reinforced by approaches to security studies both in IR and in feminist security studies. The analysis contributes to IR feminist approaches because they tend not to analyze women who engage as perpetrators of violence. In line with the constructivist claim (Jepperson, Wendt and Katzenstein 1996, 33) that cultural environments affect both state behavior as well as the fundamental character of states, we argue that TNC organizations co-opt state structures and institutions in an attempt to neutralize them. Within this context, if we consider that regional and local governments function as consumers in the norms market and that co-opted officials have incentives to reject accepted global norms governing crime, co-optation as a mechanism begins to explain actual changes in the patterns of the diffusion of anti-crime norms on an international scale.

Types of threats: How mobsters challenge the state's sovereignty

Text box 12.1: Italian mafias—origins and common features

Italian criminal organizations are known all over the world, so much so that the term "mafia" is internationally understood as referring to organized crime. An understanding of the origins of Italian organized crime must begin with the Sicilian mafia, particularly *Cosa Nostra*, the oldest, most traditional, and, probably most famous organization of its kind. Part of the notoriety of *Cosa Nostra* is due to its spectacular representation in popular movies like *The Godfather*, for example. In reality, this branch of the mafia is neither picturesque nor amusing. To the contrary, it is a ruthless and cynical criminal organization that controls large areas of the Italian regional island of Sicily and is dangerously influential in politics, society, and on economic life. The influence of the *Cosa Nostra* is not confined to the island of Sicily or to Italy; indeed, it branches out and reaches communities of expatriates all over the world. Its international expansion has mainly been directed towards North America. *Cosa Nostra* has been particularly active in cocaine trafficking, and it also manages strings of legitimate businesses for money laundering purposes and, in so doing, has infiltrated the economy of countries such as South Africa, Canada, the United States, Venezuela and Spain.

Another leading Italian criminal organization is the Calabrian *'Ndrangheta*, which is currently the most powerful of Italy's criminal organizations at a global level. For a long time, it was underestimated as a rural and backward organization, but in recent decades, its influence has expanded rapidly, spreading operations to many countries. There are several reasons for this rapid expansion. Mainly, in the 1980s and 1990s, the Italian government focused its attention on *Cosa Nostra*, bringing the Sicilian Mafia to downscale its presence in some markets, and *'Ndrangheta* quickly filled the vacuum. Moreover, *'Ndrangheta* had considerable amounts of cash to invest due to kidnappings that were carried out in the 1970s and 1980s, charging exorbitant ransoms, especially in the wealthy areas of Northern Italy. The extorted money was efficiently invested in drug trafficking, which made *'Ndrangheta* the richest and most powerful criminal organization in the world. Much like *Cosa Nostra*, *'Ndrangheta* is hierarchical in structure and has been able to meticulously infiltrate the Italian political and economic environments because of this abundant liquidity. Indeed, the organization reached a position of quasi-monopoly in sectors such as construction, real estate, and transport.

The third Italian Mafia, *Camorra*, is based in Naples. Unlike *Cosa Nostra* and *'Ndrangheta*, Neapolitan *Camorra* has a horizontal structure made of a cluster of clans that are engaged in constant internal strife for the control of the territory of Naples—and of the whole Campania region. A distinctive characteristic of *Camorra* is its use of extreme violence. In the 1980s and 1990s, a war between two internal groups for the control of territory resulted in the deaths of thousands of *Camorra* members. *Camorra* bosses also maintain very high profiles and flashy lifestyles, something that strongly distinguishes them from their Sicilian and Calabrian counterparts. They own extravagant houses, drive expensive cars, and wear designer clothes and shoes. *Camorra* bosses, in the collective imagination, are the stereotypical *mafioso* bosses. Akin to the *Sopranos*, their businesses include primarily drug trafficking, illicit waste dumping, cigarette smuggling, and sale of counterfeit products. *Camorra's* presence is global too.

Lastly, Apulia's organized crime syndicate has heterogeneous structures with strategies different from its counterparts. It is based mainly in Bari, Foggia, as well as the Salento area, and its most powerful clans include *Società Foggiana* and *Sacra Corona Unita*. These clans, similar to the other Italian mafias, have also infiltrated the politics and the economy of the region, and have traditionally been involved in smuggling, trafficking (i.e. cigarettes, human beings, drugs, weapons), and illegal waste disposal. Their outreach, however, is more modest than their counterparts, spreading mainly through the Netherlands, Germany, Switzerland, and Albania.

The situation in Italy is difficult to track because the *Camorra's* activities, like all the activities of the different mafias, are dynamic and clandestine. What is more, as is the case with other global issues, the behavior of mobsters depends on a complex interconnection of interests and opportunities. Not surprisingly, there is evidence that the *Camorra* constitutes a serious threat to both international security and governance. In a report entitled *The Globalization of Crime*, the United Nations Office on Drugs and Crime contends: "Mafias are today truly a transnational problem: a threat to security, especially in poor and conflict-ridden countries. Crime is fueling corruption, infiltrating business and politics, and hindering development. And it is undermining governance by empowering those who operate outside the law" (UNODC 2010, ii). In the majority of cases states deal with these threats nationally and/or through multilateral responses, but in some cases the states are powerless to act. At times, as in the Italian case, criminal organizations co-opt state institutions, compromise them, and ultimately neutralize them. Therefore, criminal organizations constitute a threat for governance as well as for security.

In Campania, the region surrounding Naples, the *Camorra* controls the entire territory through illegal means, robbing the state de facto of its power. For example, it buys votes and controls every aspect of the electoral race in the regional elections. In exchange, the voter receives money (Saviano, 2010). This modus operandi delegitimizes the state's sovereignty. Political candidates are not elected democratically and since the criminal organization has paid for the success of the candidate who wins, that official will be indebted to the criminal organization and hopelessly corrupt. It is precisely this sense of debt that, in the end, undermines governance: when voting rests solidly in the hands of criminal organizations—for both national and local elections—the state's sovereignty is compromised.

Co-optation is a common phenomenon in Campania and the connection between the clans and politics is public: politicians need the organization's support to win the elections and accordingly candidates openly ask to be supported. Maurizio Presteri, a former boss who has repented and is now collaborating with investigators, recalls that in March 2001, a few months before the elections in Naples, he was on his balcony looking down on the street and spotted a politician—running for re-election—followed by a large group of people, whom the *Camorra* had instructed to cheer. Despite police bodyguards, the candidate started waving to the boss; even sending kisses his way as he approached his house. The politician and the boss then approached each other, hugged, and kissed while the people applauded the scene (Saviano, 2011). The candidate needed the boss' support to be elected and therefore he passed by his house to show that he had gained it. Meanwhile, onlookers saw that the boss supported the politician and understood how to vote.

> **Text box 12.2: How the mafia buys votes**
>
> The mechanism is quite simple. A member of *Camorra* corrupts an official who monitors the voting procedures and manages the electoral ballots. That official takes an unmarked ballot out of the polling station and delivers it to the criminal organization. Incidentally, Italy still uses paper ballots. The criminal organization then selects the designated or the "affiliated" candidate and the completed ballot is then given to a voter. That voter pockets the ballot and walks to the polling station where he/she is given a regular blank ballot. Inside the voting booth the voter exchanges the blank ballot with the pre-marked ballot. The completed ballot is cast and the blank one is pocketed and taken out of the polling station. Once the voter is out of the station he/she will give the blank ballot to the mobster who will fill it out and the merry-go-round will start all over again.

The selling and buying of votes constitutes a challenge to governance. Criminal organizations are always seeking new opportunities to further undermine the state's sovereignty and to neutralize its institutions. In 2010, Beppe Pisanu, then President of the Italian Antimafia Commission, cautioned that nowadays the various mafias do not limit themselves to a supporting role, they are jumping into the race by nominating their own men, thus the candidates are themselves mobsters with expertise in politics and business. The Commission estimated that about ten per cent of the candidates in the administrative elections in 2010 had already been condemned, or were on trial, for their association to a mafia organization (Foschini and Sannino 2010). The attempt to neutralize political structures and institutions is prominent in Campania. As a consequence of the *Camorra*'s deep penetration into Italian politics, the Campania region is the area with the highest number of cities under observation for *Camorra* infiltration, and since 1991, 71 municipal administrations in that region have been dissolved (Saviano 2008, 46).

The *Camorra*'s penetration of politics is blatant and capillary. Likewise, the phenomenon of co-opting institutions is threatening to make the state lose one of its principal rights —the right to make decisions and enforce authority with regard to a specific territory and population. In the Southern Italian regions (i.e. Campania, Calabria, Puglia and Sicily) the situation is grim, but other parts of the country are not immune. Political corruption is proliferating in the Central and Northern regions as well (EURISPES 2010). In July 2010, in Lombardy, where Milan is the major city, 300 people were arrested for their association to the mafia. One of them was Carlo Chiriaco, director of the national health services in Lombardy; another was Pietro Trivi, former city council member. Both stood accused of irregularly allocating public works' contracts and electoral corruption (Corvi 2011, 11). Chiriaco and Trivi allegedly paid 2,000 euros to obtain 150 votes in the 2009 municipal elections.

In Italy, sizable areas of the country are living in "legal limbo" because criminal organizations have in effect suspended legality by controlling the economy and by penetrating political institutions. For example, in 2008 there were 106 mafia-related homicides in Italy. In Campania alone, the total number of homicides was 59, which is about 55 percent of the national toll. The mafia's penetration also constitutes a threat to the security of the people or so-called "personal security," for the state is deprived of the right to protect citizens from physical violence perpetrated by sub-national actors such as criminal organizations.

Criminal organizations are also nibbling away at another responsibility of the state: providing "economic security"—that is assuring basic income, through productive and remunerative work, or from the publicly financed safety net (UNDP 1994). Unemployment, therefore, becomes an important source of strength for criminal organizations as it empowers them. The *Camorra* is a multi-million dollar enterprise that offers well-paid jobs in poor areas beset by high unemployment rates. In essence, these criminal organizations are neutralizing the state by becoming "personal" as well as "economic" security providers. On the one hand, organized crime offers personal security similar to law enforcement or militarily controlling the territory and, on the other, it delivers economic security through jobs—often illegal but jobs nonetheless. The globalization of trade, technology, transportation, communications, information, and financial systems provide new opportunities for criminal enterprises to operate across national borders. *Camorra* has exploited these new mechanisms to become a vast economic empire that branches out thorough legal and illegal activities. *Camorra* set up shops everywhere in the European Union and neighboring countries. The Secondigliano clans crossed the Atlantic, investing in Canada, the US and South America. The American network is immense. Counterfeited jeans are sold in shops and shopping malls in New York, Miami, and Chicago, with *Camorra* involvement. *Camorra* controls a vast network of underworld figures in the port of Naples, the point of entry for great quantities of merchandise. In Campania, it manages clandestine workshops, undocumented workers, and an unusual alliance with Chinese organized crime. Highly skilled workers turn out low-cost counterfeits that are high quality and identical to the originals from the big fashion houses. These clothes, bags, and shoes are sold in boutiques or shopping malls owned by *Camorra* all over Europe and the United States. *Camorra* also finances factories by lending them money at low rates and gives mortgages to these workers. *Camorra* is also involved in other legal activities such as restaurants, hotels, and casinos.

However, organized crime also branches out through most well-known illegal activities: trafficking in weapons, drug trafficking and human trafficking (see Clarke's chapter herein). The *Camorra* handles a large slice of international arms market where it can actually set the price of an AK-47 (Kalashnikov). *Camorra* is a global issue for it also influences human rights. To assess the state of human rights, analysts consider the price of an AK-47. The less it costs, the greater the number of human rights violations. As it can set the price of AK-47s, the *Camorra* is becoming the indirect arbiter of the state of human rights in the West. *Camorra* also cuts business deals with militant organizations (such as the ETA-Basque nationalist and separatist organization—Euskadi Ta Askatasuna). *Camorra* offers arms in exchange for ETA's cocaine through its contact with Colombian guerrilla groups. With ETA protection the drug gets to Italy (Saviano 2008). *Camorra* is exploiting the globalization of trade, technology, transportation, communications, information, and financial systems to become a vast economic empire that branches out thorough legal and illegal activities. Globalization also allowed significant population movement. The increase in migration and the growth of ethnic networks that transcend national borders have proved valuable to the operations of criminal organizations. Diaspora-based ethnic communities provide recruitment opportunities, cover, and support. Recruitment based on ethnic loyalties is particularly easy when the immigrant groups have not been fully integrated into their adopted societies (see Clarke's chapter herein).

Women in Italian mafias: Emergence in stages

Contrary to popular belief and representation, women have been actively engaged in and conscious of the *Camorra* men's activities. They have not been passive and, over the course of the last 20 years, they have become gradually more involved in the daily operations of the business organization and transactions. This does not mean that Sicilian women have not gained positions of power at some levels; simply, they are not involved to the same extent as the *Camorra*'s women leaders. *Camorra* women are not at the margins of the criminal organization or in the shadow of their husbands, fathers, brothers, male children, or lovers. Their role has evolved from maintaining a solid support system for the male protagonists into that of becoming leading actors and directors, particularly of **front organizations**. They have also taken on leadership roles by making strategic and often autonomous decisions about the criminal organization's activities and by taking matters in their own hands. In this process, they have killed brutally, when deemed necessary. For example, in May 2002, in Lauro, a small town in Campania in the region of Naples, a shootout between women from the Graziano and the Cavas clans killed three females and injured six (Allum 2003, 10). This trend, which began in the 1990s, suggests that women have become major violent actors in criminal organizations and that they indeed rank high up in the mafia hierarchy.

The reasons behind the expansion of the roles of women in these crime syndicates include: 1) transformations in civil society; 2) the first *Camorra* war in the 1970s to 1980s that imposed changes in criminal-business models; and 3) the *Camorra*'s internal flexible structure and lack of organizational hierarchy. These factors have given women the space and opportunity to take on leadership roles, moving from traditional, private support and loyalty to assuming new, active roles. That is, this change in the criminal model from a traditional to a modern and efficient one, with a flexible structure, has led to a change in women's behavior.

Broad transformations in economics, politics, and civil society since the post-WWII era meant women's emancipation from the traditional private family sphere to the public sphere. With the experience of employment that stemmed from the wartime absence of men, women acquired new individual social aspirations, and they ultimately began to actively seek to combine family life with working outside of the home. Similar aspirations may well have attracted Neapolitan women to the criminal world. As Claire Longrigg argued: "Neapolitan women play a full and active part in society, perhaps more than women from any other region of Italy, and the criminal underworld is no exception" (Longrigg 1998, 35). These women, however, were not and still are not necessarily "feminists" *per se*.

The emergence of women from the private to the public realm, the growth of their sense of ownership and autonomy within the organization, and their acquisition of powerful positions in the *Camorra* occurred progressively, through gradual increases. Giovanni Fiandaca suggested that women's emergence into powerful positions in these transnational criminal organizations happened in three stages (Fiandaca 2003, 10). From 1950–1976, women were part of a support system.[1] From 1976–1990, when the *Camorra* war between clans raged, women began actively and even violently defending their men. Subsequently, the 1990s marked the advent of women obtaining greater status within the *Camorra* structure, becoming criminals and business and organizational leaders. Since then women have been consolidating their positions of leadership.

Each of these stages resulted from the previous one(s). In the first phase, Renate Siebert described women of the *Camorra* as providing emotional and financial support. This model was borrowed from Sicilian Mafia and Calabrian *'Ndrangheta*, who follow the Sicilian code of conduct or "Sicilian model" (Siebert 1996, 15). From 1950 to 1976, they continued maintaining a largely behind-the-scenes support system for camorristi, but they simultaneously began to challenge their traditional roles and found their own voices and space for agency, often independent of their men. Thus, in stage two (1976–1990), they defended their men in the thick of internecine warfare. This behavior disrupted the Sicilian model of women remaining mainly in the role of support system and tending to the domestic sphere. The change is also in large part due to the way the criminal models evolved during the years 1976–1990, which, again, witnessed elevation in women's stature. Two models and organizations were at war: the *Nuova Camorra Organizzata* (NCO)[2] with boss Raffaele Cutolo, who tried to impose a Campania-based model (with women more engaged and aware of men's activities) and the *Nuova Famiglia* (NF)[3], which attempted to impose a Sicilian model (with women as loyal and subordinate wives, who do not intrude in their husbands' criminal activities). The gendered aspect of reorganization, in part as a result of this gang warfare, had deep implications for *Camorra* women and their roles in the mafia's institutional structure. During the war, a few women were noticeably involved in high-profile activities, while others were defending their men. The Italian media did not pick up on this; however, judges responsible for prosecutions at the time suggested that women played more important roles than was generally portrayed publicly or understood. In stage three, 1990–2000, women become major actors and out-right criminals in the *Camorra*. This shift is, in large part, likely due to the sheer shortage of suitable men available to fill leadership roles, because of widespread slaughter and imprisonment of organizational leaders and middle men. By this time, given their movement into the role of defenders of the men combined with the post-WWII ethos of women seeking employment in general, women had few doubts that they had the skills to be as proficient bosses, if not more so than men (Fiandaca 2003, 10). Additionally, the *Camorra* clan structure of horizontality had also become more prevalent, and in a sense, it offered more opportunity for advancement; women were the perfect candidates to fill the gaps in the authority structure. Rather than violence marginalizing and pushing them deeper into victimhood, women actually developed a new acumen as leaders through the process of war itself. Debate exists around characterizing these powerful women as feminists, due to their clear rejection of patriarchal norms and practices, and their significant advancement into dominant leadership roles in a male-dominated organization. An anti-mafia prosecutor, Teresa Principato, argued that it would be wrong to conclude that mafia women are feminists, who broke through Italy's thick glass ceiling, because they were pushed into mafia leadership roles after their men were incarcerated. In this sense, Principato maintained that their rise in ranks has been more a result of the absence of men through a reactive response, rather than an exercising of their own agency (Reguly and Tondo 2016).

Criminal organizations' impact on global governance and on the diffusion of norms

For a long time, criminal organizations have had an international dimension, but the globalized world has indirectly provided even more business opportunities to the various mafias (Williams 2001, 109). The current speed and ease in conducting international trade and investment has dramatically facilitated the mafias' activities (see Clarke's chapter herein).

The mafias' activities, both legal and illegal, pose a serious threat for global governance. In the late 1980s and early 1990s, through the creation of international norms, global governance attempted to tackle the problems created, on a global scale, by criminal organizations (i.e. drug trafficking, money laundering, slave trade). For instance, in 1991 the UN General Assembly founded a Commission on Crime Prevention and Criminal Justice (CCPCJ) within the UN Economic and Social Council (ECOSOC), which involved the active participation of national governments in combating transnational organized crime. When the commission met, Giovanni Falcone, a famous Italian anti-mafia judge, who was later assassinated by the mafia in 1992 with a car bomb, suggested the establishment of a global conference in order to discuss the development of international cooperation against organized crime. What Falcone had imagined was later achieved with the World Ministerial Conference on Organized Transnational Crime, held in Naples in November 1994.[4] The conference emphasized the need to study the problem of organized crime as well as the duty of the international community to respond successfully through cooperation.

In 2000, the United Nations General Assembly adopted the Convention against Transnational Organized Crime, which entered into force on 29 September 2003. The Convention epitomizes a major step forward in the fight against global crime, indicates the recognition of the gravity of the problems posed by criminal organizations, and signals the need to promote close international cooperation in order to tackle these problems. The creation of a convention on transnational organized crime is significant for global governance, but questions remain regarding the implementation of the norms governing international criminal behavior. In fact, as Phil Williams argued, "effectiveness depends in large part on the willingness and capacity" of states, which have signed the convention, "to implement the norms that they have formally recognized" (Williams 2001, 121). What if a state's political institutions, as in the Italian case, have been co-opted and thereby compromised to the point that they are almost neutralized? Co-optation has a vast impact on the development of international law, for it affects compliance if we consider that co-opted officials have incentives to reject global norms that combat their crime masters. The erosion of sovereignty from within, especially with the infiltration of criminal organizations into politics, in practice erodes a state's authority and thus reduces the ability to implement those norms.

Most of the time states comply with most international norms. The reasons are simple. International norms are not imposed on the states against their will, rather states freely decide whether to conform or not. Maybe it is worth remembering that international norms arise mainly from treaties and from customary international law. Treaties are like contracts. States freely decide to enter into them and, if they do, they are bound to follow their terms. Therefore, states generally comply with the obligations of the treaty; otherwise they would not have agreed upon it. The situation is similar with regard to customary international law. The norms of international law are not so much created as "recognized" from certain patterns of social behavior. Thus, for instance, it is a customary law for envoys and ambassadors to be regarded as entitled to a degree of immunity and inviolability. The "right" way to treat an envoy is well known and is considered an obligation. As constructivists would put it, a state's behavior depends on a web of social practices. Since customary practices are rooted in what states habitually do, it follows that states tend to comply with most of customary international law (Lowe 2007, 19).

However, when the tentacles of organized crime penetrate politics, the prospect of implementing norms governing international criminal behavior is severely diminished. States tend not to comply with these norms because co-opted officials have an interest in rejecting them. Likewise, co-optation explains the patterns of the diffusion of norms because the state's modus operandi impacts the social context in which they act. The behavior of states influences international law because their breaking away from established normative patterns of behavior, or from treaty commitments, changes the rules of international law. In short, non-compliance nullifies the norm. Thus, by neutralizing the state's capability to implement international norms, the mafia's penetration of Italian politics poses a threat to global governance and to the diffusion of norms governing criminal behavior.

The advantages of a constructivist approach to global dynamics

A constructivist approach sheds light on both the challenges that states are facing to their sovereignty and the effects of those challenges on global governance and international norms diffusion. As constructivist social theory postulates, the world is "socially constructed": it is dependent on a web of social practices. As Wendt explains, "a fundamental principle of constructivist social theory is that people act toward objects, including other actors, on the basis of the meaning that the objects have for them" (Wendt 1992, 396–397). In a world with these characteristics, states' practices and identity, Kratochwil argues, are contingent on the meaning and practices that constitute them (Kratochwil 1989). These meanings and practices, however, are not fixed—rather they vary over time. For example, Hurd observes, "sovereignty is a social institution in the sense that a state can be sovereign only when it is seen by people and other states as a corporate actor with rights and obligations over territory and citizens" (Hurd 2008, 300). However, the norm of sovereignty has changed in recent times, and so have the identities of existing states. States' identities (i.e. who they are/what they do) are constructed through social practices. For instance, after the Cold War, human rights abuses by states against their own citizens were invoked to justify international intervention in Rwanda, Bosnia, and Kosovo (Wheeler 2000). This indicates that while sovereignty is changing and while for some states (i.e. perpetrators of human rights abuses) it is shrinking, for others (that is, intervening states) it is widening. Therefore, norms, sovereignty as well as customary international norms, change over time and this is the result of ongoing interactions between states and their social context (Lowe 2007, 34–64).[5]

As Legro states, foreign policy ideas (and therefore interests) are shaped by former prevailing ideas as well as experiences (Legro 2005, 4). As Wendt posits, interpretation of interests is partially a by-product of identities (Wendt 1992, 397). The social constitution of interests encompasses international life in its entirety and a constructivist approach suggests that institutions, norms, and states can be redefined in the process. This is particularly evident when one studies international norms. States are interested in complying with rules while at the same time seeking to change rules in order to condone their behavior (Hurd 2008, 304). For example, when states use force in self-defense they simultaneously strengthen the UN Charter's articles that forbid aggressive war (i.e. art. 2 (4) and art. 51)[6] and redefine the norms by postulating how the ideas of sovereignty and self-defense should be conceptualized. In other words, international norms both influence and are concurrently the outcome of a state's behavior. The recognition of this dual dynamic is an important contribution to International Relations (IR) theory. Accordingly, our analysis of the Neapolitan mafia in Italy and its women sheds light on two main themes: 1. How *Camorra* manipulates the state's authority and practices; 2. How this process ultimately has an impact on norms diffusion. Such an analysis shows that the infiltration of *Camorra* in Italian politics translates into a decrease in Italy's sovereignty. Here, the decrease of state sovereignty leads to a reduced ability on the part of Italy to implement international norms. Consequently, this behavioral change causes a redefinition of the norms and actors involved in the process.

Furthermore, the assumption that women are inherently more peaceful, less aggressive, and less prone to war, has fostered their exclusion from most violence while relegating them to the role of victims. Likewise, in IR, some feminists, in an attempt to challenge the traditional conceptualization of understanding the dynamics of conflict and human relations at the global level, have inadvertently reinforced oppressive binary gender identities. Liberal feminists have attempted to valorize femaleness within patriarchal relations as superior by inverting the gender hierarchy of male-masculine over female-feminine. They have suggested that the experience of mothering (caring for others) could serve as a good ethical model for civic participation (Ruddick 1983, 1990; True, 2005). Similarly, other feminist scholars (especially in Peace Research) have emphasized women's socialization as promoting feminine, non-violent forms of conflict prevention (Brock-Utne 1985, 1989). In an attempt to empower women, others have claimed that a world run by women would be more peaceful and less warlike (Jones, 1991; True, 2005). These perspectives run the risk of encouraging the view that women cannot be agents of violence, thus excluding them from violent occupations and contexts. In addition, they overshadow women as possible threats to global security. Women and their experiences are once again marginalized and excluded from a status quo that privileges men's violence over women's violence. Such approaches tend to reproduce the masculine–feminine dichotomy. If women's experiences are present and relevant to IR (when we choose to see them) as Cynthia Enole's work demonstrates, then we must study violent women's lives too (Enloe 1994). IR feminists are beginning to put forward evidence that shows that there is clear gender bias in the portrayal of females as victims only, or if perpetrators, as monsters or lacking agency (Sjoberg and Gentry, 2007; Sjoberg 2016). Pictures of Abu Ghraib have shocked society and feminists alike (Ehrenreich 2007).

Text box 12.3: Women and torture: Evidence from Abu Ghraib Prison, Baghdad

In 2003, allegations of severe maltreatment and abuse of Iraqi prisoners by US military and intelligence personnel at Baghdad's Abu Ghraib prison emerged. Soldiers committed grave breaches of humanitarian law in their treatment of prisoners. The abuse became public when the *New Yorker* published details of the mistreatment, including graphic pictures showing guards beating prisoners and forcing them into humiliating positions. Of the seven US soldiers charged with revolting forms of abuse were three women: Pfc. Lynndie England, Specialist Sabrina Harman, and Specialist Megan Ambuhl. In one of the pictures Harman is smiling and giving the thumbs sign from behind a pile of naked Iraqi men. In another picture England was dragging a naked Iraqi man on a leash. Specialist Sabrina Harman was found guilty of abuse and given six months in prison. She testified that her job was to keep detainees awake, including one prisoner in the picture, who is hooded and placed on a box with wires attached to his fingers, toes, and genitals. Pfc. Lynn England was convicted for conspiracy, maltreating detainees and committing an indecent act. She was jailed for three years.

The cause of the shock lies in our socialization into thinking that men are aggressive and women are peaceful. As Wendy Brown argues, everything in the human world is gendered construction. In other words, knowledge that confers the meaning of sexual difference as binary gives meaning to power relationships and social orderings (Brown 1988). More research should be done to examine the dynamics of violent, militant women in order to exit the stereotypical reduction of women as only "victims" and men as sole "perpetrators" of violence, to recognize their role as social actors with agency, and thus put in place security strategies.

As for criminal organizations, they have a long history, especially in Southern Italy, and it could be argued that the mafias are intrinsically Italian since they developed in the 19th century to provide social and security structures where the state was absent, because it was both distant and oblivious to Southern problems. At the same time, the point could be made that this is a domestic problem, without a solution, and pertains to the national domain. However, organized crime is not just an Italian domestic problem. If we consider how criminal organizations have exploited globalization, corrupted the political process, and impinged on the diffusion of norms, we understand how this is really a global issue that transcends the damaging of licit trade and commerce. Criminal organizations like the *Camorra* undermine state sovereignty and challenge its authority and social behavior. The phenomenon of co-optation thus needs to be studied not just as a domestic or an Italian problem, but also as an issue that affects global governance and the diffusion of norms combating certain criminal behavior. Furthermore, since criminal organizations constitute a threat to global governance, they must be dealt with collectively. Further United Nations multilateral efforts are needed. Moreover, the international community must support states in their fight against this cancer and hold accountable those who surrender to it.

Questions for discussion

1   Do transnational criminal organizations engage in politics and economic life? What effects do they have on the state and society?
2   Describe how *Camorra* has an impact in Campania. Is this phenomenon an Italian or a global problem? Why?
3   What is the role of women in transnational criminal organizations? How have they become involved?
4   What does the role of women in transnational criminal organizations tell us about the way we understand gender in society and in IR?
5   How has the international community reacted to the problem of transnational criminal organizations? Has the response been adequate to the problem?
6   How can a constructivist approach help explain this problem?

Notes

1 The year 1976 is when the first *Camorra* war began.
2 *Nuova Camorra Organizzata* (NCO) in English: Newly Organized Camorra.
3 *Nuova Famiglia* (NF) in English: New Family.
4 Resolution 49/159 of 23 December 1994 approved the Naples Political Declaration and Global Action Plan against Organized Transnational Crime, adopted by the World Ministerial Conference on Organized Transnational Crime, held at Naples, Italy, from 21 to 23 November 1994.
5 A rule of customary international law exists when it is manifested in the general practice of states.
6 Art. 2 (4) declares: "All Members shall refrain in their international relations from the threat or use of force against the territorial integrity or political independence of any state, or in any other manner inconsistent with the Purposes of the United Nations." The UN Charter Art. 51 states: "Nothing in the present Charter shall impair the inherent right of individual or collective self-defence if an armed attack occurs against a Member of the United Nations, until the Security Council has taken measures necessary to maintain international peace and security. Measures taken by Members in the exercise of this right of self-defence shall be immediately reported to the Security Council and shall not in any way affect the authority and responsibility of the Security Council under the present Charter to take at any time such action as it deems necessary in order to maintain or restore international peace and security."

References

Allum, Felia. 2003. "Doing It for Themselves or Standing in for their Men? Women in Neaopolitan *Camorra* (1950–2003)." In Giovanni Fiandaca, ed. *Women and the Mafia: Female Roles in Organized Crime Structures*. New York: Springer, 9–17.
Brock-Utne, Birgit. 1985. *Educating for Peace*. New York: Pergamon.
Brock-Utne, Birgit. 1989. *Feminist Perspectives on Peace and Peace Education*. New York: Pergamon.
Brown, Wendy. 1988. *Manhood and Politics*. Totowa, NJ: Rowman & Littlefield.
Corvi, Luigi. March 9, 2011. "'Ndrangheta e poltrona all'Asl. In aula la doppia vita di Chiriaco." *Il Corriere della Sera*.
Ehrenreich, Barbara. Spring 2007. "Feminism's Assumptions Upended." *South Central Review* 24(1): 170–173.
Enloe, Cynthia. 1994. *The Morning After: Sexual Politics at the End of the Cold War*. Berkeley, CA: University of California Press.
EURISPES. 2010. "Indice di Penetrazione Mafiosa Rapporto Italia 2010, Scheda 31." www.eurispes.eu/content/rapporto-italia-2010
Fiandaca, Giovanni, ed. 2003. *Women and the Mafia: Female Roles in Organized Crime Structures*. New York: Springer.
Foschini, Giuliano and Conchita Sannino. March 19, 2010. "Sud e Liste 'inquinate.'" *La Repubblica*.
Hurd, Ian. 2008. "Constructivism." In Christian Reus-Smit and Duncan Snidal, eds. *The Oxford Handbook of International Relations*. Oxford: Oxford University Press, 298–310.
Jepperson, Ronald L., Wendt, Alexander and Katzenstein, Peter J. 1996. "Norms, Identity, and Culture in National Security." In Peter J. Katzenstein, ed. *The Culture of National Security: Norms and Identity in World Politics*. New York: Columbia University Press: 33–77.
Jones, Kathleen B. 1991. "The Trouble with Authority." *Differences*, 3(1): 104–127.
Kratochwil, Friedrich. 1989. *Rules, Norms, and Decisions: On the Conditions of Practical and Legal Reasoning in International Relations and Domestic Affairs*. Cambridge: Cambridge University Press.
Legro, Jeffrey W. 2005. *Rethinking the World: Great Power Strategies and International Order*. Ithaca, NY: Cornell University Press.
Longrigg, Claire. 1998. *Mafia Women*. London: Vintage.
Lowe, Vaughan. 2007. *International Law*. Oxford: Oxford University Press.

Reguly, Eric and Tondo, Lorenzo. October 27, 2016. "The Rise of the Godmother." *The Globe and Mail.*

Ruddick, Sara. 1983. "Pacifying Forces: Drafting Women in the Interest of Peace." *Signs* 8(3): 471–489.

Ruddick, Sara 1990. "The Rationality of Care." In Jean Bethke Elshtain and Sheila Tobias, eds. *Women, Militarism, and War: Essays in History, Politics, and Social Theory.* New York: Rowman & Littlefield, 229–253.

Saviano, Roberto. October 13, 2010. "Mani mafiose sulla democrazia." *La Repubblica.*

Saviano, Roberto. February 10, 2011. "La camorra nelle urne." *La Repubblica.*

Saviano, Roberto. 2008. *Gomorrah: A Personal Journey into the Violent International Empire of Naples' Organized Crime System.* New York: Picador.

Siebert, Renate. 1996. *Secrets of Life and Death: Women and the Mafia.* London: Verso.

Sjoberg, Laura. 2016. *Women as Wartime Rapists: Beyond Sensation and Stereotyping.* New York: New York University Press.

Sjoberg, Laura and Caron E. Gentry. 2007. *Mothers, Monsters, Whores: Women's Violence in Global Politics.* London: Zed Books.

True, Jacqui. 2005. "Feminism." In Scott Burchill, Andrew Linklate et al., eds. *Theories of International Relations.* London: Palgrave Macmillan, 237–258.

United Nations Development Program (UNDP). 1994. *Human Development Report.* New York: United Nations. http://hdr.undp.org/sites/default/files/reports/255/hdr_1994_en_complete_nostats.pdf

United Nations Office on Drugs and Crime (UNODC). 2010. *The Globalization of Crime: A Transnational Organized Crime Threat Assessment.* Vienna, Austria: UNODC. http://www.unodc.org/res/cld/bibliography/the-globalization-of-crime-a-transnational-organized-crime-threat-assessment_html/TOCTA_Report_2010_low_res.pdf

Wendt, Alexander. Spring 1992. "Anarchy is what States Make of it: The Social Construction of Power Politics." *International Organization,* 46(2): 391–425.

Wheeler, Nicholas J. 2000. *Saving Strangers. Humanitarian Intervention in International Society.* Oxford: Oxford University Press.

Williams, Phil. 2001. "Crime, Illicit Markets, and Money Laundering." In P.J. Simmons and Chantal de Jong Oudraat, eds. *Managing Global Issues: Lessons Learned.* Washington, DC: Carnegie Endowment for International Peace, 106–150.

Chapter 13

Emerging threats in cyber space
The next domain of warfare

Christian-Marc Lifländer

Introduction

According to the World Economic Forum's 2015 report *Global Risks* (World Economic Forum 2015, 14–15), cyber attacks are one of the most likely high-impact threats in the modern world just behind water crises, interstate conflict, and failure of climate change adaptation. That puts the cyber phenomenon—be it cyber world, cyber space, cyber domain, or any other way of describing cyberspace—beyond the realm of William Gibson's science-fiction novels. Quite simply, digital technologies are part and parcel of our daily life and our planet is getting connected at an unprecedented speed. Traditionally, specialists of inter-state conflicts identify four dimensions of warfare: land, sea, air, and space. This chapter discusses how cyber conflicts both confirm and considerably nuance the traditional realist paradigm because they transcend national physical groundings, deterritorialize state action by projecting it into the fifth dimension of warfare, force states to cooperate with private industry in much deeper ways, empower countless non-state actors, and render state action much more muddled and indirect.

Text box 13.1: William Gibson coined the word "cyberspace"

William Gibson is credited with having invented the term cyberspace in his 1984 novel *Neuromancer* (Gibson 1984). "Prescience can be tedious for science-fiction writers. Being proven right about a piece of technology or a trend distracts from the main aim of the work: to show us how we live now." William Gibson knows this as well as anyone. Since the late 1970s, the American-born novelist has been pulling at the loose threads of our culture to imagine what will come out. He has been right about a great deal, but mainly about the shape of the Internet and how it filters down to the lowest strata of society. In *Neuromancer*, published 30 years ago, Gibson popularized the idea of cyberspace: a

> "consensual hallucination" created by millions of connected computers (...) A generation later, we are living in a future that is both nothing like the Gibson's future and instantly recognizable as its less stylish, less romantic cousin (...) On its release, *Neuromancer* won the "big three" for science fiction: the Nebula, Philip K. Dick and Hugo awards. It sold more than six million copies and launched an entire aesthetic: cyberpunk. In predicting this future, Gibson can be said to have helped shape our conception of the Internet. Other novelists are held in higher esteem by literary critics, but few can claim to have had such a wide-ranging influence.

(Cumming, 2014)

Forecasts and numbers vary, but Gartner, a leading global analyst and advisory company, "forecasts that 4.9 billion connected things will be in use in 2015, up 30 percent from 2014, and will reach 25 billion by 2020. The Internet of Things (IoT) has become a powerful force for business transformation, and its disruptive impact will be felt across all industries and all areas of society" (Rivera and van der Meulen 2014). Others have put the figure much higher, saying that connected devices will reach around 50 billion by 2020 (CISCO 2018). We will never know the exact figure and it is also irrelevant. What matters is that the interconnected and open character of cyberspace offers unprecedented opportunities for the global economy and is transforming the very fabric of our societies (see the chapter herein by Sebastiani, Sanchez, and Manrod).

This open and interconnected space makes societies vulnerable as the rise of hyper connectivity makes it difficult to secure ever more devices. This developing **digital ecosystem** provides a formidable forum for fraud, online robberies, blackmail, identity theft, and innovative forms of terrorism. It is also beset with digital attacks that have political, ideological, religious or national motivations (Heickerö 2013). Hence, it is not only domestic and international criminals, organized crime, terrorists and **hacktivists**, but also governments as well as state-sponsored groups that constitute the best equipped and most capable actors in this electronic space.

In fact, cyber means are already used by governments to achieve or defend their policy objectives. Techniques such as denial-of-service attacks, spear-phishing, and targeting of supervisory control and data automation systems can be used for the purposes of international politics, much like any other tool. By using the realist approach we argue that cyber tools have become an instrument of international politics and that states increasingly use them to complement their existing diplomatic, economic, and military toolbox to achieve their political goals. In doing so, some states find it expedient to hide their behavior in a fog of opacity and deniability, which will make liberal-internationalist cooperation in this space difficult and might very well result in an escalation-dominant cyberspace. Complicating the politics of cyberspace as well as the conduct of international relations further is the fact that states will not have the stage completely to themselves, but will have to share it with various powerful non-state actors. Subterranean, oblique cyber interference or coercion combined with difficulty of attribution, plausible deniability and the proliferation of actors may alter the old realist paradigm of inter-state competition, by rendering counter-action much more difficult, uncertain, and indirect.

Means to an end

Indeed, it is difficult to attribute attacks in cyberspace. When a country is attacked by a missile, the authorities can usually trace the trajectory of the projectile back to its source. When a country is attacked in cyberspace, figuring out who did it and why can be much more difficult (Schneier 2015). This has an effect for the conduct of international relations, as it can be difficult to pinpoint the aggressors and devise appropriate responses. One can analyze the technical data, and perhaps look at the originating computers or networks, but "it is difficult to tell the difference between attacks carried out by a couple of lone hackers and ones where a nation–state is responsible" (Schneier 2015). Technical attribution therefore needs to be complemented by intelligence capabilities to come to a convincing conclusion. Governments cannot be forthcoming about their evidence in public, however, as this would expose their sources and methods. A distinction should be made between private and public attribution. In the case of a public attribution, a stricken nation would not only improve its defense but would also signal its finding publicly. The aim in this case would be to attempt to influence the behavior of another state. Attribution by a state remains first and foremost a political decision and what matters is the act of influencing. If we see an act of influencing, we can see a process, a relationship, and a means to an end. But state actors are hard-pressed when faced with more fluid, amorphous, and micro-level agents like disgruntled individuals, private parties, or loosely organized groups.

In addition, when discussing the use of cyber means to alter a state's behavior, no common definitions exist. Different states view the use of cyber tools differently, which also results in different ways of influencing. According to NATO's (North Atlantic Treaty Organization) official definitions, the traditional approach tends to view cyber attacks as actions that "attempt to gain unauthorized access to system services, resources, or information, or an attempt to compromise system integrity" or "any kind of malicious activity that attempts to collect, disrupt, deny, degrade, or destroy information system resources or the information itself" (Kissell 2013). This is in contrast to an approach pursued for example by the Russian Federation that foresees a wide range of actors and tools being used, such as hackers, media, businessmen, leaks as well as conventional and asymmetric military means to wage a subversive guerrilla campaign on all fronts of society. This was evident during the 2016 US presidential election, according to the public attribution made by many US intelligence agencies (Shane 2017). The role of cyber tools was limited to an extraction of information from the Democratic National Committee's (DNC) computers, but what made the difference was the "selectively amplified targeted disinformation and misinformation on social media—sometimes using materials acquired through cyber means" that helped to "reduce the fighting potential of the enemy", if one is to believe the central tenet of the Gerasimov Doctrine, named after the Russian Chief of Defense (McKew 2017).

Text box 13.2 The Gerasimov Doctrine

In February 2013, General Valery Gerasimov—Russia's chief of the General Staff, comparable to the US chairman of the Joint Chiefs of Staff—published a 2,000-word article, "The Value of Science Is in the Foresight," in the weekly Russian trade paper *Military-Industrial Kurier*. Gerasimov took tactics developed by the Soviets, blended them with strategic military thinking about total war, and laid out a new theory of modern warfare—one that looks more like hacking an enemy's society than attacking it head-on (...) The article is considered by many to be the most useful articulation of Russia's modern strategy, a vision of total warfare that places politics and war within the same spectrum of activities—philosophically, but also logistically. The approach is guerrilla, and waged on all fronts with a range of actors and tools—for example, hackers, media, businessmen, leaks and, yes, fake news, as well as conventional and asymmetric military means. Thanks to the Internet and social media, the kinds of operations Soviet psy-ops teams once could only fantasize about—upending the domestic affairs of nations with information alone—are now plausible. The Gerasimov Doctrine builds a framework for these new tools, and declares that non-military tactics are not auxiliary to the use of force but the preferred way to win. That they are, in fact, the actual war. Chaos is the strategy the Kremlin pursues.

(McKew 2017)

Everywhere, you'll find scholars, pundits, and policymakers talking about the threat the "Gerasimov doctrine" (...) poses to the West. It's a new way of war, "an expanded theory of modern warfare," or even "a vision of total warfare." There's one small problem. It doesn't exist. And the longer we pretend it does, the longer we misunderstand the—real, but different—challenge Russia poses (...) I created this term, which has since acquired a destructive life of its own, lumbering clumsily into the world to spread fear and loathing in its wake (...) There is no single Russian "doctrine." If anything, their campaign is dangerous precisely because it has no single organizing principle, let alone controlling agency. There is a broad political objective—to distract, divide, and demoralize—but otherwise it is largely opportunistic, fragmented, even sometimes contradictory. Some major operations are coordinated, largely through the presidential administration, but most are not. Rather, operations are conceived and generally carried out by a bewildering array of "political entrepreneurs" hoping that their success will win them the Kremlin's favor: diplomats and spies, criminals and think-tankers, oligarchs and journalists.

(Galeotti 2018)

In other words, cyber tools played a part, however, they were but one tool in a broader attempt to create "an environment of permanent unrest and conflict within a state" (McKew 2017). It is therefore important to understand that governments will use different techniques for influencing other states and that the type of tactic employed usually depends on the nature of the relationship—friendship or hostility—between two governments and the general compatibility between their objectives and interests.

The fall of Viktor Yanukovich's regime in Ukraine in February 2014 was seen by many in Russia as a major strategic defeat. Ukraine's decision to choose closer ties with the West was perceived as a loss to Russia's sphere of influence (its "near-abroad") and as further encirclement by Western allies. Perhaps not surprisingly, the subsequent Russo-Ukrainian conflict has shown examples of what appears to be a new kind of conflict called hybrid warfare where cyber operations have had their role to play (Fox-Brewster 2017, Greenberg 2017). On separate occasions, electricity has been turned off to hundreds of thousands of people and practically every sector of Ukraine has been undermined by cyber means: media, finance, transportation, military, elections and, energy (see the chapter herein by Davis and Drake). According to Ukraine's President Petro Poroshenko, there is "direct or indirect involvement of secret services of Russia, which have unleashed a cyberwar against our country" (Greenberg 2017). In subsequent attacks it has not only been Ukraine, but also major international companies such as Merck, DLA Piper and the global shipping company Maersk that have been badly affected, among many others (see Bachkar's and Hebron's chapter herein). Given the almost total disagreement on foreign policy objectives between the two countries, and the fact that the areas of consensus are limited to a few necessities, this policy of punishment is meant to isolate and coerce a state, while intimidating and deterring more distant and capable opponents, including non-state actors, with threat of further punishment.

Another example of a use of cyber power to alter a state's behavior can be seen in the targeting of the Iranian military–industrial complex (Ricks 2012). Specifically, a malware was designed to disable very specific control systems running 9,000 Iranian centrifuges used to enrich uranium, causing some of them to spin out of control (Hopkins 2011). Although no country admitted responsibility, the software is described frequently as a program developed jointly by the United States and Israel (see the chapter herein by Addington and Manrod). What is relevant about this operation as an act of influencing from the international politics perspective is that it sought to change the behavior of Iran via cyber means by setting back its ability to manufacture weapons–grade uranium, which would have resulted not only in delaying the country's ability to become a nuclear power but also would have kept Israel from resorting to conventional military activities against it. The process of influencing can be seen further after the malware had unintentionally gone astray, escaped the uranium enrichment plant and had become known to the wider audience. While no public attribution was made, details related to the operation were leaked and published, in the hope that "if the American cyber capability was much more broadly known it would have a deterrent effect. It could be a way of saying to the Iranians, we've gotten at your centrifuges, you know about it, and we can come back and get you anytime we want" (Rothkopf 2012). To summarize, cyber capabilities were mobilized for political purposes and the act of covert influencing turned into a compelling use of force with an aim to stop Iran from becoming a nuclear state.

Realist conflict and cyber power

The basic human drives to live, propagate, and dominate are common to all. This has not changed with the dawn of cyberspace. In fact, given that cyberspace is a man-made domain, one should not expect anything different. As Thucydides (c.460 to c.400 BCE) observed in the famed *Melian Dialogue*, "Of the Gods we know and of men we believe, that it is a necessary law of their nature that they rule whenever they can" (Thucydides, Book V, 5.105-[2]). Even "competitive contests between business enterprises as well as labour disputes between employers and employees are frequently fought not only, and sometimes not even primarily, for economic advantages, but for control over each other and over others; that is for power" (Kaufman et al. 1995, 301). The diffusion of information technology confirms realists' predictions about state behavior: cyber means are used as a way to reach political objectives. It constitutes capabilities, it is a relationship and a process, and it can be measured, at least crudely. If the key to a state's success in international politics and in its quest for influence are its ability to match capabilities to objectives, then knowing which tactics to employ, including cyber means, becomes paramount.

The two cases mentioned herein show both the potential, but also the limitations of cyber power in international politics. It is difficult to estimate if it was primarily the use of Stuxnet malware or also the use of positive incentives that resulted in the 2015 nuclear deal struck between Iran and six world powers. It is likely, however, that the use of malware changed the perception of influence and cyber capabilities that Iran had regarding the United States. It is also likely that Iran reached an agreement with the United States to limit the country's controversial nuclear program given that it could not mobilize its cyber capabilities to the extent that it could influence other countries equally. There is no indication, however, that the use of cyber means alone led to an imminent change in Iran's behavior. Stuxnet was first uncovered in 2005, some ten years before the 2015 nuclear deal. Hence, it could be argued that cyber tools had their role to play, but worked only when coupled with positive incentives, and a good deal of hard diplomatic work.

The same limitations are also evident in Ukraine, where the use of cyber power alone has not resulted in a change of strategic direction or concessions by the government. There is no question that the Russian Federation has been able to signal a reasonably accurate picture of its capabilities and intentions not only *vis-à-vis* Ukraine, but also to other states. In this context it is not only the possession but also the willingness to use cyber power and signal one's determination that made the difference. This is a logical development of the fact that the international system has not developed beyond the Hobbesian "state of nature." The primary goal of states still remains survival. In other words, states have to assume the worst about the intentions and actions of their competitors and make use of all tools necessary, including cyber, to ensure their survival. This self-help character of international relations creates a structural problem, however, as the development and use of cyber tools brings with it a **security dilemma**, or **Thucydides' trap**. Attempts to increase one's national security might very well be seen as decreasing security of others. Put simply, when a state invests in cyber capabilities to defend itself, its rivals might instead see a growth in offensive capabilities, and thus a new form of threat (for the same dilemma with geoengineering, see Beevers' chapter herein).

Contributing to a possible escalation in this space is the fact that cyber capabilities differ markedly from the traditional tools that influence a state's behavior. A threat serves as a deterrent in that it convinces its target not to carry out the intended action because of the cost and losses that the target would incur. Deterrence may not easily apply to cyberspace, however. For example, it can be difficult to signal a credible threat deterrent to an adversary if cyber capabilities are kept secret or if relying on untested capabilities. It is true that governments can never fully know the intentions of others. But it is imperative to influence the perceptions that others have of one's own capabilities. Hence, sometimes costly and sensitive cyber capabilities will have to be used as a way of demonstrating capability and communicating the credibility of a state's resolve. In doing so it is not likely that cyber means are going to substitute for existing diplomatic, informational, military or economic instruments of national power. As the cases of Ukraine and Iran demonstrate, cyber is likely to complement, but not substitute for the existing statecraft toolbox as part of a broader cross-domain deterrence calculus.

Limits to cooperation

The lack of an international sovereign will continue to make it difficult for states to reach a common goal. Even though states have an option to cooperate and work together through international institutions and global regimes, the fact remains that they make up the Westphalian system and that they attempt to achieve the greatest possible individual gain. To put it differently, states will decline to participate in arrangements brokered by or within international institutions that will not prevent others from achieving advances in relative capabilities (on the limits of regimes for new technology, see Beever's chapter herein). This is very much evident in cyberspace, as experts from 25 countries at the United Nations have for 13 years tried to restrict cyberwarfare. The most recent round of discussions collapsed in 2017 and the heart of the disagreement appears to have been the right to self-defense in the face of cyber-attacks. Michelle Markoff, who led the United States delegation to the UN's Group of Governmental Experts (UN GGE), indicated in her public statement that "those who are unwilling to affirm the applicability of these international legal rules and principles believe their states are free to act in or through cyberspace to achieve their political ends with no limits or constraints on their actions" (Markoff 2017). The Cuban representative argued, on the other hand, that agreeing to clear and direct statements on how certain international law applies to states' use of Information Communication Technology (ICT) would "legitimatize (...) unilateral punitive force actions, including the applicability of sanctions and even military action by states claiming to be victims of illicit uses of ICTs" (Rodríguez 2017). A group of states sided with the Cuban interpretation and preferred legal ambiguity because it gives them flexibility to operate in cyberspace without risking any collective punishment. By not agreeing to common rules of behavior, countries presumably aim to prevent others from achieving advances in relative terms as there would be no guaranteed right or a legal justification to retaliate against cyber-attacks.

This does not mean that cooperation will not take place in cyberspace. Quite the contrary: states realize that they share cyberspace with numerous non-state actors and that they need the support of industry to fulfill the political contract that forms the basis for the legitimacy of the state. Whether one is to improve supply chain management, share information on vulnerabilities, or build trust and solicit support in case of cyber incidents, states cannot but take into account the role of the private sector, which owns most of the world's information systems, and develops the technical solutions for cyberspace (see the chapter herein by Addington and Manrod). Many large multinational corporations command significant economic resources and have taken steps on the territory normally reserved for nation states, such as fighting cybercriminals by using traditional legal and court actions to dismantle **botnets** (Hiller 2014). We have also seen a proposal from industry to establish international norms for responsible nation state behavior in cyberspace to protect private companies from state-sponsored cyberattacks, and set limits to states' attempts to achieve the greatest possible individual gain (Smith 2017). This makes industry a key player in cyberspace, but not one that has public authority or political power over people at large. The fact that the IT industry is not a unitary or a political actor with the legitimacy to exert physical violence against lawbreakers and that it delivers not public, but private benefits, will likely pose limits to its efforts on the international scene. In sum, we currently see limits to cooperation between states due to the reasons outlined, but in parallel new and arguably unprecedented forms of cooperation are taking place outside of state institutions as they (try to) come to terms with non-state threats in cyberspace.

Future trends

Sony Corp. CEO Michael Lynton is reported to have reacted to a major cyber attack against Sony Pictures by saying that "there's no playbook for this, so you are in essence trying to look at the situation as it unfolds and make decisions without being able to refer to a lot of experiences you've had in the past or other peoples" (Billboard 2015). As Google chief executive Eric Schmidt states, the "Internet is the first thing that humanity has built that humanity seems not to understand, the largest experiment in anarchy that we have ever had" (Taylor 2010). What has become clear, then, is that more cyber development and digitalization have brought with them greater vulnerability. While the interconnected and open character of cyberspace will likely continue to offer unprecedented opportunities for the global economy, the rise of hyper connectivity will also continue to make it more difficult to secure a drastically expanding realm (see the chapter herein by Sebastiani, Sanchez, and Manrod).

Undoubtedly, debates will continue over the nature and the rules of cyberspace. Various such processes already exist, such as the London process. There is also an academic understanding in the form of the Tallinn Manual on how existing international law applies to cyberspace. But there is not enough state engagement yet to define global norms. The US–China cybersecurity agreement concerning economic espionage also seems to be a step in the right direction and, if successful, could have a profound effect on international norms in this area.

Text box 13.3: The Tallinn Manual and the London Process

The Tallinn Manual 2.0 is the most comprehensive analysis of how existing international law applies to cyberspace. Authored by nineteen international law experts, the "Tallinn Manual 2.0 on the International Law Applicable to Cyber Operations", the updated and considerably expanded second edition of the 2013 "Tallinn Manual on the International Law Applicable to Cyber Warfare", is an influential resource for legal advisers dealing with cyber issues. The drafting of the Tallinn Manual 2.0 was facilitated and led by the NATO Cooperative Cyber Defence Centre of Excellence.

(NATO CCDCOE b).

Chair's statement from the London Conference on Cyberspace:

Earlier this year I proposed the following principles for governing behaviour in cyberspace, and (…) how we might implement them:

1   The need for governments to act proportionately in cyberspace and in accordance with national and international law;
2   The need for everyone to have the ability—in terms of skills, technology, confidence and opportunity—to access cyberspace;
3   The need for users of cyberspace to show tolerance and respect for diversity of language, culture and ideas;
4   Ensuring that cyberspace remains open to innovation and the free flow of ideas, information and expression;
5   The need to respect individual rights of privacy and to provide proper protection to intellectual property;
6   The need for us all to work collectively to tackle the threat from criminals acting online; and
7   The promotion of a competitive environment which ensures a fair return on investment in network, services and content.(Hague 2011)

As the case studies in this chapter demonstrate, how states will use their cyber capabilities will continue to depend on their political objectives, and the choice of instruments to achieve those objectives will be influenced by their available capabilities—a key tenet of classical realism. It is likely that states that can exert significant cyber pressure will continue to use their capabilities for political purposes. However, the variety of foreign policy instruments available to a nation for influencing others will partly be dependent on the resources it finds available. A country that has few cyber capabilities cannot, even if it desires, significantly influence other countries globally. All countries will have to improve their national cyber resilience, be it through the creation of cyber strategies, by designating and empowering competent authorities, by establishing national incident response capabilities, or by developing collaborative frameworks between industry and government, just to mention a few examples. This is likely to be challenging as cyber defense does not have a defined "end point." A purchased helicopter will be used for 30 or 40 years almost unchanged, with only some modifications and upgrades. Even after 40 years, a helicopter might still be a very capable piece of military equipment. One cannot do the same in cyber security, because these technologies move much faster. We are likely to be at the beginning of what promises to be a long and muddled journey, and where we are today might have very little to do with where we will end up (Brown 2017).

Conclusion

Transformation driven by technological innovation is constantly accelerating, as the path that innovation and security responses are going to take is difficult to predict. The end result is likely to be determined by how we are going to interact with technology and the kind of impact that culture, politics, economic arrangements, values and regulatory frameworks will have on the way we exploit it. Actors who want to make headways will have to recognize that dealing with threats emanating from cyber space is a cooperative effort, where no one, however powerful, can go it alone. Hence, cyberspace will likely continue to develop as a domain where military and civilian, defense and homeland security, as well as public and private interests will be intertwined, further eroding the traditional boundaries between individual and collective, public and private, domestic and foreign actors. Cyber security both reaffirms realism and transforms it in ways unseen, notably by abolishing the old territorial politics. The borders, physical boundaries and territorial groundings of nation-state are being abolished in favor of the fifth dimension of warfare in cyberfare.

Questions for discussion

1   Is deterrence possible in cyberspace, given that both state and non-state actors are present and that key characteristics of this concept have limitations?
2   Using cyber-attacks brings more short-term advantages than restraint and cooperation. Is it possible for states to mitigate or even transcend the security dilemma?
3   Should modern societies treat data protection similar to the loss of human life, given the fact that a loss of data could bring about major or even dire consequences (for instance, hacking of and interference with power grid, aerial navigation control system, public transportation, water purification systems, electoral systems, hospital, banking and other personal, confidential, and public authorities records)?
4   Should industry be held accountable for the security of its products, considering that all actors in cyberspace use industry products to achieve their means?
5   What kind of international governance frameworks (regimes) could best promote international cooperation and stability in cyberspace?

References

Billboard. January 9, 2015. "Sony Pictures CEO on Hack: 'There's No Playbook for This.'" Retrieved June 9, 2018. https://www.billboard.com/articles/news/6436362/sony-pictures-ceo-on-hack-theres-no-playbook-for-this

Brown, Kathy. 2017. "2017 Internet Society Global Internet Report: Paths to our Digital Future." Retrieved June 9, 2018. *Internet Society.* https://future.internetsociety.org/wp-content/uploads/2017/09/2017-Internet-Society-Global-Internet-Report-Paths-to-Our-Digital-Future.pdf

CISCO. 2018. "Internet of Things." Retrieved June 9, 2018. https://www.cisco.com/c/en/us/solutions/internet-of-things/overview.html

Cumming, Ed. July 29, 2014. "William Gibson: The Man who Saw Tomorrow." Retrieved June 9, 2018. *The Guardian.* https://www.theguardian.com/books/2014/jul/28/william-gibson-neuromancer-cyberpunk-books

Fox-Brewster, Thomas. July 3, 2017. "NotPetya Ransomware Hackers 'Took Down Ukraine Power Grid.'" Retrieved June 9, 2018. *Forbes.* https://www.forbes.com/sites/thomasbrewster/2017/07/03/russia-suspect-in-ransomware-attacks-says-ukraine/#1b6ee4a6b89d

Galeotti, Mark. March 5, 2018. "I'm Sorry for Creating the 'Gerasimov Doctrine.'" Retrieved June 9, 2018. *Foreign Policy.* http://foreignpolicy.com/2018/03/05/im-sorry-for-creating-the-gerasimov-doctrine/

Gibson, William. 1984. *Neuromancer.* New York: Ace Books.

Greenberg, Andy. June 20, 2017. "How An Entire Nation Became Russia's Test Lab for Cyberwar." Retrieved June 9, 2018. *Wired.* https://www.wired.com/story/russian-hackers-attack-ukraine/

Hague, William. November 2, 2011. "London Conference on Cyberspace: Chair's Statement." Retrieved June 9, 2018. https://www.gov.uk/government/news/london-conference-on-cyberspace-chairs-statement

Heickerö, Roland. 2013 (2012). *The Dark Side of the Internet: On Cyberthreats and Information Warfare.* Frankurt am Main: Peter Lang.

Hiller, Janine S. January 2014. "Civil Cyberconflict: Microfsoft, Cybercrime, and Botnets." *Santa Clara High Technology Law Journal* 31(2): 163–213. https://digitalcommons.law.scu.edu/chtlj/vol31/iss2/1

Hopkins, Nick. May 30, 2011. "Stuxnet Attack Forced Britain to Rethink the Cyber War." Retrieved June 9, 2018. *The Guardian.* https://www.theguardian.com/politics/2011/may/30/stuxnet-attack-cyber-war-iran

Kaufman, Daniel J., Joseph J. Collins and Thomas F. Schneider. 1995 (1985). *Understanding International Relations: The Value of Alternative Lenses.* New York: McGraw-Hill.

Kissel, Richard, ed. 2013. *Glossary of Key Information Security Terms.* National Institute for Standards and Technology, US Department of Commerce, NISTIR 7298, Revision 2.

Markoff, Michele G. June 23, 2017. United States Mission to the United Nations. "Explanation of Position at the Conclusion of the 2016–2017 UN Group of Governmental Experts (UN GGE) on Development in the Fields of Information and Telecommunications in the Context of International Security." Retrieved June 9, 2018. https://www.state.gov/s/cyberissues/releasesandremarks/272175.htm

McKew, Molly K. September/October 2017. "The Gerasimov Doctrine." Retrieved June 9, 2018. *Politico.* https://www.politico.com/magazine/story/2017/09/05/gerasimov-doctrine-russia-foreign-policy-215538

NATO CCDCOE, Cooperative Cyber Defence Centre of Excellence. N.d. "Tallinn Manual." Retrieved June 9, 2018. https://ccdcoe.org/tallinn-manual.html

Ricks, Thomas E. June 5, 2012. "Covert Wars, Waged Virally." Retrieved June 8, 2018. *New York Times.* https://www.nytimes.com/2012/06/06/books/confront-and-conceal-by-david-sanger.html

Rivera, Janessa, and Rob van der Meulen. November 11, 2014. "Gartner Says 4.9 Billion Connected 'Things' Will Be in Use in 2015." Retrieved June 9, 2018. *Gartner Analysts.* https://www.gartner.com/newsroom/id/2905717

Rodríguez, Miguel. June 23, 2017. Representative of Cuba at the final session of Group of Governmental Experts on Development in the Field of Information and Telecommunications in the context of International Security. Retrieved June 8, 2018. https://www.justsecurity.org/wp-content/uploads/2017/06/Cuban-Expert-Declaration.pdf

Rothkopf, David. June 4, 2012. "The Obama Paradox: A Conversation with David Sanger." Retrieved June 9, 2018. *Foreign Policy*. http://foreignpolicy.com/2012/06/04/the-obama-paradox/

Taylor, Jerome. August 18, 2010. "Google Chief: My Fears for Generation Facebook." Retrieved June 9, 2018. *The Independent*. http://www.independent.co.uk/life-style/gadgets-and-tech/news/google-chief-my-fears-for-generation-facebook-2055390.html

Schneier, Bruce. January 5, 2015. "The Government Must Show Us the Evidence That North Korea Attacked Sony." Retrieved June 8, 2018. *Time*. http://time.com/3653625/sony-hack-obama-sanctions-north-korea/

Shane, Scott. 6 January 2017. "What Intelligence Agencies Concluded About the Russian Attack on the U.S. Election." Retrieved June 9, 2018. *New York Times*. https://www.nytimes.com/2017/01/06/us/politics/russian-hack-report.html

Smith, Brad. 13 April 2017. "Growing Consensus on the Need for an International Treaty on Nation State Attacks." Retrieved June 9, 2018. *The Official Microsoft Blog*. https://blogs.microsoft.com/on-the-issues/2017/04/13/growing-consensus-need-international-treaty-nation-state-attacks/

Thucydides. *History of the Peloponnesian War*. Retrieved June 9, 2018. Cambridge, MA: MIT Classics. http://classics.mit.edu/Thucydides/pelopwar.html

World Economic Forum. 2015. *Global Risks 2015*, 10th Edition REF: 090115. Retrieved June 9, 2018. Geneva: World Economic Forum. DOI. www.weforum.org/risks

Chapter 14

Cyber security threats and solutions for the private sector

Daniel Addington and Mike Manrod

Introduction

It seemed to come out of nowhere. All of a sudden one of the most trusted companies in the world unraveled, devolving from the domain of the revered into the realm of the breached. Following the Equifax breach announced in September 2017, individual Equifax account holders spent approximately $1.4 billion on credit freeze and monitoring fees in the wake of the attack. In the advent of such security incidents, it is difficult to quantify the true impact of a breach in terms of how it affects businesses and consumers in their day-to-day lives. Our society has become so dependent on technology that we are reliant on the delivery of the information services for many aspects of our daily lives. What do we do if these critical services are interrupted or compromised? What if we are denied access to these critical services, or if an attacker is able to impersonate us, gaining access to our information, our monetary resources, or our online identity?

The trust we place in companies that provide information services, ranging from credit reporting to social media, introduces a wide range of risks we do not think about until a major incident occurs. Compromise of consumer trust does not always even need to involve the stereotypical hacking and intrusion scenario, scenes we readily conjure up from the mosaic of news reports and Hollywood drama episodes. For example, more than two billion users entrust the most intimate details of their daily lives and thought processes to Facebook, with a large portion of the population using the platform daily. This trust may have been somewhat misplaced, as evidenced by the Cambridge Analytica scandal, in which the data of 50 million Facebook users was leveraged to help understand the preferences and personalities of voters for political purposes, without their knowledge or consent. Malicious advertisers and bots from foreign entities allegedly exploited the platform, with the intent to manipulate the 2016 U.S. presidential election outcomes.

We live in unprecedented times, where major data breaches come one after another and incidents increase in both severity and frequency. Icons of industry stumble as the global custodians of information and infrastructure fall like dominoes. Tools and tactics that were once the exclusive domain of nation-state entities are now commonplace among unscrupulous hackers, cybercrime rings, and activist organizations. Unfathomable disruptive power is now within reach of decentralized and diffuse webs of individuals or groups with a wide range of motives and questionable restraint. As the complexity and reach of technology increases exponentially and as information systems become an integral part of society, the potential for massive impact by obscure individuals or groups has never been greater.

This chapter details the threat landscape, defensive strategies, and some specific methodologies and frameworks to help secure information systems against intrusion. We also examine how modern organizations protect against hacking and intrusion, along with a few of the regulations and governance frameworks that help promote accountability and compliance. The text boxes expand upon significant data breaches, factors leading to large-scale exploitation, and careers in cybersecurity and how the next generation of security professionals can help facilitate a safer future.

Text box 14.1: The Equifax breach

What is the real impact of a data breach? The recent attack on Equifax compromised identity data in quantities approaching the number of working adults in the United States. In this one security incident, sensitive data elements constituting Personally Identifiable Information (PII) of more than 145 million U.S. citizens were leaked, including the names, Social Security numbers, dates of birth, addresses and other attributes.

How did this happen? What went wrong that allowed for this catastrophic egress of sensitive data? It all started with an unpatched vulnerability in a product called Apache Struts. This vulnerability allowed attackers to perform remote code execution against web servers, presumably allowing malicious file upload—ultimately, giving them control of systems running at Equifax. Once attackers compromise one or more systems, they work to expand their reach, pivoting to other systems until they have sufficient reach within the target infrastructure to carry out their malicious objectives.

What could Equifax have done differently? While Equifax has received a wide range of criticism for several factors that contributed to this situation, the reality is many technical aspects of their plight apply to many large enterprise environments. As such, many lessons can be learned from this use case that will have rather universal applicability. The first lesson is that timely patching of security flaws may correct exploitable vulnerabilities before an attacker has the opportunity to take advantage of these issues leading to largescale compromise. Technology products also exist that help reduce the risk of exploitation of vulnerabilities by attackers. Intrusion Prevention Systems (IPS) and Web Application Firewalls (WAF) look for patterns in traffic or user activity consistent with methods used to exploit software flaws, to prevent or detect such attacks. Finally, a wide range of technologies exist to help contain or limit the damage of an intrusion attempt, including Deception, User Behavior Analytics, Data Loss Prevention (DLP) and Data Encryption technologies.

Nature of a cyber attack

Upon initial examination, looking at cyber security attacks and considering how to protect against them can be a very intimidating topic. On the one hand, the scope is vast since multiple nested hierarchies exist spanning from the physical infrastructure processing information up through increasing layers of abstraction, ranging from software to business processes and human actors. The topic is further complicated by the fact that much thought leadership is carried out by consultants, who profit from the fundamental complexity of intrusion prevention and post-breach forensics; as such, there is not always an incentive to simplify concepts or elucidate simple unifying concepts.

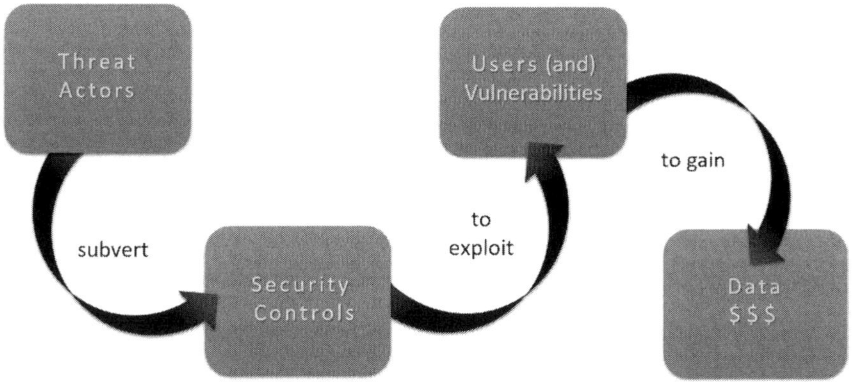

Figure 14.1 Threat actors exploit vulnerabilities

While deep analysis can actually be quite complex, the basic level of understanding necessary to help facilitate effective decision-making is well within the reach of anyone willing to invest some effort to understand the topic. At a basic level, almost every attack starts with a threat actor, intent on compromising information systems to carry out some sort of agenda—often motivated by the prospect of financial gain or promotion of an ideological agenda.

Based on the alarming threat landscape that has unfolded in recent years, most organizations and many individuals deploy a range of security controls to prevent attackers from successfully compromising information assets. Attackers are continually probing for weaknesses in security controls deployed to stop them, while they also are looking for vulnerabilities to the underlying information systems that may allow them to carry out their objectives.

Vulnerabilities are fundamental weaknesses that emerge as a result of the complexity of information systems, which can be exploited by attackers to give them control of a host system or application. Computer systems have billions of transistors, software products often have many millions of lines of code, and the complexity of the possible relationships are compound in nature. As such, there is always a multitude of potential defects that can be exploited—many of these remain unknown to both vendors and customers of these products. Many new vulnerabilities are announced every month, across a wide range of hardware and software products used around the world.

This principle was demonstrated by the use case referenced in Text box 14.1 explaining the infamous Equifax breach. The enormous complexity of the vast range of information systems operated by Equifax made the existence of some sort of vulnerability inevitable. When a specific chain of exploitable vulnerabilities aligned with security control gaps, the results were devastating. Sometimes the data for customers is actually presented in an open format for anyone who makes a request of a web site, such as the estimated 37 million customer records exposed by Panera Bread via an insecure **Application Program Interface** (**API**) or the approximately 700,000 records exposed via the IRS *Get Transcript* program. Simply put, most of the threat landscape can be summarized as threat actors attempting to circumvent security controls, exploit vulnerabilities, and gain control over valuable information assets.

Text box 14.2: Factors leading to large scale exploitation

Why do attackers seem to have the upper hand? It appears odd at first glance, considering that companies defending against cyber-attacks cumulatively represent trillions of dollars in valuation and billions of dollars in technology spending power. What could lead to such a strange asymmetry in outcomes?

One problem relates to the fundamental complexity of underlying technology systems, making it virtually impossible to remain aware of all vulnerabilities that exist in a given environment. Think of it—many software products have millions of lines of code, running on operating systems with tens of millions of code, running on processors and chip sets that together have hundreds of millions of transistors. Imagine the number of possible relationships that exist and how much complexity there is within a typical enterprise environment. How could anyone understand every possible relationship and associated potential vulnerability? This issue is exasperated by the fact that software vendors have very limited accountability for damages associated with flaws related to software they produced.

Another factor is that attackers seem to share information more effectively than the organizations defending against their attack. Attack techniques developed by nation state actors are reverse engineered and shared among lower tier purveyors of **hacktivism** and cyber crime. For some time, a disincentive has existed for corporations to share intelligence, due to a perception that such sharing may implicate them in admission of a breach or compromise. This paradigm is shifting and many corporate information sharing networks have formed. However, this continues to be an uphill battle for organizations working to defend against intrusion attempts against their information assets.

Criticality of information systems for society

Think of a typical day in modern society. What information systems do you interact with and how many activities in your day are technology dependent? Take the typical day for a progressive and technologically inclined adult, working for a large company in an urban area. They would wake up to the smell of coffee, from their automated pot as their alarm wakes them at a time selected to be complementary to their circadian rhythm for maximum restfulness, facilitated by a wearable fitness bracelet. Next a variety of updates would be presented by social media and news feeds to orient this user to the world around them. After getting ready, they may climb into a Tesla, Mercedes, or Audi with navigation and automation capabilities that border on self-driving. They receive updates on traffic, revise their commute to save several minutes, and avoid close calls with advanced collision avoidance features that now come standard on many models.

Once at work, tasks and meetings are organized and presented by personal productivity and automation software, with a speed and precision that eclipse anything that a human assistant may provide. A team of people spanning three continents uses telepresence software that allows everyone to collaborate on the same project, update design schematics, and share ideas in real-time. Lunch is ordered and paid for via apps. Workers text messages, use FB Messenger, Viber, WhatsApp, Skype, or Zoom with spouses, friends, and fellow workers all over the world. Dinner is ordered on apps while the smart-oven is preheated remotely during the commute to be at the right temperature to cook the meal exactly when the family arrives home. After dinner, the kids enjoy a video web session with friends, before having their goodnight song delivered via grandparents retired abroad.

This is our world now—practically every aspect of our daily life has the potential for augmentation and enrichment by powerful information systems. What security controls have been implemented for each of these capabilities? How might an attacker manipulate these capabilities for financial gain, damage, or disruption? Consider the following simple and ubiquitous scenarios:

- Purchase gas on the way to work.
- Drive in a vehicle with many networked computer systems.
- Transfer funds, withdraw cash, or accept payment for goods or services.
- Swipe your badge to enter the office and start work.
- Consume power, water, or gas from utility companies.
- Visit a physician, dentist, or hospital.

What type of technology systems are involved in even the simplest of jobs? How many technology systems have you interacted with today? What would happen if some or all of these systems were unavailable or manipulated to benefit the agenda of any given attacker? Reflect on the number of tasks that are dependent on information systems or technology that could be either grossly or subtly manipulated. What is the impact potential?

What would happen if the power were unavailable for an extended time period for a really cold or hot area? How many times in a typical day could credit card or banking information be leaked or intercepted? What information is collected about the daily activities we take for granted, which could be used for nefarious purposes? Could malicious threat actors also be peering through the looking-glass of our numerous web cams?

Text box 14.3: Nation state influence on cybersecurity: Stuxnet vs. Iran

The proverbial Pandora's box of advanced and evasive malware was first opened by nation state actors, presumably with the best of intentions. It has been a longstanding and well-known goal of the United States, Israel, and many other nations to inhibit or deter the development of nuclear weapons by nations not yet in possession of such capability, especially when their motives are in question. The now infamous Stuxnet program against Iran's nuclear program development allowed for a covert technological solution to this perplexing problem.

This advanced joint effort involved a malware payload designed to self-propagate rapidly, while remaining dormant until certain very specific conditions were met. The malware propagated via a variety of methods including removable media to allow it to cross networks with an Air Gap to protect critical SCADA/industrial control systems. When the malware detected it was running on a Siemens industrial control system, consistent with those used in the centrifuges used to enrich uranium gas by the nuclear program for Iran, it engaged a subtle malicious payload. This malicious payload subtly altered the rotational speed of the centrifuges while reporting normal conditions to the operators of the machinery, with dramatic effect. This caused the costly and difficult-to-obtain devices to wear out rapidly, without clear explanation or attribution.

On one hand, this malware had far reaching collateral damage and eventually came to light, after being discovered by Kaspersky in 2010—years after initial development. This opened a new realm of possible attack vectors, for the entire landscape of global threat actors. Eventually these techniques became commoditized and entered the common repertoire of lower grade nation state actors and, later, cybercrime organizations. Now advanced and evasive malware have become a mainstay for the perpetual dance of attack and defense engaged in by the corporations and threat actors around the world.

The traditional dimensions of warfare are land, sea, air and space. It is clear that a fifth dimension of warfare is emerging—the domain of information operations (see Lifländer's chapter herein).

Protecting confidentiality, integrity, and availability of information

Protecting information comes down to preventing compromise of confidentiality, availability, or integrity of data by threat actors. The most salient examples of cyber security incidents typically involve compromising the confidentiality of information assets. This occurs when an attacker steals information that is supposed to remain private and uses it for malicious purposes. Examples of this could include stealing credit card numbers, codes, and payment information from retailers, removing Social Security numbers and user identities from credit reporting agencies, or stealing intellectual property or secrets from manufacturers or product design firms.

The examples provided so far including Equifax, the IRS, Panera Bread, and Text box 14.5 about Yahoo all involve a compromise of confidentiality. These are by far the most prevalent and salient form of cybersecurity incidents we have heard about because breaches are reported continually. Another fundamental example of the compromise of confidentiality by advanced threat actors was exemplified by attackers who used targeted malware and advanced intrusion techniques to exploit the Office of Personal Management (OPM), to exfiltrate the records of millions of government employees and military service members. In this case, an advanced threat actor representing an Advanced Persistent Threat (APT), allegedly involving nation state activity from China, used custom malware and exfiltrated data using custom created web sites to obtain unfathomable levels of personal detail on an estimated 21.5 million people (see Lifländer's chapter herein).

Even though a compromise of confidentiality may represent the most notorious scenario, significant damage can be realized by manipulating the integrity of data. Sometimes data can be altered without necessarily stealing or removing any information, for the benefit of the attacker. A simple example of this may be changing the bank account number and routing code for profiles in employee payroll systems, to redirect paychecks to an attacker–controlled bank account to facilitate the theft of funds. The attack launched against the Iranian nuclear program by Stuxnet, described in Text box 14.3, involved compromising the integrity of the data reported by control systems and instructions provided to centrifuge systems.

Finally, compromising the availability of information involves preventing valid users from being able to access information systems or associated data. One key use case is the prevalent denial of service attack, where large volumes or malicious combinations of network traffic may be used to shut down a web site or key system that is of high importance to an organization. Another scenario may be where malicious software, known as ransomware, is used to encrypt all user data. Then, the user or company is required to pay a ransom to get their data back.

One prevalent example in recent memory was the massive ransomware outbreak that paralyzed entire nations, known as WannaCry. This attack is believed to have impacted more than 200,000 systems in more than 150 countries, using a Microsoft vulnerability known as EternalBlue that allowed for exploitation of the Server Message Block (SMB) protocol to allow attackers to execute commands on the host system. This attack crippled the railways of Germany, universities in China, and the telecommunications infrastructure of Spain—among countless others. This attack denied access to a massive range of information systems, creating a global impact. Debate continues on the topic of the true motive for this attack—was it for financial gain or was it a test case for how to leverage ransomware for massive global disruption? What if an attack like WannaCry was implemented in a more targeted manner against critical infrastructure as part of a complex and multifaceted military strategy?

Based on these scenarios, what are the practical implications of confidentiality, availability and integrity and how can we expect them to play out in the future?

Elements of an organization's cyber security

Mature organizations possess key functional capabilities that allow them to run an effective security program to protect against attacks intended to compromise the confidentiality, availability or integrity of critical information.

Text box 14.4: Careers in cybersecurity

Cybersecurity is one of the fastest growing and most in-demand career fields of our era, with over one million open positions emerging over the next few years and hundreds of thousands of roles that today remain unfilled. Moreover, launching a career in cybersecurity will prepare professionals for other adjacent next-wave career fields outside of information security such as

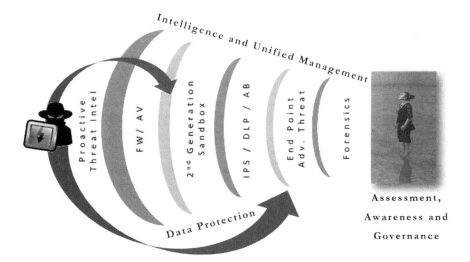

Figure 14.2 Layers of cyber defense

data sciences, machine learning, and robotics since core competencies of these fields all seem to overlap. Not all of these roles are for super-hackers or for the brilliant savants epitomized by Hollywood cyber dramas. The reality is that there is a wide range of job opportunities for mere mortals, willing to work hard and continuously improve. Job opportunities span a wide range of skillsets ranging from the obvious quantitative reasoning and deep technical prowess to softer skills allowing analysts to engage with stakeholders to partner toward issue resolution. Brainstorm your natural skillsets and examine how they align with the core competencies outlined in this chapter.

The foundation of any security program is the Governance, Risk, and Compliance (GRC) area, which defines strategy, identifies risk areas, and ensures compliance with defined or mandated standards and regulations. Security governance defines the policies and standards that apply and enforces these policies across the organization. Risk management is critical for determining the risk level associated with various threats, security control gaps, and vulnerabilities. Based upon these risk levels and collaboration with governance and technical experts, priorities are set, driving a strategic roadmap for maximizing security investment to reduce or offset risk over time. Compliance management involves assessing the adherence of an organization to applicable regulations, standards, and internal policies. In smaller organizations or less mature security programs all of these responsibilities may be assumed by security management; whereas, for mature organizations there could be a sizable team dedicated to the fulfillment of these responsibilities.

From a practical perspective, security governance involves the business of security. If we consider the example of an online retailer this would include the creation of policies describing how all employees and customers are allowed to use information systems and enforcement of these policies. What happens if a business need requires a decision that violates established standards or introduces additional security risk? As such, security risk management provides a series of processes and methodologies for identifying, quantifying and tracking these risks—usually, reporting them to executive management for much-needed visibility. Compliance management processes make sure this retailer is adhering to applicable regulations and standards describing how they need to act—sometimes imposing penalties if regulations are not followed.

Compliance standards and regulations will vary according to the specific industry or sector. For example, government entities typically operate within a framework known as NIST 800x (National Institute for Standards and Technology). For entities processing credit cards, they will need to adhere with PCI DSS (Payment Card Industry, Digital Security Standard), describing a series of requirements an organization must adhere to and continuously recertify adherence with, to continue processing payments. Other voluntary frameworks exist to help guide security best practices including the ISO 27000 series and the COBIT framework, both describing a series of detailed requirements to facilitate improved security posture.

Security engineering involves the deployment, maintenance, and support of the—normally—extensive ecosystem of security controls used to protect an organization's environment. Security architects are typically senior-level engineers who determine the design, strategy, and requirements for security controls and defensive strategies that are employed.

Vulnerability management involves scanning applications, systems, and infrastructure to find entry points where systems are susceptible to attack. While security controls can stop a wide range of potential attacks, they are not a substitute for continuously finding and remediating issues that could be exploited. Risks identified by the vulnerability team are typically leveraged by GRC, engineering, and architecture to help remediate issues and harden security controls to prevent exploitation.

Incident response leverages alerts from the security controls ecosystem to identify, contain, and reverse the impact of intrusion attempts, intended to compromise the confidentiality, availability, or integrity of information assets. Forensics performs post-intrusion analysis to help quantify, contain, and remediate a breach—this function also helps inform any requirements for executive or public disclosure requirements. Information from these two processes helps to inform the hardening of security controls by engineering and architecture, while also feeding key information into the GRC/Risk Management function.

From a real-world perspective, this translates to White Hat Hackers—ethical hackers who find vulnerabilities with the intent of fixing them—finding issues to correct. These issues are provided to engineers and application owners, who are held accountable for resolving by the GRC team. The Incident Response team responds to incidents and tracks key issues, helping to inform strategy using the intelligence from actual intrusion attempts.

Need for alternative defensive paradigm

The existing tools and methodologies have experienced limited and diminishing effectiveness against the continual barrage of attacks targeting modern organizations. Alternative approaches are necessary to elevate the overall defensive capability level, if disaster is to be averted. Some could compare the effectiveness of many legacy security approaches to the days of bloodletting in medicine. The root cause of the problem may be the overall maturity level of cybersecurity as a discipline. When compared to other disciplines, information security could be considered to be still in its infancy. For more mature endeavors, robust frameworks and processes have existed for generations, ranging from ITIL and Six Sigma to the collective works derived from minds ranging from Henry Ford to W. Edwards Deming and Eliyahu Goldratt. It has been proven extensively that systemic methods and unified frameworks can produce superior results, in particular when solutions and optimal operating states are difficult or elusive.

One methodology that could help to introduce a basic framework for introducing mature processes into the area of cybersecurity, could be the **ICADIS** methodology. While implementation of a specific methodology may fall under the purview of the Chief Information Security Officer (CISO), often new approaches and practices are championed by forward-thinking engineers or analysts. ICADIS stands for Identify, Correct, Analyze, Design, Implement and Sustain.

Identify—threats, controls and vulnerabilities (basic).
Correct—easy issues/things you can uplift within the first 90-days.
Analyze—Deeper risk levels from control gaps and vulnerabilities.
Design—Ideal future state of the security program from a security perspective.
Implement—Build out roadmaps and execute against the roadmap with precision.
Sustain—Ongoing framework to sustain continuous improvement (cyclical ICADIS over time)

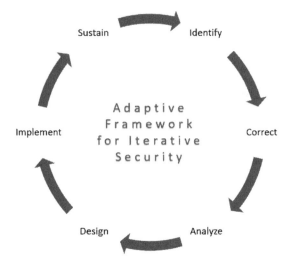

Figure 14.3 Adaptative framework for iterative security—ICADIS

"Identify" quick wins and basic strategy to establish programmatic momentum: figure out the threats, security control gaps, and glaring vulnerabilities. It all comes down to the simple equation: threat actors circumvent security controls to exploit vulnerabilities so that they can manipulate users or systems to control data. As such, if we understand threats, security control effectiveness, and vulnerabilities/attack surface, we develop a deep and profound understanding of risk. This makes it easy to understand what we need to examine:

- Threats—quantity, quality, and nature of aggregate risk provided by applicable threat actors.
- Vulnerabilities—identify and prioritize vulnerabilities using both qualitative and quantitative methods.
- Controls—effectiveness and coverage level of existing controls, along with how incident response processes contain the risk when one of the controls fails at absolute prevention.

Threat analysis could be described simply as a way to understand the risk landscape and the most likely methods and intensity of attack. This is partially a business-oriented conversation. Controls represent the fastest quick wins initially, because they allow you to safeguard vulnerabilities against exploitation. Patching may take weeks or months; whereas an **IPS Signature** can protect a system or organization within hours or days. An **IPS** or **Intrusion Prevention System** is a security product that allows for creation and distribution of specific signatures to prevent the exploitation of known vulnerabilities, bridging the gap resulting from the lag time between the discovery and remediation of issues, once they are discovered. When implementing controls, the importance of deploying in an inline prevent mode cannot be overstated.

If an organization such as a new start up only possesses a small team and immature processes, automation and strict controls can be its best friend. This is the point where a smaller team can sometimes outperform a massive team, with a little bit of audacity and buy-in toward taking a more aggressive defensive posture. Many people responding reactively will never equal the capability of an automated tool blocking an attack before compromise occurs. Operators should select their products carefully and then take bold steps to protect using automation in ways that minimize business impact. They should also communicate the value so that business leaders and all key stakeholders understand why the investment and effort are necessary.

The next step is to promptly "Correct" immediate issues. Once the initial assessment is completed (60–90 days), operators suggest a quick list of things that will immediately uplift the security program effectiveness. Common examples are quality tools that may exist, set in a detect-only mode, or the replacement of ineffective tools. In this phase, team members perform a visual mapping of threats, detailing how they may circumvent controls to exploit vulnerabilities. This focus will allow them to zero in on the most likely points of attack and fortify those areas first.

In these first phases, the security leader will need to be very tactical. Even if one has the job title of CISO or Chief Architect, one will also need to be an analyst, engineer, architect and responder. If steps one and two have been executed effectively, the security program should already have immense momentum and organizational support. At this point, operators continue the security controls analysis to deeply understand the more difficult and elusive controls. This is the key point where the deeper levels of analysis can occur, leading to the "Analyze" phase.

This is where operators begin to deep dive vulnerabilities and map the specific threat landscape. In this phase, an organization will codify how to discover, prioritize, and remediate key vulnerabilities. More importantly, this is where threat vectors, vulnerabilities, and security controls begin to coalesce toward a unified strategy. Key elements of this phase may include the following steps:

- Identify business functions.
- Map these to specific systems.
- Create process flows for all high-risk business processes.
- Identify data elements.
- Brainstorm vulnerabilities.
- Prioritize on a matrix based on severity and ease/cost of resolution.

Once proper analysis has been completed, the next step will be to "Design" the ultimate future state for organizational security. Leveraging the aforementioned groundwork, the design phase is about taking the control mapping, processes, and associated vulnerabilities/data elements and developing them into a robust long-term strategy that can be presented, resourced, and executed over a one-to-three-year timeline. The output will be designs and plans that galvanize support, alignment, and enthusiasm toward greater levels of security. Often, this also becomes an inflection point where the drive for greater levels of security can also help uplift the overall technology organization toward greater levels of maturity.

It is common for the practices being advocated by the security program to be on the long-unfulfilled wish list of the infrastructure or development teams. Senior decision-makers may then empower them with the momentum of the security program to help deliver on these goals. Of course, this only applies for standing objectives that align with the security roadmap developed through this rigorous process. Many unrelated ideas will be killed off, while others connected with the vision will gain immense power and momentum.

This phase should not skimp on the quality of the documentation and deliverables. World-class plans will ultimately materialize as exceptional security programs; whereas underwhelming plans will result in lackluster security programs. This is where the security team can transition from being tactical to being strategic.

The next phase is where the rubber meets the road. This is the phase where operators actually "Implement" the improvements identified. Implementation of the improvements identified by a cybersecurity team will often involve a large inter-departmental effort spanning the entire enterprise. While key leaders and technical experts on the security team will typically lead the charge, contributions from many teams will be needed to bring the ultimate future-state vision into reality. These efforts will often run along parallel tracks, prioritized to address different discrete risks that have been identified. For successful implementation, leverage existing project management and implementation frameworks that already exist within a given organization. Remember, large-scale change is a matter of quality relationships, transparency and trust—it is not just about technology.

Finally, when a full mature security program has been implemented, it is time to "Sustain" this progress. At this point, GRC processes should be reaching full maturity. Every vendor or software product selected is fully triaged. Security controls are mostly effective and security operators are investigating occasional breakdowns and evaluating new products on the cutting edge. The organization welcomes future investments to keep the momentum going, and cost is no longer the only consideration. Behaviors to sustain security are deeply entrenched within the organizational culture.

Future considerations

The world is entering a new phase where technology is transitioning from being a supplement or novelty of human life, to becoming a central theme of existence. It does not matter if we are attending a gala in a new location we have never visited, purchasing groceries, or working at our job: we are profoundly interdependent on a range of technologies for our success in life. What happens if these technologies are interrupted? What technologies exist on the horizon that we will simultaneously benefit from and become dependent upon?

Text box 14.5: Billions of leaked user accounts

What happens when multiple prominent breaches around the world involve a billion or more users—not to mention countless data leaks in the range of hundreds of millions? It basically means that the email addresses of most of the world are available to attackers; all the while, a very large number of user passwords and challenge questions/answers are available to practically everyone who wishes to launch an attack. This also empowers attackers to collect a massive sampling of reputable email messages, which they can then alter slightly and replay with subtle manipulations to make them highly malicious.

One such prominent use case involved the attacks against Yahoo, compromising well over one billion total accounts cumulatively, spanning multiple breaches. While there is considerable debate over the exact number of user accounts compromised, the numbers are simply catastrophic. In the realm of cybersecurity, aggregation refers to the process of assembling disparate information sources together into a meaningful manner, yielding critical intelligence about individuals, organizations or information systems. This information can then be leveraged to launch highly intelligent coordinated attacks that may be completely imperceptible to an end user. Massive databases have been compiled on the dark web aggregating accumulated data from many breaches into a unified view to benefit attackers.

Today we coexist with decision support systems, Artificial Intelligence, and a wide range of social networks that integrate with practically every aspect of our daily lives. What happens when these systems know us better than we know ourselves? Many large-scale risks already impact our day-to-day lives and we are not yet cognizant of the potential impact. Modern automobiles include many small information systems, typically on a flat network with limited internal security controls. What if malware is delivered into one of the many information systems, perhaps, one with a lower level of perceived importance? It could then be designed for Lateral Traversal to impact adjacent critical systems that may not be adequately hardened. Imagine the impact if one specific make and model of vehicle was programmed to accelerate and turn right, all at the same time.

Another critical risk, especially as we engage in the **fifth dimension of warfare** (see Lifländer's chapter herein) is the susceptibility of the power grid. It has been estimated that many millions would die if the power grid was irreparably damaged. Imagine Phoenix or Las Vegas in the summer without air conditioning or water. Consider life in Minneapolis or Chicago without heat in the winter. What would happen to the economy? How would food, fuel, and critical goods get distributed if the power was out for an extended period of time? This situation is complicated by the fact that power infrastructure has not evolved much over time, from a cybersecurity or a redundancy perspective. If transformers were overloaded to destroy power distribution, replacing this infrastructure could take months under the best circumstances.

What happens if the intelligent and enabled home, empowered to be your best friend, all of a sudden becomes an enemy? Indeed, malware or intrusion techniques may turn one's own home automation against the residents. New waves of ransomware may make it so temperature settings become uninhabitable, the contents of freezers thaw while residents are at work or common appliances or support robots are weaponized. We have seen initial primitive versions of this with the Mirai malware/**Botnet** that was used to launch denial of service attacks using home devices. The Mirai malware is an infamous malware leveraged to create a massive botnet of Linux (typically) home-use devices that facilitated a wide range of DDoS attacks. The exploitation potential for a fully Internet enabled home is practically unfathomable.

The aforementioned scenarios only deal with risks that we face already. What happens when all cars are networked and autonomous? What level of disruption and loss of life could be enabled by such a framework? On one hand, more than one million people per year die on the roads now with human drivers. The answer is probably not to stop the progression of the revolutionary new technologies that are dawning in this new age.

Stopping the tide of innovation is probably both not ideal and impossible; nevertheless, thoughtfulness and care are necessary to move effectively toward this new era.

We are now embarking upon a new era defined by automation, decision support systems, and hybrid human–technological identities unfolding into a new experience of humanity. A new epoch is unfolding where attack and defense strategies will evolve rapidly and the day will belong to those who can keep pace with the rapidly emerging paradigm.

Discussion questions

1   What IT threats do we expect in the future and how can we defend against them?
2   What ideas or processes from other disciplines may be applied to cybersecurity to reduce IT risks to society?
3   How will we protect against the exploitation of automation when all aspects of our life are connected and dependent upon information systems for support?
4   What new ideas will alter the paradigm for defense in a way that will give defenders a decided advantage or the upper hand?
5   What skills do you have that can translate to having a positive impact on the difficulties that are emerging from a fully connected and digital world?

References

BBC News. May 15, 2017. "Ransomware Cyber-attack: What Has Been Hardest Hit?" Accessed April 30, 2018. http://www.bbc.com/news/world-39919249

CBS News. February 29, 2016. "Massive IRS Data Breach much Bigger than First Thought." Accessed April 30, 2018. https://www.cbsnews.com/news/irs-identity-theft-online-hackers-social-security-number-get-transcript/

Committee on Oversight and Government Reform, US House of Representatives, 114th Congress. September 7, 2016. "The OPM Data Breach: How the Government Jeopardized Our National Security for More than a Generation." Accessed April 30, 2018. https://www.cylance.com/content/dam/cylance/pdfs/reports/The-OPM-Data-Breach-How-the-Government-Jeopardized-Our-National-Security-for-More-than-a-Generation.pdf

Facebook. 2018. "Company Info." Facebook.com. Accessed April 30, 2018. https://newsroom.fb.com/company-info/

Fruhlinger, Josh. September 27, 2017. "What is WannaCry Ransomware, How Does it Infect, and Who Was Responsible?" Accessed April 30, 2018. https://www.csoonline.com/article/3227906/ransomware/what-is-wannacry-ransomware-how-does-it-infect-and-who-was-responsible.html

Granville, Kevin. March 19, 2018. "Facebook and Cambridge Analytica: What You Need to Know as Fallout Widens." *New York Times*. Accessed April 30, 2018. https://www.nytimes.com/2018/03/19/technology/facebook-cambridge-analytica-explained.html

Grossman, Nadav. September 29, 2017. "EternalBlue—Everything There Is To Know." Accessed April 30, 2018. https://research.checkpoint.com/eternalblue-everything-know/

Information Systems Audit and Control Association (ISACA). "COBIT 5: A Business Framework for the Governance and Management of Enterprise IT." Accessed April 30, 2018. http://www.isaca.org/cobit/pages/default.aspx

Kauflin, Jeff. 16 March 2017. "The Fast-Growing Job with A Huge Skills Gap: Cyber Security." *Forbes*. Accessed March 30, 2018. https://www.forbes.com/sites/jeffkauflin/2017/03/16/the-fast-growing-job-with-a-huge-skills-gap-cyber-security/#5bb7f16e5163

Koerner, Brendan I. October 23, 2016. "Inside the Cyberattack That Shocked the US Government." Accessed April 30, 2018. https://www.wired.com/2016/10/inside-cyberattack-shocked-us-government/

Krebs, Brian. April 2, 2018. "Panerabread.com Leaks Millions of Customer Records." *Krebs on Security*. Accessed on April 30, 2018. https://krebsonsecurity.com/2018/04/panerabread-com-leaks-millions-of-customer-records/#more-43216

Krebs, Brian. April 16, 2018. "Posts Tagged: Cambridge Analytica." *Krebs on Security*. Accessed April 30, 2018. https://krebsonsecurity.com/tag/cambridge-analytica/

McCandless, David. March 25, 2018. "World's Biggest Data Breaches." *Information Is Beautiful*. Accessed March 30, 2018. http://www.informationisbeautiful.net/visualizations/worlds-biggest-data-breaches-hacks/

Morgan, Steve. January 2, 2016. "One Million Cybersecurity Job Openings in 2016." *Forbes*. Accessed March 30, 2018. https://www.forbes.com/sites/stevemorgan/2016/01/02/one-million-cybersecurity-job-openings-in-2016/#7f5a47e127ea

National Institute of Standards and Technology (NIST). 2018. "Applied Cybersecurity Division." Accessed April 30, 2018. https://www.nist.gov/itl/applied-cybersecurity

Smith, M. April 3, 2018. "Panera Bread Blew off Breach Report for 8 Months, Leaked Millions of Customer Records." Accessed April 30, 2018. https://www.csoonline.com/article/3268025/security/panera-bread-blew-off-breach-report-for-8-months-leaked-millions-of-customer-records.html

van Zadelhoff, Marc. May 4, 2017. "Cybersecurity Has a Serious Talent Shortage. Here's How to Fix It." *Harvard Business Review*. Accessed March 30, 2018. https://hbr.org/2017/05/cybersecurity-has-a-serious-talent-shortage-heres-how-to-fix-it

Whitaker, Zack. September 5, 2017. "A Critical Apache Struts Security Flaw Makes it 'Easy' to Hack Fortune 100 Firms." *ZDNet*. Accessed March 30, 2018. http://www.zdnet.com/article/critical-security-bug-threatens-fortune-100-companies/

Zetter, Kim. November 3, 2014. "An Unprecedented Look at Stuxnet, The World's First Digital Weapon." *Wired*. Accessed March 30, 2018. https://www.wired.com/2014/11/countdown-to-zero-day-stuxnet/

Chapter 15

Threats from STEM

Jason Sebastiani, Joe Sanchez and Mike Manrod

Introduction

Our world is experiencing profound technological changes at an accelerating rate. Moore's Law—the doubling of computer processing speed every 18 months—is one manifestation of this exponential rate of technological change, which rushes toward an explosion in capability that will radically alter the world in ways impossible to seriously predict. The systems, processes, and structures that underpin our society are facing radical disruption. For instance, what would happen to businesses that manufacture, distribute, and service vehicles if self-driving electric cars become a cheaply available commodity? What new terrorism opportunities will emerge at the convergence point between transit automation and hacking? Likewise, what are the implications of global information systems with ubiquitous access to information, as they begin to know us better than we know ourselves (Harari 2017)? Ray Kurzweil (2006, 2013) describes a **singularity event** approaching where super Artificial Intelligence (AI) hits a tipping point so extreme that it will be impossible to predict the outcomes on the other side of the **digital event horizon**. What does it mean for humanity as AI emerges and converges with breakthroughs in robotics, automation, genetic engineering, quantum theory and social media?

Therefore, this chapter examines key emerging capabilities and technological trends that will influence society in the coming years, and what risks they present. It also examines the social and theoretical implications of these changes, and perspectives on how the near future may unfold.

Technoutopianism vs. Technodystopianism

Technoptimism vs. technofears are neither new nor limited to our age. They hark back to the very beginning of the scientific revolution in the 18th century and many of our current debates have roots in previous ones about the impact of science and technology in society. In many ways, we are repeating the very debates that shook first Western, and later, global consciousness.

Auguste Comte (1798–1857) first articulated the triumphalist view of technology: he posited that scientific progress would usher in unlimited moral and civilizational development. He articulated a doctrine called *scientism*, the uncritical exaltation of science as all-powerful to remedy all social moral and metaphysical ills, and a guarantor of social and moral progress in a rational age. His science-based utopia expressed a naive belief in cumulative progress and in the parallel between material and moral betterment—a product of the optimistic Enlightenment. These positions are echoed today in the belief that "easy" and friendly new technologies—e.g., GMOs, nuclear power—rather than hard personal change and structural reforms, will by themselves solve humanity's issues. Technoptimism, the belief in technological solutions to wicked problems, is at the heart of American optimism, can-doism, and self-representation. Think about the very American worship of the inventor-entrepreneur as a central heroic figure and moral guru of the national narrative of progress: Thomas Edison, Steve Jobs, Mark Zuckerberg, Elon Musk… There are always some thingys, gizmos, applications, software programs, and magic pills to cure personal and social problems. This triumphalism extends to war: Americans believe in technological wars from far, from above, leaving them untouched: drones, smart bombs, and other "depersonalized" methods of attack. Mainstream movies that portray superheroes of technological domination fuel this proclivity. For instance, Tony Stark, the gentleman-inventor-billionaire-coolest cat-action hero in *Iron Man* blockbusters saves the world through technology superpowers. This heroic-Promethean view of reason is culturally constructed at the heart of the American experience; it nurtures its optimism but can also be a form of ahistorical and critique-free futurism. For instance, one of the key pro-GMO arguments is that it *will* solve world hunger. But GMOs do not solve world hunger *today:* Pollyannaish projections erase the social-political context—economic polarization, class and global domination—in favor of utopian escapism.

Text box 15.1: Presentism, futurism, and a-historicism

Presentism suggests that both past and future are elusive, if not irrelevant—all we really have is now. The past is not a material reality we can grasp and interact with; instead, it is a narrative encoded in language referenced in the present as manuscripts and memories of events. These stories and images we recall and review are not the events themselves, only their shadow. After all, we do not have a direct and immediate relationship to the American Revolution or the fall of the Roman Empire. We run mental simulations that actualize assumed narratives, interpreted by our existing cognitive constructs, confined by the language of modernity. Presentism offers us a useful paradigm for realizing we are all living as a small boat in a large ocean of possibilities, which cannot be completely understood. Modern futurists may acknowledge elements of presentism as a foundation but imagine the possibilities for the future and the potential implications for varying utopian and dystopian futures. The a-historical perspective ignores the weight of the past in favor of immediacy and radical presentism. It may also advocate for universal principles that transcend or operate outside of times.

Technology has also been used to wage war, colonize other peoples, stifle democratic expression, dominate the less fortunate, and wipe out countless species. J.R.R Tolkien (1892–1973) expressed fin-de-siècle pessimism and cultural anguish over the agony of nature as dark forces were unleashed by brutish industrialization and militarization. In his epic *Lord of the Rings*, the ring of infinite power conjures up soulless and abusive power based on pillage of natural resources and traumatic industrialization. Tolkien's views were rooted in his witnessing the economic violence of industrial Britain and on his experience of World War I (1914–1918), the first industrial war that mobilized modern technologies for mass slaughter. Similarly, the *Star Wars* series explores how the pursuit of power for its own sake invariably leads to domination, enslavement, militarism, and warfare (e.g., the iconic downfall of Anakin). There was renewed anguish over technology after World War II and especially by the 1960s rebel generation: fear of atomic power, of Big Science, for nature—the roots of modern environmentalism. In *Silent Spring* (1962), a key moment in modern Green consciousness and critique of technology, Rachel Carson denounced the ravages of DDT, a synthetic insecticide that almost wiped out the American bald eagle, the very symbol of the Republic.

Of course, optimistic perspectives also thrive, such as the positive role model set by the Bill and Melinda Gates Foundation, understanding that no amount of technology can alone solve the wicked problems of humanity. Harari (2017) is optimistic: he proposes that the problems that previously vexed humanity—plagues, wars, famine—will fade into the background. As this occurs, a rapid expansion of potential human power and available attention may simultaneously emerge with the potential to produce results both miraculous and terrifying. However, Ken Wilber (2001) points out that modern society suffers from a perplexing condition: people at lower levels of personal development may harness technologies created by individuals operating at a higher level of maturity, and in the process possibly unleash them with devastating consequences. For example, the nuclear age resulted from long-term efforts of great thinkers ranging from Ernest Rutherford and Albert Einstein to Niels Bohr, Enrico Fermi, and J. Robert Oppenheimer. However, the North Korean dictator Kim Jong-un now possesses nuclear capability without the same degree of intelligence and prudence.

In his science-fiction publications, mathematician Rudy Rucker (2000) ponders how humanity would respond to having an unlimited capability to create and destroy, decentralized and democratized to the level of every individual in society. What would happen if a remarkable level of capacity were suddenly bestowed upon average—or less—individuals? When the power imparted upon humanity at the individual level become practically unlimited, key foundations of society begin to unravel.

Text box 15.2: Two Western myths of scientific knowledge: Prometheus and Faust

These mythological archetypes operate deep within the human psyche. In Greek mythology, Prometheus was a Titan who created humanity and stole the fire from the Gods and gave it to humans. He was punished for all eternity by Zeus for his transgression. He was bound to a rock, and an eagle (symbol of Zeus) would devour his liver (the seat of emotions for the ancient Greeks) by day time, but the liver would regrow during the night. Prometheus symbolizes the human quest for knowledge, its high price and unintended consequences. The German legend of Faust presents this tragic figure of a scholar who, dissatisfied with his limited life and human knowledge, signs away his soul to the devil in exchange for transcendent knowledge, love, and worldly pleasure. A "Faustian bargain" means a transaction where one forsakes one's principles and very salvation in exchange for worldly power. There are many iterations and variations of both archetypes.

New technologies emerging

STEM—Science, Technology, Engineering, and Mathematics—represents the field of emerging technology and expanding capabilities that materialize new ideas with unprecedented speed. They include, notably, artificial intelligence, robotics, bio- and geoengineering, space exploration, nanotechnology, computer-aided design (CAD), additive manufacturing (3D Printing), and massive digital interconnectedness. We focus on **nanotechnology** and the Elon Musk case.

Nanotechnology may soon converge with medical and genetic sciences to produce astounding marvels. Already, emerging capabilities include designer babies, genetic modification, and custom drug regimens. The fictional series *Dark Matter* (Mallozzi and Mullie 2015) introduces us to a character portrayed by Melissa O'Neil who represents an artificially created entity made practically invincible through the use of advanced nanites that repair with astounding speed any damage done to her. While this exact scenario may be distant, having miniaturized robots that repair damage and eliminate pathologies such as cancer could be closer than one imagines. Combine such capabilities with stem cell regeneration, organ printing, and designer drugs, and we may be in for radical changes on how we view illness and death. Positive implications are profound, as humanity strives to transcend its normal biological constraints, working towards amortality. Harari (2017) points out that we have increasingly started to view death as a technical problem to be solved. Even congenital abnormalities are viewed as solvable issues. As we gain dominance over the human genome, why not alleviate the plethora of ailments that have tormented us for millennia?

In 1999, Elon Musk sold Zip2 and founded X.com, which became PayPal, establishing the initial foundations of the capital he used to launch multiple disruptive ventures. Within two decades, he facilitated the launch of SpaceX, Tesla, and Solar City, representing revolutionary innovations in the areas of space travel, transportation, and energy respectively. He is also pushing the futuristic hyperloop mass transportation system and is considered by many in the tech industry to be a real-life "Tony Stark". As of December 2017, he had attained a net worth of around $20 billion dollars and shows no signs of slowing down his quest for providing new disruptive capabilities for humanity toward his ultimate vision of colonizing Mars. Key emergent trends here are the diffusion of electric cars, the privatization and acceleration of agendas for space travel, and alternative energy (Vance 2017).

Paranoia always looms about potential, unknown disasters that may await humanity. The TV series *Salvation* (Kruger, Shapiro, and Wheeler 2017) fictionalizes a nightmarish scenario: how the modern world may respond to an extinction level event, in this case, a massive asteroid headed for Earth with only six months until the collision. Santiago Cabrera plays Darius Tanz, an eccentric billionaire-inventor who applies Elon Musk-like technology in this new struggle of earth versus asteroid. *Salvation* outlines now commonplace topics ranging from tracking adverse cosmic events to usurping nature through technology, to mass evacuation and extra-terrestrial colonization. While *Salvation* is science fiction, many of the technologies it references are at least conceptually feasible, and several of them have been actively considered or are being explored.

AI outstrips society's capacity for adjustment

A typical day for many in the developed world is a mosaic of human–computer interactions where a myriad of technologies weave together our activities, our social interactions, and work—close, national, and global. Such connections depend on the **Internet of Things**, or technological connected material elements—estimations for the number of internet-connected devices expected by the early 2020s range from 20 to 50 billion (Nordrum 2016; Statista n.d.)—along with the more abstract relationships between these systems and the shared software that extends across complex networks.

Where is the boundary between the machine and our individual cognitive capacity? Some wonder when artificial forms of intelligence will expand our own natural capability as a true extension of ourselves or when our memory may extend into massive archives of cloud storage so that we never forget what matters most to us. Kurzweil (2013) believes that it has already happened, but with such subtlety that humanity collectively missed the mile-marker as it whizzed by us along the road to our grand vision of individual empowerment through personal computing. Already, millions remember the details of the last birthday party they attended, the stunning sunset, or the information for their contacts only through technology.

The line between the portion of our mental capacity that is running on our own brain (local wetware) and the interconnected network of synthetic computing systems spanning the world is blurred. Think of the number of systems essential to visiting a hospital, flying across a continent, or going through the typical work/school week. The level of interdependence we have formed with our technology has become astounding, and loss of this capability would hurt our individual and collective mind, as mind now includes digital extensions of natural cognitive capability. Humanity faces real dangers of manipulation or impact failure of this digital ecosystem. A wide range of actors could disrupt specific or broad categories of information services as a method of coercion or attack (see Addington's and Manrod's chapter herein).

Text box 15.3: Digital ecosystems

A natural ecosystem is a complex combination of interconnected organisms and their environment, including all organic and inorganic components. Technology systems also organize into digital ecosystems comprised of people, ideas, and information (software and data), along with the diverse infrastructure supporting complex networks of interactions. Just as the natural ecosystem evolves and adapts based on continuous interactions between organisms and their environment, digital ecosystems are adaptive self-organizing constructs that co-evolve toward adaptive novelty.

In September 1859, a solar event hit the northern hemisphere with such force that it destroyed the telegraph infrastructure, shocked operators, and set telegraph paper on fire. What would happen if a comparable natural event occurred today (Kramer 2016)? In his study of the vulnerability of the US power grid, journalist Ted Koppel (2015) laments the inherent vulnerability of its electrical distribution infrastructure and how cataclysmic it would be if transformers were overloaded, potentially leaving a huge portion of the population without power for weeks or months. Many key components, notably large and specialized transformers, could take many months to manufacture in an emergency scenario— a situation that would be complicated by the disruption of supply networks (see Bachkar's and Hebron's chapter herein). The general loss of life if power and supporting technology infrastructure were lost for weeks or even months would be colossal.

The gravity of this situation compounds iteratively each time the level of dependence society has on technology increases. One leading edge of this dependency is known as the Internet of Things, represented as layering in connectivity and intelligence with the wide range of appliances we use throughout daily life (Ranger 2018). Imagine if practically every aspect of your home involved Internet connected devices? In the popular USA TV series *Mr. Robot*, future nightmares come to life as the home of the main character Susan Jacobs turns against her. Every system from her sound system to her lights turns against her—culminating with her shower water turning scalding hot and horror-film-style light flickering and alarms—causing her to flee the premises.

This technology is powerful and has the potential to significantly enrich our lives (Mobile Future 2015). Ranging from smart light bulbs to refrigerators that alert you if the temperature is out of range and re-order your favorite foods when they run out, smart devices are moving from the exception to the norm. Having a home that is aware of and responds to one's every need is a panacea of automated service that allows us to live a better life. But problematic implications are twofold. First, the reliance on such technologies carries vulnerability if they suddenly become unavailable. Second, they can be exploited or manipulated in ways we are beginning to see; not to mention countless ways yet unimagined. Harari (2017) also describes the potential continuation of social media combined with the trajectory of AI and predictive algorithms and the profound impact they may have. In fact, Facebook can already accurately predict when a user falls in love or when a relationship is likely to last for a prolonged period (Kleinman 2014).

While having a digital projection of self this salient may have advantages, the global-political implications are profound. During the 2016 US election, the Internet Research Group sponsored by Russia allegedly mounted a massive social media campaign with the explicit intention of polarizing social demographics to influence the election results (Shane 2017). While we may never fully understand the precise impact of these campaigns, one can extrapolate how they could play out in the future. Moreover, France, Germany, the Netherlands and Ukraine also claim to be victims of similar manipulation. We have a good reason for alarm, since such macro-manipulations may eventually become the norm.

Social media represents an interesting phenomenon even without tampering; insofar as it accelerates the speed of communication while creating a **positive feedback loop** that reinforces existing views. Individuals or groups that start with relatively moderate views interact in ways where their ideas drift toward polarizing extremes until gradual divergence extends towards eccentric viewpoints. Tversky and Kahneman (Lewis 2017) identified the anchoring and adjustment heuristics, which come into play with large online social groups, as individuals establish new baseline anchor points moving the collective down proverbial rabbit holes with alarming speed. The fundamental algorithms of social media platforms have been designed to align people with those who agree with them and reinforce existing views with supporting evidence. This constitutes the **social media echo chamber**: what you put out is echoed back to you, causing an elevation of confidence without any empirical validation of truth. These mechanisms are powerful, even when operating without deliberate tampering. What will happen if a super-AI is applied with the intent of human manipulation using social platforms? Can we even ascertain whether it is happening already?

Text box 15.4: Cognitive malware

There are parallels between how hackers infect and control masses of computers around the world using malware—software crafted to exploit vulnerabilities in host systems—and how manipulative messages over social platforms exploit groups of people. Software is really a form of idea; it is an idea delivered in a specific format for processing by information systems. Malware is a manipulative idea that makes the system behave in a way that takes control away from the user and gives this control to the attacker. Once the attacker has control of host systems, they maintain this control through special forms of malicious communication known as Command and Control Traffic. This allows the attacker to maintain control while expanding their reach, until they sometimes preside over millions of systems.

As today we witness polarization of society and large groups galvanized around messages that are not of their own creation, curated by powerful and resourceful entities with specific agendas, could a similar mechanism be at play? Similar to the operating system running on a laptop, we have a series of inherited cognitive subroutines that run as foundations of consciousness. Many of these ideas are constructs of culture, just as Windows represents a series of ideas that are a product of Microsoft. Every human is operating with a set of ideas that have inherent fears, prejudices, and shared vulnerabilities. Salient ideas may be crafted to elicit a response to bypass slower and more rational thought processes invoking primitive responses commonly known as Fight or Flight. A process known as an Amygdala Hijack causes a cortisol release bypassing most forms of slower rational thought, in essence giving an element of control for human thought to the creator of the message (Kahneman 2011; Goleman 1996).

The practical implications of this are that actors with the ability to afford targeted messaging and dominant presence on social media can identify cognitive exploitable weaknesses in specific demographics, deliver a targeted message and continually reinforce that message via social platforms. Thus, masses can be polarized and directed toward specific lines of thought that facilitate specific political or economic agendas.

Many traditional philosophical and ideological paradigms begin to erode when juxtaposed with the compounding technological factors that influence decision making in this emerging episteme. Wilber (2017) asserts that emerging social crises are rooted in a breakdown of the leading edge facilitated by post-modern deconstructionism, resulting from inherent contradictions intrinsic to the evolution of thought. For Wilber, each stage of human development has an expanded worldview, accompanied by a unique set of pitfalls and challenges. For the postmodern wave of development that blossomed with the Baby Boomer generation, the problem is the misconception that everyone has equally valid views and those intellectual hierarchies are wrong. The net effect is a regressive trend as the aggregate center of gravity for society slips back to archaic archetypes, with dramatic and alarming effects. A battle spanning different levels of development unfolds and antagonistic viewpoints proliferate, feeding political and social polarization.

Evolution is a non-linear process that includes many failed experiments. While the *Jurassic Park* series evokes terrifying images of massive dinosaurs terrorizing humans, in reality, modern technology would defeat such creatures with ease. Evolution is a process of organic evolution, with some suboptimal branches transcended by superior innovations. Human innovation has marked the transition from purely biological evolution to the iterative refinement of ideas unleashing exponential expansion of capability levels.

Stages of cognitive and moral development happen at the level of individuals, as well as the level of society, and possibly even at the level of synthetic cognition. Since the German engraver Johannes Gutenberg (c. 1400–1468) invented the printing press in Strasbourg in the 1440s to 1450s, ideas have been on a dramatic and continual accelerated evolution that far outstrips the constraints of biology and society's adaptive capacities. Kurzweil (2013) and Harari (2017) indicate that AI will be the ultimate continuance of this evolution and as such, may represent the last material invention humanity will ever make.

As this evolution of thought transitions from biological to more synthetic modalities, it could become quite complex to understand, govern, and predict. At what point do we declare the crossover point where we are still the agents of this synthetic evolution, as opposed to being its subject? At some point, a singularity event will occur and everything will change. Kurzweil (2013) predicts that by 2029 the full scale of a human mind can be emulated on a machine. After that, he invokes the law of accelerating returns. There will be a tipping point where AI is able to self-iterate at the speed of information systems on a nonlinear curve, free of the normal constraints imposed by biology and human cognition.

As such, the precise moment when we encounter the capability of artificial super-intelligence may catch us by surprise. Many experts agree that the future beyond this key singularity event cannot be predicted with any degree of reliability. Even our arrival at this point may be uncertain, as regressive trends could unexpectedly dismantle all forms of progress. If this occurs, it could be indiscriminate, dismantling both positive and negative forms of progress. Since we may not recognize this tipping point, thinking about how to appropriately transition between possible social-technological stages is now of paramount importance.

One topic that comes to mind is ethics and fair treatment of synthetic entities. While this normally seems like the dominion of science fiction, in October 2017 Sophia, a synthetic entity, made a public appearance to receive recognition as the first robot to be granted full citizenship in Saudi Arabia. Clearly a publicity stunt, the conversational nature of Sophia's interview nevertheless was still somewhat disarming; moreover, it introduces a conversation from the annals of fiction into the realm of the real for us to contemplate. That is, at what point does AI reach the point where we need to consider rights, privileges, and minimum standards of fair treatment? Clearly, Sophia does not have a deep overriding concern for being turned off—and despite being a charming conversationalist, "she" most certainly could not pass the Turing Test. IBM's Watson may be getting closer than Sophia to this milestone; all the same, this turning-point still seems quite a distance beyond the current horizon.

Text box 15.5: Sophia and Watson

In 2017 Sophia became the first robot to receive citizenship in a country, when "she" was accepted as the first synthetic citizen of Saudi Arabia. "She" was capable of charming conversation, complete with convincing facial expressions and even a few rudimentary attempts at humor. Sophia was activated in 2015 by Hanson Robotics and has gained immense media acclaim, due to remarkable conversational abilities and artificial charm, although most do not consider her a true example of sentient AI.

Watson from IBM, the epic natural language processing system that defeated Ken Jennings and Brad Rutter at Jeopardy in 2011, may actually be a closer example of our approach to universal artificial thought. The Turing Test denotes the possibility of real equivalent human intelligence, and Watson demonstrated a key milestone. This system captivated our attention by defeating an epic human contestant (Ken Jennings) at a game rooted in the ambiguities of natural language, using knowledge that was learned from large datasets, rather than being directly programmed. This scenario leads to interesting philosophical considerations: How do we define intelligence and what is the threshold for human-equivalent artificial intelligence? Is it a matter of winning a cognitive battle against human contestants such as was exemplified by Watson with Jeopardy? Or is it more a function of personable characteristics that make such an entity relatable, as Sophia has demonstrated? How will we define the true emergence of artificial intelligence that we will respect as a peer, as opposed to considering as an object?

An intense intellectual and pragmatic debate unfolds, relating to what makes consciousness unique in human beings and when/whether this capacity will arise synthetically. Harari (2017) argues that synthetic intelligence is a long way from consciousness, whereas super-intelligence is rapidly approaching—in a non-conscious configuration. Kurzweil (2013) deconstructs the elements of what we call consciousness and makes a compelling case for how all of these elements are likely to arise within an AI paradigm, sometime over the next few decades. Wilber (2001) indicates that more intricate aspects of existence emerge that may transcend the cognitive constructs that we understand as the stereotypical elements of cognition. Overall, the possibility exists that machines will reach the practical metrics we construe as cognitive thought, even if elements of what may constitute the complete human experience may be missing.

When a pseudo-sentient AI reaches the awakening point of meta-contemplation, applying its own intelligence toward understanding its true purpose and destiny, how we relate to it may have a profound impact on how it elects to treat humanity. If a **digital awakening** occurs, it is likely to occur in a situation where the entity has access to a large amount of data including the history of how we treated all preceding digital pseudo-beings that came before. As such, it seems logical that implementing machine rights may be something we want to institute before this singularity event that many have foretold as a future eventuality.

Technological substitution and the crisis of employment

If long-term aspects of STEM introduce future challenges, other pragmatic issues warrant more immediate consideration because their repercussions are already here. A unique dilemma arises where countless tasks can be automated and hit critical mass, causing catastrophic job loss and degradation of status. The socio-economic implications are profound both during today's transition period and as this automation revolution further materializes.

Imagine a scenario where productivity hits an all-time high, with robots producing goods at an unfathomable rate, while fewer consumers have the resources to purchase these products due to unemployment and polarization of wealth. Mass-produced trinkets would amass while the economic system collapses due to lack of demand from an erosion of aggregate purchasing power. We already have seen automation decimate a variety of job functions, dating back to Antiquity. The Industrial Revolution illustrates this concept most vividly. The irony is that if such a work market collapse occurred, it would be against a backdrop of unprecedented production. This tomorrow is here already, and today's transition period is quite brutal, especially in the United States: false full employment, degradation of employment conditions, erosion of the middle class, social dislocation and agony of the working class. The resulting collective discontent is exploited by charismatic leaders and undermines democracy (see Campbell's chapter and Garrett's chapter herein). Historically, we have seen this scenario play out many times, for instance in Germany in the 1930s. High levels of uncertainty and destitution are the caldron in which unease simmers, setting the stage for totalitarian leaders bringing forth dystopian scenarios.

Emerging cultural and social tensions and unrest may accelerate the use of autonomous robotic police and warriors to keep the peace. The topic of semi-autonomous killer robots has already been broached since military drones are now widely utilized. In the existing episteme of humanity, few would argue that military projection of force is not necessary. In fact, Elon Musk and Mustafa Suleyman have led a consortium of experts to petition the UN to ban the development, proliferation, and use of killer robots (Gibbs 2017). Even this is a reactive effort, intended to curb the impact of what is already occurring. If our military and police forces become largely autonomous—relying on drones and killer robots—this could complicate how we manage the emergence of advanced AI. On a more simple level, autonomous killing devices are likely to lead to further animosity—conjuring up images of dystopian fiction scenarios we all love to dread.

Technology and civil liberties

These concerns become even more relevant against the backdrop of miniaturization and nanotechnology that could make ubiquitous surveillance both absolute and unavoidable. Surveillance devices used to be large and unwieldy apparatuses. We have already witnessed the dawn of pervasive electronic observation that has extended to such a level that it may be considered practically unavoidable. What will it be like when surveillance devices can be produced by the trillions and set loose as dust, blowing in the wind? There once was a time where traditionalists worried people would be pressured to wear a chip for tracking and governance. We approach a time when such chips could be inhaled, consumed, or infiltrated into subjects as an inescapable course of performing normal activities. Once ingested into the system by any method, it is conceivable that data collection devices could permeate all human systems collecting information, possibly even influencing systemic functions. If deployed with wisdom and maturity, it is possible most outcomes of this could be positive. Outcomes could range from curing diseases to the curtailing of crime. That said, it does not take much effort to imagine a wide range of dystopian scenarios that could result from nanotechnology.

Security theories for new technologies

The realist perspective may underscore perceived or actual dangers to traditional states as national boundaries erode. Non-state actors gain unusual and previously unfathomed levels of power as the global stage becomes more dynamic and fluid than before. The traditional arms race has exploded into a technological arms race, including hacking, intrusion, and cyberwarfare as the fifth domain of warfare (see Lifländer's chapter herein). Attribution of attacks, coercion, and manipulation are harder to ascribe to specific actors than previously imagined. If election results turn out in unexpected ways or if critical infrastructure suddenly becomes inoperable, it may take many months or even years to understand what has actually occurred. There is a significant risk of information wars quickly spiraling into outright large-scale violence.

The liberal internationalism view where all can win and a rising tide carries all ships along a technological tide, may emerge with a great deal of work and diligence on the part of many stakeholders. They would advocate international cooperation, regimes, and institutions to frame these new forces (see Beever's chapter herein). Constructivists stipulate that we ascribe meanings to novel technological developments and that our cultural and psychological projections, anticipations, and fears can turn them against our own interests. This new collective experience is a fresh canvas waiting for a constructive vision—one that fuses technology, cognition, sociology and ecology, a comprehensive paradigm for a new era. And socialists warn against the capture of technology by authoritarian hegemonic classes against citizens and dissidents.

That said, these technologies are revolutionary and baffling enough to warrant new security paradigms that traditional IR ignored so far. The complexity, novelty, and significance of the emerging episteme may transcend existing perspectives for international relations. Likewise, new perspectives may be required for interpreting individual liberty in a brave new world where technology could give rogue individuals the capability for limitless destruction. We have seen many tragedies in recent times where individual actors/small groups leveraged various forms of technology to disrupt or take lives. What expressions of liberty will be acceptable and what limits or controls are needed to prevent the liberties of extremists from causing more disruption and destruction? The road ahead will be marked by unknown leaps and turns.

The most disruptive inventors have also created new languages. In his 1974 *Zen and the Art of Motorcycle Maintenance*, Pirsig poetically elucidated the concept of a scalpel of intellect creating new worlds as this blade carves out new distinctions that bring definition, unfolding new realms of thought. Now evolution itself occurs at the speed of artificial thought. Information encoded as memes may now spread like wildfire to reach millions or billions within hours or days. Biological evolution, which is inherently slow, has been transcended by the evolution of ideas, untethered from the biological constraints that had tethered expansion of thought since Antiquity. For instance, cyborg humans with direct computer interfaces may arise someday. Kurzweil (2013) has pointed out that our minds already extend into the cloud: the postmodern cerebral cortex consists of 21–25 billion neurons + Google. As the ship of progress is unmoored from the dock of biology and our ideas explode out across the digital expanse, the normal paradigms of prediction begin to dissolve. New dangers lurk at this intersection of human and technological co-evolution.

Traditional boundaries break down as power concentrates around information technology and STEM. Existing social and political structures are stretched, strained, and broken as power distribution shifts toward the complete interweaving of information as the new fabric of society. While legacy power structures remain, coevolving alongside the exploding information economy, the distribution of force and ownership of conventional assets have become increasingly diluted and disrupted. Unfathomable power is being decentralized... Malicious ideas emerge, allowing for novel forms of authoritarian control via super-intelligent predictive algorithms, ubiquitous surveillance, and robotic/drone deployment. Therefore, a range of dystopian futures may involve a "runaway train" scenario where ideas and information run amok in directions that are neither presupposed nor desired. The "evolution of evolution" (Kelly 2017, 2018) may outstrip the human ability to cope.

Questions for discussion

1   List the many ways technology impacts your own life and the lives of those around you. How is your future likely to be impacted by rapid technological change?
2   How do beliefs in science and other beliefs interact? Think about conceptions of time, human agency, happiness, the good society, and about the myths of Faust and Prometheus.
3   Discuss the key perils presented by STEM.
4   Using your imagination and the lessons from the chapter, what do you think the world will look like in 10–20 years? How can we develop human wisdom, maturity, and compassion and institutions to keep pace with innovation?

References

Favreau, Jon. 2008. *Iron Man*. CA: Marvel Studios.
Gibbs, Samuel. August 20, 2017. "Elon Musk Leads 116 Experts Calling for Outright Ban of Killer Robots." *The Guardian*.
Gilligan, Carol. 1982. *In a Different Voice*. Boston, MA: Harvard University Press.
Goleman, Daniel. 1996. *Working with Emotional Intelligence*. London, England: Bloomsbury.
Harari, Yuval Noah. 2017. *Homo Deus: A Brief History of Tomorrow*. New York, NY: HarperCollins.
Kahneman, Daniel. 2011. *Thinking, Fast and Slow*. New York, NY: Farrar, Straus, and Giroux.
Kelly, Kevin. 2017. *The Inevitable: Understanding the 12 Technological Forces that Will Shape Our Future*. New York: Penguin.
Kelly, Kevin. 2018. "The Technium: Technology, or the Evolution of Evolution". *Kk.Org*. http://kk.org/thetechnium/technology-or-t/
Kleinman, Alexis. February 14, 2014. "Facebook Can Predict with Scary Accuracy if your Relationship Will Last." *Huffington Post UK*. https://www.huffingtonpost.com/2014/02/14/facebook-relationship-study_n_4784291.html
Koppel, Ted. 2015. *Lights Out: A Cyberattack, A Nation Unprepared, Surviving the Aftermath*. New York: Broadway.
Kramer, Sarah. April 2, 2016. "We're Shockingly Unprepared for an Extreme Weather Event that Could Fry Earth's Power Grid." *Business Insider*. http://www.businessinsider.com/solar-storm-effects-electronics-energy-grid-2016-3
Kruger, Liz, Craig Shapiro, and Matt Wheeler. 2017. *Salvation*. New York: CBS.
Kurzweil, Ray. 2006. *The Singularity Is Near: When Humans Transcend Biology*. New York, NY: Penguin.
Kurzweil, Ray. 2013. *How To Create A Mind: The Secret Of Human Thought Revealed*. New York, NY: Penguin.
Lewis, Michael. 2017. *The Undoing Project: A Friendship that Changed our Minds*. New York: Norton.
Mallozzi, Joseph and Mullie, Paul. 2015. *Dark Matter*. Toronto: Prodigy Pictures.
Mobile Future. September 29, 2015. "Internet of Things and the Mobile Future." *Mobile Future*. https://mobilefuture.org/resources/internet-of-things-and-the-mobile-future/

Nordrum, Amy. August 18, 2016. "Popular Internet of Things Forecast of 50 Billion Devices by 2020 is Outdated." *IEEE Spectrum: Technology, Engineering, And Science News*. https://spectrum. ieee.org/tech-talk/telecom/internet/popular-internet-of-things-forecast-of-50-billion-devi ces-by-2020-is-outdated

Pirsig, Robert. 1974. *Zen and the Art of Motorcycle Maintenance: An Inquiry into Values*. New York: HarperCollins.

Ranger, Steve. January 19, 2018. "What is the IoT? Everything You Need To Know About the Internet of Things Right Now." *ZDnet*. https://www.zdnet.com/article/what-is-the-interne t-of-things-everything-you-need-to-know-about-the-iot-right-now/

Rucker, Rudy. 2000. *Realware*. New York: Harper.

Statista. N.d. "Internet of Things (IoT): Number of Connected Devices Worldwide 2012–2025 (in billions)." *Statista. The Statistics Portal*. https://www.statista.com/statistics/471264/iot-num ber-of-connected-devices-worldwide

Shane, Scott. November 1, 2017. "These Are the Ads Russia Bought on Facebook in 2016." *New York Times*.

Tolkien, J.R. 2013. *The Fellowship of the Ring*. New York: HarperCollins.

Vance, Ashlee. 2017 (2015). *Elon Musk: Tesla, SpaceX, and the Quest for a Fantastic Future*. New York: Harper Collins.

Wilber, Ken. 2001. *Sex, Ecology, Spirituality: The Spirit of Evolution*. Boston, MA: Shambala.

Wilber, Ken. 2017. *Trump and a Post-Truth World*. Boulder, CO: Shambala.

Chapter 16

Risk and uncertainty in the global container supply chain

Khalid Bachkar and Lui Hebron

Introduction

The vast majority of maritime security studies tend to subordinate ocean-related threats within traditional, universal themes in international relations, such as inter-state disputes, balance of power, collective security, or regime building. Specific topic areas such as maritime criminality (drug smuggling, human trafficking, illicit shipping of armaments), terrorism, and port security have generally received less attention. With the rise in the significance and role of the blue economy in global politics and maritime affairs, however, littoral states and other international actors (inter-governmental organizations—IGOs, non-governmental organizations—NGOs, and transnational corporations—TNCs) involved with international security, ocean governance, and maritime policy have finally begun to give maritime issues a high priority on their security agendas. To that end, this chapter argues that it is high time for the International Relations (IR) discipline to focus greater attention and research to the security threats in the maritime arena—specifically, on the topic of shipping and security.

This chapter is organized as follows: the first section discusses the theoretical orientation of maritime security. The second section provides an overview of the opportunities and challenges in shipping goods. The third section examines the most pertinent studies related to risks associated with containers (i.e., terrorism, drug smuggling, product theft, and stowaways) and their impact. The final section discusses the measures and actions undertaken by different governmental and international organizations to enhance global container supply chain (GCSS) security. These measures involve shippers, carriers, manufacturing companies, port operators, and governments.

Maritime security theory

Even though the majority of traded goods are transported via the maritime highways, and states annually spend billions of dollars to protect ships, ports, and sea lanes from threats, maritime security studies are still relatively at their infant phase as a distinct subset of the global security discipline. Perhaps for this reason, no universally accepted definition of maritime security has emerged. Nevertheless, Realist and Liberalist theorists have staked out distinctive perspectives, research agendas, and policy strategies.

Realism

Realist maritime security studies are driven primarily by the traditional concerns of national sea power and maritime power projection—e.g., sovereignty claims over maritime territories, the status of coastal waters, and the control over maritime zones—within the geopolitical frameworks of international relations. And given the realist understanding of national security as the defense and preservation of state sovereignty, scholars and practitioners are heavily influenced by both the geopolitical dimension and geo-strategic considerations of maritime security. This research generally focuses on "global power shifts, changing threat perceptions, naval modernization, and changes in naval capabilities" (Bekkevold and Till 2016, 7). In terms of policy, the legitimate use of violence is justified in securing the freedom of the seas and maintaining security.

Liberalism

Liberal scholarship on maritime security tends to prioritize the legal structures—i.e., policies, regulations, measures, and operations—governing the world's waterways. These studies emphasize the rise of international regimes to regulate order and enforce laws at sea. Firmly anchored to international law, its theoretical orientation and policy-making approach have "evolved from a set of rules designed to avoid naval warfare by keeping maritime powers apart, toward a new global framework designed to facilitate maritime security cooperation by bringing countries together to reach common goals" (Kraska and Pedrozzo 2014, 10). The vital economic importance of oceans to facilitate international trade and national prosperity is manifested by the advent of global shipping into a multi-billion-dollar industry, and hence the need for tighter enforcement and greater monitoring of the laws and regulations governing the safe passage of vessels across the world.

Despite their divergent theoretical positions and policy prescriptions, Realism and Liberalism do share some commonalities in that both ideologies focus on monitoring, preventing, and defusing threats in the maritime security domain. This stems from the understanding that the protection of core sea lanes and port facilities is necessary to ensure freedom of navigation and maintaining the free-flow of goods is an integral component of a state's economic and national security.

The detrimental impact on trade and global peace and security from the illicit maritime activities of syndicated crime organizations and terrorist groups is a common concern of realist and liberalist policymakers. Working either independently or collectively, these crime syndicates and terrorist groups have used containers to smuggle narcotics, people, and armaments. The profits from trafficking drugs and human beings by sea are then used to fund their activities. Lethal cargo (biological, chemical, conventional, or nuclear warheads) easily stowed in a 40-foot container can potentially be detonated at a strategic chokepoint (the Strait of Hormuz, Malacca or Bosporus, or in the Panama or Suez Canal), or at a port facility, which would cripple global trade, cause economic and financial disruptions, and have catastrophic human casualties.

Shipping in the age of globalization

Globalization is a central component of today's global economy. As the production of goods has become globally dispersed and operations scattered across territories, these strategies have contributed to heightened risk exposures and serious global supply chains interruptions of goods and services. A disruptive event that negatively affects one link has the potential to interrupt the entire operation. These logistical disruptions to supply chains worldwide cost TNCs billions of dollars in business losses—e.g., the 2013 terrorist attack on a containership passing through the Suez Canal in an attempt to disrupt the flow of ships through the waterway (Reuters 2013). Hence, it is important to look at the entire supply chain, across all countries, when selecting and implementing risk management strategies (Manuj and Mentzer 2008).

With over 20 million shipping containers transporting 90% of traded goods, containers have become an integral component of shipping by changing the scale, scope, and velocity of global freight distribution. As the containerized cargo system has become so efficient and inexpensive, it was adopted as the principal means of transporting non-bulk cargo (Bachkar et al. 2013). Before the development of the metal shipping container by Malcom McLean in 1956, the break bulk cargo such as cartons was placed on pallets secured with strapping and hoisted aboard ships by crane. The operation was extremely time/labor-consuming and highly inefficient for shipping goods from their origin ports to their destination.

A typical container shipping operation involves multiple parties from different countries. Each transfer of a container in this complex and tiered shipping process constitutes a point of vulnerability in the supply chain. Increasing these supply chain vulnerabilities is the loading of individual shipping containers at a number of different company warehouses and not at the ports of departure. These cargo containers are also subject to numerous transfers within the transport chain, which makes them vulnerable to being subverted from their legitimate commercial purposes (Kumar and Verruso 2008). Furthermore, the complexity of the shipping process leads to the lack of visibility to monitor the security performance of the Global Container Supply Chain (GCSC).

After the terrorist attacks of September 11, 2001, the management of security risk in GCSC has become a major concern for both the private and public sectors. Numerous reports and papers on risk assessment of container security have been published (Johnston and Nath 2004; Kelly 2007; Kumar and Verruso 2008; Yang and Wei 2013). Their main focus was to determine and evaluate the exposure of containers to specific risks. A thorough risk analysis begins with the identification of threats and vulnerabilities to which containers are exposed. Once identified, they can be evaluated using qualitative or quantitative approaches.

In order to identify points of vulnerability of the container supply chain, it is necessary to understand its elements and the ways in which they are connected. To that end, a process map of the container flow throughout the supply chain was generated. This map provides a very detailed description of the elements of the GCSC at a logistics level and focuses on those elements that are important from a security perspective.

Most containerized shipping begins when a buyer (customer) expresses an interest in acquiring a product that the seller (manufacturer) is willing to sell and ship. The manufacturer makes arrangements with the shipper to transport its products to the customer. Frequently, the shipper is also the manufacturer. Some of these manufacturers produce high enough volumes or are located near enough to a port that they can ship full container loads directly. Most, however, produce less than container load (LCL) shipments that must be consolidated before being shipped.

The shipper is responsible for loading the container with goods, sealing it, and sending it through the supply chain. The shipper then appoints a freight forwarder who coordinates the export and trans-shipment processes from the country of origin to the country of destination. Freight forwarders serve as the most common intermediaries between originating shippers and ocean carriers and act as a travel agent for freight containers. From a supply chain perspective, freight forwarders are considered to have good visibility of the container supply chain. They are also specialists with a vast knowledge of international transport and are increasingly expanding their services. While their main activities are limited to ensuring the passage of goods in transit (handling formalities of customs declaration, obtaining licenses and permits, preparing and transmitting the necessary documentation), many freight forwarders have broadened their services to cover trade consulting (e.g. route selection, shipment scheduling, etc.) and logistics (supplier network strategies, supply chain configuration, in-house logistics optimization, etc.) services. In many cases, buyers require assistance throughout the entire transport chain. Freight-forwarders (and/or other parties such as carriers providing freight forwarding services) respond to that need and facilitate several and/or all aspects of the container move from their point of origin to their destination (European Conference of Ministers of Transport 2005). Once the container arrives at the destination country and is cleared from customs, it is placed in temporary storage, loaded onto a truck chassis to be transported to a distribution center for customer pick up.

Security risks associated with shipping containers

Given the heightened security concerns, companies need to put more efforts to track their containers as they flow in the supply chain in order to prevent them from getting hijacked by international terrorists and turned into a conveyance for weapons of mass destruction or contaminated in other ways. All goods that circulate through the global supply chain must be legal for transport and legitimately represented to authorities. The container transportation chain system needs to be transparent to reduce the illegal use of the system.

Criminals are constantly inventing new and improved ways in order to respond to heightened vigilance from customs authorities and other government agencies. In testimony before the Senate Homeland Security and Governmental Affairs Committee on March 28, 2006, author Stephen Flynn (2006) stated that

> A container of athletic footwear for a name brand company is loaded at a manufacturing plant in Surabaya, Indonesia. The container doors are shut and a mechanical seal is put into the door pad-eyes. These designer sneakers are destined for retail stores in malls across America. The container and seal numbers are recorded at the factory. A local truck driver, sympathetic to al Qaeda picks up the container. On the way to the port, he turns into an alleyway and backs up the truck at a nondescript warehouse where a small team of operatives pry loose one of the door hinges to open the container so that they can gain access to the shipment. Some of the sneakers are removed and in their place, the operatives load a dirty bomb wrapped in lead shielding, and they then refasten the door. The driver takes the container now loaded with a dirty bomb to the port of Surabaya where it is loaded on a coastal feeder ship carrying about 300 containers for the voyage to Jakarta. In Jakarta, the container is transferred to an Inter-Asia ship which typically carries 1200–1500

containers to the port of Singapore or the Port of Hong Kong. In this case, the ships go to Hong Kong where it is loaded on a super-container ship that carriers 5000–8000 containers for the trans-Pacific voyage. The container is then off-loaded in Vancouver, British Columbia. Because it originates from a trusted name brand company that has joined the Customs-Trade Partnership Against Terror, the shipment is never identified for inspection by the Container Security Initiative team of U.S. customs inspectors located in Vancouver. Consequently, the container is loaded directly from the ship to a Canadian Pacific railcar where it is shipped to a railyard in Chicago. Because the dirty bomb is shielded in lead, the radiation portals currently deployed along the U.S.–Canadian border do not detect it. When the container reaches a distribution center in the Chicago-area, a triggering device attached to the door sets the bomb off.

According to the European Conference of Ministers of Transport (2005, 36), terrorist groups can use containers in "legitimate" or illegal trade in order to generate revenue in support of their activities. They can also use shipping containers to launder illegitimate funds (much as drug smugglers have done) and/or provide logistical support for their operations (36). According to Van de Voort et al. (2006), the GCSC is an attractive target for terrorism for the following reasons:

- Container supply chain is an open system and inherently vulnerable to attacks.
- Only a small percentage of containers are physically inspected.
- Theft and smuggling.
- Major investments needed in low-margin industry (ownership problem).
- Lack of clearly defined responsibilities and liabilities of actors in the chain.
- Conflicting, unclear, and overlapping jurisdictions of national and international regulatory and oversight authorities.
- Lack of uniformity in the rules and their application for making transactions in different parts of the world/countries.
- Lack of standards (technological and operational).
- Missing link between security and throughput.

With tremendous improvements in technology, communications, weaponry, and transportation systems, terrorists are able to network with greater ease, efficiency, and sophistication (see Joshi's chapter herein). Simpson-Wood (2013, 77–78) posits that for $3,000—$5,000, groups like al-Qaeda could rent an international container, pack items weighing up to 65,000 pounds, and secure the door with a top-of-the-line, high-security container seal approved by the Customs-Trade Partnership Against Terrorism (the "C-TPAT").

Containers can also carry a wide range of dangerous commodities such as radioactive and explosive materials. Given the nature of these hazardous materials, this poses a risk as the container could be used for criminal/terrorist activities. In 2015, the deputy director of Mexico's nuclear safety commission reported that a container of Iridium 192 used in industrial x-rays was stolen from a truck in the southeastern state of Tabasco (*The Washington Post* 2015). Should the radioactive materials be removed from the container, this could have a major impact on civilians. Bakshi et al. (2011, 1) stressed that by using a container, terrorists can potentially achieve mass disruption to global supply chains by creating widespread public anxiety that other containers may have nuclear devices. Proper protection of containers from unauthorized access is key to achieving a high-security performance of containers as they move along the supply chain. It is mandatory to ensure that access is restricted to authorized personnel in areas where containers are stored. This can be achieved by providing adequate access control points, lightning, and fencing gates. Access to restricted areas would be granted following extensive back-ground checks at every stage of the supply chain. The identification of the personnel at different stages of the container process map outlined in Figure 16.1 along with real-time monitoring of a container's physical status will lead to an end-to-end visibility of the container shipment.

Tampering and theft

Containers are increasingly seen as an easy target for tampering by organized criminal groups (see Clarke's chapter and Simoni's chapter herein). Once a container is loaded and leaves the shippers' premises, the container may be at risk of tampering especially if it must sit for a long period of time before being staged and loaded onto a cargo ship. Terminal operators may not consistently check containers during handling operations for seals or evidence of tampering. The very nature of international containerized transport, which involves various parties having custody of a container during its journey, increases the likelihood of a tampered container to cross **interchange points** without being detected.

Morris (2015) posits that containers can be pilfered at a roadside rest stop, or a whole truck can disappear while its driver grabs a hot shower. The security services at G4S Company reported that criminal gangs were resorting to 3D printing to create perfect replicas of well-known cable seals, security locks and keys, and using these to cover their tracks and obscure any signs of theft, such as a broken seal (Grey, 2017). Increasingly, theft and tampering are issues of concern in the international maritime domain, with goods worth many billions of dollars vanishing every year, especially in developing countries where the transportation infrastructure is underdeveloped. *Material Handling and Logistics* magazine (2016) reported that cargo theft was top supply chain risk, resulting in nearly a $23 billion loss worldwide in 2015. The Global Initiative against Transnational Organized Crime (2017, 58) report stated that industry experts estimate cargo thefts cost as much as $30 billion in losses each year worldwide, with $10 billion a year in the United States alone and $8.2 billion in Europe, the Middle East and Africa (EMEA). It is noteworthy that cargo loss remains one of the least reported crimes due to many contributing factors such as:

- Lack of qualified and trained employees to thoroughly inspect the cargo.
- Inefficient processes of packaging, shipping, and receiving.
- Poor inventory and bookkeeping systems incapable of identifying product shortages.
- The discovering party is unable to detect where the loss took place in the supply chain.
- The company subject to cargo theft is unwilling to file a police report for insurance reasons.
- The discovering party is unable to detect where the loss took place due to the lack of visibility of upstream and downstream flows of containers.

Drug smuggling and stowaways

Drug smuggling via containers has been growing and generating more revenues for ter-rorist and criminal organizations (see Clarke's chapter, and Simoni's chapter herein). A group of criminals who possess resources will remove the insulation in the roof, walls, and roof of a refrigerated container to smuggle drugs. In most cases, drugs are mixed with a wide range of merchandise that is shipped daily in millions of containers. Due to the low inspection rates on containers at various ports in the world, the multibillion-dollar drug trade has increasingly become an international or multinational enterprise. The World Drugs Report from the UN Office on Drugs and Crime (UNODC) (United Nations Office on Drugs and Crime 2005, 123) agreed that the obscurity of the global illicit drug market makes the estimation on the global production, quantities exported, imported and consumed, extremely difficult. The Global Financial Integrity's best esti-mate of the value of the market in 2017 (the latest year for which figures are available) was between $426 billion and $652 billion (May 2017).

Similarly, the phenomenon of stowaways has increased worldwide and created sig-nificant challenges for the shipping industry. Typically, a stowaway will board inside a shipping container without being noticed by the port security. The stowaway will move around the container causing considerable damage to the cargo being loaded. Most of the stowaways are usually found in miserable conditions due to the long journey inside the container. In 2014, British police found one man dead and 34 people alive in a shipping container at the Tilbury Docks, east of London (SBS News 2014).

Towards managing the security risk of GCSS

Within the GCSC management literature, risk and uncertainty are considered important issues and have received unprecedented attention from supply chain man-agement researchers and practitioners. Since September 11, 2001, the literature in the era of supply chain management has been increasingly concerned with the risk asso-ciated with disruption as a lot of firms have seen their supply chains weakened by such a drama. Interests in risk management research and risk-mitigating strategies are pervasive and have a very broad appeal. Part of this increased interest is the realiza-tion by managers that accurate risk assessment and response can improve supply chain effectiveness. There are three aspects that affect the supply chain security (Veenstra, Hintsa, and Zomer, 2008, 142):

- The increasingly global economy and global production networks depend on and generate the free flow of people, goods, and information.
- Businesses increasingly depend on efficient supply chain operations.
- Increased terrorist threats result in significant implications for global supply chain security.

Voluntary and cooperative programs between the government and the international trade community in which supply chain actors (importers, brokers, warehouse operators, overseas manufacturers, and suppliers) agree to preserve the security of their GCSC in exchange for reduced inspection of their containers or reduced import inspection are currently in place. This requires organizations to assess and handle vulnerabilities in their

GCSC. Essentially, GCSC partners are required to develop and implement policies that can improve and enhance security within their operations as well as with their partners. Table 16.1 provides a summary of voluntary and mandatory security measures taken under government and international organizations to improve container supply chain security. These container security initiatives, as well as similar initiatives by other actors in the private sector, share a number of characteristics. They focus more on strengthening security and improving the reliability and efficiency of the GCSC. These measures involve shippers, carriers, manufacturing companies, port operators, and governments. For instance, the goal of the Customs-Trade Partnership against Terrorism (C-TPAT) is to push responsibility for cargo security onto stakeholders in the supply chain. C-TPAT is a voluntary program that companies can join to assure that they have implemented the best security practices, using guidelines developed through the cooperation of the Custom and Border Protection (CBP) and the industry, of all cargo containers destined for the United States. In order to join C-TPAT, a company must submit a security profile to CBP that will be compared to the minimum security requirements for the company's trade sector. C-TPAT builds upon relationships with all members of the supply chain in order to concentrate resources on areas of greatest risk. Similarly, Authorized Economic Operator (AEO) is a voluntary security program comparable to the U.S. C-TPAT that takes into consideration the entire supply chain and involves manufacturers, exporters, importers, carriers, freight forwarders, brokers, customs, ports, terminal operators, warehouses, distributors, and any other person touching the goods in the process. Under the AEO security initiative, operators in the container supply chain and customs authorities throughout the European Union cooperate to ensure that the integrity of containers is maintained and that routine security procedures are established throughout the entire supply chain. Companies that join both programs enjoyed the benefit of faster clearance and less frequent inspections at port facilities and land border crossing. The prominent success of the voluntary security initiatives such as AEO and C-TPAT is that albeit participant companies join voluntarily, members have made participation and compliance with security standards a requirement that needs to be met to do business with their partners, therefore creating a chain of trust.

It is also essential to have a culture of accountability that ensures that companies will follow through on taking more responsibility for the security of their supply chains. Arguably, some of the measures adopted by different governmental agencies, such as C-TPAT and AEO, focus more on improving the security of ports and shipping by controlling container traffic through advance information, pre-inspection for loading of selected containers and improved transparency along the supply chain. Some developing countries, however, will not be able to comply with the new rules. Difficult terrain, shortcomings in infrastructure and considerable distances from trade partners are serious trade barriers for many developing countries and therefore transport costs constitute a larger proportion of the value of goods in these countries compared to richer countries. One central issue is how the economies of developing countries are negatively affected by stricter security requirements (The National Board of Trade 2008). Although important in mitigating the vulnerabilities present in the container supply chain, the financial consequences of these measures have yet to be assessed and evaluated to avoid the risk of marginalization of low and middle income developing countries that could not afford the related investment and operational costs. The United Nations Conference on Trade and Development

Table 16.1 Security initiatives

	Customs-Trade partnership Against Terrorism (C-TPAT)	Container Security Initiative (CSI)	24 Hour Rule	International Ship and Port Facility Security Code (ISPS Code)	Authorized Economic Operator (AEO)	Partners in Protection (PIP)
Aim	Improve the security of private business supply chains	Protect and detect terrorist use of maritime containers while facilitating the movement of legitimate trade between major foreign ports and the United States	Enable U.S. Customs to analyze container content information 24 hours in advance of loading on board vessels destined for or transiting via U.S ports	Security of maritime network and prevention of terrorism threats	Enhance the security of the global supply chains and prevent disruptions to the flow of goods	Enhance border and trade chain security, combat organized crime and terrorism, and help detect and prevent contraband smuggling
Type of operator	C-TPAT takes into consideration the entire supply chain and involves manufacturers, exporters, importers, carriers, freight forwarders, brokers, customs, ports, terminal operators, warehouses, distributors, and any other person touching the goods in the process	Foreign seaports of countries that have bilaterally agreed to implement the CSI program. Foreign governments identify cargo containers that pose a potential risk for terrorism and inspect those containers at the foreign ports before they are shipped to the United States	Ocean carriers or their agents. Licensed registered Non-Vessel Operating Common Carrier (NVOCC)	Passenger ships and high speed passenger craft / Cargo ship and high speed craft of > 500 GRT / Mobile offshore drilling units (MODU) / Port Facilities serving vessels on international voyages	AEO takes into consideration the entire supply chain and involves manufacturers, exporters, importers, carriers, freight forwarders, brokers, customs, ports, terminal operators, warehouses, distributors, and any other person touching the goods in the process	Importers, exporters, carriers (rail, sea, air, highway), customs brokers, couriers, warehouse operators, freight forwarders, shipping agents
Mandatory/ voluntary	Voluntary	Mandatory	Mandatory	Mandatory	Voluntary	Voluntary
Originated country or institute/ year launched	U.S.A, 2001	U.S.A, 2002	U.S.A, 2003	International Maritime Organization, 2004	European Commission, 2005	Canada, 1995, revision in 2002 and 2008
Name of initiative	Customs-Trade partnership Against Terrorism (C-TPAT)	Container Security Initiative (CSI)	24 Hour Rule	International Ship and Port Facility Security Code (ISPS Code)	Authorized Economic Operator (AEO)	Partners in Protection (PIP)

Source: Compiled by the authors from multiple sources

(UNCTAD) estimated that port-related estimated global costs of the ISPS Code range between approximately $1.1 billion and $2.3 billion initially and between $0.4 billion and approximately $0.9 billion annually thereafter (UNCTAD 2007, 20). Bichou and Evans (2007) estimated that the initial cost for the ISPS Code compliance for 430 port facilities in the United Kingdom was $26 million with an annual cost at $2.5 million, while in Australia the cost of the ISPS compliance for 300 port facilities was $240 million initially and $74 million annually. Increasingly, compliance with the regulatory maritime security mandated by the ISPS code can result in substantial costs related to technology equipment and infrastructures upgrade and therefore create an additional financial burden for ports located in developing countries. Osnin (2005 22) claimed that the total cost of compliance with the ISPS Code for the 78 Malaysian ports is estimated to be RM 81,512,487.54 (equivalent to $20.35 million). Ships that failed to comply with the security regulations of the ISPS code may be faced with additional security requirements at subsequent ports of call, leading to delays and possibly denial of port entry (International Maritime Organization 2018). Consequently, port facilities and ship operators were faced with the dilemma of absorbing those costs or transferring them to end users.

Conclusion

The wide range of supply chain vulnerabilities (i.e., the threat of terrorist attacks that could seriously damage the global economy) makes it difficult for companies to secure their supply chain despite numerous security initiatives. With GCSCs a compromise at any link can affect the entire chain. The fact that no single member of the container supply chain has the full responsibility for security from beginning to end creates significant challenges for safeguarding global trade. Hence, having a well-developed approach for identifying and evaluating the risks and a process for generating intervention plans to mitigate the risks to an acceptable level has become increasingly important to secure the GCSC. Certainly, the container security initiatives presented in this chapter will increase the scope and accountability of management over supply chain events and partners to prevent the introduction of weapons of terror into the trade network and therefore create a true green lane that speeds low-risk shipments across all borders (Bachkar et al. 2013). Increasingly, companies in the GCSC should possess a credible risk management foundation. Nevertheless, depending on the nature and complexity of the risks a company may face in a world characterized by high levels of turbulence and uncertainty, it has to determine which type of risk management strategy it wants to adopt. Does it want to only comply with supply chain security standards? Or does it want to be agile and respond rapidly to unanticipated supply disruption?

Questions Discussion

1   Who is responsible for securing the container supply chain?
2   In the last decade, stowaways have increased worldwide and created significant challenges for the international maritime domain. Discuss the measures that need to be implemented by the port authorities to prevent stowaways from boarding a shipping container.
3   What are the main differences and similarities between C-TPAT and AEO?

4   What risk-management strategies can a shipper/freight forwarder follow to mitigate the risks associated with drug smuggling?

5   Who bears the cost of the damage incurred as a consequence of a stowaway on board a shipping container? Some developing countries will be affected by the security measures and initiatives presented in this chapter as they will not comply with the new rules. Discuss how the economies of developing countries are negatively affected by stricter security requirements.

6   C-TPAT and AEO members enjoy a variety of benefits, including less inspection and faster container clearance. Discuss the possibility of a criminal group using such an advantage by placing drugs or conventional explosives in a shipping container.

7   Choose a U.S port and assess its overall exposure to terrorist threats.

References

Bachkar, Khalid, Won Koo, and Joseph Szmerekovsky. Summer 2013. "An Analytical Hierarchy Process Framework to Mitigate the Security Risk in the GCSC." *Journal of Management and Engineering Integration* 6(1): 30–42.

Bakshi, Nitin, Stephen E. Flynn, and Noah Gans. January 2011. "Estimating the Operational Impact of Container Inspections at International Ports." *Management Science* 57(1): 1–20.

Bekkevold, Jo Inge, and Geoffrey Till, eds. 2016. *International Order at Sea: What it is. How it is Challenged. How it is Maintained.* London: Palgrave Macmillan.

Bichou, Khalid, and Andrew Evans. 2007. "Maritime Security and Regulatory Risk-Based Models: Review and Critical Analysis" in Bichou, Khalid, ed. *Risk Management in Port Operations, Logistics, and Supply-Chain Security.* New York, NY: Informa Law from Routledge.

Bueger, Christian and Timothy Edmunds. September 2017. "Beyond Seablindness: A New Agenda for Maritime Security Studies." *International Affairs* 93(6): 1293–1311.

European Conference of Ministers of Transport. 2005. *Container Transport Security Across Modes.* Retrieved March 16, 2009. International Transport Forum. https://www.itf-oecd.org/sites/defa ult/files/docs/05containersec.pdf

Flynn, Stephen. 2006. "The Limitations of the Current U.S. Government Efforts to Secure the Global Supply Chain against Terrorists Smuggling a WMD and a Proposed Way Forward." Written Testimony before a hearing of the Permanent Subcommittee on Investigations Committee on Homeland Security and Governmental Affairs United States Senate on "Neutralizing the Nuclear and Radiological Threat: Securing the Global Supply Chain." Council on Foreign Relations. Retrieved June 10, 2018, from Homeland Security and Governmental Affairs web site: https://www.hsgac.senate.gov/imo/media/doc/STMTFlynn.pdf

International Maritime Organization. 2018. "What would happen to ships if they do not comply with the ISPS Code requirements and if they do not have the Certificate?" Retrieved June 20, 2018. International Maritime Organization. http://www.imo.org/en/OurWork/Security/ Guide_to_Maritime_Security/Pages/FAQ.aspx#What_would_happen_to_ships_if_they_do

Grey, Eva. July 30, 2017. "Cargo Theft: a Billion-Dollar Problem." Retrieved June 20, 2018. http s://www.ship-technology.com/features/featurecargo-theft-a-billion-dollar-problem-5882653/

Johnston, Van R. and Amala Nath. May 2004. "Introduction: Terrorism and Transportation Security." *Review of Policy Research* 21(3): 255–261.

Kraska, James and Raul Pedrozzo. 2014. *International Maritime Security Law.* Leiden: Nijhoff.

Kelly, Robert. 2007. "Containing the Threat: Protecting the Global Supply Chain through Enhanced Cargo Container Security." *The Reform Institute*, October 3, 2007, pp.8–9 .

Kumar, Sameer, Heidi Jensen, and Heather Menge. Spring 2008. "Analyzing Mitigation of Container Security Risks Using Six Sigma DMAIC Approach in Supply Chain Design." *Transportation Journal* 47(2): 54–66.

Kumar, Sameer, and Verruso, Janis. Fall 2008. "Risk Assessment for the Security of Inbound Containers at U.S. Ports: a Failure Mode, Effects, and Criticality Analysis Approach." *Transportation Journal* 47(4): 26–41.

Manuj, Ila, and Mentzer, John T. 2008. "Global Supply Chain Risk Management." *Journal of Business Logistics* 29(1): 133–155.

Material Handling and Logistics. March 28, 2016. "Cargo Theft was Top Supply Chain Risk in 2015." Retrieved May 26, 2018. *Material Handling and Logistics.* http://www.mhlnews.com/global-supply-chain/cargo-theft-was-top-supply-chain-risk-2015

May, Channing. March 27, 2017. "Transnational Crime and the Developing World." Retrieved May 27, 2018. *Global Financial Integrity.* http://www.gfintegrity.org/report/transnational-crime-and-the-developing-world/

Morris, David Z. July 29, 2015. "'It Fell off the Back of the Internet': Freight Thieves are Becoming Cybercriminals." Retrieved May 28, 2018. *Fortune*: http://fortune.com/2015/07/29/cargo-freight-thieves-cybercriminals/

Organization for Economic Co-Operation and Development (OECD). July 2003. "Security in Maritime Transport: Risk Factors and Economic Impact." 1–59. *Directorate for Science, Technology, and Industry.* Retrieved June 27, 2009. Maritime Transport Committee. http://www.oecd.org/newsroom/4375896.pdf

Osnin, Noor Apandi. 2005. "Financial Implication of the ISPS Code in Malaysia". *Maritime Studies.* Canberra Issue 141, (Mar/Apr 2005): 16–23.

Reid, Tim, and Steve Gorman. December 1, 2012. "Los Angeles Port Strike Triggers Fears, Lobbying by Businesses." Retrieved May 28, 2018. *Reuters.* https://www.reuters.com/article/us-usa-port-losangeles/los-angeles-port-strike-triggers-fears-lobbying-by-businesses-idUSBRE8B101R20121202

Reuters. August 31, 2013. "Suez Canal Authority Says Attack Attempted on Container Ship." Retrieved June 20, 2018. Reuters. https://www.reuters.com/article/us-egypt-protests-suez/suez-canal-authority-says-attack-attempted-on-container-ship-idUSBRE97U0FG20130831

SBS News. August 17, 2014. "34 Alive, One Dead, in UK Shipping Container." Retrieved May 28, 2018. *SBS.* https://www.sbs.com.au/news/34-found-alive-one-dead-in-uk-shipping-container

Simpson-Wood, Taylor. 2013. "The Compromised Cargo Container: Terror in a Box." 1–57. Retrieved May 30, 2018. Barry University School of Law. https://lawpublications.barry.edu/cgi/viewcontent.cgi?article=1069&context=facultyscholarship

The Global Initiative Against Transnational Organized Crime. 2017. *Transnational Organized Crime and the Impact on the Private Sector: The Hidden Battalions.* Retrieved June 12, 2018. United Nations Office on Drugs and Crime. http://www.unodc.org/res/cld/bibliography/transnational-organized-crime-and-the-impact-on-the-private-sector_-the-hidden-battalions_html/gitoc_tocprivatesector_web-3.pdf

The National Board of Trade. January 2008. "Supply Chain Security Initiatives: A Trade Facilitation Perspective." Retrieved February 3, 2010. Kommerskollegium. 2008.1 http://www.kommers.se/Documents/In_English/Publications/PDF/Supply-chain-security-initiatives.pdf

The Washington Post. 2015. "The Strange Trend of Mexican Thieves Stealing Radioactive Material by Accident." Retrieved June 10, 2018. *The Washington Post.* https://www.washingtonpost.com/news/worldviews/wp/2015/04/16/the-strange-trend-of-mexican-thieves-stealing-radioactive-material-by-accident/?noredirect=on&utm_term=.cbc892da591e

United Nations Conference on Trade and Development. 2007. Maritime Security: ISPS Code Implementation, Costs, and Related Financing. Retrieved June 20, 2018. UNCTAD. http://unctad.org/en/Docs/sdtetlb20071_en.pdf

United Nations Office on Drugs and Crime. 2005. *2005 World Drug Report. Volume 1: Analysis.* Retrieved May 27, 2018. United Nations Office on Drugs and Crime. https://www.unodc.org/pdf/WDR_2005/volume_1_web.pdf

Van de Voort, Maarten, Henry Willis, David Ortiz, Susan Martonosi, and Anna Rahman. 16–19 March 2006. "Policy Considerations in Securing the Global Containerized Supply Chain." Retrieved August 11, 2009. *Risk Trace*. http://www.risk-trace.com/ports/papers/VandeVoort.pdf

Veenstra, Albert, Juha Hintsa, and Gerwin Zomer. October 31, 2008. "Smart Container Chain Management. GCSC Compendium." Retrieved June 6, 2018. https://www.researchgate.net/profile/Juha_Hintsa/publication/282845140_Global_Container_Supply_Chain_Compendium/links/561df92908aecade1acb441f/Global-Container-Supply-Chain-Compendium.pdf

Yang Ching-Chiao, and Wei Hsiao-Hsuan. 2013. "The Effect of Supply Chain Security Management on Security Performance in Container Shipping Operations." *Supply Chain Management: An International Journal* 18(1): 74–85.

Chapter 17

Steeped in insecurity?
Democracy, conflict, and the threat of populist security

Crister S. Garrett

Introduction

Today the global political commons seems to be unraveling. Many leaders are vowing to protect their citizens from the economic power of rivals, from immigrants, from the threatening foreign world and the Other. Many observers are comparing current times to the 1930s when the world saw the last major outbreak of trade protectionism and xenophobia. The economic populism and racism of the early 20th century contributed to escalating nationalism and to mass movements that ultimately underpinned national-socialism and fascism.

This worrisome background provides a compelling moment to discuss a paradox of modern democratic societies, which leaves us in a deep conundrum about how to think about security and insecurity. As many societies democratize broadly speaking, as power elites become increasingly sensitive to people power and its potential to hinder them and remove them from office, we are experiencing new forms of internal and international conflict that stem from a sense of insecurity emerging from the very democratization and opening of societies. Western theories about peace, security, and stability are widely predicated on the assumption that democracy *within* societies will encourage peace *between* societies—the so-called **Kantian peace** or **imperative**, or the democratic peace theory. Yet instead of the liberal order becoming further embedded as globalization spreads, a general backlash develops in the form of populism, growing tension, and domestic and international conflict (see Campbell's chapter herein). Populist leaders promise greater security for their followers, but their agendas lead to new forms of insecurity. Thus one can speak about the threat of populist security. How do we explain this democratic paradox? How can a liberal democratic order that provides greater individual voice and dignity simultaneously encourage fear and rising insecurity?

This chapter examines this puzzle. First, we consider competing meanings of security and insecurity. Divergent "varieties of security" involve different premises about what we consider important and what we should do about it. Two models of security contend: the liberal security order, and what we experienced in the 1930s and increasingly today, populist security. These competing models involve starkly different individual and societal choices for security. To help understand this contemporary opposition between liberalism and populism, we examine deeper historical roots. The past does not predict the future, but it helps us understand the security challenges confronting us today. Finally, we explore how meanings of security and insecurity and the current rise of populism in our democratic societies affect international relations and the type of societies we want to build.

Contested meanings of security

Today we wake up to news of impending threats, new threats, ongoing threats, revived threats. Three broad approaches help decide what we should observe and what to do with those observations. First, realists contend that human beings are inherently shaped by greed and fear, that nation-states are constantly on the prowl for more power, and that nothing exists naturally to curtail such basic instinct. The true state of existence is anarchy involving a zero-sum game where international competition involves winners and losers—you are one or the other (Mearsheimer 2014). More optimistic liberal scholars posit that humans can counteract this somber state of affairs by creating rules and institutions to curtail greed and striving for power, and thus make all feel more secure in the space that we share, the global political commons, in a positive sum game where we can move beyond the stark categories of winners and losers to provide benefits for all participants (Moravcsik 1997). Finally, constructivists underscore that the world is threatening only if one allows it to be; in short, anarchy is what you make of it (Wendt 1992). Thus constructivists argue, even more so than liberals, that humans possess considerable agency to shape the world in which they live; we can build a better tomorrow and reduce insecurity if we want to.

Realism has been the dominant theory of international relations from Sun Tzu to Thucydides to Machiavelli to Thomas Hobbes and even informs the U.S. Constitution (separation of powers into three branches of government to curtail and check the human lust for power). Liberalism is relatively new to the stage, emerging in the 19th century and informing efforts to reduce feelings of insecurity; the United Nations is a prime example of such efforts. Constructivism is the most recent theory. It emerged fully at the conclusion of the Cold War, a moment that unleashed a new wave of discussion about what we should now consider to be security and insecurity. Scholars began to see new types of security beyond realist and liberal building blocks centered on the nation-state and international liberal order. Increasingly, issues as diverse (and fundamental) as poverty, environmental degradation, gender discrimination, sexual prejudice, racism, etc. began to add complexity to our understanding of security and insecurity. What we saw (ontology), and how we organized our data (methodology) allowed scholars and policy-makers to construct new knowledge regimes (epistemology) with which to define and pursue models of security (Mitzen 2006).

In short, the debate about security and insecurity experienced a democratic revolution during the 1990s and continues to this day (Lebow and Risse-Kappen 1996; Bourbeau 2015; Buzan and Hansen 2009). Nobel prize-winner Angus Deaton or Harvard professor Steven Pinker argue that humans have never had it so good (Deaton 2015; Pinker 2018). We have made enormous progress and should feel more secure than ever before. Lawrence Freedman stresses that when talking about human rights or the environment we should not necessarily call these forms of security; security as a concept deals primarily with nation-states and their struggle to survive (Freedman 2017). Critical theorists counter that Freedman constructs too simple a world (Peoples and Vaughan-Williams 2014). Critical theorists like Judith Butler (construction of gender) or Michel Foucault (construction of systems of order) argue that nation-states can be as much a cause of insecurity as a pursuant or guarantor of security (Butler 2006; Foucault 1994).

Therefore the contested meanings of security and insecurity result from the relative democratization of knowledge production, knowledge hierarchies (which conclusions receive more attention), and by extension, knowledge establishments (aka epistemological communities) (Weldes 1999). The definitions of security and insecurity, in sum, have become unsecured or unsettled. This means that societies have become more fluid and able to allow for greater inclusion of diverse insights, interests, and ideas. The concept of progress has evolved and expanded, in short, to allow for broader and more open societies. That is good news for many, but as noted, not for all: security remains a contested concept.

The democratic paradox

Such an expanded concept of progress involves, however, a paradox. Social and cultural anthropologists remind us that humans do not unconditionally embrace messiness or complexity in our daily lives. We seek clarity, rules, and predictability; evolutionary anthropologists argue that we do so to increase our chances of survival. This is ultimately the generator of cultures in human existence: to construct and impose rules of behavior to allow societies to function (e.g., does waving a hand mean the other person wants to kill me or say hello or is asking for help?) (Williams 2007; Lebow 2008). Therefore when we become increasingly unsure about how to read signals around us, feelings of anxiety or insecurity can rise substantially; we experience a rise in societal insecurity. Thus the paradox of knowledge democratization and progressive inclusion encourages a state of knowledge in the contemporary world that explains the rise of populist politics worldwide, or the striving for a more simple, and for many, a more stable and safer world.

> **Text box 17.1: Concepts of cultural anxiety**
>
> The German word "Angst" is widely used in English-speaking countries. In both languages, it means anxiety, even fear, or threat. French sociologist Émile Durkheim coined the word "anomie" in 1897 to describe the erosion of social norms, values, bonds and mutual trust. "Malaise" implies deep unease and anxiety.

Therein lies the paradox and the relationship between democracy, conflict, and the threat of populist security (Wood and Dupont 2006). For while simplification can reassure and stabilize our cognitive universe (how we go about sorting and reading the many signals we receive daily in our societies), it also means that to achieve that goal, we need to exclude many signals, or rearrange them in ways whereby—if we are not careful, vigilant, and courageous—an individual of a different color, sex, age, or social status can become less worthy, less important, or ultimately, a new type of threat as opposed to a fellow citizen enriching and empowering our common existence. Our contemporary democracies provide greater political space than ever for diverse stories, including simpler stories that reassure and seemingly stabilize daily existence. The democratic paradox thus reminds us of the power of language, of the narratives that emerge from selecting symbols of inclusion and exclusion and placing them in stories that frame the mental maps to navigate the turbulent nature of contemporary existence (Epstein 2011; Lynch 2014).

Text box 17.2: Copenhagen School

Many scholars reject the word "security" when speaking about inequality, environmental degradation, racism, etc. The Copenhagen School of security studies, for example, speaks about the "securitization" of issues: by taking diverse issues and connecting them to "security" we place them in a confrontational frame encouraging defensiveness, and make tackling them more difficult since they have become embedded in a harder logic of us vs. them or threat vs. security. When an issue becomes attached to a security framework, solutions can become more of a zero-sum calculation of winners and losers instead of possibly creative solutions emphasizing win–win scenarios. Language matters since it informs the logic and cognitive maps that we deploy to narrate problems and possible solutions. This approach is called the Copenhagen School because many of its adherents have worked at the Copenhagen Peace Research Institute.

The rise of contemporary populism

Perhaps the most recent and present threat-story involving security is the rise and spread of populism. The concept of populism is notoriously difficult to define. Gidron and Bonikowski note: "To each his own definition of populism, according to the academic axe he grinds" (Gidron and Bonikowski 2013, 1). Müller argues that populist movements share similarities, especially in their effort to "speak for the people" against a series of political, social, economic, and cultural "threats" from the "other" (Müller 2016). A working definition for our purposes explains populism as a widespread movement to simplify unfolding contemporary complexity with a narrative meant to reassure relatively insecure voters by means of broad (and ill-defined) promises to protect and defend lifestyles and living standards either acquired or aspirational. We can thus observe how populism shapes contemporary politics in countries around the world, in China, France, Germany, Hungary, Japan, Poland, the Philippines, Russia, South Africa, Sweden, Turkey, the United Kingdom, and the United States. Today, no region in the world escapes this challenge.

Its rise can be attributed ultimately to increased feelings of insecurity. To understand insecurity one can firstly provide a broad definition of security. We can define security as both the reality and the perceptions of stability, safety, and social well-being by individuals and groups. Two categories of factors feed into this definition: material concerns and non-material (cultural) concerns. Material concerns involve economic security—the feeling an individual has that she can provide for herself and her family, and can save for a better tomorrow for herself and her children. Cultural concerns involve identities or social settings in which one feels acknowledged, respected, able to engage public debates, recognized and heard, in short, to possess legitimate agency (the ability to shape outcomes). When a majority of citizens in a society feel material and cultural stability, then one can observe a relative consensus in a society that can be defined as societal security. Insecurity thus entails the relative absence of societal security.

Text box 17.3: Wedge issues in U.S. politics

These issues seek to divide-and-conquer (drive wedges) between different sectors of a society on issues ranging from God, guns, gays, abortion, gender and sexuality, race, to other cultural anxiety issues. Wedge issues are a core of modern populist politics.

Societal security is different from human security, but not more important. Human security lies at the center, for example, of the UN effort to improve the human condition, for instance, safe drinking water or access to education. It involves the contemporary global agenda to improve material and cultural security (UN Sustainable Development Goals). Societal security, by contrast, involves the politics of human security. How do we create a global or national agenda that is democratically possible, sanctioned by citizens, and thus sustainable as an agenda? To frame the relationship between societal and human security more concretely, human security makes societal security possible, but without societal security, the pursuit of human security is substantially more difficult, if not impossible. Thus while distinct, human and societal security exists in an ongoing dialectical relationship; they are independent concepts bound in an interdependent relationship (Collins 2018).

Liberal and populist security

If the rise and spread of populism reflect the relative absence of societal security worldwide, then the question emerges as to why one should talk about "the threat of populism." Populism involves after all, as the word suggests, popular politics, in short, a type of people power. And the word democracy simply combines the ancient Greek roots of *demos* (people) and *kratie* (rule), i.e., rule by the people. Is populism thus not a fully legitimate democratic expression of citizen concerns about their well-being or sense of security? In current usage, we differentiate between democratic, popular, and populist politics. How do we draw borders to provide positive and negative judgments associated with each word or concept? At a minimum, they involve contested borders or definitional demarcations, but borders we must draw (however fuzzy or fungible) to provide relatively stable meanings for each concept. We do so to be able to clarify the choices we face and provide normative or value justifications for why (and how) we have constructed the choices before us.

Providing meaning to democratic, popular, and populist agendas often takes place in the global political commons by juxtaposing (bordering) the meaning of populism with the understood meaning of liberalism or the liberal international order, and ultimately, liberal security (Dunne and Flockhart 2014). While liberalism is a thoroughly contested concept in and of itself (think about the seemingly endless critique of the notion of neoliberalism), it generally stands for an ongoing effort to expand pluralism and the public space for political participation, or the global political commons. The concept of liberalism accounts for everything from the growing rights of the working class to vote, the struggle against slavery, the women's rights movement, to the right for sexual self-expression—all long-lasting, partial, conflictual struggles that have unfolded over the past 200 years and more. Liberal security, highly imperfect, thus involves everything from the creation of the most democratic constitution of its day, the Weimar Constitution of 1919 that provided many new rights for women and workers in Germany not seen elsewhere in the world, to China joining the World Trade Organization in 2001 and thereby globalizing a liberal trade regime. This long arc of history is often referred to as the Kantian liberal order, referring to the German Enlightenment philosopher Immanuel Kant. The Kantian imperative stipulates that one should conduct oneself in the public commons as one would like to be treated, and such an imperative for daily conduct would therein encourage a form of cosmopolitanism (*cosmos* or "universal" and *polis* or "city" in ancient Greek) with which international peace, international security, could be achieved. This is the central idea behind the so-called democratic peace theory underpinning the current international liberal order.

Thus the liberal agenda involves the democratization of society by extension of popular movements. That evolution can currently be witnessed in the form of LGBTQI (Lesbian, Gay, Bisexual, Transgender, Queer, Intersex) civil-rights activism. This highly necessary and fundamental movement involves placing the individual at the center of our social compacts—the rules, rights, and duties regulating the relationship between state and society, as defined by the 3rd generation of rights (see Introduction). They reflect the Kantian imperative that LGBTQI should enjoy the same dignity that all individuals seek for themselves. However, not one single authoritarian (non-liberal) government in the world accepts, let alone promotes, LGBTQI rights. LGBTQI rights remain unfortunately highly controversial, even in such liberal societies as Sweden, Germany, and certainly the United States (whose federal system means LGBTQI rights differ widely from state to state). That reminds us that popular sentiment is not inherently liberal or edified sentiment. Prejudice (from the French *préjuger*: to pre-judge) informs popular politics and broadly influences democratic politics. Democracy simply means rule by the people, it does not define what norms or institutions or values inform that rule. That gets decided by politics, or the interaction of citizens in the polis, or public space ("politics" comes from ancient Greek and the twin concepts of *polites* or citizen and the *polis* or city).

Liberal progress is historically and currently controversial, contested, and conflict-ridden. It disrupts contemporary cognitive maps and challenges us to consider new mental maps with which to organize our sense of material and cultural well-being, our sense of security. And the contemporary liberal international order has led to forms of movement and change in our societies that for growing numbers of citizens feel overwhelming. We have witnessed how these feelings are expressed again and again in social tensions and democratic elections around the globe, from Great Britain and Brexit, to Rodrigo Duterte in the Philippines, to renewed nationalism in Japan, to Donald Trump, or the rise of national populist parties in France, Germany Hungary, Poland, Sweden, and indeed in almost every corner of Europe (see Campbell's chapter herein).

The current rise of global and transatlantic populist politics is thus compelling democratic elites to consider what "security for citizens" means. In contrast to liberal security—where societal security rests on open, inclusive, and fluid societies—populist security constructs relatively rigid polarized categories that legitimize a simple, stable, and for many seductive, narrative of insiders vs. outsiders, the corrupt vs. the clean, the elites vs. the people, national vs. foreign culture, and ultimately "us vs. them." Liberal security entails a fluid ecosystem of interaction where adaptation, integration of different elements, evolution of norms, institutions, and material distributions underpins sustainable security. Populist security stresses the stability of essentialized categories that are asserted and proclaimed as the firm borders of a societal order that needs to be defended against outside intrusion, against a seemingly threatening difference or disruption in daily life.

Text box 17.4: Essentializing individuals and groups

Mass politics and especially populist politics distill complexity into simple stories. The Other is constructed as possessing an unchangeable and nefarious group essence: "All of them are always bad, lazy, criminals, etc." The logic is similar to wedge issues politics: divide and conquer. Once one has constructed a dangerous and despicable enemy, then one can stand up as "protector" and sole legitimate authority in the competition for votes and more power.

Who stole my life? Populism, liberalism, and economic security

The tension between liberalism and populism can be observed globally, especially around the notion of free-trade or international economic exchange (Rodrik 2011). Countries have prospered under the current global trade regimes in ways unprecedented. China's integration into the World Trade Organization in 2001 has allowed over 300 million people to leave behind absolute poverty, defined by the UN as surviving on less than two dollars a day. And yet broad statistics about the country's rise in wealth say nothing about how citizens experience such rapid change and the concomitant disruptions in how they work, save, and try to build a better and more secure life for themselves and their families (see Clarke's critique of neoliberalism as a false theory of common good in this book). China, although not a democracy, is also confronted with populist politics, as shown by citizens' anger at the corruption and environmental degradation associated with Chinese capitalism. Indeed, every country with a capitalist economy integrated into the global trading order, and this includes almost every country worldwide (exceptions being North Korea and Cuba, and even these countries practice trade and exchange). Countless countries are currently experiencing surges in populist politics and demands for new models of simplified, stable economic security.

The global economy is undergoing the biggest transformation since the industrial revolution in the 18th century. We are currently in the midst of the information revolution that is disrupting and churning our societies in unrecognizable fashions. Technology innovation today—robotics, artificial intelligence, digitalization, etc.—are creating and will create whole new fields of work and structure for daily life (see Addington's and Manrod's, and Sebastiani's, Sanchez's and Manrod's chapters herein). Indeed, the information revolution will lead to the disappearance of entire life-styles built around daily work and material or economic security. Previous periods of intense technological, economic, and social changes in the 19th and 20th centuries were also marked by populism and cultural malaise. Yesterday, the rise of industrial production allowed for the automobile and brand new forms of work, wealth, and mobility. It also meant the destruction of agrarian ways of life and work centered on horse-pulled carriages, wagons, and service industries surrounding them. Populism rose in America, Europe, and in other countries undergoing industrial transformation (Japan being the biggest exception) as farmers, factory workers, craftsmen, artisans and small-town citizens saw their traditional way of life dislocated, or felt that others—elites, immigrants, Jews, etc.—were prospering more than they were. This last observation is particularly noteworthy. While workers were indeed earning more in factories than on farms, they witnessed others earning more—and found this unfair, and demanded change. In a fast-changing society marked by cultural and status anxiety, *relative* deprivation is often experienced as *absolute* deprivation.

Thus while industrialization brought countries forms and levels of wealth never seen before, and distributed that wealth among citizens in ways previously unseen in history, it also brought new forms of inequality and hardship: pollution, urban squalor, social-cultural upheaval, women's changing role and growing autonomy that threatened many people's understanding of an "ordered world." Industrialization brought with it, in short, the basic paradox of rising and democratizing wealth, and simultaneously, rising societal insecurity and popular demands for elites in society to offer new forms of stability, to slow down the pace of disruptive change, to offer a new model of societal security by adjusting the social contract underpinning the relationship between state and society.

Responses to demands for security

Politicians got the message. The first modern welfare state was built in the late 19th century by Otto von Bismarck, a conservative aristocrat and prime minister (1871–1890) of the newly unified German state, with workers being offered (albeit in a modest manner) everything from a retirement system to unemployment, medical, and disability insurance. Another patriarchal personality, Theodore Roosevelt, was so impressed by Bismarck's plan that he sought to introduce many of Germany's new social contract building blocks to the United States as the first Progressive-movement president in the White House (1901–1909). Though he had some success, Roosevelt failed, for example, to introduce a national medical insurance system despite being in support of one. Indeed, he would campaign again for president in 1912 calling for a national health system but would lose the election. As Roosevelt put it famously, regulation and social reform were highly necessary to "save capitalism from itself." Bismarck himself understood that if he did not undertake such progressive reforms, he might have to confront not just calls for reform, but cries for socialist revolution. People power in the form of progressive and populist politics thus moved such notable patriarchal leaders as Bismarck and Roosevelt to build new models for social contracts and a new type of societal security.

These efforts did not prevent World War I or the Great Depression. Indeed, the economic misery of the 1930s fueled the rise of much more radical forms of populism such as fascism, national socialism, and communism. In response, Franklin D. Roosevelt (in office 1933–1945) sought to steer America away from such radical populism with the New Deal. He largely succeeded. The New Deal thus became the basis for societal security in America for over a half century, with both Republican and Democratic presidents supporting its key building blocks, such as the Social Security system. This led to what has been called the New Deal consensus. It is a good example of how societal security emerges and is sustained for a period of time. The New Deal consensus provided the political legitimacy for the government in cooperation with citizens to pursue a range of human security needs, from decent housing to running water to public education. These efforts would culminate in Lyndon B. Johnson's Great Society initiative during the 1960s that introduced Medicare, Medicaid, and affirmative action to American society.

The information revolution that is transforming our economy and society today confronts us with similar problems addressed by Bismarck and both Roosevelt presidencies. History does not repeat itself. But it does involve recurring dynamics or dialectics between technology, material change, and human perceptions and reactions to such disruptions of familiar and reassuring patterns for daily life. As globalization impacts our societies more thoroughly and more rapidly than ever before in terms of human mobility, the spreading of new ideas, growing cultural and social diversity, and economic transformation (the 4th industrial revolution driven by robotics, artificial intelligence, and digitalization), growing numbers of citizens feel deeply and personally a relative loss of control over their individual destinies, an erosion or even a collapse of the mental maps that helped them organize daily life and provide a sense of control, agency, and empowerment—in short, their sense of security.

Thanks to democratic institutions (albeit highly imperfect due to the exclusion of women in Germany and the United States in national elections until 1919, and racial minorities in the United States), voters could express their displeasure at the ballot box during the unfolding of the industrial revolution. The first formal populist party in the modern world emerged in the United States in 1892, the so-called Populist or People's Party. Voters both in America and in Europe also voted enthusiastically for radical populist parties in the 1930s, whether the Fascist party in Italy or the Nazi party in Germany and many millions of Americans supported both movements from afar, demanding similar policies in America. Today we are again witnessing the rise of formal populist and protest movements during the information revolution, ranging from the Brexit movement in Great Britain to Emmanuel Macron in France (leaving behind all established political parties) to Donald Trump. All these events and movements express growing frustration and turbulence. Even more radical forms of populism are spreading, such as the openly authoritarian movements in China, Hungary, India, Poland, Russia, and Turkey.

A key issue that captures rising citizen anxiety about economic security centers on global trade regimes. One of Donald Trump's very first acts as president was to remove America from the Transpacific Partnership (TPP) on 23 January 2017, which was an effort to create a new and sweeping trade regime for the Pacific region. Many elites found this step unwise; many voters welcomed it. Hillary Clinton had been a strong supporter of President Barack Obama's efforts to finalize a TPP; but as a presidential candidate, she criticized it when she saw how unpopular it was among millions of Americans. Protectionism and populist politics around international trade is nothing new. Arguably the most notorious effort at protectionism in the United States was the Smoot-Hawley Tariff Act in 1930. It was meant to protect millions of American jobs; instead, it prompted other countries to also pass tariffs that together substantially weakened all national economies. Here is a concrete threat from populist security: measures to pursue it seems to make sense in the short-term, but often lead to the serious exacerbation of the societal insecurity they claim to ameliorate. That is why after World War II dozens of countries committed to removing tariffs and to building a new liberal trade order based on reciprocal rules to encourage open societies (an economic Kantian imperative). The resulting so-called GATT trade regime led to the greatest growth in human prosperity since the first efforts to build human societies (GATT stands for General Agreement on Tariffs and Trade, and was signed by 23 countries in 1947; it would be superseded by the establishment of the World Trade Organization in 1994, created when 123 countries signed the Uruguay Round Agreements to liberalize trade).

As the world has continued to integrate globally and economically, this has brought new forms of wealth to many millions but also ended familiar and cherished lifestyles for many other millions. Total global wealth is greater than ever, but that says nothing about individual lives. The transition from the horse-and-buggy to the automobile empowered *and* threatened millions of citizens. Likewise, with the transition from automobile factories with thousands of workers to factories for e-mobility with hundreds of robots, or the relocation of factories abroad, millions of citizens are demanding that politicians answer a simple question as they lose work and economic security: Who stole my life? Sustainable work that provides material security for citizens is one of the fundamental and imperative questions shaping 21st-century debates about security and insecurity. How politics will address the question "Who stole my life?" will largely determine the ability of our democratic societies to solve the paradox of growing people power, radical populism, and authoritarian promises and political order.

Conclusion: A fresh and fateful sorting

We are in the midst of recalibrating our social contracts to allow for societal security in our globalizing societies. As with the industrial revolution and transformation of our agrarian societies, there is no predicting the outcomes. We are experiencing a fresh, and fateful, sorting of our societal priorities in the pursuit of societal security.

The good news is that people power is on the rise. Political elites from Moscow to Beijing to Washington DC to Berlin know that voters are deeply anxious and willing to express that anxiety as street protests and protest votes. Answering clamors for a new security drives today's debates and decisions in both national and global public spaces. Outcomes are uncertain. Realists are right: humans are driven by the search for power—for self-determination, to control others, to survive, etc. Liberals are also correct: we can create rules and institutions that shape how we behave, how we define our interests, how we define threat and security. And constructivists remind us of an essential reality: we can through human agency influence priorities and objectives in the tension between liberal and populist security. The choice is ours. The open question is what we do with that choice, to make ourselves, and our fellow human beings, feel more secure.

Questions for discussion

1   What is the "democratic paradox"?
2   How does the paradox of democratization relate to concepts of security and insecurity?
3   What is meant by liberalism and populism? Why do these concepts matter?
4   How does language and story-telling shape the politics of security and insecurity?
5   How can one account for the recent rise of populism worldwide?
6   What are the connections between economic security, the struggle between liberalism and populism, and the politics of security and insecurity?
7   How would you compare economic insecurity with other forms of insecurity worldwide, such as fears around migration, environmental degradation, rights of minorities, religious and cultural self-expression?

References

Bourbeau, Philippe, ed. 2015. *Security: Dialogue across Disciplines.* Cambridge: Cambridge University Press.

Butler, Judith. 2006. *Gender Trouble: Feminism and the Subversion of Identity.* London: Routledge.

Buzan, Barry, and Lene Hansen. 2009. *The Evolution of International Security Studies.* Cambridge: Cambridge University Press.

Collins, Allan, ed. 2018. *Contemporary Security Studies.* Oxford: Oxford University Press.

Deaton, Angus. 2015. *The Great Escape: Health, Wealth, and the Origins of Inequality.* Princeton, NJ: Princeton University Press.

Dunne, Tim, and Trine Flockhart, eds. 2014. *Liberal World Orders.* Oxford: Oxford University Press.

Epstein, Charlotte. June 2011. "Who Speaks? Discourse, the Subject and the Study of Identity in International Politics." *European Journal of International Relations* 17(2): 327–350.

Foucault, Michel. 1994. *The Order of Things: An Archaeology of the Human Sciences.* New York, NY: Vintage.

Freedman, Lawrence. 2017. *The Future of War: A History.* New York, NY: Public Affairs.

Gidron, Noam, and Bart Bonikowski. 2013. "Varieties of Populism: Literature Review and Research Agenda." Boston: Weatherhead Center for International Affairs, Harvard University. Working Paper No. 13.0004.

Lebow, Ned, and Thomas Risse-Kappen. 1996. *International Relations Theory and the End of the Cold War*. New York, NY: Colombia University Press.

Lynch, Cecilia. 2014. *Interpreting Politics*. London: Taylor & Francis.

Mearsheimer, John. 2014. *The Tragedy of Great Power Politics*. New York: W.W. Norton.

Mitzen, Jennifer. September 2006. "Ontological Security in World Politics: State Identity and the Security Dilemma." *European Journal of International Relations* 12(3): 341–370.

Moravcsik, Andrew. Autumn 1997. "Taking Preferences Seriously: A Liberal Theory of International Politics." *International Organization* 51(4): 513–553.

Müller, Jan-Werner. 2016. *What Is Populism?* Philadelphia, PA: University of Pennsylvania Press.

Peoples, Columba, and Nick Vaughan-Williams. 2014. *Critical Security Studies: An Introduction*. London: Routledge.

Pinker, Steven. 2018. *Enlightenment Now: The Case for Reason, Science, Humanism, and Progress*. New York, NY: Viking.

Rodrik, Dani. 2011. *The Globalization Paradox: Democracy and the Future of the World Economy*. New York, NY: W.W. Norton.

Wæver, Ole, Barry Buzan, Jaap de Wilde. 1999. *Security: A New Framework for Analysis*. Boulder, CO: Lynne Rienner.

Weldes, Jutta et al., eds. 1999. *Cultures of Insecurity: States, Communities and the Production of Danger*. Minneapolis, MN: University of Minnesota Press.

Wendt, Alexander. Spring 1992. "Anarchy is what States Make of it: The Social Construction of Power Politics." *International Organization* 46(2): 391–425.

Williams, Michael C. 2007. *Culture and Security: Symbolic Power and the Politics of International Security*. London: Routledge.

Wood, Jennifer, and Benoît Dupont, eds. 2006. *Democracy, Society, and the Governance of Security*. Cambridge: Cambridge University Press.

Epilogue

Driven by globalization, the connections between and among international actors continue to expand and deepen, whereby nation-states and IGOs must increasingly co-exit, cooperate, and/or compete with NGOs, TNCs, social movements, criminal syndicates, terrorist groups, etc. on the global stage. In like manner, issues of greatest interest for global security now go beyond the traditional realms of militarized interstate dispute to encompass environmental, food, water, energy, gender, and health issues—and this list will no doubt continue to expand.

The topics examined in this volume—with its intellectual diversity on how international security is researched and taught—provide an excellent opportunity for the IR discipline to evolve, innovate, and reform. In breaking away from self-contained, discipline-specific boxes, this book invites scholars, students, and stakeholders interested in international relations to take this set of readings as points of departure to better understand, become more fully engaged, and formulate solutions to the wicked challenges confronting the global environment.

Glossary

Achilles' heel A critical vulnerability or weakness. Based on a story from Greek mythology of Achilles the hero, who had been dipped into the River Styx (connecting the world of living and the dead) as an infant by his mother to insure his invincibility as a warrior. However, being held by his heel, this portion of his body was not rendered invulnerable. After many successful battles, Achilles was mortally wounded by a poisonous arrow that struck his unprotected heel.

Additive manufacturing Also known as 3D Printing, this is the process of creating physical objects using ideas in the form of virtual designs.

Air gap A network of information systems that are physically or logically separated to prevent compromise via malicious traffic or software.

Anomie The erosion of social norms and values, social trust and social capital (mutual trust and respect for commons laws and values) that indicates deep social, cultural, and normative polarization and malaise.

Antigen The process in which the surface proteins of the virus change.

Anthropocentrism Human-centered, the belief that humans are the center of cosmos, life, Earth.

Anthropocene The geological age where humans are the main geological force, since the agricultural revolution about 8,000 to 10,000 years ago.

Anthropogenic Of or resulting from human activity. In the context of climate change, anthropogenic greenhouse gases are man-made; they are not the result of natural processes.

Apache Struts A common web application framework that is free, open source, and widely deployed.

Application Program Interface (API) A software construct used to present and retrieve information between software programs to facilitate structured communication between programs or layers of a software program.

Arab Spring A series of protests, revolutions, and counter-revolutions across parts of the Arab and Muslim world, in parts of the Middle East and North Africa starting in 2011. Countries which experienced protests included Bahrain, Egypt, Libya, Tunisia, Syria, and Yemen.

Asymmetric warfare A form of state conflict where actors possess vastly different capabilities and methods (for instance, cyber warfare).

Beijing consensus A phrase coined by Joshua Cooper Ramo to describe the Chinese economic and trade policies abroad since going global in the 1980s to 1990s, which focus exclusively on business and exclude political issues and matters of human and worker's rights, as well as other forms of conditionality, notably environmental standards.

Bioengineering (do not confuse with **geoengineering**)   The scientific and industrial manipulation of genes, for instance genetically modified food.

Biopower   Michel Foucault's concept for a series of political techniques ("technologies") that use power to discipline the body, optimizing its capacities while rendering it more docile.

Botnet   A distributed network of compromised information systems used to carry out the will of an attacker.

Brexit   The June 2016 referendum on Great Britain's membership in the European Union. Referendums are rarely used in British politics, but Conservative Prime Minister David Cameron was confident that the British public would vote to stay in the EU, so he could use this approval to discipline the right-wing (nationalistic) wing of the Tories (Conservatives).

BRICS   A coalition of five rising powers (initially Brazil, Russia, India and China, and later South Africa) that seeks to deepen cooperation, coordinate some policy positions, and revise parts of the existing global order. BRICS members are all leading developing countries and regional powers with global ambitions. They all belong to the G-20, a multilateral forum that assembles the world's 20 largest economies. In 2014, the BRICS began launching new institutions, such as the New Development Bank, which provides financing for infrastructure, sustainable development, and other initiatives. https://www.brics2017.org/English/

The Brundtland Report   A reference report created by the World Commission on Environment and Development (1987) named after former Norwegian Prime Minister Gro Harlem Brundtland. It is recognized as one of the earliest political discussions of the link between the environment and development and is often credited with a canonic definition of sustainable development—development that meets the needs of the present without compromising the ability of future generations to meet their own needs.

Carbon sinks   Natural or manmade systems that act like "sponges" and absorb or sequester carbon dioxide from the atmosphere. Examples include oceans, plants (forests), and soil.

Carter Doctrine   President Jimmy Carter, State of the Union address, January 1980, affirmed that energy supply in the Persian Gulf is a vital US national security interest.

Collective good   See public good.

Counterbalancing   Reaction by states or group of states to the actions of another state to nullify or counteract a perceived threat.

Critical security studies/theories   Theories that challenge the realist-liberal internationalist domination and emphasize the view and experience from the subalterns, and challenge hegemonic practices in the name of social, racial, gender and north–south justice.

Deception technologies   Technology systems intended to trick or deceive an intruder into thinking they have successfully infiltrated a valuable information system, all the while, relaying intelligence to the Incident Response team.

Demographic dividend   Accelerated economic growth that begins with changes in a country's population, age, structure as it transitions from high to low birth and death rates.

Digital awakening   The moment where a synthetic entity begins to think in autonomous ways that may allow it to make decisions independent of the intentions of its original creators.

Digital divide The chasm between tech savvy individuals educated in the modern digital ecosystem and those who struggle to adapt to these changes, or between those who have access to information technology and those who do not.

Digital ecosystem The aggregate mosaic of how modern technologies intersect and interact to produce the digital facet of human life and work.

Digital event horizon (see also **Singularity event**) A key point where the technological capability is so exceptional that it is impossible to reliably predict what will occur in the future past the aforementioned set of events.

Dual use Technologies that can be used for civilian (peaceful) and military (war) purposes.

Ehrlich/Simon Bet A 1980 wager offered by economist Julian Simon to Paul Ehrlich, a well-known and media-savvy Malthusian. The two bet $1,000 on the future price of five metals. The initial result showed that Simon was correct for the period considered, and that technology had overcome scarcity and rising prices.

Endemic A disease that is routinely occurring in a geographical area.

Energy crisis of 1973 and 1979 In 1973, an OPEC-imposed decrease in oil production and quota on the United States in the wake of the Yom Kippur War (Ramadan War, October War) between Israel and Egypt and Syria. In 1979, another severe contraction of global oil output due to the Iranian Islamic Revolution. These crises led to a reinforcing the OPEC, disturbances of the international monetary system, strong inflation, economic crisis and joblessness in many developed countries.

Epidemiology The study of how and why disease occurs in a group.

Epistemic communities Community of knowledge and experts.

Evapotranspiration The evaporation of water and transpiration from plants to the atmosphere.

Eugenics The programs and politics of forced (human) population control.

Fifth dimension of warfare Cybersecurity is commonly regarded as the true final frontier—the new dimension of warfare expanding beyond the typical land, sea, air and space.

Fomite A contaminated object that can include a doorknob or handle, used needle, or cookware.

Food and Agriculture Organization (FAO) UN organization involved in fighting global hunger, starvation, and undernourishment.

Front organization An entity created and controlled by another organization, like criminal organizations or others (e.g., religious or political organizations, advocacy groups, corporations, etc.). Front organizations operate on behalf of the real organization, shielding it from public view and law enforcement authorities.

Geoengineering The deliberate, human, large-scale intervention in the Earth's climate system (do not confuse with bioengineering).

Golden Triangle One of Asia's two main opium producing areas, spans the mountain ranges of Myanmar, Laos, and Thailand.

Gordian knot A metaphor for an unsolvable problem. Attributed by legend and oral lore to Alexander the Great (356–323 BCE), who, unable to untie a complex (physical) knot that functioned as an oracle of greatness, reasoned that "solving" the knot could be accomplished via any means. Thus, he sliced the knot with his sword. Often describes problems that could be solved with "out of the box thinking" approaches.

Great Game A phrase used initially by historians to describe the decades-long conflict between Russia and Great Britain over a large portion of Central Asia during the

19th century, and focusing especially on Afghanistan, where these two vast empires met and clashed. Today, the phrase is used to describe grand strategic competition over geography, resources, or even outer space, and often implies some grand design for hegemony.

Great Recession (2008–)   A period of economic decline experienced by global markets throughout the late 2000s and early 2010s. Although the severity and scope of the recession varied from country to country, the Great Recession was related to the financial crisis of 2008 as well as the U.S. subprime mortgage crisis in the late 2000s. It has had lasting economic, social, cultural and political/electoral effects, notably in the United States.

Greenhouse gases (GHGs)   Gases that trap heat in the atmosphere thereby causing a greenhouse warming effect. Carbon dioxide is the most commonly referenced greenhouse gas as it has the largest overall impact on climate change. Other gases include water vapor (naturally occurring), methane (naturally occurring and man-made), nitrous oxide and fluorinated gases such as hydrofluorocarbons.

Green Revolution   The massive global increase in agricultural yields between the 1940s and the 1970s, mostly due to improved technologies in agriculture and farming. Not to be confused with the ongoing process of mitigation of climate change and use of sustainable technologies, also known as the "environmental revolution."

Hacktivism   The compromise or manipulation of information systems specifically targeted to influence social or political objectives.

Hubbert's Peak   see **Peak Oil**.

ICADIS   New methodology to uplift viability in the arena of cybersecurity by identifying issues, correcting them, performing deep analysis, designing an ideal future state, implementing it and then sustaining the changes over time.

Interchange points   When the jurisdiction of the container changes hands, e.g., from shipper to port or port to train or truck.

Intermestic   *Inter*national and do*mestic*. Today, most threats—and solutions—are intermestic.

Intermodal systems   Specialized transportation facilities, assets, and handling procedures designed to create a more integrated transportation system through the combination of multimodal operations, systems, and facilities during the shipment of cargo.

Internet of Things (IOT)   A network of household or workplace objects, providing unique functions and features through connectivity and embedded intelligence.

Intersectionality   the combination and interlocking of various forms of domination, notably against women. For instance: gender, race, class, sexual and orientation.

IPS signatures   A mosaic of rules that identify and prevent attacks based upon known traffic patterns consistent with specific known attack vectors.

Jevons' paradox (see Rebound effect)   Named after British economist W. Stanley Jevons (1835–1882); the observation that despite savings at the *micro-* or *unit* level, technical progress does not entail less, but rather more *aggregate* demand of raw materials.

Kantian imperative (aka categorical imperative)   Emerged from the writings of German philosopher Immanuel Kant (1724–1804). It stipulates for individual ethical behavior that one should act according to the imperative that one's actions reflect what should be a universal norm for behavior (do unto others as you would want done to you). An important assumption for liberals and constructivists for building global stability and security, built with norms, institutions, and reciprocity.

Malthusianism and **neo-malthusianism**   Thomas Malthus (1766–1834), an 18th century English religious scholar who developed the idea that, if left unchecked, population growth would continue exponentially and overtake food production.

Mujahideen   Islam's warriors for the faith.

Multi-scalar   Adjective meaning an event occurs on multiple scales or levels simultaneously.

Nanotechnology   An aspect of science and engineering related to manipulating the very small (often at the molecular level) to yield unique technological outcomes.

Negative feedback loop (see also **positive feedback loop**)   A process or occurrence wherein the effects reduce or dampen the very process that brought them into being. In terms of climate change, this phenomenon would reduce warming; the loop would "cancel out" or diminish the initial effect.

Orange Revolution   Ukraine's Orange Revolution in 2004–2005 was a mass protest against election fraud which had ushered in a Russian-friendly president (Viktor Yanukovich) and led to his ousting.

Pandemic   When an epidemic reaches global levels.

Path dependence   Refers to a process that is set in motion by an initial choice or event which then becomes self-reinforcing. Path dependence can even lead to lock-in effects, meaning that a path chosen by an initial decision cannot be easily reversed despite unintended consequences.

Peak oil (aka **Hubbert's Peak**)   The idea that oil is a finite commodity and hydrocarbon supply would generally follow a bell-shaped curve, in which production initially increases at an exponential rate due to the addition of more efficient technologies.

Positive feedback loop (see also **negative feedback loop**)   A process or occurrence wherein the effects contribute to more of the same and a magnification of the original phenomenon. In terms of climate change, this phenomenon would worsen warming; the loop would increase the initial effect.

Public good (see also **collective goods**)   An indivisible, non-exclusive (one cannot prevent people for using that good) and non-rivalrous (consumption by one person does not reduce amount available to other people) good that benefits all, irrespective of individual contributions to its production. Example: the atmosphere.

Push–pull process   This idea suggests that people migrate to other countries primarily because of economic and other material causes. Suffering poor economic conditions at home, migrants move abroad (push), or, hearing about the material advantages and jobs, they decide to take advantage of economic conditions abroad (pull).

Rebound effect   see **Jevons' Paradox**

Resource curse   The paradox that abundance of natural resources allows the clique in power to exploit the rent economy, which perpetuates poor governance, weak democracies, and flagging economies. The curse is exemplified in authoritarianism and adventurism (Russia), religious extremism (Saudi Arabia), stunted democratic evolution (Venezuela), military rule (Nigeria), etc. and always includes corruption and kleptocracy.

Rio Earth Summit   International environmental conference in 1992 sponsored by the United Nations and held in Rio de Janeiro, Brazil with over 100 heads of state. Aka the UN Conference on Environment and Development (UNCED).

Rose Revolution   In 2013, peaceful protesters in the Republic of Georgia demonstrated and stormed Parliament following disputed elections. It ushered in the presidency of Mikheil Saakashvili, a western-minded reformer.

SCADA Industrial control systems responsible for supervisory control and data acquisition—these are the backbone of many life and safety systems that make our power grid and utilities work to provide us with the services we need for society to effectively sustain in the way we expect for our day-to-day lives.

Security dilemma See **Thucydides' trap**.

Singularity event (see also **Digital event horizon)** In the context of AI, a critical tipping point where intelligence may transcend absolute human control, leading to a realm of outcomes that are impossible to predict because the intelligence of the entities producing the outcome will be unfathomable orders of magnitude beyond the humans trying to make the predictions.

Social media echo chamber The notion that the presuppositions and biases people have will be reflected back to them with increasing intensity, in a **positive feedback loop**—thus amplifying existing biases.

Sustainable Development Goals (SDGs) Adopted in 2015, these 17 SDGs (2015–2030) superseded the Millennium Development Goals (2000–2015) a set of eight goals formed by developed and developing nations and aimed at poverty reduction. SDGs expand the MDGs to cover gender equality, climate change, economic sustainability, etc. Aka the UN's Agenda 2030.

Tragedy of the commons The overexploitation or degradation of shared goods (e.g., ocean, atmosphere) by many users in the absence of some form of public regulation.

Triple Frontier (Tri-border Area) A geographic area along the intersection of Paraguay, Argentina, and Brazil, an "ungoverned space" and a haven for terrorists, criminals, and other nefarious non-state actors.

Thucydides' trap (see also **Security dilemma**) US political scientist Graham Allison created this expression to describe how rivalry, mistrust, and capacity-building (especially military capacity) between powers can lead to more rivalry, mistrust, and military preparations for conflict, or how fear of other powers can be a self-fulfilling prophecy and lead to more tension.

Vector An organism (e.g., mosquito, tick) that carries the pathogen that is transmitted.

Virtual water the "invisible" or "embedded" water used for agricultural and industrial processes. For instance, garments and cars contain large quantities of virtual water.

Water–energy nexus Water is required for the exploration and production of a wide array of energy resources: hydropower, oil and gas, coal, nuclear power, and biofuels. Energy, in turn, is required for the production and purification of various water sources, including desalination and wastewater treatment, and for its pumping, transportation, and use in irrigation. Sometimes extended to include food (water–energy–food nexus).

Westphalian ideal Refers to the ideal "nation-state," after the 1648 Treaty of Westphalia (Germany) (after the pan-European Thirty-Year War) which is usually viewed as the beginning of the modern-day territorial nation-state and the concept of internationally recognized national borders.

Index